Lecture Notes in Computer Science   13000

More information about this subseries at http://www.springer.com/series/7409

William F. Lawless · James Llinas ·
Donald A. Sofge · Ranjeev Mittu (Eds.)

Engineering Artificially Intelligent Systems

A Systems Engineering Approach to Realizing
Synergistic Capabilities

 Springer

Editors
William F. Lawless ⓘ
Paine College
Augusta, GA, USA

Donald A. Sofge ⓘ
U.S. Naval Research Laboratory
Washington, DC, USA

James Llinas ·
University at Buffalo, Director Emeritus,
Center for Multi-source Information Fusion
Buffalo, NY, USA

Ranjeev Mittu
U.S. Naval Research Laboratory
Washington, DC, USA

ISSN 0302-9743   ISSN 1611-3349 (electronic)
Lecture Notes in Computer Science
ISBN 978-3-030-89384-2   ISBN 978-3-030-89385-9 (eBook)
https://doi.org/10.1007/978-3-030-89385-9

LNCS Sublibrary: SL3 – Information Systems and Applications, incl. Internet/Web, and HCI

Preface

Jay Forrester, creator of system dynamics, remarked we "live in a complex world of nested feedback loops," involving cascading interdependencies across these loops that vary in complexity, space, and time. Many, if not most, of the current AI/machine learning algorithms, data and information fusion processes, and related methods are attempting, in software, to estimate situations in this complex world. Hence, these algorithms and processes must gracefully and efficiently adapt to the technical challenges (e.g., data quality) induced by nested feedback loops and interdependencies.

To realize effective and efficient designs of these computational systems, a systems engineering perspective may provide a framework for identifying the interrelationships and patterns of change between components, rather than static snapshots, as systems engineering methods are about seeing "wholes." The increasing prevalence of intelligent systems within society will reveal yet more interdependencies, in that AI-enabled intelligent systems have both upstream processes impacting them and downstream processes they affect. The benefits of studying cascading interdependencies through a systems engineering perspective are essential to understanding their behavior and for the adoption of complex system-of-systems in society. Knowledge about the world is needed for multiple applications.

Models of complex situations (e.g., patterns of life) are typically attacked with reductionism. However, in the absence of modeling dynamics and evolving interrelationships, these strategies fall short. If causal models of feedback loops and interrelations can be developed, then system modeling, and the ability to estimate system dynamics, will be as correct as possible. However, real-world situations of Forrester's "nested feedback loops" involve uncertainty and incompleteness, impeding the calculation of accurate estimates. These topics continue to be researched by the data and information fusion communities, whose processes form snapshots and estimates about component entities and situational states. However, the data and information fusion communities should also seek opportunities (where appropriate) for employing AI/machine learning beyond these component-level estimates, toward modeling synergies and dependencies within and across estimation loops to achieve maximum situational awareness.

The genesis of this book was the scholarly presentations given at the Association for the Advancement of Artificial Intelligence (AAAI) Spring Symposium, held during March 22–24, 2021, titled "Leveraging Systems Engineering to Realize Synergistic AI/Machine Learning Capabilities". However, we decided to refocus the title of the book to Engineering Artificially Intelligent Systems to emphasize pragmatic aspects. More information about the AAAI 2021 Spring Symposium series can be found online (https://aaai.org/Symposia/Spring/sss21.php).

Due to the worldwide COVID-19 pandemic the symposium was held virtually. We invited leading experts from around the world to explore the effects of cascading interdependencies, real-world dynamics, and subsequent opportunities to leverage systems engineering principles to design and develop AI/machine learning and data and information fusion estimation processes that accurately represent complex world states. These relationships are exacerbated by the unpredictability of human decision-makers, uncertainty in raw and fused data, and the large trade space of algorithm permutations orchestrated to solve given problems. The field of systems engineering brings opportunities to address and model the full range of complex, synergistic feedback loops in modern complex systems, toward the realization of cost-effective designs.

The chapters of this book are extensions of abstracts and presentations from the AAAI 2021 Spring Symposium on Leveraging Systems Engineering to Realize Synergistic AI/Machine Learning Capabilities. The topics included AI, machine learning and reasoning, data and information fusion, systems engineering, interdependence, human systems, human biases and limitations, trust and complex AI systems, and ethics. In particular, the call for papers sought contributions on the following:

- Artificial Intelligence, Machine Learning, and Reasoning
- Data and Information Fusion
- Systems Engineering of Complex Interdependent Subsystems
- Systems Engineering for Artificial Intelligence
- Artificial Intelligence for Systems Engineering
- Systems Engineering and Federated Learning
- Human Systems Integration and Visualizations
- Human Biases, Limitations, and Capabilities with Large Scale AI-based Systems
- Trust and Acceptance of Complex AI-based Systems
- Emergence in Complex System-of-Systems
- Ethics in Deploying Complex AI-based systems
- Societal Consequences of Interacting Complex AI-based systems
- Explainability and Interpretability of Artificial Intelligence
- Uncertainty Propagation in AI-based Complex Systems
- Modeling User Interactions with Large Scale AI-based Systems

More details about the symposium, including the full program, can be found on our webpage (https://sites.google.com/view/systems-engineering-ai-ml/home). In addition, we invited additional authors, who did not participate in our symposium, to join us by contributing chapters to this book.

In our deliberations and preparations for the symposium and the LNCS book, we were assisted by our Program Committee, some of whom became presenters at our symposium and contributors to this LNCS book. We thank them, we thank our invited speakers, and we thank our regular speakers.

August 2021

William F. Lawless
James Llinas
Donald A. Sofge
Ranjeev Mittu

Organization

Organizing Committee

W. F. Lawless   Paine College, USA
Ranjeev Mittu   U.S. Naval Research Laboratory, USA
Donald A. Sofge   U.S. Naval Research Laboratory, USA
Thomas Shortell   Lockheed Martin Company, USA
Thomas McDermott   Stevens Institute of Technology, USA
James Llinas (Chair)   University at Buffalo, USA
Julie L. Marble   Johns Hopkins University, USA

Publication Chair

W. F. Lawless   Paine College, USA

Program Committee

Raj Dasgupta   U.S. Naval Research Laboratory, USA
Ali K. Raz   Purdue University, USA
Erik Blasch   Air Force Office of Scientific Research, USA
Edward Waltz   Naval Postgraduate School, USA
Will Williamson   Naval Postgraduate School, USA
Ken Hintz   George Mason University/Perquire Research Co., USA
Noelle Brown   U.S. Naval Research Laboratory, USA
Michael Floyd   Knexus Research Corporation, USA
Rino Falcone   Institute of Cognitive Sciences and Technologies, Italy
Paul Robinette   University of Massachusetts Lowell, USA
Ciara Sibley   U.S. Naval Research Laboratory, USA

Addendum

The Association for the Advancement of Artificial Intelligence (AAAI) Symposium in the spring of 2021, originally scheduled to be held at Stanford University, USA, was instead converted into a virtual symposium conducted over Zoom as a result of the COVID-19 pandemic. Its reduced two-day agenda consisted of eight invited speakers who gave hour-long presentations and eight regular speakers who gave half hour presentations, along with the two speakers who gave opening comments on both days. All of the symposium papers were submitted to the lead organizer via EasyChair, who conducted a review of each paper that was accepted for presentation, assisted by the co-organizers (reducing potential conflicts of interest, the lead organizer did not give a talk at the symposium). In a normal year not affected by COVID-19, we would have had more speakers participating on the regularly scheduled third day of the symposium (usually a half-day).

Of the 18 speakers at the AAAI Spring Symposium, 10 papers were expanded into chapters and submitted to the lead editor of this LNCS book. An 11th chapter contributed by the lead organizer gives an introduction, an overview of the science, and a review of the chapters contributed, which was only reviewed by the lead editor of the book. Of the 10 content chapters, four were written by invited speakers at the symposium. Each of these 10 chapters was thus triple-reviewed: for the symposium, following editing for inclusion in this LNCS book, and for review comments as part of the introductions to each chapter.

Finally, having collected only 10 content chapters, a shortfall that we attributed partly to the COVID-19 pandemic, we invited five additional authors to contribute to the LNCS book. These invited chapters were reviewed twice, once by the LNCS lead editor for editorial content, and once by the symposium's lead organizer for the introduction to each chapter. All of the chapter contributors were asked to address all of the editorial comments, which they did.

The editorial process was arduous, but it assured that the contents of the book were uniformly edited, that conflicts of interest were prevented or minimized, and that the state of the science was advanced.

Contents

Motivations for and Initiatives on AI Engineering

James Llinas[✉]

Center for Multi-Source Information Fusion, University at Buffalo,
311 Bell Hall, Buffalo, NY 14260-5030, USA
llinas@buffalo.edu

1 Introduction: Urgencies for AI Engineering

There are evolving perspectives from a wide range of authors and documented sources that an urgency exists for defining and developing what will likely be an entirely new systems engineering paradigm for the engineering of artificially-intelligent (AI) systems. These perspectives evolve from many viewpoints related to complexities ranging from issues in data and data engineering to the challenges of realizing ethical and legal employment of autonomous system capabilities that are highly reliant on artificial intelligence technologies. Motivation also comes from accumulating experience that the fielding of AI-based systems is sorely lagging; opinions regarding the impact of AI are changing from the early euphoria to much more pragmatic concerns. From a recent Forbes website report[1] we see:

> "The percentage of firms investing greater than $50 million in Big Data and AI initiatives is up to 64.8% in 2020 from just 39.7% in 2018, with a total of 98.8% of firms investing; only 51.9% of firms are accelerating their rate of investment, in stark contrast to the 91.6% who were accelerating their pace of investment in 2019; only 14.6% of firms report that they have deployed AI capabilities into widespread production, and the percentage of firms naming AI as the most disruptive technology declined from 80.0% in 2019 to 69.5% in 2020; 73.4% of firms cite big data adoption as an ongoing challenge and only 37.8% report that they have thus far created a data-driven organization;......."

There are various assertions as to why AI deployment is having difficulties. To start with, we need to clarify what it means to "deploy" AI or Machine-Learning (ML) technology. In an extended web article, Samiullah[2] asserts that "The deployment of machine learning models is the process for making your models available in production environments, where they can provide predictions to other software systems. *It is only once models are deployed to production that they start adding value,* making deployment

---

[1] https://www.forbes.com/sites/gilpress/2020/01/13/ai-stats-news-only-146-of-firms-have-dep loyed-ai-capabilities-in-production/?sh=1c9dd41c2650.

[2] https://christophergs.com/machine%20learning/2019/03/17/how-to-deploy-machine-lea rning-models/.

© Springer Nature Switzerland AG 2021
W. F. Lawless et al. (Eds.): Engineering Artificially Intelligent Systems, LNCS 13000, pp. 1–18, 2021.
https://doi.org/10.1007/978-3-030-89385-9_1

a crucial step." Deployment of a tightly-focused, narrowly-purposed AI or ML tool is one thing (even these deployments suffer from development centered on "first to market" pressures and incomplete validation; see (Llinas et al. 2020)), but more typically the AI/ML component is a part—often a small part—of a larger total-systems architecture. What this means is that you cannot think about <u>model</u> deployment in isolation, you need to plan it at a <u>system</u> level. The initial deployment is not really the hard part (although it can be challenging). It is the ongoing system maintenance, the updates and experiments, the auditing and the monitoring that are where the real technical complexity starts to build up. These larger-systems environments entail much more complexity in engineering development, interfaces, and in requirements for testing, verification, and validation. In a highly-cited paper, Sculley et al. (2015) discuss the ramifications of "technical debt," a metaphor introduced in the 90's to help reason about the long-term costs (debt in life-cycle costs) incurred by moving too quickly in software engineering. Similarly, in a highly-cited editorial (Kruchten 2012), the various concerns for technical debt as related to AI/ML software development are discussed; Fig. 1 shows the "Technical Debt Landscape" derived from that work, showing that some concerns are not obvious ("mostly invisible" in the figure), and can be difficult to prevent, leading to life-cycle cost impacts.

Fig. 1. The Technical Debt Landscape (derived from (Kruchten 2012))

Effective and efficient deployment also relies on a development community having matured to the point where it has the accumulated knowledge to specify effective and efficient design patterns and even, ideally, notions of reference architectures that provide the systemic and design foundations for life-cycle-based development. Samiullah (see Footnote 2) also points out that there is some knowledge beginning to accumulate about recurring design patterns in ML systems, such as shared databases and streaming designs. Large companies are also exploring reference architectures; Rodriguez[3] points out that Google, Facebook, Uber, DataBricks, and others are evolving concepts of reference architectures, and IBM has published an in-depth technical report on an AI Infrastructure Reference Architecture (Lui 2018).

With the widespread interest, research, and development of AI spread across individuals and organizations of strong reputation and knowledge, many having varied opinions

---

[3] https://medium.com/dataseries/machine-learning-reference-architectures-from-google-facebook-uber-databricks-and-others-58191cf82b98.

on the range of issues surrounding AI, such as the reasons for the declining statistics reported by Forbes, it is difficult to develop defendable, substantiated views on how to improve these statistics. All of the articles cited related to deployment point to improved systems engineering methods, but what the role of improved systems engineering should be, and what the shape of a new engineering methodological foundation for designing and developing AI-based systems going forward should look like, are open for discussion and a central theme of this book. One source drawn on here was the report of the U.S. National Security Commission on Artificial Intelligence titled "Key Considerations for Responsible Development and Fielding of Artificial Intelligence" (Schmidt 2021). The first section of the report, "Aligning Systems and Uses with American Values and the Rule of Law," provides guidance specific to implementing systems that abide by American values, most of which are shared by democratic nations. (It will be seen that Chapter 11 of this book, "Risk Reduction for Autonomous Systems" by Gillespie, addresses some of the issues related to the Commission's emphasis on ethics and law in AI system development.) The four following sections in the Commission report are on Engineering Practices, System Performance, Human-AI Interaction, and Accountability & Governance that outline practices needed to develop and field systems that are trustworthy, understandable, reliable, and robust. Another source of opinion that we choose to draw on is from the initiative motivated by the U.S. Office of the Director of National Intelligence (ODNI) that set in motion a program at Carnegie-Mellon University's Software Engineering Institute (CMU/SEI) on AI Engineering. Even this term of AI Engineering is new, apparently headed toward replacing Systems Engineering for AI (SE4AI) and AI for Systems Engineering (AI4SE) that have been used recently.

As regards engineering practices, the National Commission recommends adopting recommended practices for creating and maintaining trustworthy and robust AI systems that are (quoting):

- auditable (able to be interrogated and yield information at each stage of the AI lifecycle to determine compliance with policy, standards, or regulations);
- traceable (to understand the technology, development processes, and operational methods applicable to AI capabilities;
- interpretable (to understand the value and accuracy of system output, and,
- reliable (to perform in the intended manner within the intended domain of use).

The report asserts that there are no broadly directed best practices or standards to guide organizations in the building of AI systems that are consistent with these principles, but candidate approaches are available. A not-unexpected area of expressed concern in this report relates to security and vulnerability, especially of ML systems but broadly also to both AI and ML that are subject to intentional (adversarially-based) and unintentional failures, such as reward-hacking and distributional shifts. They also point out the concerns that current engineering practices do not address, or do not address well, related to integrated multi-AI/ML elements where inter-element complex interactions lead to unexpected or poorly characterized behaviors. Emergent behavior leads to such unexpected behaviors, and ML processes typically employ/embody neural networks that are known to have inherent emergent behavior. There are many definitions and taxonomies of emergence (Fromm 2005; Chalmers 2006), but the focus of concern related to engineering practice is on the *effects* of emergence, not emergence per se. This report does not elaborate much on recommendations regarding specifics of engineering practice but does address what could be called quality control in recommending the incorporation of methods for risk assessments, documentation, security-related improvements, and traceability through the engineering processes. One area emphasized is with regard to human-AI interaction. Methods in support of effective human-AI interaction can help AI systems understand when and how to engage humans for assistance, when AI systems should take initiative to assist human operators, and, more generally, how to support the creation of effective human-AI teams. The report urges the incorporation of methods to deal with known human failure modes and biases, and to recognize and respond to the potential for costly human biases of judgment and decision making in specific settings. As part of effective teaming, it is suggested that AI systems can be endowed with the ability to detect the focus of attention, workload, and interrupt-ability of human operators and consider these inferences in decisions about when and how to engage with operators. (Methods addressing human-system issues are discussed in Chapters 5, 6, 8, 13, 14 and 15, and is a central issue in this LNCS book). A final comment drawn from this report is that there are no agencies that serve as a clearinghouse and unified point of guidance as regards engineering practice for effective and efficient design and development of AI systems. The International Council on Systems Engineering (INCOSE) has an AI Systems Working Group that is targeted on "**providing expertise across SE functions and lifecycle management that can be used by industry to promote the development of AI Systems**,"[4] and is involved with AI *for* systems engineering by promoting conferences on this topic[5].

Driven by national security concerns involved with AI/ML systems, the U.S. Office of the Director of National Intelligence (ODNI) has sponsored an initiative in late 2020 at Carnegie-Mellon's Software Engineering Institute (CMU/SEI), a federally-funded research and development center (FFRDC) in the U.S., to have SEI lead a national initiative to advance the discipline of artificial intelligence (AI) engineering for defense and national security. (The National Security Commission on Artificial Intelligence specifically referenced this ODNI–SEI effort in its Second Quarter 2020Recommendations.) Although this initiative can be expected to focus on security issues, the viewpoint taken by SEI will encompass the full engineering life cycle; coupled with SEI's reputation in software and systems engineering, it can be expected that this initiative will have a wide-ranging impact.

As a first step in reacting to this assignment, the SEI has been putting out papers on their viewpoints regarding the formalization of a discipline of AI Engineering (we will abbreviate this as AIE going forward). The earliest papers were related to first thoughts on the "pillars" of AIE: three initial pillars of artificial intelligence (AI) engineering: human centered, scalable, and robust and secure, elaborated below. These build upon a

---

[4] https://www.incose.org/incose-member-resources/working-groups/transformational/artificial-intelligence-systems.

[5] E.g., https://www.incose.org/events-and-news/search-events/2020/10/13/default-calendar/artificial-intelligence-for-systems-engineering---ai4se-2020.

prior SEI report addressing "Eleven Foundational Practices: Recommendations for decision makers from experts in software engineering, cybersecurity, and applied artificial intelligence" (Horneman 2019), also remarked on below. The three initial *pillars* are described as follows (quoting)[6]:

- **Human-centered AI**

  o Key to the implementation of AI in context is a deep understanding of the people who will use the technology. This pillar examines how AI systems are designed to align with humans, their behaviors, and their values.

- **Scalable AI**

  o Effective AI systems require large investments of time and money to develop. This pillar examines how AI infrastructure, data, and models may be reused across problem domains and deployments.

- **Robust and Secure AI**

  o One of the biggest challenges facing the broad adoption of AI technologies and systems is knowing that AI systems will work as expected when they are deployed outside of closely controlled development, laboratory, and test environments. This pillar examines how we develop and test resilient AI systems.

The eleven principles published earlier (Horneman 2019) are summarized here, with some brief remarks of our own on each:

1. **Ensure you have a problem that both can and should be solved by AI**

An interesting principle that challenges our knowledge of how well we understand AI problem-space-to-solution-space mappings. It also challenges the understanding of AI solution capabilities and boundaries, so that one knows that the entire problem as specified is covered or bounded by an AI-only solution.

2. **Include highly integrated subject matter experts, data scientists, and data architects in your software engineering teams**

This principle emphasizes that, especially today and especially when dealing with the new and special needs of complete AI solutions (explanation, V&V, etc.), that a design/development team needs to be an interdisciplinary team.

3. **Take your data seriously to prevent it from consuming your project**

The data engineering processes are complex and these complexities require a comprehensive data management strategy and oversight function.

---

[6] https://www.sei.cmu.edu/news-events/news/article.cfm?assetId=735477.

4. **Choose algorithms based on what you need your model to do, not on their popularity**

This would seem normal and should be part of good AIE.

5. **Secure AI systems by applying highly integrated monitoring and mitigation strategies**

Cybersecurity is of extraordinary interest today, and the so-called "attack surface" or digital footprint of software systems continues to expand; an AIE engineering team must understand attack vectors such as data poisoning attacks and model stealing techniques.

6. **Define checkpoints to account for the potential needs of recovery, traceability, and decision justification**

The need here relates to the topic of technical debt and the invisible and subtle factors that can affect interdependencies across software functions and versions; the need for version changes in AI applications is typically frequent, and versions can also have time dependencies.

7. **Incorporate user experience and interaction to constantly validate and evolve models and architecture**

Human-system interaction and interdependencies is always a key issue and this is especially true in AI applications that may have degrees of autonomous capability. Users and user feedback both in real-time and offline can be critical to both performance and adjustments in an AI system.

8. **Design for the interpretation of the inherent ambiguity in the output**

AI systems are trying to deal with real-world problems that typically involve varying degrees of uncertainty and ambiguity; popular examples of AI misclassification abound, showing the reality of current-day performance. AI engineers need to decide on the bounds of planned capability from assisted intelligence to autonomous intelligence.

9. **Implement loosely coupled solutions that can be extended or replaced to adapt to ruthless and inevitable data and model changes and algorithm innovations**

This principle interrelates to that of the 6th principle dealing with interdependencies within AI processes and systems; known software design schemes related to containerization apply here for control of dependencies.

10. **Commit sufficient time and expertise for constant and enduring change over the life of the system**

All the evolving principles of AI Devops apply here. AI engineers need to take and commit to a life-cycle perspective from the beginning, if successful deployments are to be realized; sensitivity to technical debt is again involved.

11. Treat ethics as both a software design consideration and a policy concern

As remarked previously in citing the National Commission's report, a commitment and adherence to American values, ethics, and laws will be an overriding focus that has to be visible in the way we do AIE.

The CMU/SEI effort is just getting underway, but it can be expected to be a centerpoint of R&D related to the formation of an integrated methodology for AIE.

At these high and strategic levels, there is also something else to pay attention to: the just-formed National Artificial Intelligence Initiative (NAII) was established by the National Artificial Intelligence Initiative Act of 2020 (NAIIA) (DIVISION E, SEC. 5001) – bipartisan legislation enacted it on January 1, 2021. The website[7] describes the objectives of this law as: "The main purposes of the initiative are to ensure continued US leadership in AI R&D; lead the world in the development and use of trustworthy AI systems in public and private sectors; prepare the present and future US workforce for the integration of artificial intelligence systems across all sectors of the economy and society; and coordinate ongoing AI activities across all Federal agencies, to ensure that each informs the work of the others." This initiative has already published some 70 documents addressing many strategic issues that will bear on the formation of the AIE discipline[8]. They have issued Requests for Information and thus likely will be funding a number of relevant programs that will influence the formation of AIE.

It would also be expected that the International Council on Systems Engineering (INCOSE) would be addressing the issues surrounding the engineering processes that would be involved with AIE. While no singular INCOSE publication seems to fully provide an integrated view of what AIE is and what it should comprise as an engineering discipline, there are several papers that address closely-related issues; most are from the INCOSE publication called Insight[9]. Overarching viewpoints related to AIE are summarized in sections of the Systems Engineering Body of Knowledge (SEBOK)[10] where perspectives on SE4AI and AI4SE are also described. Under the SE4AI section, the major challenges that an SE methodology needs to address are asserted as (quoted):

1. **New failure modes not previously experienced in the engineering of systems**. The AI community recognizes that there are there are five main failure modes that cause the AI systems to not behave safely and as expected. These new failure modes include negative side effects, reward hacking, scalable oversight, unsafe exploration, and distributional shift.

---

[7] https://www.ai.gov/.

[8] See https://www.ai.gov/documents/ and https://www.ai.gov/publications/.

[9] See https://onlinelibrary.wiley.com/journal/21564868.

[10] https://www.sebokwiki.org/wiki/Artificial_Intelligence.

2. **The unpredictability of performance due to non-deterministic and evolving behavior**. ML systems initially learn from predetermined data and through the activity of validation, system engineers check the compliance of the system performance against its intended purpose, captured in a Systems Specification. The challenge with AI, and specifically ML, is predicting the performance and behavior of the AI algorithm on unseen data in future operations. ML systems exhibit non-deterministic performance, with the performance of some systems evolving as the system learns (changes performance) during operations. This presents challenges in validating system compliance before the system enters operations.

3. **Lack of trust and robustness in future systems performance**. System validation is based on a basic four step approach: obtaining results from a validation test, comparing the measured results to expect results, deducing the degree of compliance, and deciding on the acceptability of this compliance. A key aspect in deciding the acceptability of compliance is expert judgement. Expert judgement requires an understanding of the result as compared to the relevance of the context of use, and therefore the results need to be explainable. Explainable behavior of AI Systems is problematic, and therefore determining a level of trust and robustness in future systems performance is challenging.

It can be seen in this list that new methods for testing and validation will be critical in the formation of AIE methods; very interesting articles related to these topics are in the INCOSE publications by Freeman on T&E for AI[11], in Collopy et al. on Validation testing for autonomous systems,[12] and a thorough paper on a research roadmap for both SE4AI and AI4SE in McDermott et al.[13].

Not unexpectedly, AIE is also a topic of international concern. A sampling of international thinking on AIE can be seen in a Swedish paper by Bosch et al. (Bosch 2020) that brings us back to the issue of deployment, where these authors suggest a deployment-type model (they call it an AI Evolution model) that depicts a phased approach, evolving from experimentation to autonomous component operations. For each deployment phase, they comment on the AIE activities that they see for each; the following Table 1 shows the phase-to-phase association:

Building upon an extensive survey of AI system development efforts and deployments, Bosch et al. build a framework for a research agenda for AIE. For each real-world case studied, they enumerate the problems in each and then categorize these problems into four categories: Data Quality Management, Design Methods and Processes, Model Performance, and Deployment and Compliance. To address these problem areas, they suggest a research agenda that has three main components: Data Science—AI Engineering—Domain-specific AI Engineering. Their breakout of AIE has three elements: Architecture—Development—Process. Arguments are made in the paper that AIE will have application-domain-specific aspects; their categorization of these application domains are: cyber-physical systems—safety-critical systems—autonomously improving systems.

---

[11] https://onlinelibrary.wiley.com/doi/abs/10.1002/inst.12281.

[12] https://onlinelibrary.wiley.com/doi/10.1002/inst.12285.

[13] https://onlinelibrary.wiley.com/doi/10.1002/inst.12278.

Table 1. Correlation of AIE activities and AI evolution process

Deployment phase	AI activities	Remarks
Experimentation and prototyping	None	Research phase
Non-critical deployment	ML/Deep Learning (DL) Models deployed but only in non-critical system flows	AI Technology isolated
Critical deployment	ML/DL processes integrated into system-level critical paths	System failures dependent on ML/DL functioning
Cascading deployment	Chained, interdependent connected ML/DL processes	Possibly dealing with emergence
Autonomous ML/DL components	ML/DL models monitor their own behavior, automatically initiate retraining	Facing assured autonomy challenges

AIE clearly has strong dependencies on the engineering processes for good software engineering. A paper claimed to be the most extensive survey of software engineering methods and practices as a part of systems engineering for AI applications (SE4AI) is that of Martinez-Fernandez (2021) that offers an extensive survey of papers on various topics related to the issue of software engineering of AI systems. Each area studied is categorized according to the "knowledge areas" of the Software Engineering Body of Knowledge (SWEBOK) report put out by the IEEE (Bourque 2014). In the conclusions of this report, it is interesting to note that only 20% of the papers reviewed were from industry; most were academic papers. In spite of the concerns for the international AI race, the papers in this survey were dominated by U.S. publications. The most important conclusion regarding AIE aspects is that few of the papers were for a systemic level; on the other hand, most were related to software testing and software quality, which are relevant but not of a systemic viewpoint.

Finally, a comment about AIE education. In addition to CMU/SEI, and again reflecting the international concern for AIE, educational initiatives are evolving both in Sweden and in Germany, possibly among others. In Germany, CC-KING is the competence center for AI Systems Engineering in Karlsruhe that is related to a network of research centers in the region and will be supporting AIE R&D and will be holding workshops and conferences on AI Systems Engineering[14]. Jönköping University in Sweden is offering a Master's program in AIE, focusing on the development of intelligent software products and services. This program has 12 courses spread over 2 years but again none on engineering per se[15]. In the USA, Duke University offers a Product Innovation Master of Engineering program with 10 courses that include Business fundamentals and management, Sourcing data, modeling, algorithms, Building products using Deep Learning, and Ethical implications of AI that seem to be a better balance directed to successful

---

[14] See https://www.ki-engineering.eu/en.html.

[15] See https://ju.se/en/study-at-ju/our-programmes/master-programmes/ai-engineering.html.

deployment at the system level[16]. IBM is offering a certificate in AIE through Coursera, comprising 6 courses but none are about engineering per se[17]; reviewing Coursera courses in AI, this seems to be the only one on AIE. While these programs have titles using the AIE phrasing, most seem to focused on AI technologies and methods more so than the engineering aspects of developing, testing, and deploying AI capability.

2   AIE Status Summary

It is clear that there is widespread acknowledgement of the need for an integrated AIE process that the AI/ML communities will take up in a committed way to inculcate AIE across the communities of practice. The criticality of defining and employing such engineering procedures to especially include approaches for testing and evaluation, as well as methods of assuring that system performance is recognized will be crucial for assuring system performance and quality. Failure to define and employ AIE will threaten the future success of the AI/ML field. What this AIE process is and what its components are, seem to have a degree of convergence toward a consensus view, but so far only high-level principles and foundational ideas have been developed; much more needs to be done. The technological societies have roles to play here to foster discussion but also to push to closure for an AIE body of knowledge, and for the employment of that body of knowledge. Systemic-level specification of AIE will be complex and viewpoints on each AIE component will abound.

3   Overview of the LNCS Book

This book is one of a series of books being published by Springer whose contents are in part drawn from expanded versions of papers for the proceedings of the Spring Symposia of the Association for the Advancement of Artificial Intelligence (AAAI), in this case the Spring 2021 Symposium. Some chapters however, are original works submitted by invited authors who were not part of the symposium. In the following section, we provide short synopsis of each chapter.

4   Chapter Synopses

Chapter 2: In Chapter 2, Kenneth Hintz describes the architecting process of an integrated scheme to optimally collect data from multiple sensors in any system application that must develop an information management approach in the face of competing goals. Important in these applications is the development of a scheme by which information value is weighed; Hintz develops a unique weighting approach that maximizes the "expected information value rate", an approach that not only assigns value to the information

---

[16] See https://pratt.duke.edu/artificial-intelligence-product-innovation-master-engineering?utm_source=search&utm_medium=cpc&utm_campaign=ai&utm_content=ai&gclid=CjwKCAjwj dOIBhA_EiwAHz8xm415dgrxIvA_KZMfDoXuqJ5YE4vHXfqpAu8WjwltQq8kBtmnw8Ry ixoCaLUQAvD_BwE.

[17] See https://www.coursera.org/professional-certificates/ai-engineer#courses.

collected by a sensor but also the rate at which that information value is collected. Hintz develop a "goal lattice" structure that allows the control process to effectively arbitrate over competing mission goals that are posting information needs. Hintz's scheme, the "Information based Sensor Management (IBSM)" process, addresses the constraints for a heterogenous sensor management process contending with the primary constraint that constrain sensors are constrained in measurement, computation, and/or data space. That is, a sensor cannot sense from all directions and all sources at the same time.

The process architecture is developed by utilizing a single optimization criterion based on the following four criteria with commensurate units of measure:

- Transfer information not just data
- Mission-value the information
- Maximize the probability of obtaining the information
- Obtain the information in a timely manner

This IBSM architecture has been employed in some limited applications and with good results. IBSM is a satisficing solution for the management of heterogeneous sensors in that it does the best it can under the real-time constraints without seeking the real-time global maximum type solutions that in many, if not most cases, are unworkable and not computable in realistic applications.

Chapter 3: AI and ML are clearly foundational technologies for processes that are information-dependent. In cases where there are adversaries, where an adversary could be nature, it is of interest to be able to assess the information position of each agent in relation to the other. Understanding the information positions of each agent would clearly be helpful toward the engineering of AI/ML system designs. Chapter 3, led by Erik Blasch, provides a framework and line of thinking to quantitatively make such assessments. The method actually spawns off ideas that trace back to the 1980's when Col. John Boyd formulated his well-known "OODA Loop", describing a closed-loop situation control process comprising of four parts: Observe-Orient-Decide-Act. This process has been employed and further developed by many researchers, both in defense applications, business, and a variety of non-defense applications. Building on a related idea formulated by Boyd called "Energy-Maneuverability" theory, Blasch, et al. extract ideas about *information power* and *information maneuverability*. The result is a measure, similar to specific energy in physics, that allows for comparisons between the information positions of two or more entities and thus, determine which agent has the superior information position. This transition from physical entropy and specific energy to proposed information equivalents is consistent with robust artificial intelligence (AI)/machine learning (ML) methods. The chapter introduces the concepts of "strong" and "weak" information positions for an agent as compared to an adversary or competitor – hence the chapter develops ideas and measures related to "information maneuverability" that derive from the agent-specific assessments. The chapter provides a mathematical framework to formalize the information-centric maneuverability concept that can be exploited in adversarial AI/ML contexts, and clearly can be exploited in trading-off alternative designs that employ AI/ML technologies.

Chapter 4: In Chapter 4, a BioSecure Digital Twin approach is described for cyber-protection to improve the resilience and security of the biopharma industrial supply chain and production processes. To effectively develop and deploy a Digital Twin, Mylrea's team performs an applicability and gap analysis via a framework of "Consequence-driven Cyber-informed Engineering (CCE)". Consequence-driven Cyber-informed Engineering is a rigorous process for applying Cyber-informed Engineering (CIE) principles to a specific organization, facility, or mission by identifying their most critical functions, methods and means that an adversary would likely use to manipulate or compromise them and determining the most effective means of removing or mitigating those risks. The CIE approach emphasizes the removal of potential risk in key areas, in part by prioritizing cyber events that have the greatest impact on system performance and operations. After this consequence analysis, a systems of system analysis of the BioSecure Digital Twin model needs to be conducted to define the system's boundary conditions.

The proposed BioSecure Digital Twin is engineered to create an industrial immune system to improve manufacturing and to rapidly identify anomalies and mitigate the behavior that deviates from normal operations, both in the cybersecurity dimension and in process fidelity control. The BioSecure Digital Twin monitors every step in the supply chain, the production process and it introduces security controls while detecting and mitigating cyber vulnerabilities.

Chapter 5: Chapter 5 by Fouad et al. provides a high-level insight into the engineering issues for the Design of Synergistic Human-Centric Complex Systems. The authors examine three interrelated topics that can be viewed as working in synergy towards the development of human-centric complex systems: (1) Artificial Intelligence for Systems Engineering (AI4SE); (2) Systems Engineering for Artificial Intelligence (SE4AI); and (3) Human Centered Design (HCD) and Human Factors (HF). For each topic addressed, they highlight the viewpoints between the three approaches and they discuss possible research opportunities that may begin addressing the gaps within and across each discipline. Their exploration over these topics is in a sense about exploring synergistic capabilities in human-centric complex systems, since synergistic system operations yield: mutually reinforcing system functions, improved effectiveness and efficiency, and human-system role optimization. The lead author of this chapter is a scientist at the U.S. Naval Research Laboratory (NRL) who has demonstrated the ability of attention management strategies to significantly improve operator performance in multitasking environments; attention-management is also addressed in Chapter 14, and is an important aspect of human-system dynamics for AI, ML, and autonomous system operations. Information value, the entropically-based measures related to information value is also addressed here. Workflow process modeling and design is discussed as part of the methodological toolkit for exploring and ultimately designing human-system interfaces and operations.

Chapter 6: The Brownian motion paradigm has proven very agile across a wide range of modeling applications from its traditional use in fluid physics to stock price prediction. In Chapter 6 on Agent Team Action, Brownian Motion and Gambler's Ruin, Ira S. Moskowitz exploits this approach to model various probabilities concerning a group of agents, or more simply put, a Team. The approach builds on a series of prior works cited in the chapter. The chapter is broken into two main parts, presenting the mathematics first and then describing the Team problem from a behavioral point of view separate from the mathematical proofs. The team behavior is modeled using Brownian methods, where each team-member has two modeled characteristics, skill level and level of cooperation. Moskowitz uses the notion of team diffusion as a measure of how well the Team is working together, where a team with good cooperation is expected to have a small diffusion rate, and vice versa. The notion of interdependence among team-members (also treated in Chapter 8 and 15) is also integrated into the modeling approach. This modeling-centric chapter concentrates on modeling the probability of a Team reaching the correct decision and performing a task correctly but leaves the time rate of this process for future research.

Chapter 7: The training of deep learning models often takes advantage of cloud computing services for that purpose. But as Chapter 7 by Bykov et al. shows, choosing the right configuration on a public cloud for model training is not an easy task. As described there, surfing through the cloud shows that there are hundreds of different virtual machines available with a wide variety of CPU core counts, memory, disk type, network speed, and of course graphics card (GPU) options. Using a set of use-case training benchmarks across image-processing, natural language processing, and recommendation applications, they took the most popular cloud provider Amazon Web Services (AWS) and ran a set of benchmarks on all of the available single GPU instances. Performance was highly irregular; for example, they showed that: "goofy" VM configurations can give both the best price and performance, and that the cheapest instances for one network can be the most expensive for others. The lessons learned here are that cloud configuration decisions for DN training can be complex and yield unexpected results.

Chapter 8: While it seems clear that the notions of teams and teamwork will be central to the engineering of many AI/ML systems, especially in the case of autonomous systems, understanding what teamwork really is and how to model and analyze it is proving to be a challenge to AI/ML/Autonomous system communities. Chapter 8, "How Interdependence Explains the World of Teamwork", by Matthew Johnson and Jeffrey M. Bradshaw, proposes that "interdependence" is the key principle for understanding teamwork in the broad sense but also the means of framing seemingly disparate research perspectives. They posit that "providing effective support for team members as they fulfill joint requirements is the *sine qua non* of designing and developing successful human-machine team performance". In their view, teamwork is facilitated if joint activity is supported by some combination of observability (team members can observe the role of others), predictability (of intentions), and directability (of one member by another). They point out that these three interdependence relationships are consistent with principles of human-centered design.

Chapter 9: Interactive Machine Learning (IML) is the focus of Chapter 9 by Jaelle Scheuerman. She applies it to an application involving the labeling of GIS data for systems exploring airfield change detection, geographic region digitization, and digital map editing. IML systems start with little to no training data, and iteratively improve runtime performance through interactions with the user. This process of active learning updates the underlying baseline uncertainty model to reduce uncertainty, helping the model to converge more quickly. Challenges in this research involve methods to optimize the amount of editing required by the analyst, and thereby increasing the speed of model convergence. Among various challenges is the design of the means to communicate uncertainty to analysts, and bounding the regions displayed for label editing to balance overall speed and comprehensiveness in performance. Also important is to capture cognitive feedback from the analyst, which can be done by self-reporting, eye-tracking, or other means. Overarching design features that need to be balanced are cognitive load, vigilance, speed and accuracy; these features collectively represent a significant challenge to the exploitation of IML methods.

Chapter 10: Largely because AI and ML algorithms and processes can be so complex and opaque as regards an understanding, explanation services have arisen as an often-needed function to aid users both in understanding such processes and also as a means to engender trust. Explainable Artificial Intelligence (XAI) refers to systems that try to explain how a black-box AI or ML model produces its outcomes. "Post-hoc" explanation methods approximate the behavior of an AI/ML process. One of the ways this can be approached is by understanding the influence of the features used in an ML scheme. Chapter 10, on "Faithful Post-hoc Explanation of Recommendation using Optimally Selected Features" by Shun Morisawa and Hayato Yamana offers thoughts on the design and development of a post-hoc explanation scheme. Their approach is a ML-model-agnostic approach that explains the recommendation (baseline system) result by training the input-output pairs of the recommendation model with an "interpretable" model that treat the recommendation model as a black box. This type of an approach explains the recommendation results without modifying the base recommendation model. A tradeoff here is that the post-hoc approach does not provide a completely accurate explanation because the interpretation and recommendation models may differ. However, this approach does not require existing ML recommendation systems to be modified, allowing a more straightforward path to closure between the two models. Building on a popular post-hoc model (LIME-RS), Morisawa and Yamana derive improvements based on optimal feature selection for the interpretable model.

Chapter 11: Systems that have AI/ML and/or autonomous characteristics will very likely have emergent or some type of unpredictable behavior. Such characteristics can also be the result of poor systems engineering and/or test and evaluation procedures. No matter the cause, if such behaviors are expected, system designers need to be concerned that system behavior adheres to therules of both law and ethics. In Chapter 11 Gillespie addresses such issues, raising three critical questions that a technologist needs to be concerned with: what is the relevant legal framework; how to model non-deterministic behavior; and how actions are authorized. Contemplating these questions leads Gillespie to assert that there must be a separation of ML-based decisions and authorizations to act. The rate of development of AI/ML-based systems is moving much faster that the development of meaningful and correctly-tuned laws, and developers cannot wait for future standards and regulations due to commercial timescales. They must base their work on current legal instruments, keeping a close eye on the future. This chapter provides a provocative review of the currently-fuzzy landscape that borders the intersection of law and ethics and non-deterministic behaviors.

Chapter 12: In a detailed review of a use case in the sensitive area intersecting AI/ML technologies and health-based systems, in Chapter 12, Das et al. provide a detailed step-through of an agile development process used in the real-world. In formulating their approach, it is emphasized that both the specification and the expected outcomes of a new AI/ML system in a computational AI system are often vague; such conditions are incompatible with the traditional "waterfall" software development process. Das describes a scrum-based agile approach to the development of a real-world health services system that has considerable interactions with users/patients. The development team is cross-functional in nature with analysts, developers, and data scientists. A big part of most of these projects is to prepare the data, labelled by team analysts, and typically employing supervised machine learning to achieve a higher accuracy, but at the high cost of labeling upfront. The scrum process is a short pause in development that assesses the necessary adaptations needed; this is followed by a "sprint" that involves fairly short-period development of scrum-judged improvements. There are many software tools that exist to expedite these interleaved steps, as described in the chapter.

Chapter 13: Bidirectional trust, wherein humans come to trust system technologies, and where system technologies trust human interactions, may be the most overarching issue governing the success or failure of the current wave of AI/ML. In Chapter 13, Marble, et al., address the question of how to provide a research and test infrastructure that provides a basis for insightful exploration of these issues. A key issue in such an exploration is providing a framework that allows assessing an agent's trust in another agent when near ecologically-valid risk is presented. Since test environments cannot sometimes present realistic (e.g., life-threatening) risks to the participants, an analogous environment is needed where such issues can be effectively simulated. The overall research area related to trust assessment is confounded by many factors/issues such as context, system capability and reliability. In the chapter, it is argued that these confounds can be addressed through the use of virtual reality and immersive gaming systems. The chapter discusses two such prototype laboratory systems. These prototypes are part of the infrastructure of the Johns Hopkins University Applied Physics Laboratory that is developing Platforms for Assessing Relationships. The specific simulators are called PAR-TNER for studying Trust with Near Ecologically-valid Risk, and PARTI, for the exploration of human collaboration with autonomous systems. The chapter describes the issues in developing and also using these research tools, and shows some of the difficulties related to this type of research.

Chapter 14: Chapter 5 addressed some of the issues related to the important topic of human operator attention. Here, in Chapter 14, Nicosia and Kristensson discuss this issue in the critically-important application area of safety-critical systems. This chapter addresses key human-machine challenges intrinsic in this design problem and distills six design principles based on a functional design of a general AI-assisted attention-aware system for target identification. Along with the design principles, the chapter contributes a functional architecture of an AI-assisted target identification system. The authors put forward four challenges that need to be addressed in the design of an AI-assisted target identification system, such as dealing with distracting information. They also point out the crucial balance between balancing operator attention and when to intervene to direct the analyst to key information. The roles for AI are directed to the functions of inferring the target identity and the prioritization of given targets in the system field of view.

Chapter 15: Lawless and Sofge bring interdependence forward in Chapter 15, offering some overarching perspectives on this area of study, and introducing the topic of vulnerability, reminding that "States of interdependence transmit both positive (constructive) and negative (destructive) effects in the interaction." They also add perspective to this field of study in relation to the framework of social interdependence-based analyses that are stated as faulty in the inability to predict outcomes and also in not proving to be a sound foundation for a theoretical basis. Building on an entropy-based foundation, Chapter 15 explores the topic of interdependence and vulnerability. Vulnerability is of course of keen interest in business contexts regarding competitors, military settings involving adversaries, and a wide range of other use cases. In the mathematical treatment of the chapter, vulnerability is characterized mathematically by an increase in structural entropy generation and a decrease in a team's productivity. Development of this theoretical base allows teams and organizations to pursue avoidance behaviors, to engage in exploitative behavior, or to create a vulnerability in an opponent. This entropy-based, mathematical approach is argued for as an organizing principle for formal studies in the domain of social interaction.

Chapter 16: "Principles of decision and sense-making for virtual minds," was written by Olivier Bartheye and Laurent Chaudron. Bartheye is with CREA, the French Air Force Academy (FAFA) Research Center in France. FAFA is a Public Industrial and Commercial Establishment. Chaudron, formerly with the Office National d'Études et de Recherches Aérospatiales (ONERA), is now at THEORIK-LAB, also in France. In their chapter, building on prior research, Bartheye and Chaudron approach the sense-making needed to construct a cognitive context with a geometrical perspective of decision logic that generalizes from perception to action at the individual to the group level to determine logically the collective "mind" of an assembled team of intelligent agents (akin to the geometric reach of interdependence). Their approach uses the logic of topology. With this logic, their question is how can different intelligent agents reach consensus? They start with the mind of a virtual agent, and they proceed epistemologically to address the validity of a context using temporal logic and sense-making along with cross-representations from individuals to a team. A co-algebra, causal algebra and Hopf algebra are introduced, but they must also confront a causal break. This causal break thwarts their aim by not allowing them to embed logical switchings from perception to action inside of an automorphism algebra that provides completeness.

5 A Tabular Review

Finally, to try and link the chapter-wise content to the opening remarks on AI Engineering, we provide a cross-reference table of chapter-wise Keywords to the Pillars and Principles of AI Engineering as described in the cited CMU/SEI documents, as in Table 2 below:

Table 2. Chapter Keywords and AI Engineering Pillars and Principles

Chapter	Key analysis—Engineering phrases	Pillars and principles of AI engineering
2	• Architectural design for information collection • Maximizing the information value rate of information gathering	Scalable architectures
3	• Information Maneuverability • Relative information power	Take information/data seriously
4	• Consequence-driven Cyber-informed Engineering • Secure Digital Twins	Robust and secure AI
5	• Synergistic capabilities in human-centric complex systems • Attention management strategies	Human-centered AI
6	• Brownian motion studies of team behavior • Interdependencies in teams	Human-centered AI
7	• Training of deep learning models • Public cloud design choices for model training	Taking data seriously
8	• Interdependence and teamwork • Observability--predictability--directability	Human-centered AI
9	• Interactive machine learning • Speed—Comprehensiveness--Convergence	
10	• Explainable Artificial Intelligence; Post-hoc Cases • Issue of interpretability	Traceability, justification
11	• Addressing Legal/Ethical aspects of emergent/unpredictable behavior • Dealing with the Current Legal Landscape	Ethics in design and policy
12	• Design and development of AI/ML technologies for health-based systems • Agile development: scrums and sprints	Scalable architectures
13	• Research and test infrastructure for exploring human trust • Achieving ecologically-based trust	Human-centered AI
14	• AI-assisted attention-aware system • Dealing with distractions and intervention	Human-centered AI
15	• Organizing principles for social interaction analysis • Interdependence and vulnerability	Human-centered AI
16	• Intelligent agent consensus processes	Human-centered AI

References

Bosch, J., Crnkovic, I., Holmstrom Olsson, H.: Engineering AI Systems: A Research Agenda. arXiv:2001.07522, January 2020. http://arxiv.org/abs/2001.07522

Bourque, P., Richard, E. (eds.): Software Engineering Body of Knowledge, (SWEBOK) Version 3.0. IEEE, ISBN-10: 0-7695-5166-1 (2014)

Chalmers, D.J.: Strong and weak emergence. In: Clayton, P., Davies, P. (eds.) The Re-emergence of Emergence. Oxford University Press, Oxford, pp. 244–256 (2006)

Fromm, J.: Types and forms of emergence, Distributed Systems Group, Universität Kassel, Germany (2005). http://arxiv.org/ftp/nlin/papers/0506/0506028.pdf

Horneman, A., Mellinger, A., Ozkaya, I.: AI Engineering: 11 Foundational Practices. Technical Report. Software Engineering Institute, Carnegie Mellon University, Pittsburgh, PA (2019)

Kruchten, P., Nord, R.L., Ozkaya, I.: Technical debt: from metaphor to theory and practice. IEEE Softw. **29**(6), 18–21 (2012)

Llinas, J., Fouad, H., Mittu, R.: Systems Engineering for Artificial Intelligence-based Systems: A Review in Time, Chapter 6. In: Lawless, W., et al. (eds.) Systems Engineering and Artificial Intelligence, to be published 2021 by Springer (2021)

Lui, K., Karmiol, J.: AI Infrastructure Reference Architecture-IBM Systems, June 2018. https://www.ibm.com/downloads/cas/W1JQBNJV

Martínez-Fernández, S., Bogner, J., Franch, X., et al.: Software Engineering for AI-Based Systems: A Survey arXiv:2105.01984 (2021)

Schmidt, E., et al.: Final Report, National Security Commission on Artificial Intelligence, March 2021. https://www.nscai.gov/wp-content/uploads/2021/03/Full-Report-Digital-1.pdf

Sculley, D., et al.: Hidden technical debt in machine learning systems. In: Neural Information Processing Systems (NIPS) (2015)

Architecting Information Acquisition to Satisfy Competing Goals

Kenneth J. Hintz[1,2]([email]) [iD]

[1] George Mason University, Fairfax, VA 22030, USA
[2] Perquire Research, Savannah, GA 31410, USA
ken.hintz@perquire.com

Abstract. There has been a slow and persistent progression of data acquisition (sensor) systems from isolated, independent, and single-purpose sensors to federated, networked, integrated, multi-modal, and agile sensors with which to provide data for situation assessment (SA). Associated with this progression is the inexorable increase in the quantity, quality, and diversity of data which these systems provide. In order to provide a minimal uncertainty, mission-valued situation assessment on which decision makers can order their choices it was necessary to design a sensor/information-source system architecture based on a new application of information theory and take a system of systems (SoS) approach. The resulting Information-Based Sensor/source Management system (IBSM) is predicated on viewing sensors (including data/information sources) as communications channels between the real world and a probabilistic model of the world. In this context, information is measured by the expected decrease in uncertainty in our situation assessment probabilistic model as weighted by its mission value and the time it takes to acquire the information. This paper briefly introduces IBSM, the functions of the partitioned model, and the goal lattice which effectively combines competing, independent, orthogonal, and dependent goals into a mission value with which to value competing sensor functions. It is also shown how machine learning can be applied to assist the internal operations of the human-on-the-loop (HOL) system as well as to provide the situation awareness of potential adversary behaviors.

Keywords: Heterogenous sensor management · Information · Sensors · IBSM · Situation assessment · Goal Lattice

1 Motivation for IBSM: Requirements and Constraints

The system design goal is to provide the decision maker with the maximum mission valued, minimum uncertainty model of the world in a timely manner through the effective use of heterogeneous, multi-modal sensors operating in physical, social, and cyber space on one or more platforms. We focus here on the single platform case for simplicity. That is, we desire a situation assessment of *what* comprises a situation as opposed to the situation awareness which provides the *why* of a situation. Both situation assessment and situation awareness are provided by IBSM. For a complete discussion of sensor

© Springer Nature Switzerland AG 2021
W. F. Lawless et al. (Eds.): Engineering Artificially Intelligent Systems, LNCS 13000, pp. 19–33, 2021.
https://doi.org/10.1007/978-3-030-89385-9_2

management in intelligence, surveillance and reconnaissance (ISR), the reader is referred to a recent book by the author [1]. We focus here on the motivation for, and thus the requirements and constraints for, the design of the IBSM architecture.

Sensor suites were initially designed to optimize the data acquisition capabilities of each individual sensor with individual operators reporting their observations. The fusion of the single sensor data with other sensors or *a priori* knowledge was in the minds of a sensor operator. In the case of the WW-II Chain Home Air Defense radar network, the data from the spatially dispersed radars were fused in the minds of the commanders in a central analysis center where target positions were manually positioned on a large table. As the complexity of sensors both in terms of capability and modes of operation increased, manual operations needed to give way to automated sensor scheduling which some erroneously viewed as sensor management.

It also became clear that a single sensor could not provide enough information about the situation as different electromagnetic (EM) sensors interacted differently with the environment depending on the wavelengths sensed. Sensors at one wavelength could provide long range coverage, others short range. There are many other examples of wavelength dependent capability which we will not list here. So there was a move away from optimizing the usage of a single sensor to maximize the flow of data toward maximizing the flow of data from multiple heterogeneous sensors observing a situation into a common operating picture (COP) of that situation for decision makers.

The constraints that we are operating under in heterogenous sensor management are many but the primary one is that sensors are constrained in measurement, computation, and, or data space [2]. That is, a sensor cannot sense from all directions and all sources at the same time. For example, an omnidirectional EM sensor has a short range. To improve detection range, energy must be focused to a narrow beamwidth, but this is at the expense of not being able to observe targets outside of that beamwidth at the same time. This limitation may also be computational in that there is not enough computing power with which to process the amount of data that can be obtained by a sensor. Recognizing these limitations, one needs to make a decision about what to observe from a multiple sensor system point of view, not from a myopic, single sensor point of view. That is, the optimum sensor schedule (from the sensor's point of view) may not provide the information needed to properly assess a situation in a timely manner or with enough accuracy. These individual sensors must behave in "subservient autonomy" to higher authority in order to make a more efficacious system of systems (SoS).

The most effective way in which to transfer data from the real world into a model of that world for use by decision makers is to obtain valuable, timely, actionable intelligence. This acquisition can be done by utilizing a single optimization criterion based on four criteria with commensurate units of measure:

- Transfer information, not just data
- Mission-value the information
- Maximize the probability of obtaining the information
- Obtain the information in a timely manner

That is, we seek a sensor manager which maximizes the expected information value rate (EIVR). This EIVR will be explained in more detail later, particularly the fact that

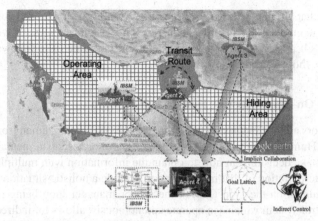

Fig. 1. Notional model of 4 agents surveilling an operating area, a hiding area, and a transit route between the two areas [2].

there are two different types of information to be considered, sensor information and situation information.

At the same time, we must be aware of implementation considerations such as the need for the sensor manager to be computable in real-time or to have a reasonable planning horizon, to be scalable (*i.e.,* be comprised of a single model that can be used and integrated among multiple intelligence levels), to reduce communications bandwidth (*i.e.,* operate with data pull rather than data push), and to have a firm theoretical basis for design guidance with which to make tradeoffs.

An additional motivation for this design is that all of the components of IBSM are amenable to machine learning and real-time adaptation to the current environment. This adaptability is important because the situation is never as we expect it to be since there are both natural interference (in the sense of random noise and events) and intelligent adversaries (in the sense of intentional deceptive maneuvers or radiated signals).

The result of applying the following design principles results in a software system which can be encapsulated in a container, instantiated multiple times in parallel either in the cloud or locally, and needs only the goal lattice to be particularized for the platform and mission. The second useful result is that IBSM can be utilized at any level of the command and control (C2) hierarchy because one hierarchical level's sensors are the goals of a lower layer. At a strategic level, a sensor is a squadron; at a squadron level a sensor is an aircraft; and at an aircraft level, a sensor might be a radar. But at all these levels, IBSM works the same. A cartoon of a typical sensor management problem as viewed from a command authority is shown in Fig. 1. Individual and essentially identical IBSMs are implemented at the area commander level as well as on each of the platforms.

2   Design Considerations

While the stated goal is the maximization of the flow of mission-valued information from the real world into a mathematical model of that world, there is no conventional guidance on how to do that. To that end, we have specified certain constraints and considerations which helped to guide us and insure that the resulting system is realizable with traceable behavior as well as a system which can operate in real time. The following sections briefly explain those considerations.

2.1 Human-On-The-Loop Vice Human-In-The-Loop

Both the sensors and the environment require the removal of the human from inside the control loop. Human reaction time is not fast enough nor is human mental bandwidth sufficient to make decisions on how to obtain the information with multiple sensors as well as the interpretation of that information to provide a holistic situation assessment. Placing the human-on-the-loop (HOL), the sensor manager loop being essentially a feedback control system which can operate autonomously, allows for indirect control of the behavior of the loop without the need for the human to directly "twiddle the knobs" internal to the system. The human tells the IBSM system the relative mission value of what is desired rather than how to obtain it. This indirect control is exercised by the operator in the form of adjustments of the relative weights of the topmost goals of the mission goal lattice (GL) which is detailed later in this Chapter.

2.2 Partition the System into Orthogonal Components

Often systems are designed as an *ad hoc* collection of interconnections between functions or sensors with many of these connections arising as an afterthought to solve a problem. It is not unusual to discover during development that a function needs specific non-local data so that it is directly connected to the source. The resulting spaghetti diagram is not suitable for incremental improvement, and major changes require replacement rather than refinement or evolution. By partitioning the sensor management system into orthogonal components with well defined, bidirectional interfaces, any one of the components can be replaced without regard to the others provided it meets the interface requirements. This partitioning is much like the use of hardware design language with declared interfaces (like the function definitions in *.h files in the C programming language or the architectures in *.vhd files in VHDL) being separated from the definitions (like the function implementation *.c files in C and the entities *.vhd files in VHDL) which instantiate the declared function. With this approach, IBSM can individually implement components with simplified definitions which can be enhanced and fully developed in parallel while at the same time providing functionality for incremental simulation of the entire IBSM system with increasing fidelity to a finally deployable system.

2.3 Probabilistic World Model

Since we do not know anything in the world with absolute certainty, it seems reasonable to use a probabilistic model of the world. As we will see later, a probabilistic model allows us to compute the amount of information which will be acquired when these probabilities change as a result of obtaining data. The choice of which probabilistic model to use is only guided by the need to be able to predict the amount of change that will occur if we were to obtain certain data. For IBSM, we have chosen to use two causal Bayesian networks [3], one representing the situation assessment encapsulating our knowledge of the situation as it exists, and a second representing the situation awareness encapsulating our knowledge of how the situation could evolve and the possible situations to which the current situation could lead (or be precluded).

2.4   Partitioned Components Are Interconnected by Bidirectional Interfaces

While IBSM could launch observation requests to sensors and wait for the data to be returned, it makes more sense for there to be component-to-component bidirectional interfaces such that each transfer function in the loop can immediately feed back to the earlier transfer function whether it can, indeed, perform the function. If it cannot perform the function, the earlier transfer function (which may have had several choices of functions that can meet its requirements) can immediately send another request which may meet its needs, even if not with as high an expected information value rate. This approach will make more sense after viewing the IBSM block diagram and the brief top-level explanation of how it operates.

2.5   Data, Information, and Knowledge

Since the terms data, information, and knowledge are often used somewhat interchangeably in common language, it is necessary for the design of a heterogeneous sensor management system to define them less ambiguously. For our usage, we follow the lead of Waltz [4] and modify his definitions slightly for our usage as follows:

- Data: individual observations, measurements, and primitive messages: Data are the result of sensor observations or cyber accesses which are combined into measurements and affect the uncertainty about a process or event. In order to obtain data we make one or more observations and combine them or fuse them with other data or knowledge to produce a measurement.
- Information: an organized set of data: Information is a change in uncertainty about a random variable or its underlying probability distribution.
- Knowledge: information once analyzed, understood, and explained. A causal Bayesian net (BN) is an example of a knowledge repository.

That is, data can be acquired and used to decrease our uncertainty about a dynamic process resulting in information which can flow into or out of a BN resulting in a change in the knowledge about a situation.

It is important to note that our usage of information is not in the Shannon sense of encoding data to be transmitted through a communications channel. Shannon was agnostic about message content, value, or meaning and confined his work to coding of data through a noisy, bandwidth-limited communications channel. Our non-Shannon sense of information is related to the choice of what data to send down a channel, namely the choice of those data which will produce the greatest decrease in our uncertainty about a node in a probabilistic representation of the world.

The value of focusing on information as a component of a sensor/source management system is that it is a commensurate measure with which to compare alternatives. One can compute the information amount of search, track, identification, likelihood of a cyber attack, or the size of an unknown organization based on changes in probabilities associated with these nodes resulting from the acquisition of data. It is only these probabilities we need to consider independent of their actual units of measure.

Information

We make no distinction among the data obtained by physical measurements of a process and the data obtained by querying a database, the state of a controller on a supervisory control and data acquisition (SCADA) connection, or activities on a physical or social network. They all can be viewed as sensors which obtain data that may or may not provide our model with information. There are a variety of measures of information among which are Fisher's information [5], Renyi's information [6], Kullback-Leibler (KL) divergence [7], and Shannon entropy [8] where the KL and Shannon measures of information can be derived from Renyi's information.

For IBSM we chose to utilize the change in entropy as a measure of information [9] because it is familiar, ubiquitous, and easy to compute both when computing sensor information and situation information. The entropy, $H(X)$, can be computed as

$$H(N_j) = - \sum_{i=1}^{n} P(x_i) log_b P(x_i) \tag{1}$$

where $P(x_i)$ is the probability of a random variable, x_i, and b is the base of the logarithm (a value of 2 yields information measured in bits). The amount of information resulting from a change in probabilities (a change in entropy) being,

$$I^+ = H^- - H^+ \tag{2}$$

where the negative sign in the entropy is replaced by reordering the entropies such that the information after (I^+) is the difference between the entropy before, H^-, and the entropy after, H^+.

We must make a distinction between two computationally similar but interpretationally different types of information in sensor management. First, there is the information associated with the fundamental change in the uncertainty associated with a process in the environment (the sensor information, I_{sen}), and second, there is a change in uncertainty about the situation itself which is comprised of the uncertainty about many (possibly related) processes (the situation information, I_{sit}).

It should also be noted that information does not exist on its own. You cannot "look up" information because information is a change in uncertainty and different users with different existing knowledge may or may not acquire information from the same observation of a process. The same data may provide information to one user and none to another.

Sensor Information

Physical, cyber, and social sensors are all methods for obtaining data about a process whose state is uncertain. The state can either be an enumerable quantity with a probability of being in a state associated with it or a random variable (RV) which has a probabilistic representation. For brevity we will simply use the term random variable when referring to either. Generally an uncertainty associated with an RV increases with time if an RV is not observed. If one uses a Kalman filter state estimator (or any other method which can propagate uncertainty into the future), then the amount of information obtained by a sensor, I_{sen}, as a result of that observation is the difference (*e.g.*, using K-filter terminology [10]) between the conformal norms of the a priori and a posteriori error covariance matrices as [11],

$$I_k = -log\big[\,\|P_k^-\| - \|P_k^+\|\,\big] \tag{3}$$

Situation Information

If information is defined as a change in entropy, then there can be positive and negative information flows [12]. If we assume that a situation assessment causal Bayesian network is used to represent the probabilities associated with the multiple dynamic processes of the situation of interest, then there is a temporal loss of information associated with the lack of data to reduce or maintain our uncertainty. This loss is because many of the processes which we are estimating are represented by random variables whose future states are inherently less certain than their current states. As a result, and because many nodes of a causal BN are connected by conditional relationships, situation information must be computed as a global change in entropy of the entire Bayesian network [12]. With no measurements, the information flow is negative. With measurements, the information flow can be negative, zero, or positive. That is, with no measurements, our knowledge of the situation decreases over time. With measurements over time, our knowledge may decrease, increase, or remain the same.

2.6 Mission Value and Competing, Interdependent Goals

It is common to have an objective function which is comprised of a weighted sum of non-commensurate criteria. For example, while the probability of detection of a target, P_d, and the probability of avoiding detection by the target must both be considered, a weighted sum of these two is of little value. What is needed is a nondimensional value which is a measure of the mission value of accomplishing a goal. A hierarchical goal tree is not sufficient since many low-level goals can simultaneously contribute to the accomplishment of several higher level mission goals. However, if we put the mission goals in the mathematical form of a lattice and then adjoin to each of the goals a computed mission value, we have a goal lattice [13] which can be used to assign a mission-value to an information need.

To form a mathematical goal lattice (GL), we need a set of goals, S, and an ordering relation, $\leq$,

$$Lattice = \{S, \leq\} \tag{4}$$

In our case, the set of goals are the mission goals and the ordering relation is considered to be *is necessary for the accomplishment of*. This ordering relation leads to the interpretation of the lattice as the highest goals (the most inclusive) being soft and

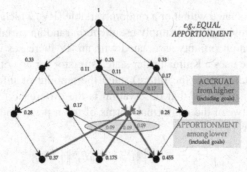

Fig. 2. A numerical example of an atypical GL in which mission values are equally apportioned among the included goals. Equal apportionment is generally not the case.

abstract with the bottommost goals being the real, measurable actions which can be taken to accomplish the higher level goals. To produce a mission goal lattice, a web based server-client tool [14] is used to first enter goals and then to specify their relationship or that they are unrelated. The goal lattice engine then combines these specific pair-wise or n-wise relations into a lattice.

Having now a lattice of mission goals, we assume that the topmost goal of accomplishing the mission has a value of 1. This value is apportioned among the goals in the next "layer" of the lattice in a zero sum manner. The values of the goals of this layer are then apportioned to the goals in the next layer and so on. While the value of a goal is distributed downward to its included goals, the value of a lower goal is the sum of the values that are apportioned to it. That is, a lower (included) goal, may contribute to the accomplishment of more than one higher level goal and accrue value from each. For a simple example of this apportionment, see Fig. 2.

While a goal lattice itself may look complex and require significant *a priori* construction effort, in practice, the pre-mission and mission adjustments are only in the topmost relative goal values. During the mission, the calculation of the mission values of the various real, measurable sensor actions which are available is in the form of a straightforward matrix multiplication.

3   IBSM Architecture

With reference to the block diagram of Fig. 3, there are six main components to the partitioned IBSM:

- Goal lattice (GL) assigns mission values to situation information needs as well as to alternative sensing functions to satisfy those needs
- Situation information expected value network (SIEV-net) incorporates contextual information into the situation information needs evaluation through conditional probabilities
- Information instantiator (II) utilizes the AFT to map situation information needs to sensor functions

- Applicable function table (AFT) maintains a dynamic list of available sensor functions for use by the information instantiator
- Sensor scheduler maps sensor functions to sensor observations utilizing an on-line, greedy, urgency drive, pre-emptive scheduling algorithm (OGUPSA)
- Communications Manager (CM) transmits and receives non-local information requests and goal values

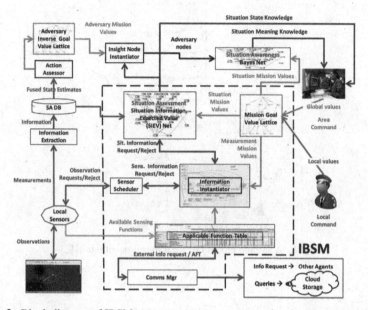

Fig. 3. Block diagram of IBSM sensor management system showing the components.

As all of these components are described in detail in a recent book [1] by the author with references to the papers which describe them in detail, we only briefly describe their relevance to the system design of IBSM.

3.1 Goal Lattice

The goal lattice [2, 13] is a hierarchical ordering of mission goals from the highest level which are the soft, difficult to define overall goals. The lowest level goals are the real, measurable sensor actions. All of these goals have adjoined to them the mission value which is traceable through the GL in a manner shown in Fig. 2. The approach is to define the GL and its value apportionment in pre-mission planning with the relative values of the topmost goals adjusted in real-time by the local command authority with the ability of higher level authority to add additional top-level goals during a mission. Gross changes in relative mission values can be implemented by preprogrammed mission values such as for surveillance, self-defense, or attack phases. Single button pushes can be used to immediately switch from one relative set of goals to another and thereby change the entire behavior of the IBSM to provide the best EIVR for that type of mission phase. A partial goal lattice for a maritime mission is shown in Fig. 4.

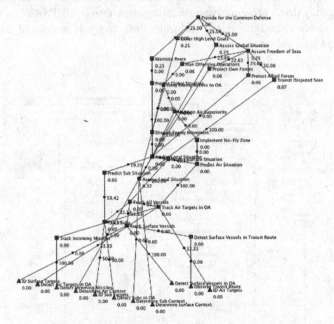

Fig. 4. A sample global GL for a maritime situation [2].

3.2 Situation Information Expected Value Network

The situation information expected value network (SIEV-net) is an enhancement of a causal Bayesian network which encapsulates and values our knowledge of the situation. It also associates topmost mission values with the situation assessment nodes and has functions to compute $EI_{sit}VR$. As shown in Fig. 5, the BN itself is divided among three layers, the non-managed nodes which are data provided by outside sources over which we have no control, the situation nodes which are of interest to us and are our current situation assessment, and the managed nodes which are the sensor information functions that we can request through the information instantiator. The SIEV-net is also dynamic in that as targets are detected or lost, their nodes are automatically instantiated or de-instantiated through a process of inserting net-frags (network fragments) along with their associated connectivity into the SIEV-net.

3.3 Information Instantiator

The information instantiator (II) [15] converts situation information requests received from the SIEV-net and downselects from the set of available sensing functions as stored in the applicable function table (AFT) to those which are able to satisfy the situation

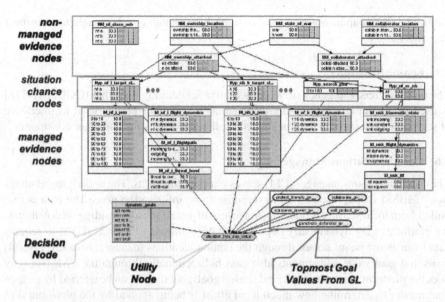

Fig. 5. Example of a small SIEV-net showing the three different types of nodes.

information request. This subset of sensor functions is then evaluated utilizing their parameters to produce the $EI_{sen}VR$ of each sensing function and order these. This highest valued sensor function and temporal constraints are then sent as an observation request to the detailed sensor scheduler. Should the sensor scheduler not be able to fulfill the request, a rejection is sent back to the II, and the next lower $EI_{sen}VR$-valued observation request is sent to the sensor scheduler. If there is no admissible function available, the II reject the information request and the SIEV-net knows immediately that the information instantiator, and hence the sensor system, is not able to obtain it.

3.4 Applicable Function Table

At initialization, the applicable function table (AFT) [16] is empty. As sensors come on-line on the platform, they transmit a sensor modeling language (SensorML) description of their capabilities with which to populate the AFT [17]. The AFT is a tabular listing of the specific sensing functions that each sensor can perform along with the parameters associated with those functions. During the mission, the AFT is dynamically updated as sensor functions come on-line, degrade, or fail. Notice that we use the term sensing functions since multiple sensors of the same or different type may be able to acquire the data we seek. We leave it to the sensor scheduler to determine which sensor is the best usage of the available sensors to make the actual observation. That is, the information instantiator does not micromanage the acquisition of data.

We further assume that all new sensors are provided by the supplier with a SensorML description of the functions it can perform. IBSM does not care how the sensing function is performed, but only needs to know the sensors' capabilities and limitations for use by the II, and these can be best specified in a machine readable and parsable form using a SensorML.

3.5 Sensor Scheduler

The on-line, greedy, urgency drive, pre-emptive scheduling algorithm (OGUPSA) [18] is used in our initial design. Any other suitable scheduler can be used to interleave observation requests such that they meet deadline requirements and other constraints.

3.6 Communications Manager

The communications manager (CM) serves multiple functions. The underlying assumption of IBSM is that of data-pull in response to an information need. The data is first pulled from local sensors if possible, however, off-board sensors residing on collaborating platforms may dynamically populate the AFT allowing the local IBSM to request data from an off-board sensor through the communications manager. Area level (local) goals and goal value adjustments also pass bidirectionally through the CM. Not only does the platform receive specific and shared goals, but its GL can be queried by an area commander to determine how much local effort is being applied by the platform(s) to the accomplishment of a shared goal. It has to be recognized that a local commander may adjust the GL relative values in order to maximize self preservation or other mission goals at the expense of off-board requests of a lower priority. The CM can also communicate with cloud-based databases with which to populate the non-managed nodes of the SIEV-net.

4 IBSM Operational Narrative

Referring to Fig. 3, the IBSM components can be seen in the dashed box. The relative mission values in the GL can be adjusted by the local command as well as the area command. The topmost values are available to the SIEV-net to determine the $EI_{sit}VR$ and order the situation information requests. Originally there was one SIEV-net which combines both situation assessment and situation awareness. However, it is convenient to differentiate between the situation assessment BN and the situation awareness BN so they are shown separately in the figure. The managed node with the highest $EI_{sit}VR$ is passed to the information instantiator (II). The II determines which observation to request from the sensors by applying the bottommost GL values to the admissible set of sensor functions as listed in the applicable function table. The admissible sensor functions are multiplied by their GL values to determine the possible $EI_{sen}VR$ and then prioritize them. If a suitable observation function is not available, the II rejects the situation information request and an alternative or different information request can then be sent to it by the SIEV-net. If there is an admissible observation request, the observation request is then sent from the II to the sensor scheduler (SS). The SS schedules the observation among the multiple heterogenous sensors utilizing an OGUPSA algorithm. The sensor makes the observation, the data are sent to the information extraction (data fusion) component, and this measurement is then used to update the BN in the situation assessment SIEV-net.

That is, the process is closed loop and real-time with the HOL implemented through relative goal management by local and area commanders.

5   Machine Learning in IBSM

Again with reference to Fig. 3, there are blocks which are outside of the IBSM dashed line but which are components of any sensor system. The information extraction block on the left recognizes that data fusion and the method by which this is done are not within the domain of IBSM. There are other hooks into the system which take the information request and use it to specify the kind of processing which is to be done in the information extraction block since the extraction of information is not only data and context dependent, but also dependent on how that data are processed.

Just as a goal lattice encapsulates the user's mission goals, so can the methodology be used to determine the GL of the adversary by implementing an inverse GL as shown in the upper left of Fig. 3. This inverse GL is populated from the bottom up by the observations of the real-measurable actions which are taken by an adversary. From this inverse GL, the insight-node instantiator (INI) is implemented by AI or ML to determine possible courses of action by the adversary. These alternative scenarios are used to populate nodes of the situation awareness BN. These nodes and their probabilities are used to inform the user about possible courses of action by the adversary which may result in the user's adjustment of the IBSM GL values.

Not shown here is the generation of one or more log files by an IBSM daemon which operates in the background. This methodology captures the sequence of measurements that were made in support of informing a node and thereby allows one to retrospectively understand the means by which the system came to its decision. Unlike other systems whose operations are opaque, IBSM is fully transparent, and the decisions that are made as to which information to seek, which sensor to use, and the mission value of each action are available for retrospective analysis.

Since the parameters embedded in IBSM are based on hardware specifications, receiver operating curves (ROC), environmental attenuation, possible jamming amounts and effectiveness as well as historical data on the probability of obtaining situation information in response to a situation information request, there is a lot of room for the addition of machine learning to refine these parameters in real-time during operations.

6   Conclusion

It remains to summarize the features and benefits of the IBSM approach to sensor management and they are several:

- IBSM is a satisficing solution to the management of heterogeneous sensors in that it does the best it can under the real-time constraints without seeking the "incomputable in real time" global maximum.
- IBSM operates in real-time, and is a scalable and collaborative system which can provide individual platform sensor management as well as provide management of battlespace reconnaissance assets.
- IBSM is predicated on maximizing the expected information value rate (EIVR) to minimize uncertainty in the world model while maximizing mission value which has firm theoretical bases.

- IBSM provides the highest-valued, lowest-uncertainty, and context-sensitive, situation assessment from which to make command decisions.
- IBSM is a closed loop, context sensitive control system which is indirectly controlled through the use of a dynamic mission-oriented goal lattice.
- IBSM is dynamically reconfigurable and fault tolerant through the use of the applicable (sensor) function table.
- The IBSM architecture allows for one sensor management model to be the framework for multiple diverse platforms and hierarchical levels of resource management.
- Sensors can be added or removed in real time without redesigning the system. This capability provides for graceful degradation and robust behavior in dynamic, stressing environments.
- IBSM is amenable to the application of artificial intelligence or machine learning to improve real-time behavior.
- IBSM behaves with subservient autonomy to its higher level goals.

References

1. Hintz, K.J.: Sensor Management in ISR. Artech House, Boston (2020)
2. Hintz, K.J., Kadar, I.: Implicit collaboration of intelligent agents through shared goals. In: SS14 Sensor, Resources, and Process Management for Information Fusion Systems, FUSION2016, IEEE/ISIF, Heidelberg (2016)
3. Pearl, J.: Causality, Models, Reasoning, and Inference, 2nd edn. Cambridge University Press, New York (2009)
4. Waltz, E.: Knowledge Management in the Intelligence Enterprise. Artech House, Boston (2003)
5. Fisher, R.A.: On the mathematical foundations of theoretical statistics. Philos. Trans. Royal Soc. **222**, 309–368 (1922)
6. Renyi, A.: On measures of information and entropy. In: Proceedings of the fourth Berkeley Symposium on Mathematics, Statistics and Probability, Berkeley, pp. 547–561 (1960)
7. Kullback, S., Leibler, R.A.: On information and sufficiency. Ann. Math. Statistics **22**, 79–86 (1951)
8. Shannon, C.E., Weaver, W.: The Mathematical Theory of Communication. University of Illinois Press, Urbana (1949)
9. Hintz, K.J., Darcy, S.: Cross-domain pseudo-sensor information measure. In: 2018 21st International Conference on Information Fusion (FUSION), Cambridge, UK (2018)
10. Gelb, A.: Applied Optimal Estimation. MIT Press, Cambridge (1974)
11. Hintz, K., McVey, E.: Multi-process constrained estimation. IEEE Trans. Syst. Man Cybern. **21**(1), 237–244 (1991)
12. Hintz, K., Darcy, S.: Temporal bayes net information & knowledge entropy. J. Adv. Inf. Fusion **13**(2) (2018)
13. Hintz, K.J., McIntyre, G.A.: Goal lattices for sensor management. In: SPIE 3720, Signal Processing, Sensor Fusion, and Target Recognition VIII, Orando, FL (1999)
14. Hintz, K.J., Hintz, A.S.: Creating goal lattices with GMUGLE. In: Signal Processing, Sensor Fusion, and Target Recognition XI, Orlando, FL (2002)
15. Hintz, K., McIntyre, G.: Information instantiation in sensor management. In: Proceedings Signal Processing, Sensor Fusion, and Target Recognition VII, vol. 3374, pp. 38–47. SPIE (1998)

16. Hintz, K.: Utilizing information-based sensor management to reduce the power consumption of networked unattended ground sensors. In: Signal Processing, Sensor Fusion, and Target Recognition XXI, SPIE Defense Symposium, vol. 8392. SPIE, Orlando (2012)
17. Hintz, K., Brannon, S., Williamson, W., Scrofani, J.: Cross-domain pseudo-sensors in IBSM. In: 21st International Conference on Information Fusion, Fusion2018. IEEE/ISIF, Cambridge (2018)
18. McIntyre, G.A., Hintz, K.J.: Sensor measurement scheduling: an enhanced dynamic preemptive algorithm. Opt. Eng. 37(2), 517–523 (1998)

Trusted Entropy-Based Information Maneuverability for AI Information Systems Engineering

Erik Blasch[1]([⊠]), Tod Schuck[2], and Oliver B. Gagne[3]

[1] MOVEJ Analytics, Dayton, OH, USA
[2] Lockheed Martin RMS, Moorestown, NJ, USA
tod.m.schuck@lmco.com
[3] US Army, Enfield, Connecticut, USA
oliver.b.gagne.mil@mail.mil

Abstract. Future battle conflicts will be fought in information space as opposed to a classical physical space. The purpose of the Chapter highlights the overlap of Electromagnetic Maneuver Warfare (EMW) and cyber warfare (CW) concepts with the measures of *information power* and *information maneuverability*. Specifically, the Chapter utilizes Col. John Boyd's Observe-Orient-Decide-Act (OODA) process and his "Destruction and Creation" thesis where he originated "Energy-Maneuverability" (EM) theory towards *information power* and *information maneuverability*. With the proliferation of EMW/CW, there is a need to transition from physical entropy and specific energy to proposed information equivalents. The entropy approach to energy analysis is consistent with robust artificial intelligence (AI)/machine learning (ML) methods. Introducing the concepts of "strong" and "weak" information positions as compared to an adversary or competitor – hence "information maneuverability" (IM), the Chapter lists the theoretical background to develop IM. Decision speed is a hallmark of superior agility and autonomy systems within the systems engineering information domain. Results demonstrate from force ratio use cases the importance of trusted information, achieving a five-fold increase on force structure analytics.

Keywords: Information maneuverability · Information power · Data fusion · Trust · Entropy · Machine learning

1 Introduction

Recent advances in artificial intelligence and machine learning (AI/ML) have developed methods for deep learning that shown remarkable success in object classification of imagery, entity resolution in text, as well characterization of methods for communications [1–3]. These AI/ML techniques are tools that would reside in a systems engineering design and hence need to accommodate various concerns of data collection, user support, and operational sustainment [4]. Hence, there is a need to consider the availability, quality, and trust in the data; especially for systems with human-in-the-loop technology [5, 6].

© Springer Nature Switzerland AG 2021
W. F. Lawless et al. (Eds.): Engineering Artificially Intelligent Systems, LNCS 13000, pp. 34–52, 2021.
https://doi.org/10.1007/978-3-030-89385-9_3

The elements of *data trust* for AI/ML within complex environments require appreciation of the data security (e.g., blockchain methods [7, 8]), the context [9], semantic uncertainty [10], as well as the electromagnetic spectrum. While these AI/ML concepts are being developed, there is also concern on how to effectively use the AI/ML technology, or rather, how the AI/ML technology affects the force ratio analysis between those with the technology and those without. One example is the use of AI/ML in electronic warfare.

In July 2015, the United States Defense Science Board (DSB) of the Office of the Under Secretary of Defense for Acquisition, Technology, and Logistics (OUSD ATL) released a study titled "21st Century Military Operations in a Complex Electromagnetic Environment" [11]. The purpose of this study, according to the DSB, was to "examine both offensive and defensive electronic warfare (EW) needs and opportunities over the next two decades". The concepts are general to improve efficiency and effectiveness of operations. Specifically, the DSB report lists three needs that emerged during the study, which are the following:

1. *Need to dynamically manage the use of the electromagnetic spectrum;*
2. *Need to achieve near real-time system adaptation; and*
3. *Need to switch to a more offensive EW position.*

All three of these needs of the electromagnetic (EM) spectrum (manage, adapt, and act) can be described within the framework of Boyd's Observe-Orient-Decide-Act (OODA) loop [12]. The OODA loop was developed for tactical decision making; but in the context of the information space, the observation-to-action is assessed from the use of Intelligence, Surveillance, and Reconnaissance (ISR) multidomain command and control (MDC2). For example, the DSB report states that for Need 2, "taking advantage of opportunities, far faster than can be currently done", and Need 3, "the need to shift more to offence because responding to every problem defensively will never get ahead of the adversary...".

Using the DSB statement on Need 2, it can be further refined to state that the *speed of adaptation only needs to be faster than the adversary can adapt*. Figure 1 graphically shows *proactive* and *preventative* maneuver OODA cycle (of us) that increases decision speed as compared to the adversary (them) [13]. The multiple OODA-loop concept has well been reported for 20 years such as a cognitive-OODA (C-OODA) to include knowledge reasoning [14] and contextual analysis [15]. Effectively if all agents (actors, equipment, planners, etc.) have an OODA-loop, then there are multiple sources of information and assessment being conducted simultaneously. Some agents interact together such as human and a machine (e.g., Boyd's original concept as applied to a pilot in an aircraft), a human with another human (e.g., ground informant reports back to a commander), or a machine to a machine (e.g., equipment response to the environmental sensors). With the complexity of the battle increasing with the internet of battle things (IoBT), edge devices will be tasked with autonomous capabilities to support effects-based operations. Many times, human-decision making will be slower to act than that of a machine from which the information maneuverability would require humans to impart general commands of operations for machine execution. Clearly, the future will entail AI/ML concepts to meet these coordinated "speed of decisions".

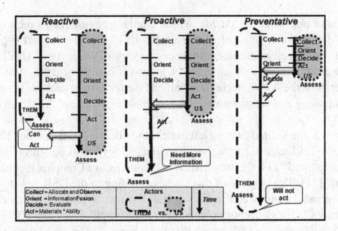

Fig. 1. Preventative maneuver enabled by a superior information position

The DSB states the need to *maneuver* as a foundational power projection strategy and expands the concept via the following:

> *The U.S. has placed increasingly significant importance on information superiority as one of the keys to prevailing in conflict against other forces throughout the world. That superiority is built upon the sensing of ISR assets, the ability to communicate what these sensors see to all required elements of the fight, the geographic and temporal coordination of military forces, and using all of that to outmaneuver the actions of potential adversaries. The dependence on information has not gone unnoticed in the rest of the world and some adversaries have spent significant time, effort, and resources toward lessening the U.S. ability to gather, distribute, coordinate, and act on that information* [11].

When considering the electromagnetic spectrum (EMS), the DSB states the need to *maneuver* as a foundational information strategy need,

> *This dynamic management of the EMS is sometimes described as treating the spectrum as a "maneuver space". It is an interesting concept, because the EM maneuver space has two important characteristics it does not share with the four spatial domains. First, one can change frequency discontinuously and without trend, meaning that agility in the EM domain is possible in a way that is impossible in the four spatial domains. This agility is used in frequency hopping radios, but otherwise largely unexploited in U.S. systems today. It could be a critical enabler of future success* [11].

This Chapter proposes the concept of *information power* and *information maneuverability* that provides a mathematical framework to formalize the information-centric maneuverability concept. The concepts are built upon Boyd's development of **Energy-Maneuverability (EM) theory** first published in March of 1966 by Eglin Air Force Base (AFB) in a report and released to the public in 2013 [12]. By extending Boyd's work based on the context of maneuver to the information domain via Shannon and Ashby's work in information theory; there is an ability to examine the importance of information. The result is a measure, similar to specific energy (E_s) in EM theory, that allows for comparisons between the information positions of two or more entities and thus, which agent has the superior information position. The new measure of *information maneuverability* (IM) extends to new research areas in Cognitive Electronic Warfare and spectrum management [16–19] for information operations [20]. Examples of work with recent AI/ML efforts in Electro-Optical [21] and Radar [22] sensing demonstrate the decision speed and accuracy that foster similar approaches for communications and EW.

Building on the recent efforts of sensor-data fusion, AI/ML, and information maneuverability, the combination of these efforts include systems-of-systems loops that process the data flowing in a scenario. A sensor-data-control loop structure helps for coordinating and modularizing data which is a hallmark of system engineering approaches. Efforts of cognitive computing towards efficiency [23], cognitive assessment to reduce bias [24], and cognitive coordination to maximize usability [25] are trends to bring together AI/ML techniques with deployed data fusion systems. Additional challenges on reliance of AI/ML systems is that they are prone to adversarial attack from which data transfer and resiliency are needed for users to trust developments [26]. Likewise, channel-aware [27] methods assessing the data rate, quality, and availability would enable 5/6G communications for decentralized sensor data fusion systems [28].

The Chapter is developed with the following sections. Section 2 provides a background on information power and maneuverability. Section 3 presents an initial study using force ratios, Sect. 4 engages in an overall discussion of the work thus far, and Sect. 5 discusses conclusions and applications for future work and research.

2 Information Power and Maneuverability

Colonel John R. Boyd, USAF retired, is credited with the development of EM theory as part of the OODA method. Col. Boyd and his co-authors popularized their EM concepts to optimize aircraft design in terms of their ability to maximize maneuverability based on energy state [12]. Boyd *et al.* introduce the concept of *aircraft maneuverability* as "the ability to change direction and/or magnitude of the velocity vector". Applications of the OODA loop are found beyond air-to-air combat in various aerospace texts and competitive enterprises such as business, sports, and electronic games.

EM is introduced to the reader from the Boyd report in the following way. The aircraft altitude, airspeed, and dynamic changes thereto are directly dependent upon the system's forces acting along, and normal to, the flight path. By mathematically manipulating the expressions describing this force system, altitude (h) and airspeed (v) are related through the expression for specific energy (E_s) [12],

$$E_s = h + \frac{v^2}{2g} \tag{1}$$

where g is the gravity acceleration constant.

Thus, EM theory provides a method to understand the relationship between altitude and the kinetic energy of an aircraft to define aircraft maneuverability. It is noted that the units of E_s result in a distance such as length (meters, feet, etc.).

Further, Boyd states that "for an offensive maneuvering advantage, a fighter pilot must be at a higher energy level or be able to gain energy more quickly than his adversary before the maneuver and counter-maneuver portion of the battle begins." Eq. (1) is the flight path determination that gives a pilot an advantage over an adversary.

Boyd references the method of E. S. Rutowski that provides an approximate method for finding the "best flight path" (the Rutowski path [29]) for gaining maneuvering energy. Here, energy gain is maximum "at the points where E_s contours are tangent to the specific excess power (P_s) contours" [12]. P_s is formulated according to the following with its force and velocity equivalent and the assumption that mass change is negligible ($dm/dt = 0$).

$$P_s = \left[\frac{T-D}{W}\right]V = [Force] \times Velocity \tag{2}$$

where Specific Power (P_s) (the time rate of doing work) is equal to Thrust (T) minus Drag (D) divided by the aircraft's Weight (W) multiplied by its current Velocity (V).

The forces in Eq. (2) are illustrated in Fig. 2:

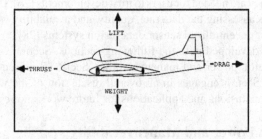

Fig. 2. Principal forces on an aircraft

There are also similar formulations for power such as Ohm's Law:

$$P = EI = Force \times Velocity \tag{3}$$

where: Power (P) = Electromotive Force (E) × Velocity (V) and the units are Power (watts), Electromotive Force (volts) × Velocity (current (I) in amperes = 1 C/s).

Using Eq. (2) and (3), any power/force relationship can be generated in any domain according to the following framework:

$$P = \left[\frac{Force\ Adders - Subtractors}{Resistance\ to\ inertia(change)}\right]System\ Velocity \tag{4}$$

Therefore, based on inspection of Eq. (4), *information power* (P_I) is formulated according to the following (from Shannon's Theory):

$$P_I = \left[\frac{N_S - H}{(1/C)}\right]V = [Force] \times Velocity \tag{5}$$

where: N_S = Number of allowed signals of specific duration.

H = Information entropy (where min = 0), and
C = Channel capacity (bits/sec)
V = velocity of information (bits/sec, messages/sec)

and

$$H = -K \sum_{i=0}^{Ns} p_i \log_2 p_i \qquad (6)$$

where: K = arbitrary positive constant (e.g., system availability)
p_i = probability of an event occurring

and

$$\left(C = \lim_{T \to \infty} \frac{\log Ns}{T} \right) \qquad (7)$$

where: T = signal duration.

With the formulation of P_I (Eq. (5)), the concept of information maneuverability can be derived from the illustration of a simple mechanical system. If a mechanical system has no losses, then the input power must equal the output power. So, let's describe the input power to a device be a force (F_A) acting on a point that moves with velocity (V_A) and the output power be a force (F_B) that acts on a point that moves with velocity (V_B). If there are no losses in the system, then:

$$P = F_B V_B = F_A V_A \qquad (8)$$

and the *mechanical advantage* (*MA*) of the system (output force per input force) is given by $MA = F_B/F_A$, which is equivalent to a P_I ratio:

$$MA(\text{or } IM) = \frac{F_B}{F_A} = \frac{V_A}{V_B} \equiv \frac{P_{IB}}{P_{IA}} \qquad (9)$$

where: IM = information maneuverability.

An application using the Shannon formulation of Hick-Hyman [30, 31], and Fitts' Law [32] sheds further insight into the concept of information maneuverability and how Eq. (9) is determined. Specifically, Fitts applied the Shannon formulation for channel capacity (information amount, noise, channel capacity, and rate of information transmission) to the concept of human perceptual-motor functions and formulated his *index of difficulty* (I_d) shown as:

$$I_d = -\log_2 \left(\frac{W_S}{2A} \right) \qquad (10)$$

where: I_d is measured in bits/response.
w_S = the movement tolerance range (inches or equivalent).
A = average amplitude of the movements (distance of the move).

Revisiting the Shannon formulation of information channel capacity [33] per the development in MacKenzie [34], there is the following formulation for channel capacity:

$$C = (BW) \log_2 \left(\frac{S}{N} + 1 \right) \qquad (11)$$

where: C = channel capacity (bits/sec).

BW = channel bandwidth (1 cycle/s or Hz).

S = Signal power (watts).

N = Noise power (watts).

From Eq. (11), an individual demonstrates information transfer in some form with human movement amplitudes equating to signals and their target tolerances (e.g., noise). Continuing with this analysis, the Fitts I_d can be represented as the following Shannon formulation [33]:

$$I_d = \log_2\left(\frac{A}{W_T} + 1\right) \tag{12}$$

where S and N in Eq. (11) are replaced by amplitude (A) and target width (W_T) which are both distances, and BW is no longer considered to maintain a unitless index.

The example of "difficulty" can be used to re-examine the formulation in Eq. (5), which is not entirely satisfactory. The channel capacity is defined in the same context as N_S (number of signals of duration (t)) and does not provide insight into the characteristics of a transmission medium, like a communications link over the air or in a cable. However, substituting in Eq. (11) for the channel, C, formulation in Eq. (5) now defines information power P_I as a function of number of messages, channel bandwidth, and signal to noise power ratio of the channel (S/N). So, an alternative formulation of Eq. (5) is to insert Eq. (11) for channel capacity C.

Also, the method to fully quantify entropy in the context of Eq. (5) is difficult. The scale of the amount of entropy, the value for K, and how it might subtract from N_S (or BW and S/N) for P_I calculations is not well bounded. One possible method to overcome the need to quantity information entropy is to use the *Probability Information Content* (*PIC*) metric as a substitute for an unbounded H. The PIC normalizes entropy between 0 (maximum entropy) and 1 (minimum entropy). The PIC is defined by Sudano [35] where given a probability measure P on a set $A = \{a_1, a_2, \ldots, a_N\}$ with respective probabilities $\{P(a_1), P(a_2), \ldots, P(a_N)\}$, such that *PIC* is defined as:

$$PIC(A) \cong 1 + \frac{\sum_{i=1}^{N_S} P(a_i) \log_2[P(a_i)]}{\log_2[N_S]} \tag{13}$$

We assert that the definition of entropy, Eq. (13) can constrain Eq. (5) versus a traditional approach. Shannon defined entropy H, of a discrete random variable A, with positive values $\{a_1, a_2, \ldots, a_N\}$ and a probability mass function P(A) becomes:

$$H(A) = E[I(A)] = E\left[-\log_2(P(A))\right] \tag{14}$$

where: $E[I(A)]$ = the *expected value of information content* $I(A)$. Entropy then is:

$$H(A) = -\sum_{i=1}^{N_S} P(a_i)I(a_i) \tag{15}$$

$$H(A) = -\sum_{i=1}^{N_S} P(a_i)\log_2[P(a_i)] \tag{16}$$

Substituting in Eq. (13), then

$$PIC(A) \cong 1 + \frac{-H(A)}{\log_2[N_S]} \tag{17}$$

Rearranging yields:

$$H(A) = -[PIC(A) - 1]\log_2[N_S] \tag{18}$$

And then substituting into Eq. (5) gives,

$$P_I = -\left[\frac{N_S - [PIC(A) - 1]\log_2[N_S]}{1/C}\right]V \tag{19}$$

$$P_I = -\{N_S - [PIC(A) - 1]\log_2[N_S]\}CV \tag{20}$$

$$P_I = -CVN_S + CV\{(PIC(A)\log_2[N_S]\} - CV\log_2[N_S] \tag{21}$$

For example, if $\Sigma(P(a_i)) = 1$, and all a_i are equiprobable (e.g. if $A = \{0.25, 0.25, 0.25, 0.25\}$) then the $PIC = 0$ (no information is conveyed). So, if by considering Eq. (18) and consider P_I as a positive quantity since it is used in a ratio:

$$P_I = CV[N_S - H] = CV[N_S - 2] \tag{22}$$

If $A = \{1,0,0,0...\}$, then $H(A) = 0$ as there is no uncertainty and the $PIC = 1$ and the full amount of P_I emerges per the capacities of N_S, C, and V; where,

$$P_I = CVN_S \tag{23}$$

Finally, by substituting for C with Eq. (11), Eq. (23) becomes:

$$P_I = (BW) \log_2\left(\frac{S}{N_S} + 1\right)VN_S \tag{24}$$

which can also be done in Eqs. (19–21) when $H \neq 0$. Hence, the information power, P_I (Eq. 24), relates to the information uncertainty, and the ratio of P_I (s) (Eq. 9) gives *information maneuverability*.

3   Machine Learning Combat Power Study

As an example, a force ratio calculator uses information maneuverability to assess how *relative combat power* is calculated during complex engagement planning and wargaming. If sensor fusion, machine learning, and power analysis are employed in future conflicts, the dissemination of effects are important [36]. Hence, using traditional approaches for equipment status needs to further consider the value of information. Figure 3 shows a capture of a US Army (USA) force calculation spread sheet [37]. The warfighter has the option of generating physical force ratios based upon how he/she would need to represent estimated friendly and hostile force structures.

Combat Power is the total means of destructive, constructive, and information capabilities that a military unit or formation can apply at a given time [38]. From the modeling spreadsheet, the following is a description of the determination of relative combat power [37].

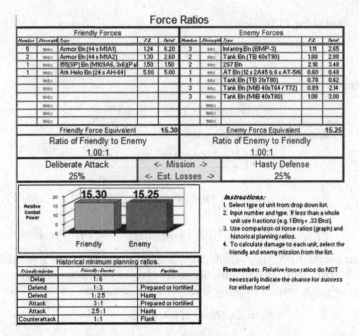

Fig. 3. Force ratio calculation example.

Combat power is the effect created by combining maneuver, firepower, protection, and leadership, the dynamics of combat power, in combat against the enemy. By integrating and applying the effects of these elements with any other potential combat multipliers (Combat Service and Combat Service Support arms as well as other service assets available) against the enemy, the commander can generate overwhelming combat power to achieve victory at minimal cost. This task is difficult, at best. It requires an assessment of both tangible and intangible factors as well as consideration of an inordinate number of those factors either directly or indirectly affecting the potential outcome of the battle.

Further,

Although some numeric relationships are used in this process, it is not like the former-Soviet mathematically substantiated computation for the correlation of forces. Rather, it is only a largely subjective estimate. The (Course of Action) COAs must not be based strictly on mathematical analyses. Pure, logical approaches are often predictable, sacrificing the surprise that bold, audacious action can achieve.

The current method of determining *relative combat power* [37] contains no information power (P_I) predictions or considers P_I effects. So, any assumptions of combat power as shown in Fig. 3 are based upon expected force equivalents where the "dynamics of combat power" are not based on information maneuverability. If the information knowledge is considered in the force ratio, it would better characterize the actual environment. For example, much of the force structure (e.g., tanks, personnel) are operating based on the information they receive and thus, need to be assured that the information available is accurate, complete, resilient, and trusted.

Broadly speaking, the units listed in a US Army Force Ratio Worksheet do not operate autonomously and are increasingly reliant on complex distributed information systems in order achieve a greater force equivalency value (i.e., combat multiplier). Because information must be shared across common networks to synchronize combat power, it is critical that users also account for the status of these networks independently (e.g., IM) when assessing combat power.

Recent technology has been demonstrated for electronic attack from which electronic countermeasures are needed. For example, systems can employ jamming, spoofing, and data manipulation [39]. For jamming, there is a complete loss of signal from which the power of information could be lost. For spoofing, an incomplete or deceptive understanding would cause disruption and confusion. Finally, for data manipulation, the information that was being transferred could be of the same integrity, but the content is changed to mislead efforts. Hence, new technology is being deployed to challenge the information exchange for situational awareness. The technology can affect many platforms from tanks to unmanned aerial vehicles [40]. The data integrity, trust, and explainability would be always of concern in future battlespace environments.

We modified the force ratio calculator to include the effect of *relative information power* (hence P_I) between corps-level[1] entities based upon hypothetical force ratios. In doing so, Force Equivalencies (FE) are adjusted for the speed and/or quality (degradation) of information utilized by Friendly and Enemy forces.

3.1 Example 1: Data Transfer

Our prior work focused on data completeness and data resiliency [41]. The transfer of data is an important aspect of distributed information fusion systems; however, data may come at different resolutions, intervals, and completeness. Recent efforts of AI/ML applied to edge services [42] utilize data fusion [43] from which data completeness determines the credibility in the decision assessment.

Let's assume there are two situations of three reports of equal value, but the information transfer is (CASE A – Fig. 4) **incomplete** and (CASE B – Fig. 5) **resilient**.

CASE A: **Incomplete**. In this scenario, three reporting sources provide information, but the channels do not have complete transfer of information such that each channel is not able to transfer all the required information at the same time.

CASE B: **Resilient**. In this scenario, three reporting sources can report their information simultaneously with the available data transfer.

Comparing an **incomplete scenario** with **resilient scenario**; it is noted that the incomplete data transfer has different probabilities of available information $P_A(x) = \{0.2, 0.3, 0.5\}$ while the available transfer has $P_B(x) = \{0.33, 0.33, 0.33\}$. The information power of the scenarios is $1.58 > 1.49$ which is $|P_{IB}| > |P_{IA}|$ and the information maneuverability is $|IM_B| > |IM_A|$.

---

[1] Ideally, relative information power, P_I, would begin to be calculated starting at the lowest echelon which owns a complete information network.

The Force Ratio Worksheet calculation results are presented in Figs. 4 and 5 for incomplete and resilient scenarios.

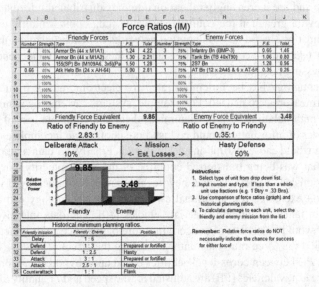

Fig. 4. Force ratio worksheet with IM (CASE A)

Holding all of the other variables constant, as shown in Fig. 5, the course of action (COA) for this situation is validated as suitable for the operating approach based on the assumptions used in the analysis.

By multiplying the sum of Force Equivalencies by the IM value, a heuristic technique is created to model relative combat power in degraded or contested electromagnetic operating environments. When applying the IM values presented in CASE A and CASE B with the Force Ratio Calculation example, one can see that IM has affected a potential deliberate attack to the point where a Commander may want to consider a different COA as the Friendly to Enemy ratio changes from 3.22:1 to 2.83:1.

In the case presented, IM increases the force ratio in favor of the Friendly forces. However, the opposite could be true when the Enemy has the ability to affect the IM for themselves, either with better technology or disrupting the Friendly content of information. While these capabilities might be current approaches of jamming, the future of AI/MI would change the information landscape offering a host of alternatives to consider – especially with adversarial machine learning (AML) techniques.

The AML classic example includes manipulating signs such that a classifier detects a completely different object. To that end, there could be multiple situations in which the force ratio is not an accurate representation of the force structure. For example, by manipulating the signature of a tank, the "tank classification" from AI/ML results could be altered such that the information knowledge about the opposing force is inaccurate. Hence, there is a need to update the IM concepts to also consider the trust in the data that is used for the force ratio analysis. To increase trust in the decision, methods of sensor

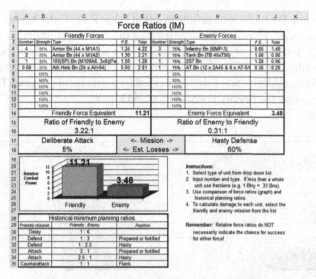

Fig. 5. Force ratio worksheet with IM (CASE B)

data fusion offer the ability to determine information conflicts (e.g., when the results do not match), reduce uncertainty (e.g., combining multiple looks), and increase trust (e.g., verifying consistent results).

3.2 Example 2: Data Trust

Building on the data transfer results, there is a concern with the trust in the sources of information using AI/ML methods. Hence, to determine information maneuverability, the fusion of information can increase trust and the quality of the results. The trust elements can be a scale from well trusted to untrusted. Within an authenticated known group (e.g., Friendly Force), the data and information can be verified and trusted. On the other hand, if the sensed information on the opposing force cannot be verified (say from data fusion); then even if the information reported (or reporter) can be trusted, there is still uncertainty in the results. If there is a reasonable set of trust in the data, but it is only collected from a small piece of evidence, the trust is unsure, and the entropy is high. There are the cases in which data provided has no trust reported as from the ambiguity of the information. Finally, the information could be untrusted as coming from an unreliable source, concerns of whether the information manipulated or is incomplete. In the case of untrusted, the uncertainty is high.

Given the need for trusted, verified, and corroborated information for effective decision making, the force ratios need to consider situations in which these needs are not satisfied. Building on Example 1, another scenario was run with the uncertainty analysis with and without data fusion. For the data fusion case, it is assumed that the information is verified and remains the same for the Friendly Force (as to a representation from Example 1). However, if multiple pieces of evidence are not the same, then variations of trust (by way of uncertainty) are re-calculated.

Translating the IM calculation results from the Force Ratio Calculations, information maneuverability was calculated for scenarios of different trust attributes as shown in Figs. 7 and 8. From Fig. 7, the trusted results offer a situation in which the Force ratio favors the Friendly Force; however, when there is high uncertainty as determined from multiple conflicting information being processed by a data fusion engine (Table 1), then the force ratio favors the Enemy Force (Fig. 6 and Fig. 8).

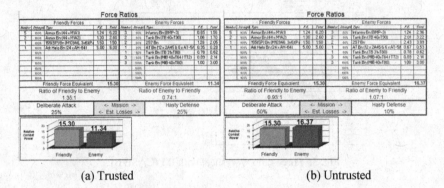

(a) Trusted   (b) Untrusted

Fig. 6. Force ratio worksheet for (a) trusted and (b) untrusted data scenarios

Table 1 presents a notional example. In the case of verified, it is the same as the force ratio worksheet. A trusted result is still high with a small uncertainty. Moving to a situation in which the report is somewhat trusted, but not confirmed or verified (such as one source of evidence of four being in conflict), the results are unsure, but could be a case for action. However, when there is no trust of the source of information, then a conservative estimate would be to add uncertainty. Finally, the case of untrust is when there is good reason to expect some attributes of an AML situation and concern is placed on whether the information is even correct. The untrust case might come from a situation in which new evidence contradicts the *a piori* estimates of force structures.

Note, while this is a notional example, the purpose of the exercise is to look at information maneuverability and information power ratios in the context of advances in sensor data fusion (SDF) AI/ML. Thus, it is assumed with advances in computational power and SDF AI/ML, that more rigor can be placed on the information being transferred from the edge to the central decision maker of force structures and force ratios.

Table 1. Scenarios from the Force Ratio Calculator

	Verified	Trusted	Unsure	NoTrust	UnTrust
	1	0.9	0.6	0.3	0.1
Friendly	15.31	**15.31**	15.31	15.31	15.31
Enemy	11.34	11.90	13.58	**15.25**	16.37

Figure 7 plots the perspectives of the information maneuverability ratio (IMR) between the Friendly Force and the Enemy Force. Two things are revealed. The first is that the Friendly Force has an advantage when the data is trusted based on the force structure assessments; and the second is that the Enemy Force has an advantage with information maneuverability by way of increasing the uncertainty associated with the untrusted data. Hence, it is advantageous to not only disrupt information maneuverability, but also disrupt the power of the information. Again, the notional examples present the case in which the high uncertainty with the IM and IP cause confusion. Figure 7 shows where the ratio of 1.23 (Friendly to Enemy) is better than 0.8 (Enemy to Friendly) giving an advantage to the Friendly Force. On the other hand, the ratios become nearly equal with the high uncertainty.

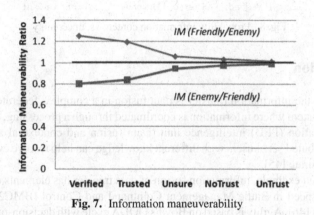

Fig. 7. Information maneuverability

Figure 8 tells a similar story in that the PIC begins with an advantage to the Friendly Forces, but quickly favors the Enemy Force when the data is untrusted. As the PIC is grounded in sensor data fusion, the results indicate a benefit to the Friendly Force when the information is verified, but then favors the Enemy Force when the data is untrusted.

The results indicate that future methods need to consider the advances in AI/ML processing, uncertainty analysis, and entropy information measures. Different scenarios produce different results. When there are variations in the force assessments of technology, then other considerations are needed, such as that of EW and CW. The force capability only begins with the available equipment, but how the knowledge of the force technology is deployed is based on the sensing and knowledge capturing. Thus, decision makers need to consider the conservative/aggressive, optimistic/pessimistic, and verified/unverified data assessments in their course of actions.

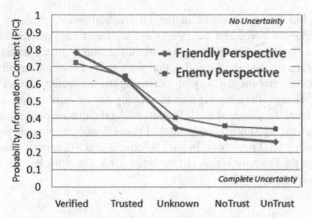

Fig. 8. Probability information content vs. uncertainty

4 Discussion

Analogous to the information transfer is data fusion in a complex, federated command and control system where information is coordinated through a processing, exploitation, and dissemination (PED) intelligence unit. Data fusion and contextual analysis [44] across a distributed set of users with different knowledge can help resolve events quicker and more accurate [45].

As a related example, information fusion of data transfer has elements of IP and IM for decision speed in Battle Management Command and Control (BMC2) operations such as agility [46]. Agility is based on Boyd's OODA cycle with decision-oriented value assessment for scenario/situation assessment [47]. *Agility* is the ability to successfully effect, cope with, and/or exploit changes in circumstances. In a real-world situation, as an example, the opposing force will have their own multiplier for IM, so it is important to react quickly to change.

Agility involves gathering and recognizing changes in the environment and developing the ability to respond approximately. The core elements of agility include responsiveness, versatility, flexibility, resilience, innovativeness, and adaptability. An example of agility in practice is network security that provides the dynamic responsiveness and resilience to adapt to moving challenges. By considering the suitability of different command and control (C2) approaches for the conduct of different types of situations, the paradigm of C2 agility can be directly linked to the situational leadership. Using the C2 agility paradigm [48], there is a need to understand how Battle Management (BM) is developed with new systems and architectures in total system development such as for Command, Control, Communications, Computers, and Intelligence (C4I).

The realities of next generation warfare have transformed the information environment into a battlefield. Information operations, systems, and electronic warfare pose a grave threat to the Department of Defense, combatant commands, and Service components. Conversely, when leveraged effectively, the information domain can serve as a force multiplier.

Taking a page out of the Boyd playbook, Col. Matthew Kelly (USMC), once the US Government flight test director for the F-35 program, writes that the OODA loop has evolved beyond its original "mechanical" basis [49]. Instead of altitude and airspeed, the F-35 works the OODA loop in the information domain which, considering its 20:1 kill ratio in Red Flag exercises in 2017, which offers evidence for IM and IP as OODA 2.0 [50].

Classical fighter "dogfighting" from Boyd's OODA concept derivation is not the most important activity with next generation of warfare equipment (e.g., planes, tanks), rather information dogfighting is the activity that is now needed. The realities of next generation warfare have transformed the information environment into a battlefield. Information operations, systems, and electronic warfare pose a grave threat to the situational understanding as well as situation and threat assessment – across all domains from space, air, ground, sea, and cyber elements. Conversely, when leveraged effectively, the information domain can serve as a force multiplier [51]. As from Boyd, the requirement to prosecute an adversary's position is already lost; if the time to act on information is limited to when a pilot can visually identify his or her objective. Likewise, the same holds true for the general force ratio analysis. Instantaneous information space transcends distances that the physical cannot. The IM concepts can be further developed with AI/ML to enable the understanding information superiority in future conflicts across all domains [52].

5   Conclusions

The Chapter highlighted the importance of information maneuverability (IM) and Information Power (IP) in the context of developments in systems engineering, AI/ML, and sensor data fusion for Electromagnetic Maneuver Warfare (EMW) and cyber warfare (CW) domains. Using force ratios, multiple scenarios were presented to formulate and evaluate relative combat power, IM, and IP interactions where the enemy/adversary IM/IP position is dynamic and challenging to measure and predict. Two scenarios were presented to highlight the importance of assessing the information for completeness and resiliency as well as that of verified and trusted results afforded from sensor data fusion, advanced computing, and AI/ML. The IM/IP ratios complement that of decision speed.

Future work will consider the variations of decision speed, methods of SDF for surveillance, EMW, and CW based on collected information, as well as that of estimates of AI/ML methods to enhance complex scenarios. Complementing these efforts would be to work with users towards effective methods of human-machine teaming for real-time force estimates for effective and efficient orchestration of equipment and technology.

References

1. Majumder, U., Blasch, E., Garren, D.: Deep Learning for Radar and Communications Automatic Target Recognition. Artech House, New York (2020)
2. Zhao, Q., Liu, J., Sullivan, N., Chang, K., et al.: Anomaly detection of unstructured big data via semantic analysis and dynamic knowledge graph construction. In: Proceedings SPIE vol. 11756 (2021)

3. Zheng, Y., Blasch, E., Liu, Z.: Multispectral Image Fusion and Colorization. SPIE Press, Bellingham (2018)
4. Blasch, E., Sung, J., Nguyen, T.: Multisource AI Scorecard Table for System Evaluation. AAAI FSS-20: Artificial Intelligence in Government and Public Sector, Washington, DC, USA. arXiv:2102.03985 (2020)
5. Lawless, W.F., Mittu, R., Sofge, D., Hiatt, L.: Artificial intelligence, autonomy, and human-machine teams: interdependence, context, and explainable AI. AI Mag. **40**(3), 5–13 (2019)
6. Lawless, W.F.: Quantum-Like interdependence theory advances autonomous human–machine teams (A-HMTs). Entropy **22**, 1227 (2020)
7. Chen, N., Chen, Y., et al.: Enabling smart urban surveillance at the edge. In: IEEE International Conference on Smart Cloud (SmartCloud), pp. 109–119 (2017)
8. Lawless, W., Mittu, R., Sofge, D., Moskowitz, S.R. (eds.): Artificial Intelligence for the Internet of Everything. Academic Press, Cambridge (2019)
9. Blasch, E.: Context aided sensor and human-based information fusion. In: IEEE National Aerospace and Electronics (NAECON) (2014)
10. Blasch, E., Laskey, K.B., Joussselme, A.-L., Dragos, V., Costa, P.C.G., Dezert, J.: URREF reliability versus credibility in information fusion (STANAG 2511). In: International Conf. on Info Fusion (2013)
11. Defense Science Board Study: 21st Century Military Operations in a Complex Electromagnetic Environment. Office of the Under Secretary of Defense for Acquisition, Technology, and Logistics, Washington, D.C., July 2015
12. Boyd, J.R., Christie, T.P., Gibson, J.E.: Energy-Maneuverability. USAF, Eglin AFB (1966)
13. Blasch, E.P., Bosse, E., Lambert, D.A.: High-Level Information Fusion Management and Systems Design. Artech House, Norwood (2012)
14. Blasch, E., Breton, R., Valin, P.: Using the C-OODA Model for CIMIC Analysis. In: Proceedings IEEE National Aerospace Electronics Conference (NAECON) (2011)
15. Snidaro, L., García, J., Llinas, J., Blasch, E. (eds.): Context-Enhanced Information Fusion. ACVPR, Springer, Cham (2016). https://doi.org/10.1007/978-3-319-28971-7
16. Snidaro, L., Garcia, J., Llinas, J., et al.: Recent Trends in Context Exploitation for Information Fusion and AI. AI Mag. **40**(3), 14–27 (2019)
17. Blasch, E., Busch, T., Kumar, S., Pham, K.: Trends in survivable/secure cognitive networks. In: IEEE International Conference on Computing, Networking, and Communications (2013)
18. Wang, G., Pham, K., Blasch, E., Nguyen, T.M., Shen, D., et al.: Cognitive radio unified spectral efficiency and energy efficiency trade-off analysis. In: IEEE MILCOM (2015)
19. Tian, Z., Blasch, E., Li, W., Chen, G., Li, X.: Performance evaluation of distributed compressed wideband sensing for cognitive radio networks. In: International Conference on Info Fusion (2008)
20. Joint Publication 3–13. Information Operations, (Change 1 20 November 2014).https://www.jcs.mil/Portals/36/Documents/Doctrine/pubs/jp3_13.pdf. Accessed 14 July 2021
21. Liu, S., Liu, H., John, V., Liu, Z., et al.: Enhanced situation awareness through CNN-based deep multimodal image fusion. Optical Eng. **59**(5), 053103 (2020)
22. Roy, D., Mukherjee, T., Chatterjee, M., et al.: RFAL: adversarial learning for RF transmitter identification and classification. IEEE Trans. Cogn. Commun. Networking **6**(2), 783–801 (2020)
23. Preece, A., Cerutti, F., Braines, D., Chakraborty, S., Srivastava, M.: Cognitive computing for coalition situational understanding. IEEE Ubiquitous Intell. Comput. (2017)
24. Raz, A.K., Llinas, J., Mittu, R., Lawless, W.F.: Chapter 12 - Engineering for emergence in information fusion systems: a review of some challenges. In: Lawless, W.F., Mittu, R., Sofge, D.A. (eds.) Human-Machine Shared Contexts, Academic Press, pp. 241–255 (2020)

25. Raz, A.K., Blasch, E.P., Guariniello, C., Mian, Z.T.: An Overview of Systems Engineering Challenges for Designing AI-Enabled Aerospace Systems. AIAA Scitech, Forum, p. 0564, (2021)
26. Caballero, W.N., Friend, M., et al.: Adversarial machine learning and adversarial risk analysis in multi-source command and control. In: Proc. SPIE 11756 (2021)
27. Lin, C.H., Lin, S.C., et al.: TULVCAN: terahertz ultra-broadband learning vehicular channel-aware networking. In: IEEE INFOCOM (2021)
28. Shen, D., Lu, J., Chen, G., Zulch, P., et al.: On-device implementation of JML based decentralized data fusion with non-permissive communications. In: IEEE Aerospace Conference (2021)
29. Johnson, D.T.: Evaluation of Energy Maneuverability Procedures in Aircraft Flight Path Optimization and Performance Estimation. Technical Report AFFDL-72–58 (1972)
30. Hick, W.E.: On the rate of gain of information. Q. J. Experimental Psychol. 4(1), 11–26 (1952)
31. Hyman, R.: Stimulus information as a determinant of reaction time. J. Experimental Psych. 45(3), 188–196 (1953)
32. Fitts, P.M.: The information capacity of the human motor system in controlling the amplitude of movement. J. Experimental Psychol. 47(6), 381–391 (1954)
33. Shannon, C.: A mathematical theory of communication. The Bell Syst. Tech. J. 27, 379–423 (1948)
34. MacKenzie, I.S.: A note on the validity of the Shannon formulation for Fitts' index of difficulty. Open J. Appl. Sci. 3, 360–368 (2013)
35. Sudano, J.: The system probability information content (PIC) relationship to contributing components, combining independent multi-source beliefs, hybrid and pedigree pignistic probabilities. In: International Conference on Information Fusion (2002)
36. Blasch, E., Cruise, B.: Information fusion management: collection to diffusion. In: IEEE National Aerospace and Electronics Conference (2016)
37. US Army Command and General Staff College. Student Text 100–3: Battle Book. Fort Leavenworth, KS: USACGSC (2000)
38. Headquarters, Department of the Army. Army Doctrine Reference Publication 1-02: Terms and Military Symbols. Department of the Army, Washington, D.C., November (2016)
39. Blasch, E., et al.: Cyber awareness trends in avionics. In: IEEE/AIAA 38th Digital Avionics Systems Conference (DASC) (2019)
40. Ozberk, T.: Aselsan delivers electronic attack system to Turkish Army. C4ISR. (2021). https://www.c4isrnet.com/electronic-warfare/2021/07/15/aselsan-delivers-electronic-attack-system-to-turkish-army/. Accessed 20 July 2021
41. Schuck, T.M., Blasch, E., Gagne, O.B.: Information maneuverability and the transformation of the warfighting environment. In: IEEE/AIAA Aerospace (2021)
42. Sun, H., Chen, Y., Aved, A., et al.: Collaborative multi-object tracking as an edge service using transfer learning. In: IEEE 18th International Conference on Smart City (2020)
43. Munir, A., Blasch, E., Kwon, J., Kong, J., Aved, A.: Artificial intelligence and data fusion at the edge. IEEE Aerosp. Electron. Syst. Mag. 36(7), 62–78 (2021)
44. Blasch, E.P., et al.: Resolving events through multi-intelligence fusion. J. DoD Res. Eng. 2(1), 2–15 (2019)
45. Blasch, E., Nagy, J., Aved, A., Pottenger, W.M., Schneider, M., et al.: Context aided Video-to-Text information fusion. In: International Conference on Information Fusion (2014)
46. Blasch, E., Bélanger, M.: Agile battle management efficiency for command, control, communications, computers and intelligence (C4I). In: Proceedings SPIE, vol. 9842 (2016)
47. Alberts, D.S.: The Agility Advantage: A Survival Guide for Complex Enterprises and Endeavors, CCRP Pub. Series (2011)
48. Alberts, D.S., Huber, R.K., Moffat, J.: NATO NEC C2 Maturity Model, CCRP (2010)

49. Kelly, M.G.: The F-35s new OODA loop. In: Proceedings of the US Naval Institute, March, pp. 24–28 (2016)
50. Shuck, T., Blasch, E.: OODA Loop 2.0: Information, Not Agility, is Life. Breaking Defense, 11 May 2017
51. Blasch, E., Ravela, S., Aved, A. (eds.): Handbook of Dynamic Data Driven Applications Systems. Springer, Cham (2018). https://doi.org/10.1007/978-3-319-95504-9
52. Blasch, E., et al.: Machine learning/artificial intelligence for sensor data fusion-opportunities and challenges. IEEE Aerosp. Electron. Syst. Mag. **36**(7), 80–93 (2021)

BioSecure Digital Twin: Manufacturing Innovation and Cybersecurity Resilience

Michael Mylrea[1]([∅]), Charles Fracchia[2], Howard Grimes[3], Wayne Austad[4],
Gregory Shannon[5], Bill Reid[1], and Nathan Case[1]

[1] National Resilience Inc., La Jolla, CA 92037, USA
Michael.mylrea@resilience.com
[2] BioBright, Boston, MA 02114, USA
[3] The Cybersecurity Manufacturing Innovation Institute, University of Texas at San Antonio,
San Antonio, TX 78249, USA
Howard.grimes@CyManii.org
[4] The Cybersecurity Manufacturing Innovation Institute, Idaho National Laboratory,
Idaho Falls, ID 83415, USA
[5] The Cybersecurity Manufacturing Innovation Institute, Carnegie Mellon University,
Pittsburgh, PA 15213, USA

Abstract. U.S. national security, prosperity, economy, and well-being require secure, flexible, and resilient Biopharmaceutical Manufacturing. The COVID-19 pandemic reaffirmed that the biomedical production value-chain is vulnerable to disruption and has been under attack from sophisticated nation-state adversaries. Current cyber defenses are inadequate, and the integrity of critical production systems and processes are inherently vulnerable to cyber-attacks, human error, and supply chain disruptions. The following chapter explores *how* a BioSecure Digital Twin will improve U.S. manufacturing resilience and preparedness to respond to these hazards by significantly improving monitoring, integrity, security, and agility of our manufacturing infrastructure and systems. The BioSecure Digital Twin combines a scalable manufacturing framework with a robust platform for monitoring and control to increase U.S. biopharma manufacturing resilience. Then, the chapter discusses some of the inherent vulnerabilities and challenges at the nexus of health and advanced manufacturing. Next, the chapter highlights that as the Pandemic evolves, we need agility and resilience to overcome significant obstacles. This section highlights an innovative application of Cyber Informed Engineering to developing and deploying a BioSecure Digital Twin to improve the resilience and security of the biopharma industrial supply chain and production processes. Finally, the chapter concludes with a process framework to complement the Digital Twin platform, called the Biopharma (Observe, Orient, Decide, Act) OODA Loop Framework **(BOLF), a four-step approach to decision-making outputs from the Digital Twin**. The BOLF will help end users leverage twin technology by distilling the available information, focusing the data on context, and rapidly making the best decision while remaining cognizant of changes that can be made as more data becomes available.

This work was partially funded by the Department of Energy under contract DOE-EE0009046.

Keywords: Digital Twin · Critical infrastructure · Cybersecurity · Resilience · Advanced manufacturing · Cyber informed engineering · OODA Loop

1 Introduction

All modern organizations and nations require the health and well-being of their population to function. The COVID-19 pandemic was a grim reminder of how fragile our infrastructure and systems are when the health sector fails to keep us healthy. The United States' national security, economy and well-being require secure, resilient, and agile capabilities to respond to coronavirus health and economic threats. As a critical national capability for coronavirus events, the current state of cyber-physical security in biopharma manufacturing requires a more resilient approach to improve the security, visibility, and control of the rapid disease response, therapeutic resilience, and economic opportunities created by modern digitally supported biological systems. The following chapter highlights a high-impact research and development effort underway to move this sector toward increased resilience, while also improving the competitiveness, integrity, visibility of the manufacturing process via a high-fidelity BioSecure Digital Twin. A Digital Twin is defined as a high-fidelity virtual model or representation of the physical environment, including the data exchange, communication, interaction, and behavior between converged physical and virtual spaces. The virtual or cyber part of the twin collects, aggregates, and analyzes performance behavior data throughout the production life-cycle of the physical systems and sensors. The Digital Twin allows digital verification of products to ensure the latest technologies are deployed across the entire manufacturing ecosystem. Machine learning helps distill and recognize patterns in the data from multiple sources (e.g., sensor, model, domain expertise) to predict behavior and optimize performance. Digital Twin use cases are increasing from GE's Digital Ghost for cyber-physical anomaly detection combined with cycle power plants to real-time monitoring and predictive maintenance of aircraft and various defense platforms, [1] from predictive maintenance on the factory floor to dual optimization in manufacturing where the physical systems provide intelligence for the virtual mirror to continuously evolve [2].

The proposed BioSecure Digital Twin, Fig. 1, will create an industrial immune system to improve manufacturing to rapidly identify anomalies and mitigate the behavior that deviates from normal operations, both in the cybersecurity dimension and in process fidelity control. It creates a digital infrastructure that is portable and can be deployed as a virtualized testbed for both simulation, analytic, control, and optimization. Potential use cases for applying Digital Twin solutions to improve cybersecurity are numerous, from cyber wargaming to enhanced workforce development, where end users can learn and experiment on a high-fidelity twin. In the realization of these objectives, this research has the potential to transform and improve biopharma cybersecurity resilience, integrity and monitoring of the supply chain and production lifecycle while improving:

- **Monitoring and Agility.** Improved monitoring and agility with a high-fidelity Digital Twin will help improve biopharma production system simulation, analytics, optimization, and security.

- **Acceleration, Efficiency and Scale.** The competitiveness of the US bioeconomy on the global stage depends on improving real-time visibility and analytic capabilities of the biopharma production lifecycle. A BioSecure Digital Twin will help realize these acceleration and efficiency objectives in addition to various cybersecurity objectives – pervasive, unobtrusive, resilient, and economical – will drive the U.S. bioeconomy into global leadership position.
- **Cybersecurity, Integrity and Resilience.** Strengthen our national security by developing next-generation defensive capabilities for the critical healthcare and bioeconomy sector.

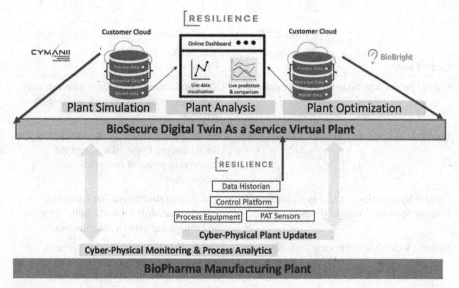

Fig. 1. Illustrative BioSecure Digital Twin to improve monitoring and agility, accelerate US bioeconomy competitiveness and move the sector towards cyber-physical resilience [3].

2 Problem

At present, biopharma and other advanced manufacturing platforms are vulnerable to catastrophic attacks, supply chain shortages, human error and other naturally occurring disasters capable of wiping out most of the U.S. bioeconomy. Our bioeconomy is currently estimated at more than 5% of U.S. GDP ($950B) annually, according to Safeguarding the Bioeconomy, a 2020 report from the National Academy of Sciences, Engineering and Medicine. Our nation's ability to respond to pandemic events, compete on the global stage, and realize the full potential of the bioeconomy depends on our ability to monitor, predict, and protect its underlying cyber-physical infrastructure. We must better control the process machine states, strongly verify product integrity through its entire chain of custody, and compare machine and workflow states across geographies and history. In the realization of these goals, the BioSecure Digital Twin for critical biopharma processes and supply chains will employ CyManII's "Secure BioPharma Architectures" (SBPA) based on the Secure Manufacturing Architectures (SMA) that CyManII is developing and implementing for other manufacturing sectors.

Biopharma infrastructure is vulnerable to a host of adversaries and naturally occurring hazards, ranging from cyber threats to supply chain shortages, access issues directly related to the pandemic, and to simple human errors. The current state of biopharma manufacturing systems and processes vulnerabilities exacerbates these challenges and undermines the preparedness and competitiveness of the US bioeconomy. The vulnerabilities in the current state and R&D and validated advances for a future state, shown in Table 1, constitute the focus areas of this ongoing research.

Table 1. Current and future state.

Current state	Future state
Critical production systems are not monitored	The BioSecure Digital Twin monitors every step in the supply chain and the production process
Currently systems use insecure architectures	Secure BioPharma Architectures ensure that the Biosecure Digital Twin, and the underlying physical processes, are cybersecure
Current Systems Lack Security Controls and Contain Multiple Vulnerabilities	The Secure BioPharma Architectures introduce security controls while detecting and mitigating cyber vulnerabilities
Systems lack basic cybersecurity analysis tools	CyManII will develop and implement integrous tools for biopharma on systems deployed by National Resilience and BioBright
Systems have NO traceable Bio Integrity	The Secure BioPharma Architecture introduces CyManII's "cyber physical passport" to create supply chains that are rooted in trust and data integrity

BioPharma Operational Technology & Industrial Control Systems. A digital transformation of manufacturing is rapidly digitizing, networking and automating the biopharma-value chain. Today's smart manufacturing systems unlock value in modernizing processes and systems that are increasingly interoperable, connected to cloud and associated microservices at the edge of the control plane. While this modernization has unlocked significant value in process efficiency, it also presents new security challenges for critical production systems and operational technology (OT) that were never designed to be connected to the Internet. The rapid digital transformation of our critical systems has significantly increased their attack surfaces by combining cyber-physical systems, software and hardware, information technology (IT) and OT. This situation or combination has created new challenges to identify, monitor and protect these critical systems [4]. A BioSecure Digital Twin can help fill these gaps by providing real-time cyber-physical situational awareness monitor the cyber threats and anomalies across the cyber-physical, IT and OT attack surface [1].

However, even as Digital Twin technology helps improve cybersecurity defenses, the attack surfaces of biopharma and other advanced manufacturing has expanded significantly, introducing, and leaving several major cyber gaps. For one, most cyber-defenses and monitoring solutions are ineffective in detecting sophisticated attacks targeting operational technology. This problem is especially true for insider and supply chain attacks, zero-day exploits and other stealthy threats that continue to evade and defeat cyber defenses and intrusion detection systems. These systems originated from securing information technology across a business enterprise and defending against known malware, malicious packets and other attacks that are easy to catalogue in a library as signature heuristics. However, the OT found in various biopharma production systems present new challenges as the protocol, malware signatures, tactics, techniques, and procedures used by adversaries also differ significantly. Moreover, manufacturing plants lack basic cybersecurity defenses to identify and monitor their critical cyber-OT assets. Thus, the detection of sophisticated adversaries is limited – usually too late or reactive, only occurring after the damage has been done – enabling them to persist and pivot their malicious activities in critical systems and networks too often without being detected for long periods of time.

To overcome these limitations, solutions must advance from security to resilience to provide more holistic cover for critical OT in critical manufacturing. Cyber defense of critical infrastructure continues to evolve, but cyber adversaries often have the upper hand as their offensive tools improve faster as the attack surface available to them expands. Cyber challenges remain for policies, technology, and people (workforce and expertise). To change this equation, new paradigms, formal methods, and advances in threat mitigation technology need to be developed. Even as cyber defense technology improves, workforce development, especially in the area of OT cybersecurity, remains a major gap. The confidentiality, integrity, and availability triad that has defined cybersecurity in the last 20 years continues to be pressured by the digital transformation underway. The digital transformation in the biopharmaceutical sector has prioritized interoperability and connectivity, with the increased automation often leaving core cybersecurity concerns behind. As we digitize, automate, and connect systems in critical infrastructure to the internet, this also expands the cyber-physical attack surface, which we must protect or risk losing a dominant opportunity in the global bioeconomy.

To improve the current state of the art in biopharma cyber-defense requires moving beyond the cybersecurity triad paradigm in favor of cyber resilience. A BioSecure Digital Twin will help improve the ability to identify, detect, respond, and recover from cyber threats and vulnerabilities in under sub-second times. Cyber resilience requires both a hardened perimeter as well as the ability to neutralize sophisticated attacks once they have been found. In short, a defense in depth approach must be adapted for use in the critical sector of the bioeconomy.

Advances of innovative threat mitigation solutions help to move the industry towards cyber resilience. However, the design and implementation of these advances, such as machine-learning algorithms, require the distillation of large data sets to be intelligently fused with operations. The form of the cyber-defense technology needs to be complemented by a process function in a way that helps transform data into intelligence and production insight. Through this information fusion, human-machine teams can increase both their autonomy and effectiveness to evolve their defenses to be more cyber resilient in response to sophisticated and evolving threats. The effective design and deployment of the next generation BioSecure Digital Twin to mitigate threats in a more effective and autonomous way also require prioritization. To effectively develop and deploy a Digital Twin, we perform an applicability and gap analysis with a framework of Consequence-driven Cyber-informed Engineering (CCE) methodology focused on securing the nation's critical infrastructure systems.

3 Applying Cyber-Informed Engineering (CIE) to Effectively Develop and Deploy a Digital Twin for BioPharma Manufacturing

Applying a CCE framework is important as it recognizes that the biopharma manufacturing is inherently vulnerable and that a skilled and determined adversary has the capability to sabotage a manufacturing system, process, and infrastructure. Consequence-driven Cyber-informed Engineering is a rigorous process for applying CIE's core principles to a specific organization, facility, or mission; it does this by identifying most critical functions, methods and means an adversary would likely use to manipulate or compromise them and by determining the most effective means of removing or mitigating those risks. The Cyber-Informed Engineering (CIE) framework and body of knowledge drives the inclusion of cybersecurity as a foundational element of risk management for engineering of functions aided by digital technology. CIE emphasizes the removal of potential risk in key areas, as well as by ensuring resiliency and response maturity within the design of the engineered system. CCE walks an organization through core components of CIE in CCE's 4-phase process (shown in Fig. 2 [5]) to evaluate, remove or mitigate weaknesses in its critical functions.

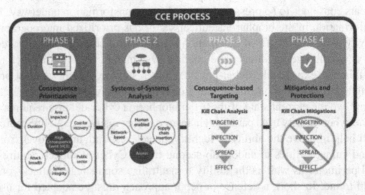

Fig. 2. An outline of a CCE process in a way that can help guide effective Digital Twin deployment.

Exploring Digital Twin use cases through a CCE framework provides valuable insight into how to deploy a BioSecure Digital Twin, thus providing manufacturing stakeholders a more focused bottom-line approach to: a) determine most critical functions; b) evaluate complex systems and dependencies to deliver those functions; c) identify methods an adversary could use to target and compromise these systems; and, d) apply proven engineering, protection, and mitigation strategies to isolate and protect the most critical assets [6]. The key to CCE is focus on physical processes in the context of cyber threats and not just the security of the bits/bytes to engineer resilience into a complex systems of systems. Since Digital Twins use both the original engineering design models and new forms of complex physical process for optimization/prediction with machine learning, the Digital Twins are complementary to CCE approaches. This provides a valuable framework in determining the use case, what is being modeled, and how to effectively deploy a BioSecure Digital Twin to secure critical manufacturing systems and infrastructure.

Consequence Prioritization. Deploying a Digital Twin for every production system and associated network would degrade the fidelity of data and the ability to model, analyze and effectively draw insights and intelligence from the operation. Leveraging CCE requirements with a comprehensive design can be developed for a BioSecure Digital Twin. During the design phase, it is essential to scope the target system and define the sub-systems that are prioritized based on their potential consequence (shown in Fig. 3 [7]) or impact should the system be sabotaged or taken offline.

Fig. 3. Consequence Prioritization helps focus the Digital Twin on modeling and related use cases to predict and prevent cyber events that have the greatest potential impact [7].

For example, if a production system produced a vaccine that was sabotaged, and no alarms or malicious behaviors were detected, the damage could be catastrophic resulting, possibly in the loss of life, reputation, and prohibitive damage that could shut down most manufacturing plants. Digital Twin consequence-driven prioritization will leverage domain expertise to determine the vulnerabilities that could be exploited to cause such an event by using a supervised machine learning approach to determine what the behaviors look like behind the anomaly that would lead to such an event. With the understanding of what normal operations look like combined with a detailed understanding of anomalies from faults, cyber-attacks, naturally occurring ambient changes and degradation curves, an operator, or system's owner can start training the Digital Twin and establish boundary conditions for modeling and simulation for the improved detection and mitigation of stealthy cyber-attacks.

Systems of Systems of Analysis. After the consequence analysis helps to select the production environment, a systems of system analysis of the BioSecure Digital Twin model needs to be tested, exercised, and trained to define the system's boundary conditions. A range of normal and abnormal spaces are selected with various levels of actionable deviations based on naturally occurring ambient conditions and other norms within the operating manifold.

Consequence-Based Targeting. A high-fidelity model of cyber-attack versus fault analysis within the operating spaces is essential to help reduce false positives and to improve the accuracy of the Digital Twin's detection capability. Consequence-based targeting analysis creates a framework to exercise, train, and test the machine-learning algorithms against different scenarios to determine the paths, targets, access, and information an adversary would need to achieve their adverse events. This Kill Chain Analysis can be reverse engineered to further test the algorithms for defenses against stealthy attacks. Machine learning algorithms developed from these attacks is intended to differentiate between a naturally occurring system fault, degradation, human error, and outsider attacks. Historical data obtained from BioPharma manufacturing environment is reviewed to establish the key system monitoring nodes for detecting and localizing events, which is especially important in a transient closed-loop system with stochastic behavior.

Mitigation and Protections. Kill chain analysis supports associated mitigations by establishing the decision boundary between normal and abnormal operating spaces. This can help improve performance predictions that are generated based on an optimal decision boundary. The optimal decision boundary may also evolve as the cyber threat is complex, non-linear, and rapidly changing. It is essential that boundary and learning algorithms are updated as the system evolves via real-time learning and adaptation algorithms. Performance and data-fidelity of the BioSecure Digital Twin needs to be continuously reviewed and monitored throughout the biopharma production lifecycle [1]. We perform the kill chain analysis and propose mitigations to find that it is important to understand the system level vulnerabilities and security gaps that are often found in BioPharma production systems.

4   Biopharma System Level Security Gaps

Technology Gaps. The following four areas are technology gaps that need to be closed: (i) Operational technology includes a large and diverse attack surface that is often connected through both internet protocols (IP), serial, bluetooth, and other connections unlike IT solutions which are easy to enumerate and inventory by scanning. (ii) Proprietary protocols initially designed for intellectual property purposes are often vulnerable by design as vendors prioritize functionality, ease of use and cost over security. (iii) Firewalls, network, and host intrusion detection systems are rarely implemented by the vendor and are left to be installed by the customer. Thus, even moderately sophisticated attackers using brute force, polymorphic, AI-generated, or insider attacks are virtually impossible to detect with current field-accepted technologies. Zero-day exploits targeting operational technology are very difficult to block with most existing attack detection solutions let alone taking into account the hundreds of custom software, firmware and hardware solutions deployed in the field by vendors who have not historically considered the cybersecurity attack surface. (iv) Finally, resource intensive tuning can be required for AI defense-critical solutions to be integrated into existing technology stacks for Security Information and Event Management (SIEM).

Process and Policy Gaps. As AI solutions improve attack detections, it will increase the speed, size, and fidelity of logging critical machine state integrity as well as other network and system outputs. Thus, monitoring policies and process updates need to intelligently distill and fuse these findings for this data to create actionable cyber intelligence. Often, cyber defenders have policies and processes in place to monitor and log their critical cyber assets as defined by Food and Drug Administration (FDA) requirements; however, they often do not read these logs. Moreover, additional networks or systems that are connected to these critical cyber assets can provide an attack pathway if they are not secured and are not currently sufficiently considered when demonstrating ongoing compliance to pharmaceutical quality standard as defined by FDA.

An additional major gap in policy is FDA's current definition of what constitutes a "medical device." Currently, devices used in the biopharmaceutical production workflow are not considered part of the Center for Devices and Radiological Health (CDRH) purview, instead, managed by the Center for Biological Evaluation and Research (CBER) [8, 9]. In practice, this leaves a gaping hole in the evolving security measures applied to devices that are crucial to biopharmaceutical production and national disease response. We strongly recommend that the department of Health and Human Services (HHS) give FDA's Center for Biological Evaluation and Research (CBER) the resources to build strong and perennial cybersecurity expertise. Without it, we are condemning ourselves to a two-speed security improvement regime and a lack of understanding of unique biopharmaceutical and bioeconomy threats.

We further recommend that the Biomedical Advanced Research and Development Authority (BARDA) and the office of the Assistant Secretary for Preparedness and Response (ASPR) be given the resources to build similar core competency and the understanding of digital biosecurity and cybersecurity concerns. These resources must be made perennial in the form of an office for cybersecurity or digital security. This does not need to be expensive by limiting it to a small staff of 4–5 people each, but it needs to be in dedicated offices reporting to the director and assistant secretary, respectively, to ensure the appropriate responsiveness and escalation to mitigate attacks.

The administration resources outlined above should engage in an inter-agency process to leverage knowledge from the Department of Defense (DoD) and Department of

Homeland Security (DHS) to help them adapt to their unique biomedical sector needs and threats.

People Gaps. Machine learning algorithms that have high-false positive rates create prohibitive operations and maintenance requirements for security teams. Cybersecurity teams have been traditionally IT focused, however, the convergence of IT/OT in critical infrastructures has increased the responsibilities and created new workforce development challenges for them. Innovative new tools require training, and adding another tool creates information fusion challenges. Finally, AI solutions that are tuned and learn what is normal on networks and systems that are already infected may be providing a false sense of security to their operators. Advances in invariant learning and humble AI explored in this chapter highlight how researchers are overcoming these gaps.

5   Digital Twin R&D, Testbeds, and Benefits

The BioSecure Digital Twin accomplishes two important outcomes. First, it significantly and efficiently improves bio-integrity of the U.S. biopharma manufacturing sector. Second, it results in greatly improved operational cybersecurity in the U.S. biopharma manufacturing. It does this by: a) making critical production systems more visible in both the biological and cybersecurity dimensions; b) enabling continuous and improved parallel modeling, integrity, analytics, and control of biopharma processes; c) introducing secure BioPharma architectures that will move the biopharma manufacturing sector toward cyber-physical resilience; d) providing a strong, cryptographically auditable trail designed to provide multiple, out-of-band, parallel paths for traceable audits of processes; and e) developing continuous testing of quality, integrity, and security through the entire production lifecycle. These areas are explained in more detail below.

The BioSecure Digital Twin Project advances effective and efficient bio-integrity and cybersecurity for the biopharma industry that is critical to coronavirus detection and response. It also builds on the cybersecurity innovations being introduced by the Cybersecurity Manufacturing Innovation Institute (CyManII) in its developing and implementing cyber-inspired, secure by design architectures that will protect and enhance U.S. manufacturers. Table 2 describes how the R&D and Testbed contributions enable us to respond effectively to the Coronavirus challenges and provide benefits with each of our project objectives. These R&D objectives drive the outcomes for a BioSecure Digital Twin.

(A) Visibility into Cyber-Physical Processes – Benefits. *Make critical production systems visible in both the biological and cybersecurity dimensions.* In the biological dimension it enables a continuous quality approach that is data-driven and real-time linked to high fidelity process models. In the cyber dimension, it provides strong logging, improves attacker detection dramatically based on physical behaviors, and makes it harder for unsophisticated attackers to have an impact.

This contribution directly addresses the fact that no monitoring of critical production systems currently occurs. Monitoring in the biomanufacturing sector largely follows historical definitions of pharmaceutical quality, with an emphasis on paper records and strong change-management processes. This is similar to what CyManII is addressing in

Table 2. R&D Objectives. Our R&D objectives drive outcomes relevant to pandemics such as a coronavirus.

BioSecure Digital Twin - R&D Objectives and examples of Coronavirus impacts					Summary outcomes
A. Visibility into Cyber & Physical Processes	B. Parallel Modeling & Analysis	C. Secure BioPharma Architectures	D. Traceable & Secure Audit Trails	E. Continuous Quality & Security	High fidelity process controls
Make critical productions systems for coronavirus detection, treatment, and prevention visible for both physical quality & cybersecurity	Enable continuously-improved parallel modeling, integrity checks, performance analytics, and control of biopharma processes used in coronavirus	Create new secure biopharma architectures and systems that will move bio manufacturing for coronavirus response and health-care therapeutics towards cyber-physical resilience	Provide a cryptographic auditable trail designed to preserve data lineage and provenance for both physical and cyber properties in corona virus therapeutics	Establish continuous testing of quality, integrity, and security through the production lifecycle of coronavirus detection, treatment, and prevention products	Detect and mitigate both anomalies and vulnerabilities Accelerate new production processes Introduce trust, integrity, & resilience for Bio Manufacturing Optimize production across sites, geographies, and CDMOs

BioSecure Digital Twin created using Secure by Design Lifecycle
and CyManII's SMA Framework

other manufacturing sectors with an integrated technical approach to a new Secure Manufacturing Architecture. While essential, these processes have not taken advantage of modern monitoring technologies and capabilities. This lack has biological implications such as long lead times (often several days) to identify root cases for batch deviations, difficulty in comparing real-time conditions with all historical batches, and near-total reliance on individual staff's historical experience and memory. In the cyber domain, this lack of modern monitoring represents an enormous advantage for adversaries: it makes detection difficult; attribution is significantly more complex; lateral movement by attackers within networks is simplified; and adversaries can use less sophisticated methods. But, creating high fidelity cyber-physical visibility with Digital Twins provides the following benefits:

1. **Improved Scale-Up Process Characterization.** By continuously collecting and processing data from all of the digital instrumentation that underpins the biological scale-up process, we enable an unprecedented level of process characterization. This in turn enables us to improve the state-of-the-art in batch comparison, inter-operator variabilities, identification of anomalies, and differences in batch conditions (PV, RPM, feed timing, feed nature, feed concentration, respiratory parameters, etc.).

Our approach provides data-driven feeds for all of the digital data collected from the process in near real-time thus making the process analyzable and machine learnable in a way that was not previously possible.

2. **Transform Digital Biosecurity Monitoring and Attacker Detection.** By collecting all of the biological scale-up process data, we enable a new level of data-driven digital biosecurity monitoring. With this process data at our disposal in a reproducible way (API, structured data) and at scale (100's of instruments), we can create digital tripwires to identify, characterize and rapidly respond against attackers who attempt to infiltrate these key processes. The combination of process and traditional cybersecurity endpoint data enables us to develop true digital biosecurity detection mechanisms leveraging features that cross the cyberphysical/cyber-biological domains.

(B) Parallel Cyber-Physical Modeling & Analysis – Benefits. *Enable continuously improved parallel modeling, integrity checks, performance analytics, and control of processes used in coronavirus pharmaceuticals.*

The BioSecure Digital Twin creates a framework that is both secure by design and aligned to the needs of the modern industrial biological age. Our framework incorporates the need of process and workflow biologists at its very core, striking a balance between security and useability in the facilities. This is important as legacy biological instrumentation will continue to be a source of vulnerability for several years until all vendors make cybersecurity an important part of the design lifecycle. A Digital Twin that operates in "shadow mode" to the physical process can inform and protect the workflow that scientists are operating. The major benefits of a BioSecure Digital Twin that enables parallel modeling, integrity, analytics, and control of the biopharma process are:

1. **Security Lifecycle Support.** Our BioSecure Digital Twin also enables improvements in design through advancing modeling and the analytics for critical processes. For example, the impact of patching a system or adjusting a batch volume can be understood via modeling simulation on a high-fidelity system without making physical changes to a live batch process.

2. **Adapt to the Constraints of Biomanufacturing Workflows**. Real-time access to a Digital Twin provides continuous insights into the physical processes that scientists are running. It enables them to run and compare models "in silico" to interrogate future states without placing any new requirements or workflow changes in their environment. The BioSecure Digital Twin is automatically populated with new data in the background by the secure infrastructure. New models and analyses are also updated in the back-end and made available to their scientists via a series of web-based dashboards.

(C) Secure BioPharma Architectures – Benefits. *Create a framework and build process that is secure by design, resilient, and aligned to the needs of the industrial biological technology lifecycle.* A major factor that leads to structural insecurity of the biomanufacturing and public health response sectors is the lack of security attention that is paid to the key infrastructural devices and systems. These instruments and systems have a long shelf-life (10+ years), high CAPEX ($1M+ per many instruments), and software that is often treated as an afterthought by the vendors. Vendors often subcontract the software development to the lowest bidder and to teams established in countries (e.g., Ukraine, China, India, Singapore, Bulgaria) that pose additional threat concerns; software quality, let alone security, is almost never considered. BioBright and CyManII national lab partners (Idaho National Laboratory, Sandia National Labs) have identified and disclosed many of these vulnerabilities to the relevant authorities in these areas. To add to this challenge, the historical focus on pharmaceutical quality led to the development of rigid processes that are woefully inadequate in the digital age. Processes that ensured integrity during a paper notebook paradigm have become leverageable and mortal vulnerabilities in the digital age of automation. This problem has led to a crisis of trust in modern biopharmaceutical workflows.

Current systems were not designed with cybersecurity in mind, and are now interconnected with more systems and control data. Finally, the signature heuristics in current intrusion detection systems and firewalls do not recognize sophisticated attacks, such as insider exploits that enable privileged insiders access to critical supply chains and production systems. The average amount of time to detect that an organization has been hacked is currently 280 days. In the biopharmaceutical field, due to its complex logistics, 280 days can represent the success or failure of a drug candidate; is at stake in the case of smaller, more innovative companies, the very survival of that enterprise. The problem is compounded by the lack of biosecure and bio-aware monitoring or detection tools, effectively affording adversaries an unimpeded and undetectable reign of attack. By developing Secure BioPharma Architectures and Systems we provide:

1. **Effective Operational Cybersecurity**. Secure BioPharma Architectures and Systems will move biopharma manufacturing sector towards cyber-physical resilience with real time monitoring. Instead of a detection signature being a 1 or 0 heuristic, we are taking a more holistic approach to monitoring anomalies by examining the metadata from bioreactors as well as the physical signatures (ambient, frequency, voltage) that are very difficult to spoof. When considering the stochastic nature of biology, together with cyber and physical signatures, it is difficult for a human to analyze these prodigious data sets to find patterns. The proposed approach leverages a machine learning (ML) algorithm to illuminate these patterns. Thus, the complexity of these systems can create the next generation of defense as certain behaviors become impossible. They can quickly be detected, localized, and mitigated, however, including faults, attacks, human error and even naturally occurring changes in ambient conditions.

2. **Enhanced Security Controls.** Meaningful and verifiable security controls and systems are non-existent in the biomanufacturing field, instruments are riddled with exploitable vulnerabilities and historical data integrity controls are easily circumventable. Existing verification and validation procedures (including paper backups) are vulnerable. In one incident that this team has dealt with, the technological means used to produce and print the paper trail was relying on outdated and vulnerable digital platforms. This posed an existential threat to the trustworthiness of even their paper batch records. In addition, all of the digital process data are easy to exfiltrate, manipulate and destroy. In contrast, after creating robust security controls by design,

the proposed BioSecure Digital Twin improves the control and redundancy of critical systems.

(D) Secure and Traceable Audit Trails – Benefits. *Produce a BioSecure Digital Twin that provides a strong, cryptographically auditable trail that is designed to provide multiple, out-of-band, parallel ways to audit a process.*

The reality is that the industry cannot track, trace, or validate the integrity of a production lifecycle with a level of assurance adequate for today's threat landscape. Moreover, existing regulatory guidance and compliance processes have not adapted to digital threats and can in fact cause major downtimes that exacerbate cybersecurity attacks. For example, existing security solutions that monitor production systems for vulnerabilities may create new validation requirements if they change the logs or function of the system. Finally, it is often impossible to attest that a security control is in place and working without continuously testing those controls. This is addressed with:

1. **Traceable Bio Integrity.** Developing the continuous testing of quality, integrity, and security through the production lifecycle. This creates a framework that other manufactures can use to design, deploy, and manage systems with a defense-in-depth approach improving resilience as well as data integrity and non-repudiation. It will be possible to build supply chains that can be trusted.
2. **Seed for a Secure Standard for Data Collection & Auditing.** The BioSecure Digital Twin design provides strong primitives and capabilities that can, with proper federal collaboration and input (e.g., NIST, FDA, ASPR, BARDA and DARPA), evolved into industry standards that would represent a giant leap in the resilience and verifiable auditability of biological processes. These contributions would help FDA's Center for Biologics Evaluation and Research and its Center for Drug Evaluation and Research create strong and auditable trust for all coronavirus countermeasures.
3. **Next Generation – Real Time Audits.** Next generation regulation and audit of these system by FDA and other regulators could leverage a high-fidelity virtual representation of the physical state of the machine to improve efficiency and visibility remotely and in real time.

(E) Continuous Quality & Security – Benefits. *Improve the understanding, identification, and control of bio-physical anomalies inducible from cyber threats to bio-digital systems.* Identifying, baselining, and monitoring what normal looks like using Digital Twins enables improved analytics and anomaly detection in biopharma processes. Overcoming this complexity with an improved understanding and control of sophisticated sensor suites in production systems also provides new opportunities for production efficiencies through predictive prognostics and inherent functional expandability, providing win-win incentives for manufacturers to adopt such systems. In the realization of these goals, the Biosecure Digital Twin will improve the current state of the art in several ways:

1. Trust and integrity of processes will be enhanced via preventative maintenance and by enabling continuous data quality assurance.

2. Introducing predictive quality analytics by collecting ground truth data at scale and leveraging modern, secure data-driven systems for building novel predictive models.
3. Applying cyber-physical anomaly detection to biopharma thus improving the ability to adjust machine settings to improve output quality.

BioSecure Digital Twin enables continuous and predictive quality by monitoring the state of the industrial equipment (asset condition monitoring) and by predicting failures (predictive maintenance), while also monitoring the quality of manufactured product during all of the steps of production. In Fig. 4, a cyber-physical anomaly detection engine will ingest DarwinSync metadata collected from critical production systems and then analyze various out-of-band signals that deviate from what normal looks like. These anomalies will be detected, analyzed, and then used to continuously train the detection and mitigation ML algorithms. To improve the accuracy and to better understand the cause of the behavior that triggered the anomaly, we will perform inferential correlations in comparing commands from production workstations with the physics dictated by supervisory control and data acquisition systems (SCADA) to the controllers (cyber and physical). These will be compared with quality measurements from the bioproduction process examining anomalies, such as spikes in glucose, metabolic and other biologic stochastic changes. This stochastic complexity when run through inference analysis can improve the explainability and measurement of quality; there are certain events or outputs that can be ruled out compared to what normal looks like in biology, cyber and physical systems.

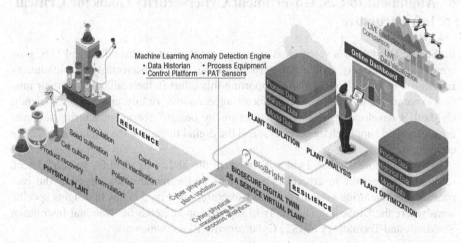

Fig. 4. Cyber physical anomaly detection of machine state integrity reference architecture.

A BioSecure Digital Twin will also to help improve analytics for the understanding of physical outputs that should never result from certain digital commands and/or functions. This can prevent stealthy replay, supply chain and man-in-the middle attacks as well as human error, while improving production efficiencies and the continuous monitoring of machine state integrity and quality of production. Actionable insights on machine state integrity also helps to improve predictive quality analytics of biopharma production process. By collecting, aggregating, analyzing, and running ML inference, we can rule out certain faults versus attack, environmental or human error, giving us a higher fidelity view into the machine state's integrity and quality of product. There is value beyond the technology and platform, in the formal methods and framework that enable us to draw the inference, to measure what normal looks like, and scale a Digital Twin or physical attestation in virtual form.

Building a framework around this model will help to scale and advance security and integrity monitoring in the biopharma sector. Solving this problem requires advances in the current state of the art in control, optimization, and monitoring. Anomalies can be caused by numerous factors and thus detection alone is not a sound solution. To prevent prohibitive number of false positives and to improve actionable and even predictive insight, we need to understand the behavior—including biological in nature—behind the anomalies; this will give us the ability to detect, localize and perform remedial action in a more predictive way. This is key to improving integrity and quality in biopharma manufacturing. This capability can help to prevent manipulation and error in manufacturing COVID-19 and future vaccines or biopharmaceutical countermeasures. Moreover, this would also help to detect stealthy supply-chain attacks that continue to target the biopharma manufacturing value chain with increasing frequency and sophistication. Currently, these production systems lack basic encryption, authentication and/or ability to detect these potentially catastrophic attacks.

6 Alignment to U.S. Government Cybersecurity Goals for Critical Infrastructure

BioSecure Digital Twin research is a strong complement to several critical U.S. government cybersecurity critical infrastructure areas. The Cybersecurity Manufacturing Innovation Institute (CyManII) is supporting this effort in the realization of their mission to secure the future of U.S. manufacturing, economic vitality, and energy efficiency. CyManII's developing the future of "secure by design" for manufacturing automation, advanced supply chain networks, and the digital threads in the engineering design ecosystem.

The BioSecure Digital Twin will improve the ability to identify, protect, detect, respond, and recover to critical cyber threats and vulnerabilities targeting the biopharma manufacturing systems and infrastructure. The Fig. 5 below highlights specific areas where the BioSecure Digital Twin supports and extends the National Institute of Standards and Technology (NIST) Cybersecurity Risk Framework.

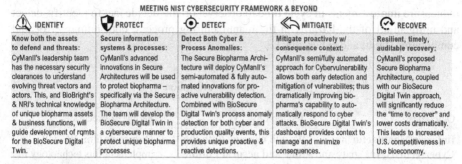

MEETING NIST CYBERSECURITY FRAMEWORK & BEYOND				
⚠ IDENTIFY	🛡 PROTECT	◉ DETECT	🢤 MITIGATE	✅ RECOVER
Know both the assets to defend and threats: CyManII's leadership team has the necessary security clearances to understand evolving threat vectors and actors. This, and BioBright's & NRI's technical knowledge of unique biopharma assets & business functions, will guide development of rqmts for the BioSecure Digital Twin.	Secure information systems & processes: CyManII's advanced innovations in Secure Architectures will be used to protect biopharma – specifically via the Secure Biopharma Architecture. The team will develop the BioSecure Digital Twin in a cybersecure manner to protect unique biopharma processes.	Detect Both Cyber & Process Anomalies: The Secure Biopharma Architecture will deploy CyManII's semi-automated & fully automated innovations for pro-active vulnerability detection. Combined with BioSecure Digital Twin's process anomaly detection for both cyber and production quality events, this provides unique proactive & reactive detections.	Mitigate proactively w/ consequence context: CyManII's semi/fully automated approach for Cybervulnerability allows both early detection and mitigation of vulnerabilites; thus dramatically improving bio-pharma's capability to auto-matically respond to cyber attacks. BioSecure Digital Twin's dashboard provides context to manage and minimize consequences.	Resilient, timely, auditable recovery: CyManII's proposed Secure Biopharma Architecture, coupled with our BioSecure Digital Twin approach, will significantly reduce the "time to recover" and lower costs dramatically. This leads to increased U.S. competitiveness in the bioeconomy.

Fig. 5. Highlights how the BioSecure Digital Twin supports and extends the NIST Cybersecurity Risk Framework.

7 Project Impact, Outcomes, Dissemination

The BioSecure Digital Twin will create an industrial immune system to improve manufacturing's ability to rapidly identify anomalies and mitigate the behavior that deviates from the norm, both in the cybersecurity dimension and in process fidelity control. It creates a digital infrastructure that is portable and can be deployed as a virtual testbed for both cyber wargaming and enhanced workforce development.

In the biological dimension, the BioSecure Digital Twin will, a) provide enhanced process control techniques that leverage all digital data sources; b) create reproducible and portable reference infrastructure deployable to any biomanufacturing facility in the US; c) enable higher quality and faster training of biomanufacturing staff; and, d) generate a novel dataset that represents scaled-up biomanufacturing processes with unprecedented fidelity in time and detail. In the cyber dimension, the BioSecure Digital Twin will, a) create models capable of detecting cyber intruders and attackers in biomanufacturing environments; b) create an infrastructure capable of alerting key operators when these events are triggered; and, c) create a reference implementation portable and deployable to any US biomanufacturing facility. Through these contributions, the BioSecure Digital Twin will provide the ability to reproduce medical countermeasures with higher assurance and in a more distributed manner. It strengthens the resilience of the biomanufacturing infrastructure at the local and national level by providing increased cybersecurity alerting and control. Finally, this proposal creates portable infrastructure and virtual testbeds that enable high-fidelity scenario building (including red/blue teaming) to increase the quality and speed of workforce development. This leap in integrity is necessary for our country's ability to prevent, prepare, and respond to the coronavirus pandemic in the face of increased adversarial interference.

8 Responding to the Current Coronavirus and Preparing for the Next Potential Pandemic

In addition to the BioSecure Digital Twin, we are developing a BioSecure OODA (Observe, Orient, Decide, Act) Loop Framework (BOLF) to be used for the evaluation metrics shown in Table 3. It will include a scalable and exportable methodology to measure improvements in cycle time to observe–orient–decide–act to identify, detect and mitigate all of the hazards in the manufacturing process, both human error and computation, fault, and cyber-attack.

Table 3. Outcomes evaluation.

Outcomes	Technology	People & process
Improve Manufacturing Cybersecurity, Integrity and Resilience. The BioSecure Digital Twin provides an Industrial Immune System to rapidly identify anomalies and mitigate maliciously-induced behavior. This meets a national advanced manufacturing need in Pandemic response. It is timely because U.S. production is under attack and vulnerable to supply chain and natural hazards that limit an effective response	We will measure **both the time and accuracy of the Digital Twin** to identify, detect and mitigate manufacturing anomalies and associated hazards. The accuracy will examine the number of false positives detected by ML algorithms with the goal of achieving 98% accuracy and to improve awareness of machine state and process integrity. Training sets will be harvested from a) real facilities' attacks, and b) virtual twin environments with in-vitro exploits	**Dissemination.** We will implement this technology in key biopharma clusters, including those on the front lines of the Pandemic response. We will share successes via BIO-ISAC, NIIMBL and CyManII's large consortium of critical manufacturers
Accelerate and improve Efficiency and Scale of biopharma manufacturing process. The BioSecure Digital Twin provides the ability to experiment and perform real time analytics to enhance the industrial competitiveness and economic growth through improving real-time visibility and analytic capabilities of the production lifecycle. It enables researchers to experiment, scale and find other operational efficiencies and gaps without impacting production systems in the loop	The effort will improve resilience for critical systems and processes by detecting and mitigating stealthy cyber-attacks, faults, human error, and other hazards that current defenses cannot detect. **We will measure the number of stealthy attacks and hidden faults detected**, the mean time to detection as well as the cost savings from being able to test patches and diagnostics to a system without taking them offline	**We will measure the cost savings** from hardware in the loop, the number of people trained on the twin as well as risk mitigation in having this redundancy

(continued)

Table 3. (*continued*)

Outcomes	Technology	People & process
Lower Cost and National Test Bed Access. The BioSecure Digital Twin considerably lowers the capital costs and increases access to lab and test bed facilities; as they are available in a virtual form for experimentation, process improvement and other critical analytic capabilities	The proposed solution **enables access to critical lab and test bed infrastructure** to NRI and BioBright manufacturing stakeholders as well as a CyManII's and NIIMBL's consortium of academic institutions and students	We will **measure these cost savings** and highlight how secure cloud, virtualization, and advanced monitoring testbeds advance U.S manufacturing capabilities

9 Conclusion

BioSecure Digital Twin research and development efforts discussed in this chapter are an imperative response to securing critical health and manufacturing infrastructure as the frequency, severity and sophistication of cyber-attacks has increased exponentially during the current pandemic. Current digital biosecurity and monitoring deficiencies allow nation state backed adversaries low-cost and deniable cyber-attacks with a potentially catastrophic impact on public health, economy, and national security. The COVID-19 crisis has accelerated the convergence of these two fields; it coincides with the emergence of high impact and persistent digital biosecurity attacks. Even relatively simple attacks can cause daily losses in the millions of dollars and cause months of catastrophic downtime due to regulatory and supply chain constraints unique to the bioeconomy. Unfortunately, the entire bioeconomy is currently vulnerable to a wide range of attacks that include targeted ransomware, industrial control system vulnerabilities, and bioeconomy-specific laboratory instrumentation vulnerabilities. Unchecked and insecure, our adversaries can hold U.S. citizens hostage to future pandemics or any other public health event, crippling our economy and global competitiveness. While the BioSecure Digital Twin is not a panacea, it presents an innovative approach to increase efficiency, competitiveness and move our nation's manufacturing and health infrastructure towards resilience. This is a timely and critical response as no modern organization could operate effectively during a pandemic if the Bioeconomy and associated infrastructure was significantly compromised by a major cyber-attack.

References

1. Mylrea, M., Nielsen, M., Justin, J., Abbaszadeh, M.: AI driven cyber physical industrial immune system for critical infrastructures. In: Lawless, W.F., Sofge, D.A., Mittu, R. (eds.), Systems Engineering and Artificial Intelligence. Springer (2021, forthcoming)
2. Tao, F., Zhang, M.: Digital twin shop-floor: a new shop-floor paradigm towards smart manufacturing. IEEE Access **5**, 20418–20427 (2017)

3. Mylrea, M.: AI systems engineering approach to digital twin for cyber physical anomaly detection. AAAI Presentation Abstract. 24 March 2021

4. Mylrea, M., Gourisetti, S.N.G.: Cybersecurity and optimization in smart "autonomous" buildings. In: Lawless, W., Mittu, R., Sofge, D., Russell, S. (eds.) Autonomy and Artificial Intelligence: A Threat or Savior?, pp. 263–294. Springer, Cham (2017). https://doi.org/10.1007/978-3-319-59719-5_12

5. Idaho National Laboratory. Cyber-informed Engineering Website. https://inl.gov/cce/. Accessed 28 July 2021

6. Bochman, A.A., Freeman, S.: Countering Cyber Sabotage: Introducing Consequence-driven, Cyber-informed Engineering [CCE]. CRC Press (2021)

7. Freeman, S.G., St Michel, C., Smith, R., Assante, M.: Consequence-driven cyber-informed engineering [CCE]. No. INL/EXT-16-39212. Idaho National Lab. [INL], Idaho Falls, ID [United States] (2016)

8. https://www.fda.gov/medical-devices/classify-your-medical-device/device-classification-panels

9. https://www.fda.gov/medical-devices/overview-device-regulation/classify-your-medical-device

Finding the Path Toward Design of Synergistic Human-Centric Complex Systems

Hesham Y. Fouad[1]([✉]), Ali K. Raz[2], James Llinas[3], William F. Lawless[4], and Ranjeev Mittu[1]

[1] Information Management and Decision Architectures Branch, Code 5580 Naval Research Laboratory, 4555 Overlook Avenue, SW, Washington, DC 20375, USA
hesham.fouad@nrl.navy.mil
[2] Aeronautics and Astronautics Department, Purdue University, West Lafayette, IN 47906, USA
[3] Center for Multisource Information Fusion, University at Buffalo, Buffalo, NY, USA
[4] School of Arts and Sciences Paine College, Augusta, GA 20901, USA

Abstract. Modern decision support systems are becoming increasingly sophisticated due to the unprecedented volume of data that must be processed through their underlying information architectures. As advances are made in artificial intelligence and machine learning (AI/ML), a natural expectation would be to assume that the complexity and sophistication of these systems will become daunting in terms of comprehending their design complexity, effective operations, and managing total lifecycle costs. Considering the fact that such systems operate holistically with humans, the interdependencies created between the information architectures, AI/ML processes and humans begs that a fundamental question be asked – "how do we design complex systems such as to yield and exploit effective and efficient human-machine interdependencies and synergies?" A simple example of these interdependencies may include the effects of human actions changing the behavior of algorithms and vice-versa. The algorithms may serve in the extraction and fusion of heterogeneous data, employ a variety of AI/ML algorithms that range from hand crafted, supervised and unsupervised approaches coupled with federated models and simulations to reason and infer about future outcomes.

The purpose of this chapter is to gain a high-level insight into such interdependencies by examining three interrelated topics that can be viewed as working in synergy towards the development of human-centric complex systems: Artificial Intelligence for Systems Engineering (AI4SE), Systems Engineering for Artificial Intelligence (SE4AI), and Human Centered Design (HCD) and Human Factors (HF). From the viewpoint of AI4SE, topics for consideration may include approaches for identifying the design parameters associated with a complex system to ensure code maintainability, to minimize unexpected system failures, and to ensure that the assumptions associated with the algorithms are consistent with the required input data while optimizing the appropriate level of interaction and feedback from the human. Considering SE4AI, how

W. F. Lawless et al. (Eds.): Engineering Artificially Intelligent Systems, LNCS 13000, pp. 73–89, 2021.
https://doi.org/10.1007/978-3-030-89385-9_5

can the synergies between different AI/ML approaches from handcrafted rules to strictly data-driven learning within the data-to-decisions information pipeline be realized, again while maximally leveraging human inputs? From the lens of HCD and HF, a system is likely to be necessarily complex, and a key aspect of the designer may be to ensure an optimal balance between the human systems or software developer and the end-user. For instance, can principles from HCD/HF engineering permit us to design better systems that enhance end-users' strengths (e.g., intuition, novel thinking) while helping to overcome their limitations (e.g., helping a user maintain focus and attention during tasks that require significant multi-tasking)?

Keywords: Artificial intelligence · Machine learning · Systems engineering · Human centered design

1   Introduction

The complexity associated with decision support systems is increasing in sophistication due to new requirements for ingesting and processing large amounts of heterogeneous sources of data. The resulting system complexity is directly correlated with the development and integration of new approaches to data and information fusion, analytics driven by artificial intelligence (AI) and machine learning (ML), and novel architectures such as cloud computing. However, these opportunities also impute design and development challenges. For example, choosing the best combination of algorithms to solve a given problem is challenging due to the large solution space. Furthermore, the interdependencies between the algorithms and the human user create additional complexities and design tradeoffs. Our hypotheses are as follows: (1) due to design space complexity and various interdependencies in a complex system, new Systems Engineering for AI (SE4AI) methods may offer valuable insight for optimizing a large-scale system comprised of a workflow of various information fusion and AI/ML technologies; and, (2) AI for Systems Engineering (AI4SE) may provide new tools for SE that develop insights into optimizing the design and engineering of a larger "system-of-systems." Furthermore, there may be opportunities to optimize these systems such that they not only provide an optimized design space (e.g., software maintenance costs, minimizing system failures, constructing workflows of AI/ML algorithms that perform superior as a sum-of-parts), but also is balanced for human centered design (e.g., minimize workload, increase situational awareness, manage attention).

This chapter will begin by discussing the general approach used by the SE community to design a complex system against a set of metrics that enable the maintenance of that system through its lifecycle, i.e., SE4AI. Next, we will discuss the related topic of AI4SE that addresses the use of AI to support the SE process in designing large-scale enterprise systems. We will then discuss perspectives from the HCD/HF community on how a system ought to be engineered for usability, with implications for both SE4AI and AI4SE. Following this discussion, we will highlight the viewpoints between the three approaches and discuss possible research opportunities that may begin addressing the gaps across each discipline. The chapter will close with brief conclusions and a discussion of future research opportunities and synergies between SE4AI, AI4SE and HCD.

Our goal in exploring engineering methodologies for realizing synergistic capabilities in human-centric complex systems is related to the meaningful positive effects that synergistic system operations yield: mutually reinforcing system functions, improved effectiveness and efficiency, and human-system role optimization. The overarching goal is effective performance while maintaining cost-effective usability over a system's lifetime; to achieve this at least in part will require a human-centered design approach.

We will briefly describe an oversimplified example that demonstrates the importance of examining the interdependencies among the three disciplines. The defense research community has identified certain benefits of using AI and ML, but also realizes the current limitations of these approaches such as the need for large training data and black box techniques that lack explainability and transparency. If there is a roadmap for adoption by the defense community, it must include capabilities for exhaustively exploring the design space to ensure that such limitations are addressed. However, the ability to generate and analyze an exhaustive set of designs may be intractable, but necessary given that the environments where these systems will be expected to operate are high stakes in which a poor design could lead to the loss of life. Hence, HCD principles must be explored versus an enumeration of all possible designs to ensure the enterprise system is globally optimal and not in one aspect at the expense of another.

The ISO 9241-210 standard defines human-centered design (HCD) as "an approach to systems design and development that aims to make interactive systems more usable by focusing on the use of the system and applying human factors/ergonomics and usability knowledge and techniques." This standard also asserts that for a design to be HCD compliant requires that: (1) The design is based upon an explicit understanding of users, tasks, and environments; (2) Users are involved throughout design and development; (3) The design is driven and refined by user-centered evaluation; (4) The process is iterative; (5) The design addresses the whole user experience; and (6) The design team includes multidisciplinary skills and perspectives. For systems having AI/ML capabilities, this user/human-centric aspect also relates to the criticality of incorporating well-designed "explanation" capabilities that serve as the means for humans to understand, deal with, and effectively use the opaque internal operations of AI/ML components and subsystems (e.g., see [1–3]). It should also be noted that the inherent emergent properties of AI/ML processes impute a need to address both accommodation and exploitation of these properties within the system engineering methods employed in development. This is because emergence can have a range of properties from strong to weak [4], corresponding to undesirable behavior that possibly yields unintended or unsafe operations, as well as desirable properties such as self-healing or positive performance-adaptive behaviors.

SE methods have been proposed for purposefully engineering weak emergence into system designs by Neace and Chipkevich [5].

2   State of the Art in Systems Engineering for Complex Systems and Human Integration

2.1   Systems Engineering and Role of Artificial Intelligence Techniques for Complex Systems

The International Council on Systems Engineering (INCOSE) defines systems engineering as "a transdisciplinary and integrative approach to enable the successful realization, use, and retirement of engineered systems, using systems principles and concepts, and scientific, technological, and management methods" [6]. The definition of systems engineering, in its present form, remains broadly applicable to any engineered system but our focus here is on complex engineered systems inclusive of human participants. Complexity as an attribute of an engineering system is viewed from a variety of perspectives. Systems comprised of a large number of components with first and second order effects of the interactions between their parts are considered complex systems, along with systems where there is unpredictability in cause and effect that are also labeled as complex systems [7]. Moreover, seemingly simple systems, such as a bicycle where the number of parts is not large and the interaction between the parts are well understood, become complex when a rider is considered as part of the system as human behavior and actions would seem to be largely unpredictable (see Sect. 2.2 for more on this issue).

Most engineered systems today exhibit traits of a complex system in both multi-order interactions and their interface with a human and/or teams of humans. One of the primary roles of SE of complex systems is to not only identify the nature of the interactions, but also to ensure the optimization of a set of criteria that are important either to the developer or user of the system [8].

The emerging field of AI provides a unique potential and challenge for complex systems and SE as AI is becoming an integral part of "scientific [and] technological [methods]" for realization of these systems while also being a part of those systems' components itself. This demands "systems principles and concepts" for successful realization per the SE definition. Hence, AI adds to systems engineering processes while itself requiring systems engineering processes for its incorporation into systems. These two facets of AI and SE are called AI4SE and SE4AI, respectively, as previously noted.

To highlight the roles of AI4SE in a system and how AI can add to and reduce system complexity, Fig. 1 provides a conceptual illustration of a system's decomposition and its interfaces. In its simplest form, a system is composed of interdependent sub-systems that perform one or more functions to achieve the system capability. Systems rarely exist in isolation, and in their operation, they interact with humans and external environments, which may include other systems [6]. AI4SE is about introducing AI to help engineer systems and includes

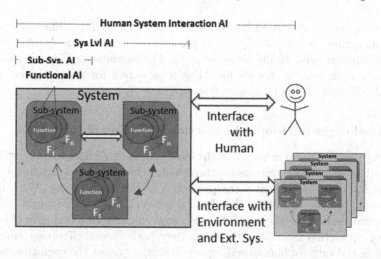

Fig. 1. Levels of AI in a system.

performing system functions, and the interaction of sub-system interfaces and those systems' interfaces with humans and the environment. Although the current advancements in AI are increasingly finding application at the functional level where many functions performed by the sub-systems now include the various forms of supervised, unsupervised, and reinforcement learning, AI4SE purports a broader role of AI at the sub-system level, the system level and the interface level with humans and environments. A significant challenge here is that these levels remain interdependent of one another as functions within a sub-system that share input/output with other sub-systems that are influenced by the humans and the systems' environment. From an HCD standpoint, it is important to recognize this coupling and to engineer solutions that aid humans with its cognizance. However, increasing capability of systems is accompanied with a non-linear increase in the complexity of interactions. The goal for AI4SE, then, is to decipher this complexity and create viable solutions across the different levels including the human interaction with a complex system.

While the goals of the AI4SE paradigm is to make AI as part of the "systems principles and concepts" for identifying, managing, and engineering human and complex systems interactions, this goal cannot be achieved without a discussion of the SE4AI which seeks to introduce "systems principles and concepts" for AI. AI development has remained focused on algorithmic advancement hitherto, which is being recognized as an impediment to the wider adoption of AI in complex systems [9]. Higginbotham identifies that there is a lack of process models for documenting and developing AI algorithms despite being a common practice in software engineering [10]. Sculley et al. describe the hidden technical debt of machine learning algorithms and attribute it to a lack of operational considerations when developing the algorithms [11], resulting in serious implications for life-cycle costs. SE of any product or system (static, interactive, or intelligent) begins with the identification of needs and takes it through the lifecycle starting with conceptual design, development, production, verification, validation, utilization, support, and finally retirement [6]. The fundamental idea of SE4AI is to develop such process models for AI as a precursor for AI's adoption in SE (i.e., AI4SE) and HCD of complex systems.

2.2   Challenges of Human Interaction with Complex Systems

As briefly touched upon in Sect. 2.2, the most elusive challenges in understanding the behavior of complex systems are those where the human is a significant "forcing function" that complicates the prediction of human behavior. With regard to behavioral unpredictability, the physical network scientist, Barabàsi [12], and the modern game theorists would disagree, so even the notion of degree of human behavior prediction is in flux. However, they both base their disagreement by dismissing the value of human self-reports (i.e., they reject the cognitive model). With the goal of control [13], by rejecting the cognitive model, physical network scientists and game theorists dramatically improve the predictability of behavior in situations where beliefs are suppressed, in low-risk environments, or for economic beliefs in highly certain environments. However, the predictability achieved by these models fails in the presence of uncertainty [14] or conflict [15], exactly where interdependence theory thrives [19]. For example, facing uncertainty, debate exploits the bistable views of reality that exist to explore interdependently the tradeoffs that test, or search, for the best paths forward. Generalizing, reducing uncertainty for a system necessitates that human and machine teammates are both able to explain, however imperfectly, each other's past actions and future plans in causal terms [17,18]. Further, in that no single human or machine agent can determine context alone, resolving uncertain contexts requires a theory of interdependence to build and operate safely and ethically autonomous human-machine systems [19]. According to Cummings [20], the best science teams are fully interdependent. Cooke [21] locates a team's intelligence in the interdependence among teammates. We extend these findings to the open-ended debates that explore tradeoffs seeking to maximize a system's production of entropy (MEP) in highly competitive but uncertain environments.

SE and AI have core concepts or issues, as we have asserted. In SE, it is a synergistic concept where "the whole is greater than the sum of its parts" [6]. In AI, an issue raised by a leading researcher, is the need for AI to address cause and effect in explaining its results [17]. Here, we introduce the third dimension to be addressed in forming a path to a holistic SE approach: the challenges associated with human interaction in systems. We address three cases to make some points:

Case 1: We consider the human and machine as a system. AI's Machine Learning (ML) can learn patterns sufficiently to drive an Uber car, but in 2018, a self-driving Uber car was unable to alert its human operator when its sensors acquired an obstacle in the road, not only killing a pedestrian [22], but also making it a poor team player [19]. The latter is an example of dysergy, the opposite of synergy. Unlike the rational choice model which breaks down with conflict [15], interdependence thrives, encompassing synergy and dysergy.

Case 2: In 2017–18, BMW's human-robot teams were functioning synergisti-cally, motivating BMW to add new employees and machines. In compari-son, Tesla's all-robot factory struggled to meet its quota of 5000 cars per quarter, a dysergic system effect that Tesla's human operators and robots could not analyze on the fly. To make his quota, Elon Musk replaced many of Tesla's robots with humans. Later analysis discovered that humans did not see that the machines were dysfunctional in different orientations on the assembly line. This problem was solved with the use of improved robotic vision. Tesla's robots evolved and the resulting synergy increased Tesla's pro-duction beyond its original quota to over 80,000 in 2018's Quarter 3, contin-uing in 2019 (reviewed in https://www.wsj.com/articles/ludicrous-review-a-revolutionary-old-product-11566945826).

Case 3: In another project, seeking the true promise of AI by solving a well-defined problem to integrate expert human decision making in AI applications for well defined, limited domains of knowledge. The authors focused both on managing the attention of an operator working in a highly multitasked environment, and supporting the rapid recovery of situation awareness for operators who leave and reenter that environment [35]. Once a solution with AI has been found for an independent part of a complex system, however, that independent part has to be integrated back into the full system to test for unexpected, dysergic, or synergistic interdependent effects.

The effort discussed in Case 3 above provides a good example of a dysergic human interaction with a complex system and how a human centered design could remediate the dysergy. In an effort to reduce manpower, the US Navy introduced an advanced information console known as the Common Display System (CDS) to shipboard Combat Information Systems (CICs) in all new platforms as well as in existing platforms through the AEGIS modernization program. The CDS gives watchstanders access to multiple tasks from a single seat and a three-fold increase in visual display space. While this technology allows a single watchstander to perform multiple tasks at the same time, con-currency among critical tasks in shipboard CICs results in increased operator workload and requires operators to resort to multitasking strategies that lower situation awareness (SA). Watchstanders are expected to interact with multi-ple shipboard systems simultaneously, while also interacting with multiple chat message threads (up to 30 concurrent threads have been observed) and moni-toring up to five voice communication channels. What was observed and docu-mented in multiple studies [24,25] is that, instead of a synergistic effect leading to higher operator efficiencies, significant performance degradations resulted. These included increased cognitive load, fatigue, and higher error rates.

Research conducted at the U.S. Naval Research Laboratory (NRL) has demonstrated the ability of attention management strategies to significantly improve operator performance in highly multitasking environments such as CICs. Viewing human attention as a limited resource, this research attempts to manage an operator's attention through serialized guidance, thus freeing the operator to completely attend to one task at a time. NRL has already shown the merit of mediated attention management for concurrent radio communications monitoring in CICs through an extended series of human performance studies. Measures of attention to data, comprehension, and effort improve dramatically when competing communications circuits are buffered and played sequentially at accelerated rates of speech to ensure that transmissions on each circuit are fully presented [26, 27].

An attention management strategy, however, must include a task prioritization model that can inform serialized guidance so that operators address the most critical amongst competing primary tasks. Additionally, this model must provide for operator-centered control that enables the operators to affect how tasks are prioritized based on their current operational needs. This is a challenging problem as both operational and user contexts must be considered when assessing the value of incoming information.

Approaches for automatically assessing the value of information given operational and user contexts, especially for the micro text comprising chat messages, remain in a nascent state. Instead, an automated variation of the Analytic Hierarchy Process (AHP) [28] was utilized to capture the information value assessments of watchstander subject matter experts. AHP is a well-studied and highly utilized approach for structured decision-making and SE. The process begins with a group of subject matter experts (SME) examining a decision space to 1) determine a goal (what's to be decided); 2) define a set of criteria along with respective weights for each that can be used to rate the decision choices (the weights indicate how relevant a criteria is to the goal); and 3) a set of weights for each decision choice relative to each of the defined criteria. In our approach, we derived the criteria weights through a human subject study with CIC watchstander SMEs. The choice weights are calculated automatically at runtime and are used to prioritize incoming information. More details on this approach can be found in [35].

In general, solutions to complex problems arise from the widest exploration of potential solutions until a synergistic signal suggests the potential for maximum entropy production [29]. Difficult problems are constrained by available energy, time, and intelligence, especially for teams [21]; e.g., affecting the search for patents and the size of, or skills on, a team [19]. Teams are more productive than individuals, the most productive teams being the most interdependent [20]. Thus, managing interdependence for autonomous or human-machine systems is critical.

2.3 Perspectives on Synergy

Synergy is a term that notionally implies a special type of cooperation among two or more agents that yields a result greater than any single agent could have achieved alone. To achieve synergy in system design, the system components involved need to be designed such that a mutual advantage to each component can be realized from some cooperative act; ideally, these actions result in a type of mutual reinforcement toward an objective. Following [1], synergy can be expressed and quantified in terms of systems architecting theory by correlated changes across the systems' design space that yield some measure of improved utility or reduced cost.

3 Engineering Synergy Between Human and Complex Systems

3.1 Systems Engineering for Human-Centric Design

Well-defined and proven SE4AI is a capability yet to be developed. Both the SE and AI communities are searching for the best intersection of what they each do, toward an ability to specify, design, develop, deploy, and operate systems that perform well and realize bounded life-cycle costs. Part of the problem in achieving this capability is a consequence of history in the AI domain when, until recently (but even to a degree still today), AI and ML were fields largely based in an R&D framework. As a result, there was no urgency for efficient, effective, and formalized methods for developing systems that might be employed in a critical or otherwise very important context. Today, because of broadened receptivity to new technologies and because of a range of successes in applications, systems containing AI and ML components are evermore being considered for a wide range of application, some very exacting, some of high-consequence, even some involving life-and-death consequences. As a result, there is a new urgency to define how to build, test, and operate such systems.

Among the challenges toward realizing formal methods of SE are those that are a consequence of the characteristics of AI and ML processes. Emergence is one such characteristic (probabilistic and non-deterministic behaviors are other complications). Here we prefer the definition of emergence given as a property of a complex system: "a property of a complex system is said to be 'emergent' and it arises out of the properties and relations characterizing the system's simpler constituents, but it is neither predictable from, nor reducible to, these lower-level characteristics" [see: https://www.sebokwiki.org/wiki/Emergence]. There are many other definitions and taxonomies of emergence [4,30,31], but our focus is on the effects of emergence, not emergence per se. Such effects can be either, or both, unintended and unexpected behaviors but some emergent behaviors such as self-healing or desirable self-adaptation can be purposefully engineered into a system, so there are good and bad consequences of emergence.

Developing SE4AI will involve aspects of software engineering as a central part, since AI and ML capabilities are largely realized in software. Because AI/ML history was R&D-centered, software design was largely developed from an inductively-based approach, shifting the perspective of the engineer from a software engineer to a data scientist. As discussed by Sculley et al. [11], this approach can then lead to a hidden "technical debt"; the notion of technical debt is related to the idea of hidden long-term maintenance costs for software. A key point is that, as regards to lifecycle costs, the development phase is a relatively small part. Further, as we are still in the "AI Spring," the reality of lifecycle costs for systems involving AI/ML technologies has not yet been experienced. While the distribution of the degree of AI/ML functionalities in real-world systems is not very well known, Sculley et al. [11] assert that even though AI/ML typically comprises a relatively small part of a larger system, the within-AI/ML and AI/ML-system complexities and their pathologies can lead to high lifecycle costs.

Even basic aspects of SE, such as specifications and requirements definition and development, are issues being struggled with in the evolution of SE practice for AI/ML development. Belani et al. [32] suggest that a new paradigm is needed for AI/ML requirements elicitation, and also that there are new types of requirements for AI/ML such as explainability[1] On the back end, as regards test and evaluation (T&E) of AI/ML, there is a bifurcation of the issues, as the AI and ML processes are different. For the ML that largely delivers a classification type capability, the T&E processes and metrics have the advantage of a long history of classifier testing and associated metrics. But even so, there are complications and issues because it has to be appreciated that many of the traditional metrics compute measures from different points of view and therefore measure different properties; Flach [33] gives a good summary of these points. For AI, one can get immediately ensnared in the question of what intelligence is and how to measure it. Many testing approaches today take a task-orientation, assessing whether the AI capability allowed a task to be done well; see Hernández-Orallo [34] for remarks on this point of view.

Space does not allow a complete discussion on this SE4AI topic; it can hopefully be appreciated from these limited remarks that there is a long way to go to formalize mature and reusable methods and practices for "good" SE4AI. One final and non-trivial remark has to do with the fact that it is not only SE, usually focused on system development, that is of concern today. Today we see a major thrust toward what is called "DevOps," meaning a synthesis combining SE and post-system-deployment Operations into a new integrated engineering process. The SE4AI issue may only solve the first part of the challenge.

3.2 Complex System View from a Human Prespective

Modern software systems have moved away from a monolithic systems approach towards a "system of systems" approach, where a cloud based, software-as-a-service (SaaS) model enables system designers to assemble complex software systems through the composition of cloud-based services.

In [35], we propose a multi-agent, intelligent system that uses Emergent Configurations (EC) [36] as the organizing principle for compositing data from a disparate set of Internet-of-Things (IoT) sensors to distill information for a user in an as-needed fashion.

---

[1] The complexities and resultant opaqueness of AI/ML processes have demanded that an explanation utility be delivered with these processes to aid users in understanding, trusting, and operating systems with these complex operations; see ([3]) as an example.

One can envision a generalization of this approach for the creation of intelligent systems that use EC principles to self-organize autonomous agents into a complex system of systems that use the SaaS model to acquire and digest the services and information needed to form a complex intelligent system. This approach abstracts the SE problem away from that of designing a complex intelligent system to that of designing the rules by which complex intelligent systems emerge into a form that addresses a given goal. Such an approach has the advantage of providing a single design that can address a class of problems through the EC approach. The problem becomes that of finding an appropriate design principle that can manage the complexity inherent in using EC to dynamically create and compose autonomous agents into a coherent intelligent system. Prior work by Simon [37] and later by Valckenars [38] could provide a basis for such a design principle.

In his seminal work on the Sciences of the Artificial, Simon explores the laws that bound artificial systems. His goal was to develop a corollary to the laws of physics, but applied to artificial systems. Simon outlines three assumptions that, when holding true, require that any successful artificial system be characterized by a pyramidal structure; a Holonic system. Simon's first assumption is that intelligent systems have a bounded, or limited, capacity for computation and communication. As the limits of that capacity are approached, adding more resources produces diminishing returns. The implication is that real-world intelligent systems must be able to make decisions based on imperfect information and limited computations. Simon's second assumption is that intelligent systems will operate in demanding environments. Intelligent systems must address nontrivial problems, make effective use of the resources available to them, and grow in complexity only in service of achieving a successful outcome. Systems that cannot do this invariably fail and are replaced by more successful systems. His final assumption is that intelligent systems must be able to operate in a dynamic environment. Operating in a highly dynamic environment requires that systems have the capacity to evolve to adapt to changing contexts. This requirement has implications for the idea of optimality. In a fast-changing environment, the time required to design and develop a solution that approaches optimality makes a system obsolete before it can be deployed. Developing optimal systems has been the holy grail of computer science since its inception. Forgoing that goal in service of agility requires rethinking how software systems are engineered.

In a Holonic system of autonomous agents, information flows upwards from leaf node agents towards the apex. Furthermore, each layer of agents is only aware of agents directly below them in the hierarchy. In fact, in our proposed EC scheme, each layer of agents is responsible for the creation of the next, lower level of agents needed to fulfill an informational or computational requirement. Agents that no longer serve a function are destroyed by the agents that created them.

This approach provides a number of advantages, especially when user context is considered: (1) the interaction is bounded to each layer of the pyramid. In other words, in designing the behavior of agents on one level of the pyramid,

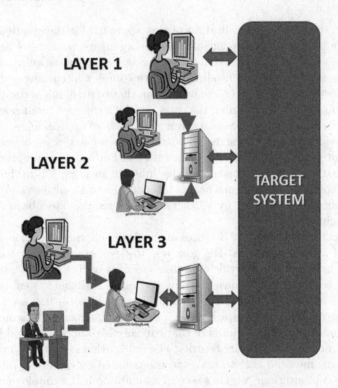

Fig. 2. Three layers of human-machine interaction [38]

we are only concerned with that layer's interaction with the layer immediately below them; (2) the overall system complexity is proportional to the problem being addressed. The agent configuration created through the EC process will only be as complex as required by the service being provided; and (3) such a system provides multiple insertion points for user interaction at different levels of abstraction. Furthermore, the decision of how and when to interact with a system is made locally at the agent level.

3.3 Synergistic Design of Human-Centered Complex Systems

There are interesting notions of possible frameworks for human-centered, human-machine cooperation and achieving possible synergies. Moradi et al. [39] remind us that the "layering" of humans and machines can be complicated in certain cases, as in Fig. 2 that shows where: a) humans are directly interfacing with a target system, b) human-machine workstations interfacing with the target system, and c) yet other "layers" through which humans interact with the target system.

This characterization imputes a need to factor in workflow processes into the overarching design of such complex systems. The modeling and design of workflows is a rapidly-evolving area of study to understand, organize, and often automate the processes upon which a human-centric complex system is operated and used. It is clear that system design and workflow design are co-dependent and add to the challenges of defining an overarching approach to the SE of such complex systems.

In a new paper, Stephanidis et al. [40], provide a major overview of the "grand challenges" for human-computer-interaction (HCI) design; the paper is too large to summarize here but we offer a few interesting remarks drawn from the paper. One interesting topic is that of "meaningful human control" as a principle that goes beyond any specific protocol; it advocates that humans, not computers and their algorithms, should ultimately remain in control of, and thus be morally responsible for, actions mediated by autonomous systems. To achieve such human control, important features of complex systems are transparency, understandability (relates to explainability) and accountability, these features also contribute towards building a relationship of trust improved performance of the human-automation team. The paper offers a nice summary of the wide range of challenges toward realizing human-machine symbiosis/synergy to show that the issues are complex and multi-faceted, extending beyond technical boundaries to a multi-disciplinary approach with the aim to also address compelling ethical, societal, and philosophical issues. Achieving this symbiosis will entail a number of considerations, such as incorporating human values in the design choices and trade-offs, taking into account the social dynamics involved, and combining these concerns with a number of practical influences.

In thinking about "human centered design (HCD)" in the context of complex systems, the philosophical distinctions for the concurrent creation and development of artifacts (concepts and/or technology), together with the people and organizations that relate to them, have to be jointly considered [41]. This chapter and others that take a top-level view of the HCD issue for complex systems make

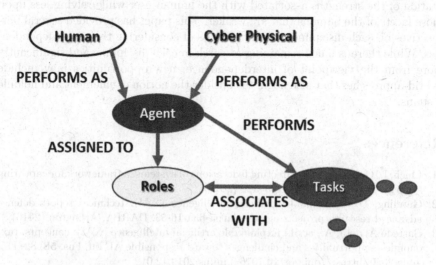

Fig. 3. Human-machine teaming ontology [41]

clear that the design thinking is an evolutionary state. For example, the very ontology of a "Human-Machine Team" is discussed in [42] and shown in Sect. 3.

If we are truly striving for achieving synergistic human-machine operations in designing human machine systems in complex frameworks, the question of how to measure synergy will arise. Virtually all of the literature on this topic relates synergy to the multivariate information measures descriptive of, or involved with, the functions of the contributing processes. If such information measures are bivariate, the synergy measures are clear; but if the measures are multivariate, a variety of offerings exist on synergy metrics. One summary paper on this topic is [42]. It points out that a crucial topic related to the use of multivariate information measures is the distinction between synergy and redundancy. Timme et al. [42] provide a nice review of different strategies used, not only to assess synergy and redundancy, but also interaction between contributing processes.

4 Conclusions and Path Forward

Artificial Intelligence (AI), Human Centered Design (HCD), and Systems Engineering (SE) are typically considered as three distinct disciplines. However, AI is rapidly changing the complexity of systems and the nature of how we begin to consider the role of the human. The interdependencies of all three disciplines has the potential to create a design space that can easily become too difficult to jointly optimize. Our claim is that the identification of the key design metrics within a complex system (based on an SE perspective) and how those affect (and are affected by) metrics critical to the performance of the human (examined from the viewpoint of HCD) creates an opportunity to yield a "balanced" system. We further hypothesize that achieving such a balance will provide efficiencies in software maintainability and cost, system performance, and best utilization of the strengths associated with the human user while relying less upon those facets of the humans that are weaker. This paper has provided several perspectives on each discipline and the benefits of considering their interdependencies. While there is much remaining research in each discipline, and significantly more from the viewpoint of interdependence, new opportunities may include hybrid-approaches that also begin to consider the notion of emergent and holonic systems.

References

1. Lluch, I., Golkar, A.: Architecting federations of systems: a framework for capturing synergy. Syst. Eng. **22**(4), 295–312 (2019)
2. Gunning, D.: Explainable artificial intelligence (XAI): technical report defense advanced research projects agency darpa-baa-16-53. DARPA, Arlington (2016)
3. Barredo Arrieta, A., et al.: Explainable artificial intelligence (XAI): concepts, taxonomies, opportunities and challenges toward responsible AI. Inf. Fus. **58**, 82–115, June 2020. https://doi.org/10.1016/j.inffus.2019.12.012

4. Chalmers, D.J.: Strong and weak emergence. In: Davies, P., Clayton, P. (eds.) The Re-Emergence of Emergence: The Emergentist Hypothesis From Science to Religion, Oxford University Press, Oxford (2006)
5. Neace, K.S., Chipkevich, M.B.A.: Designed complex adaptive systems exhibiting weak emergence. In: IEEE National Aerospace and Electronics Conference, NAECON 2018, pp. 214–221. July 2018. https://doi.org/10.1109/NAECON.2018.8556693
6. INCOSE. INCOSE Systems Engineering Handbook: A Guide for System Life Cycle Processes and Activities, 4 edn, Wiley, Hoboken (2015)
7. Rouse, W.B.: Complex engineered, organizational and natural systems: issues underlying the complexity of systems and fundamental research needed to address these issues. Syst. Eng. **10**(3), 260–271 (2007)
8. Raz, A.K., Kenley, C.R., DeLaurentis, D.A.: System architecting and design space characterization. ChSyst. Eng. **21**(3), 227–242 (2018)
9. Raz, A.K., Llinas, J., Mittu, R., Lawless, W.: Engineering for emergence in information fusion systems: a review of some challenges. In: 2019 22th International Conference on Information Fusion (FUSION), pp. 1–8. July 2019
10. Higginbotham Hey, S.: Data scientists: show your machine-learning work. IEEE Spectrum
11. Sculley, D., et al.: Hidden technical debt in machine learning systems. In: Cortes, C., Lawrence, N.D.D., Lee, D., Sugiyama, M., Garnett, R. (eds.) Advances in Neural Information Processing Systems, vol. 28, pp. 2503–2511. Curran Associates Inc., Red Hook (2015)
12. Barabàsi, A.L.: Network science: understanding the internal organization of complex systems (Invited Talk). In: 2012 AAAI Spring Symposium Series, March 2012, https://www.aaai.org/ocs/index.php/SSS/SSS12/paper/view/4333. Accessed 29 Apr 2020
13. Liu, Y.-Y. Barabási, A.-L.: Control principles of complex systems. Rev. Mod. Phys. **88**(3), 035006, September 2016. https://doi.org/10.1103/RevModPhys.88.035006
14. Hansen, L.P.: Nobel lecture: uncertainty outside and inside economic models. J. Polit. Econ **122**(5), 945–987 (2014). https://doi.org/10.1086/678456
15. Mann, R.P.: Collective decision making by rational individuals. PNAS 115(44) (2018)
16. Lawless, W.F.: The interdependence of autonomous human-machine teams: the entropy of teams, but not individuals. Adv. Sci. Entropy **21**(12), 1195 (2019)
17. Pearl, J.: Reasoning with cause and effect. AI Mag. **23**(1), 95–95 (2002). https://doi.org/10.1609/aimag.v23i1.1612
18. Pearl, J., Mackenzie, D.: AI can't reason why. Wall Street J. (2018). https://www.wsj.com/articles/ai-cant-reason-why-1526657442. Accessed 27 Apr 2020
19. Lawless, W.F., Mittu, R., Sofge, D., Hiatt, L.: Artificial intelligence, autonomy, and human-machine teams – interdependence, context, and explainable AI. AI Mag. **40**(3), 5–13 (2019)
20. Cummings, J.: Team Science successes and challenges. In: National Science Foundation Sponsored Workshop on Fundamentals of Team Science and the Science of Team Science, Bethesda (2015)
21. Cooke, N.: Effective human-artificial intelligence teaming. In: AAAI-2020 Spring Symposium, Stanford (2020)
22. NTSB: Preliminary Report Released for Crash Involving Pedestrian, Uber Technologies Inc., Test Vehicle. https://www.ntsb.gov/news/press-releases/Pages/NR20180524.aspx. Accessed 13 Mar 2019

23. Fouad, H., Moskowitz, I., Brock, D., Scott, M.: Integrating expert human decision-making in artificial intelligence applications. In: Lawless, W.F., Ranjeev, M., Sofge, D. (eds.) Human-machine Shared Contexts, Elsevier, London (2020)
24. Marois, R., Ivanoff, J.: Capacity limits of information processing in the brain. Trends Cogn. Sci. **9**(6), 296–305 (2005). https://doi.org/10.1016/j.tics.2005.04.010
25. Chérif, L., Wood, V., Marois, A., Labonté, K., Vachon, F.: Multitasking in the military: cognitive consequences and potential solutions. Appl. Cogn. Psychol. **32**(4), 429–439 (2018). https://doi.org/10.1002/acp.3415
26. Brock, D., Wasylyshyn, C., McClimens, B., Perzanowski, B.: Facilitating the watch-stander's voice communications task in future Navy operations. In: 2011 - MILCOM 2011 Military Communications Conference, pp. 2222–2226, November 2021
27. Brock, S.C., McClimens, P.B., McClimens, B., Radivilova, T., Bulakh, V.: Evaluating Listeners' Attention to, and Comprehension of, Serially Interleaved, Rate-accelerated Speech (2012)
28. Saaty, T.L.: The Analytic Hierarchy Process. McGraw-Hill, New York (1980)
29. Martyushev, L.M.: Entropy and entropy production: old misconceptions and new breakthroughs. Entropy **15**(4), 1152–1170 (2013). https://doi.org/10.3390/e15041152
30. Holland, O.T.: Taxonomy for the modeling and simulation of emergent behavior systems. In: Proceedings of the 2007 Spring Simulation Multiconference, vol. 2, pp. 28–35 (2007)
31. Fromm, J.: On engineering and emergence (2006)
32. Belani, H., Vuković, M.Ž., Car, M.: Requirements engineering challenges in building AI-based complex systems (2020). arXiv:1908.11791 [cs], Accessed 29 Apr 2020
33. Flach, P.: performance evaluation in machine learning: the good, the bad, the ugly, and the way forward. In: Proceedings of the AAAI Conference on Artificial Intelligence, vol. 33, pp. 9808–9814 (2019). https://doi.org/10.1609/aaai.v33i01.33019808
34. Hernández-Orallo, J.: Evaluation in artificial intelligence: from task-oriented to ability-oriented measurement. Artif. Intell. Rev. **48**(3), 397–447 (2016). https://doi.org/10.1007/s10462-016-9505-7
35. Fouad, H., Moskowitz, I.S.: Meta-agents: using multi-agent networks to manage dynamic changes in the internet of things. In: Lawless, W., Mittu, R., Sofge, D., Moskowitz, I.S., Russell, S. (eds.) Artificial Intelligence for the Internet of Everything, Academic Press, pp. 271–281 (2019)
36. Mihailescu, R.-C., Spalazzese, R., Heyer, C., Davidsson. P.: A role-based approach for orchestrating emergent configurations in the internet of things. Internet of Things, arXiv:1809.09870 [cs], September 2018
37. Simon, J.: The Sciences of the artificial. MIT Press, Cambridge (2019)
38. Valckenaers, P., Brussel, H.V., Holvoet, T.: Fundamentals of holonic systems and their implications for self-adaptive and self-organizing systems. In: 2008 Second IEEE International Conference on Self-Adaptive and Self-Organizing Systems Workshops, pp. 168–173 October 2008
39. Moradi, M., Moradi, M., Bayat, F., Nadjaran Toosi, A.: Collective hybrid intelligence: towards a conceptual framework. Int. J. Crowd Sci. **3**(2), 198–220, January 2019. https://doi.org/10.1108/IJCS-03-2019-0012
40. Stephanidis, C.C., et al. : Seven HCI Grand Challenges. Int. J. Hum. Comput. Int. **35** (14), 1229–1269, August 2019. https://doi.org/10.1080/10447318.2019.1619259
41. Boy, G.A.: Human-centered design of complex systems: an experience-based approach. Des. Sci. **3** (2017)

42. Madni, A.M., Madni, C.C.: Architectural framework for exploring adaptive human-machine teaming options in simulated dynamic environments. Systems **6**(4), 44 (2018). https://doi.org/10.3390/systems6040044

43. Timme, N., Alford, W., Flecker, B., Beggs, J.M.: Multivariate information measures: an experimentalist's perspective, August 2012. arXiv:1111.6857 [physics, stat], http://arxiv.org/abs/1111.6857. Accessed 29 Apr 2020

Agent Team Action, Brownian Motion and Gambler's Ruin

Ira S. Moskowitz[✉]

Information Management and Decision Architectures Branch, Code 5580,
Naval Research Laboratory, 4555 Overlook Avenue, SW, Washington DC 20375, USA
ira.moskowitz@nrl.navy.mil

Abstract. In this chapter, we discuss how to use Brownian motion to
model various probabilities concerning a group of agents, or more simply
put, a Team. We discuss the limiting behavior of probabilities of interest
and also discuss how an information geometric approach can assist in
analyzing various situations of interest.

Keywords: Agents · Team · Wiener process · Brownian motion ·
Differential geometry

1   Introduction

Brownian motion (1-dimensional) is the infinitesimal generalization of a
(1-dimensional) random walk. It had its origins in the natural sciences [6].
Einstein [14] obtained the major results on diffusion equations and Brownian
motion. However, we do not concentrate on the physics' aspect of Brownian
motion; rather, we look at artificial intelligence (AI) uses of Brownian motion
concerning modeling human behavior in a group of agents or a Team. In [29],
we concentrated on using Ratcliff diffusion [34–36] to model how a single person makes quick decisions. In [29], we also touched upon Team science. In this
chapter, we discuss Teams, and more generally, agent behavior in terms of Brownian motion. We also consider the information we may learn from the geometry
of the curves and surfaces under consideration. Analyzing the formulas without
visual clues misses some important and interesting aspects of the probabilities
under consideration.

The stochastic processes in this chapter are for continuous time t, $t \in
[0,T], 0 < T \leq \infty$. Much of our terminology is freely borrowed from [29].

1.1   Agent/Team Behavior in Brief

We assume that we have a Team of agents, people, etc., who are attempting to
perform a joint task. The task can be mundane, such as a restaurant crew working
together in a kitchen, or more machine oriented, such as sensors attempting to
find something. The Team, over time, produces an output. When the output

W. F. Lawless et al. (Eds.): Engineering Artificially Intelligent Systems, LNCS 13000, pp. 90–108, 2021.
https://doi.org/10.1007/978-3-030-89385-9_6

reaches the value $A \in \mathbb{R}$ (success), the process stops. If the output instead reaches the value $0 \in \mathbb{R}$ (not successful), the process also stops. Note that the process stops when it reaches 0 or A. If it reaches A first, we assume that the Team has had a success; if it reaches 0 first, we take that as a failure. At time 0, the output is an initial value $Z, 0 \leq Z \leq A$. We have normalized our values to 0, A and Z, to facilitate the mathematics; of course, one may shift and renormalize.

We have decided to go through the mathematics first and then describe the Team problem with the mathematics for two reasons; 1-We give some novel insights into the mathematics, and 2-This allows us to concentrate on the Team behavior separately from the mathematical proofs.

2   Stochastic Processes

Definition 1. *A stochastic process X_t is said to be* **Gaussian** *if for any $t_1, ..., t_k$ the joint distribution of $X_{t_1}, ..., X_{t_k}$ is multivariate normal.*

Note 1. *Keep in mind that a Gaussian process is completely determined by its mean and covariance properties, since for a multivariate normal random variable, we only need its covariance matrix and mean to uniquely determine it [11, p. 71].*

Definition 2. *A stochastic process S_t has stationary increments if the distribution of the random variable $S_b - S_a$, where $b \geq a$, only depends on $b - a$. This is equivalent to $S_b - S_a$, where $b \geq a$, having the same distribution as S_{b-a}.*

Definition 3. *A Wiener process $\mathscr{W}(t)$ for $t \geq 0$ is a Gaussian process with stationary increments and continuous sample paths[1] such that:*

1) The expectation, $E(\mathscr{W}(t)) = 0$
2) The covariance, $Cov(\mathscr{W}(S), \mathscr{W}(T)) = \min(S, T)$.

We can easily see that for a Wiener process $\mathscr{W}(t)$, the variance is $Var(\mathscr{W}(t), \mathscr{W}(t)) = t$. Of course, the covariance between a random variable and itself is simply referred to as the variance.

Theorem 1. *The following is an equivalent definition of a Wiener process: We say that a stochastic process $\mathscr{W}(t), t \geq 0$ is a Wiener process [16] if*

---

[1] That is, sample paths are continuous with probability 1. Of course there are the 0 probability pathological occurrences, such as the process being 1 at rational numbers, and -1 at irrational numbers. We find it noteworthy that the term "continuous stochastic process" refers to the fact that the stochastic process is indexed by a non-zero measurable set of the reals. However, the common mathematical definition of continuous is still captured by having continuous sample paths. We further observe as an interesting fact, but will not prove, that the sample paths of a Wiener process are not differentiable.

- $\mathcal{W}_0 = 0$.
- With probability 1, the function $t \to \mathcal{W}_t$ is continuous in t.
- The stochastic process $\{\mathcal{W}_t\}, t \geq 0$ has stationary, independent increments.
- The increment $\mathcal{W}_{t+s} - \mathcal{W}_s$ has the distribution of the standard normal random variable $N(0, t)$ (this later part of the definition tells us that $\mathcal{W}_t$ has the distribution of $N(0, t)$).

Proof. See the literature.   □

Since $E(\mathcal{W}(t)) = 0$ and $Var(W(t), W(t)) = t$, we see that the Wiener process is modeled on the standard normal random variable $N(0, 1)$. Furthermore, one can show that the Wiener process exists and can be easily simulated (see [29] where the literature is more fully reviewed in this matter). We note that a Wiener process is more than a stochastic process, where each X_t is a normal random variable with mean 0 and variance t. A Wiener process has stationary increments and continuous sample paths.

To generalize the Wiener process, we model on the normal random variable with mean μ and variance σ^2, or $N(\mu, \sigma^2)$, instead of the previous $N(0, 1)$. This generalization defines Brownian motion, or BM (taken from [29]).

Definition 4. We say that the stochastic process $\mathcal{B}(t), t \geq 0$ is Brownian motion if for real μ and $\sigma > 0$, and $\mathcal{W}(t)$ the Wiener process, then

$$\mathcal{B}(t) = \mu t + \sigma \mathcal{W}(t). \tag{1}$$

We call μ the drift (coefficient) and σ the diffusion (coefficient).

Note 2. The diffusion is sometimes called scale, volatility (economics) or variance. Observe that when we use the term Wiener process, many others use the term Brownian motion, and when we use Brownian motion, many others use the term Brownian motion with drift. We find this confusing and just view the Wiener process as Brownian motion with drift 0 and diffusion of 1. The drift can be thought of as the slope, and the diffusion as the spread.

Brownian motion has the same properties as a Wiener process except that the increment $\mathcal{B}(t + s) - \mathcal{B}(t)$ has the distribution $N(\mu s, \sigma^2 s)$ instead of $N(0, s)$.

In particular, a Brownian motion $\mathcal{B}(t)$ with drift μ and diffusion σ has the properties found in [5, Def. 12.5, p 250].

Theorem 2. The increments $\mathcal{B}(t + s) - \mathcal{B}(t)$, with $t, s \geq 0$ are

1) independent,
2) normally distributed and with

$$E(\mathcal{B}(t + s) - \mathcal{B}(t)) = s\mu; \; Var(\mathcal{B}(t + s) - \mathcal{B}(t)) = s\sigma^2; \; and$$

3) $Cov(\mathcal{B}(S), \mathcal{B}(T)) = \sigma^2 \cdot \min(S, T)$.

When we wish to denote the parameters μ, σ more specifically, we express the Brownian motion as $\mathcal{B}_{\mu,\sigma}(t)$. If $\mu = 0$, we more simply write $\mathcal{B}_\sigma(t)$. Obviously $\mathcal{B}_1(t) = \mathscr{W}(t)$.

3 Gambler's Ruin

Brownian motion is the continuous version of a random walk. Many of the results from random walks transition into results for Brownian motion.

In this chapter, we are concerned with a Brownian motion from a starting point Z instead of 0. We denote this new stochastic process as $\mathscr{B}$, where for some Brownian motion, $\mathcal{B}(t)$, we have

$$\mathscr{B}(t) = \mathcal{B}(t) + Z \tag{2}$$

Thus, $\mathscr{B}(0) = Z$; we have just shifted from 0 to Z. In relation to the gambler's ruin, Z can be thought of as the initial pot of money. The drift can be viewed as the probability of winning from the pot, and the diffusion as the possible spread of the winnings. This logic is all addressed thoroughly in [13]. In [13], it is heuristically shown how the gambler's ruin problem turns into the absorption problem for a Brownian motion with a starting point. However, to prove the results fully, one must use optional sampling theory [12] and exponential martingales [38] (Fig. 1).

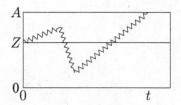

Fig. 1. Brownian motion $\mathscr{B}(t)$ starting at Z and with absorbing boundaries at A (top) and 0 (bottom).

If $\mathscr{B}(t)$ starts off at Z and bounces around, it will eventually hit either the bottom boundary 0 (the gambler has run out of money) or the top boundary A (the gambler has won the entire pot of money). Let $P_Z(\partial = 0)$ be the probability that $\mathcal{B}(t)$ hits the bottom boundary first, then, $P_Z(\partial = A) = 1 - P_Z(\partial = 0)$ be the probability that it hits the top boundary first. These probabilities are derived from the stopping probabilities, and we use L'Hôpital's rule for $\mu = 0$ (see [13, 29, 34, 38] for the details).

$$P_Z(\partial = 0) = \begin{cases} \dfrac{e^{-\frac{2A\mu}{\sigma^2}} - e^{-\frac{2Z\mu}{\sigma^2}}}{e^{-\frac{2A\mu}{\sigma^2}} - 1}, & \text{if } \mu \neq 0 \\ 1 - \dfrac{Z}{A}, & \mu = 0 \end{cases} \tag{3}$$

and

$$P_Z(\eth = A) = \begin{cases} \dfrac{e^{-\frac{2Z\mu}{\sigma^2}}-1}{e^{-\frac{2A\mu}{\sigma^2}}-1}, & \text{if } \mu \neq 0 \\[2ex] \dfrac{Z}{A}, & \mu = 0 \end{cases} \tag{4}$$

It is interesting that when $\mu = 0$, the value of σ does not affect the probabilities. This result makes sense since up and down actions are averaged out with a zero drift. If $\mu = 0$ and $Z = A/2$, we have that both probabilities are $1/2$, which also makes physical sense since we start right in the middle of failure and success, and nothing is weighted (to drift) one way or the other.

3.1 Some Analysis

Consider

$$f(x) := \frac{e^{Bx}-1}{e^{Ax}-1}, A > B > 0, x \neq 0 .$$

It is obvious that as $x \to -\infty, f(x) \to 1^-$, and as $x \to \infty, f(x) \to 0^+$. We can make $f(x)$ a continuous function by applying L'Hôpital's rule at 0 and defining $f(0) := B/A < 1$. We will prove that the function is decreasing. Since it is now continuous at 0, it suffices to show that it is decreasing for $x < 0$ and for $x > 0$ (Fig. 2).

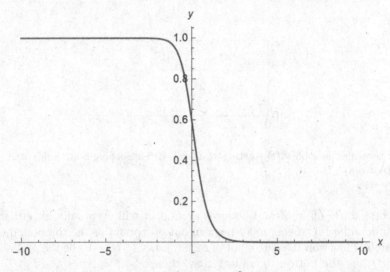

Fig. 2. Plot of $y = \frac{e^{3x}-1}{e^{5x}-1}$.

Theorem 3. For $x \neq 0$, $f(x) = \frac{e^{Bx}-1}{e^{Ax}-1}$, and with $A > B > 0$, we have that $f'(x) < 0$.

Proof. (We are grateful to Paul Cotae of UDC for supplying the clever idea behind this proof.)

Let $A = KB, K > 1$; and let $0 < u(x) = e^{Bx}$, then $f(x) = \frac{u(x)-1}{u(x)^K-1}$; therefore $f'(x) = \frac{df}{du} \cdot u'(x) = \frac{df}{du} \cdot Be^{Bx}$. Since $Be^{Bx} > 0$, it suffices to show that $\frac{df}{du} < 0$.

$$\frac{df}{du} = \frac{d}{du}\left(\frac{u-1}{u^K-1}\right)$$
$$= \frac{(u^K-1) - Ku^{K-1}(u-1)}{(u^K-1)^2}$$
$$= \frac{u^K - Ku^K - 1 + Ku^{K-1}}{(u^K-1)^2}$$
$$= \frac{(1-K)u^K + Ku^{K-1} - 1}{(u^K-1)^2}.$$

Therefore, if we can show that in the numerator of the above,

$$g(u) := (1-K)u^K + Ku^{K-1} - 1 < 0, \text{ for } u \neq 1$$

we will be done with our proof, since $u = 1 \iff x = 0$. Please observe that $g(1) = 0$, so we will show that $g(u) < 0$ for $u \neq 1$ by analyzing $\frac{dg}{du}$.

$$\frac{dg}{du} = K(1-K)u^{K-1} + (K-1)Ku^{K-2}$$
$$= K(K-1)(u^{K-2} - u^{K-1})$$
$$= K(K-1)u^{K-2}(1-u).$$

We see that for $u < 1$, $\frac{dg}{du} > 0$; for $u = 1$, $\frac{dg}{du} = 0$; and for $u > 1$, $\frac{dg}{du} < 0$. Therefore, the value $g(1) = 0$ is an isolated maximum for $g(u)$, and as we desired, $g(u) < 0$ for $u \neq 1$; hence, $f(x)$ is decreasing for $x \neq 0$. Through the continuity of the extended definition of $f(x)$ to include $x = 0$, we have found that $f(x)$ is a decreasing function. $\qquad\square$

Now, consider $h(x) := \frac{e^{-Bx}-1}{e^{-Ax}-1}, A > B > 0$; we see from this that $h(x)$ is an increasing function since it is $f(x)$ "run backwards," or, we can apply the chain rule as above and use $\frac{d}{dx}e^{-Bx} < 0$ to obtain an increasing function (Fig. 3).

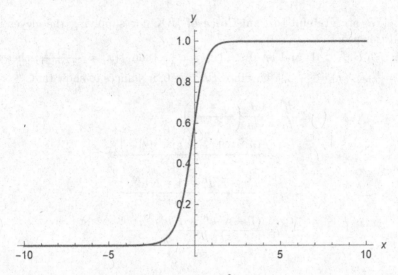

Fig. 3. Plot of $y = \frac{e^{-3x}-1}{e^{-5x}-1}, x \in \mathbb{R}$.

Corollary 3.1. For $h(x) = \frac{e^{-Bx}-1}{e^{-Ax}-1}, A > B > 0, x \neq 0$, we have that $h'(x) > 0$. Thus, $h(x)$ is an increasing function as x grows, and we set $h(0) = B/A$ to obtain an increasing continuous function on the reals going from 0 to 1.

Now consider $c(x) := \frac{e^{-B/x}-1}{e^{-A/x}-1}, A > B > 0$; as x increases, the exponential terms go from $-\infty$ to 0, so $c(x)$ behaves similarly to $f(x)$ in the theorem and thus decreases as x grows. Therefore, as $x \to \infty$, we must apply L'Hôpital's rule to see that the function approaches B/A (Fig. 4).

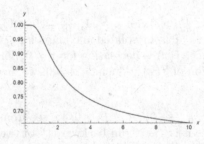

Fig. 4. Plot of $y = \frac{e^{-3/x}-1}{e^{-5/x}-1}, x > 0$.

Corollary 3.2. For $c(x) := \frac{e^{-B/x}-1}{e^{-A/x}-1}, A > B > 0$, we have a decreasing function on the positive reals going from 1 to B/A.

We are left with seeing how $\frac{e^{-B/x}-1}{e^{-A/x}-1}, A > B > 0$, behaves when $x < 0$. Similar to our other results (L'Hopital's rule at $\pm\infty$ and one-sided limits at 0), we have (Fig. 5):

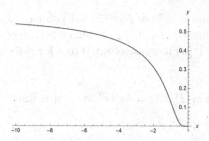

Fig. 5. Plot of $y = \frac{e^{-3/x}-1}{e^{-5/x}-1}, x < 0$.

Corollary 3.3. *For* $w(x) := \frac{e^{-B/x}-1}{e^{-A/x}-1}, A > B > 0,$ *we have a decreasing function on the negative reals going from B/A to 0.*

Therefore, $\frac{e^{-B/x}-1}{e^{-A/x}-1}$ has an essential singularity at $x = 0$.

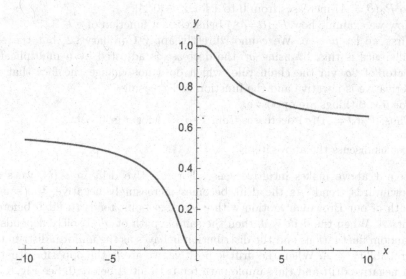

Fig. 6. Plot of $y = \frac{e^{-3/x}-1}{e^{-5/x}-1}, x \in \mathbb{R} - 0$.

3.2   Effects of Parameters on Absorbing Probabilities

We concentrate on Eq. 4 (in general, we **now assume** L'Hôpital's rule has been applied and all functions are extended to remove singularities). We use $P_Z(\eth = A) = \frac{e^{-\frac{2Z\mu}{\sigma^2}}-1}{e^{-\frac{2A\mu}{\sigma^2}}-1}$ in our analysis since it is the simpler of the pair, and we have the complementary behavior $1 - P_Z(\eth = A) = P_Z(\eth = 0)$.

1) Let us start by examining how $P_Z(\partial = A)$ behaves as a function of $\mu \in \mathbb{R}$. To do this we just use the result of Corollary 3.1, since $\left(\frac{2A}{\sigma^2}\right) > \left(\frac{2Z}{\sigma^2}\right) > 0$. Therefore, $P_Z(\partial = A)(u)$ increases from 0 to 1 for $\mu \in [-\infty, \infty]$, with $P_Z(\partial = A)(0) = Z/A$.

2) Now we examine how $P_Z(\partial = A)$ behaves as a function of $Z \in [0, A]$. We have that for $\mu \neq 0$

$$\frac{d}{dZ} P_Z(\partial = A) = \frac{d}{dZ} \frac{e^{-\frac{2\mu}{\sigma^2} Z} - 1}{e^{-\frac{2A\mu}{\sigma^2}} - 1} = \frac{-\frac{2\mu}{\sigma^2} e^{-\frac{2\mu}{\sigma^2} Z}}{e^{-\frac{2A\mu}{\sigma^2}} - 1} \tag{5}$$

and for $\mu = 0$, we apply L'Hôpital's rule to the above to get

$$\left. \frac{d}{dZ} \right|_{\mu=0} P_Z(\partial = A) = 1/A \tag{6}$$

Thus we see that for any value of μ that $\frac{d}{dZ} P_Z(\partial = A) > 0$.
So $P_Z(\partial = A)$ increases from 0 to 1 for $Z \in [0, A]$.

3) Now we examine how $P_Z(\partial = A)$ behaves as a function of $\sigma \in \mathbb{R}^+$.
First we let $\mu > 0$. We cannot directly apply Corollary 3.2, but the only difference is that by using σ^2 the decrease is adjusted by a multiplicative factor of 2σ via the chain rule, which does not change the fact that the derivative is negative and the function is decreasing.
For $\mu < 0$ things are opposite.
Thus, $P_Z(\partial = A)(\sigma)$ decreases from 1 to Z/A for $\sigma \in [0, \infty]$. .

Let us discuss the above items.

a. Item 1 above makes intuitive sense. For negative drift in $\mathcal{B}(t)$, we see a downwards trend. As the drift becomes increasingly negative, the sample path of our Brownian motion with a starting point tends to hit 0 before it hits A. When the drift is 0, then the sample path of $\mathcal{B}(t)$ solely depends on random fluctuations and the distribution behaves as the uniform distribution probability Z/A. When the drift is positive, we are in the opposite situation of negative drift and the sample path tends to hit A before 0. See Fig. 6.

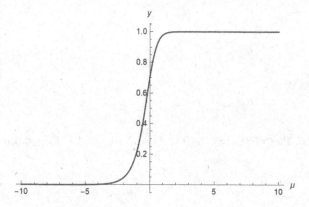

Fig. 7. Plot of $f(\mu) = P_Z(\partial = A)$: for $A = 10, Z = 7, \sigma = 2$. Note $\lim_{\mu \to -\infty} f(\mu) = 0, f(0) = 7/10, \lim_{\mu \to \infty} f(\mu) = 1$.

b. Now we look at Item 2 above. When $Z = 0$ there is nothing left to happen. The sample path of $\mathscr{B}(t)$ never moves from 0, so the probability of hitting A first is 0. Conversely, when $Z = A$ there is again no movement, and the probability of hitting A first is 1. As Z moves from 0 to A, the probability of hitting A first increases. See Figs. 7, 8, 9, 10 and 11.

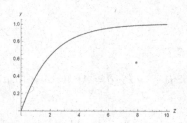

Fig. 8. Plot of $f(Z) = P_Z(\partial = A)$: for $A = 10, \mu = 1, \sigma = 2$.

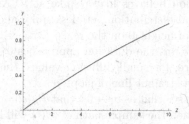

Fig. 9. Plot of $f(Z) = P_Z(\partial = A)$: for $A = 10, \mu = 0.1, \sigma = 2$.

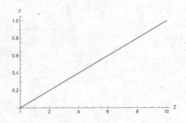

Fig. 10. Plot of $f(Z) = P_Z(\partial = A) = Z/10$: for $A = 10, \mu = 0, \sigma = 2$.

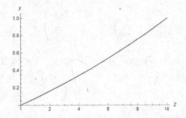

Fig. 11. Plot of $f(Z) = P_Z(\partial = A)$: for $A = 10, \mu = -0.1, \sigma = 2$.

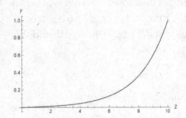

Fig. 12. Plot of $f(Z) = P_Z(\partial = A)$: for $A = 10, \mu = -1, \sigma = 2$.

c. Item 3 above is interesting. One should think of the normal distribution $N(\mu, \sigma^2)$ by way of an analogy. When the standard deviation σ is small, the normal distribution behaves like a spike at μ. As the standard deviation grows, the normal distribution gets less spiky and starts to approach a uniform distribution of height 0 on the reals.

For $P_Z(\partial = A)(\sigma)$ as the diffusion approaches 0^+, $\mathscr{B}(t)$ has decreasing fluctuations. Therefore, for small diffusion values, the sample path of $\mathscr{B}(t)$ tends to behave like a straight line of slope μ.

If $\mu > 0$, then we see that as $\sigma \to 0^+$ that $P_Z(\partial = A)(\sigma) \to 1$; regardless, $Z > 0$. If σ is large, then the sample path of $\mathscr{B}(t)$ will have large fluctuations and the probability of hitting A before 0 decreases. Notably, when there are essentially infinite fluctuations, we are again in a situation of the normal distribution and $P_Z(\partial = A)(\sigma) \to Z/A$ as $\sigma \to \infty$.

If $\mu < 0$, then the probabilities behave in an opposite manner. A small diffusion cannot counteract a negative drift, but a large diffusion normalizes the probability to the ratio Z/A.

Therefore, a small diffusion for $\mathscr{B}(t)$ is analogous to a small standard deviation (or variance) for a normal distribution. When a normal distribution has small standard deviation, it tends to cluster tightly around the mean. Likewise, when $\mathscr{B}(t)$ has a small diffusion, its sample path tends to cluster tightly along the straight line μt. See Figs. 12 and 13.

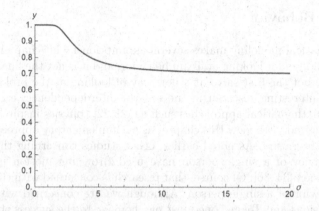

Fig. 13. Plot of $f(\sigma) = P_Z(\vartheta = A)$: for $A = 10, Z = 7, \mu = 1$.

Considering Fig. 12, we see that for a small standard deviation the sample path tends to follow the positive drift to the upper absorbing boundary A. However, as the standard deviation grows, the distribution in which $\mathscr{B}(t)$ is absorbed first starts behaving like a uniform distribution and the probability $P_Z(\vartheta = A)$ approaches 7/10.

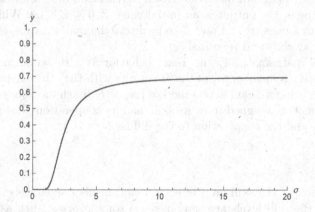

Fig. 14. Plot of $f(\sigma) = P_Z(\vartheta = A)$: for $A = 10, Z = 7, \mu = -1$.

Considering Fig. 13, we see that for a small standard deviation the sample path tends to follow the negative drift to the lower absorbing boundary 0. However, as the standard deviation grows, the distribution in which $\mathscr{B}(t)$ is absorbed first starts behaving like a uniform distribution and the probability $P_Z(\vartheta = A)$ again approaches 7/10.

4 Team Behavior

Our mathematical modeling makes several assumptions. This chapter is written as a new paradigm for looking at Team behavior, and it is not the final answer to the question, but the first salvo at a new way of looking at the problem. There is certainly interesting research in the area of interdependence, e.g. [31], and some novel mathematical approaches such as [21, 22] (physics inspired) and [27] (Shannon inspired). We view this chapter as a complementary approach to what exists in the literature. As noted earlier, other studies concerning the decision-making behavior of a single person have used Brownian motion in terms of Ratcliff diffusion [34–36]. Of course, that research is concerned with the decision-making behavior of a single person. Although we are concerned with different types of decisions and Teams, one must pay homage to the success that Ratcliff diffusion has had in the psychological sciences.

As discussed at the beginning of this chapter, we assumed that we have a Team of agents, people, UAVs, etc., who are attempting to perform a joint task. The task can be mundane, such as a restaurant crew in a kitchen, or more machine oriented, such as attempting to find something. The Team over time produces an output. When the output reaches the value $A \in \mathbb{R}$ (for success), the process stops. If the output instead reaches the value $0 \in \mathbb{R}$, the process also stops. Note that the process stops when it reaches 0 of A. If it reaches A first, we assume that the Team has a success, if it reaches 0 first, we take that as a failure. At time 0, the output is an initial value $Z, 0 \leq Z \leq A$. While we have normalized our values to 0, A and Z to facilitate the mathematics, of course, as before, one may shift and renormalize.

We model mathematically the Team behavior as a Brownian motion $\mathscr{B}(t)$ starting at Z. Each member m_i of the Team acts with the other Team members; the net result being a Team action modeled as $\mathscr{B}(t)$. Each member of the Team has two parameters assigned to it: its skill, and its cooperation. The skill relates to the drift μ and the cooperation to the diffusion σ.

4.1 Drift

We do not look at the skill level of each Team member separately. Rather, we assume that the skill levels are combined via some process, such as the mean, min/max values, etc., to arrive at a drift value μ for the Team. Even if every Team member is highly skilled, we still assume that there is a finite maximal drift. If the Team members are, on average, unskilled, we assume that the drift is 0. If there are some Team members who are anti-skilled (bad at their task), we are now into the arena of negative drift, and again we assume there is a finite minimal value. We realize that these modeling assumptions along with the ones we will present for diffusion call for a discussion. Again, we remind the reader this chapter is a first step in this approach (Fig. 15).

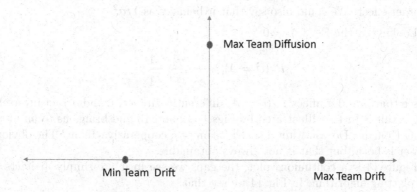

Fig. 15. Team drift and diffusion in $\mathbb{R} \times \mathbb{R}^+$.

There is no reason to assume that the maximum and minimum Team drift are equal, up to absolute value. In general we feel that most Teams will in fact have positive drift.

4.2   Diffusion

Team diffusion is a measure of how well the Team is working together. A Team with good cooperation is expected to have a small diffusion, while a Team with poor cooperation would have a large, but not infinite, diffusion.

The concept of interdependence as discussed above is a hot topic in Team science. There seems to be no definition accepted by all. The community takes interdependence to be how well a Team works together. Therefore, we propose using diffusion as a measure of Team interdependence. That is:

A Team with good/high interdependence has low diffusion, whereas a Team with bad/low interdependence has high diffusion.

We further assume that no Team is ever perfectly interdependent, that is, the diffusion $\sigma > 0$. Similarly, no Team has $\sigma = \infty$. We do not illustrate the lower bound for Team diffusion in Fig. 13 because it is not clear how close to 0 it may get.

5   Discussion

Based on the above reasoning we assume that:

- Team skill $\approx \mu$. Skilled is $\mu > 0$, No Skill is $\mu = 0$, Anti-Skilled is $\mu < 0$.
- Team Interdependence/Cooperation $\approx 1/\sigma$—This assumption is a second order effect. We could also say that it behaves as $1/\sigma^2$.

Looking at the Eq. 4, $\mu \neq 0$

$$P_Z(\eth = A) = \frac{e^{-\frac{2Z\mu}{\sigma^2}} - 1}{e^{-\frac{2A\mu}{\sigma^2}} - 1}$$

we see that μ and σ affect $P_Z(\eth = A)$ differently. In fact, μ and σ^2 act inversely. This result is further illustrated by Figs. 6, 12 and 13 and brings us to an interesting thought: Do you want a smart Team or a cooperative Team? The obvious answer is both, but that is not always obtainable.

Figure 14 is a continuous plot; the gaps we see in it are simply artifacts of the plotting algorithm. In Fig. 14 we see that:

- The line at average Team skill ($\mu = 0$), where we get the same answer of $P_7(\eth = 10) = 7/10$, regardless of what the degree of cooperation/interdependence (σ) is.
- As the Team skill (μ) increases, so does $P_7(\eth = 10)$, with the value asymptotically approaching 1.
- For Team skill $\mu > 0$, as the Interdependence/Cooperation decreases (σ increases), the probability decreases from 1 to the limiting value of 7/10.
- For Team skill $\mu < 0$, as the Interdependence/Cooperation decreases (σ increases), the probability increases from 0 to the limiting value of 7/10 (Fig. 16).

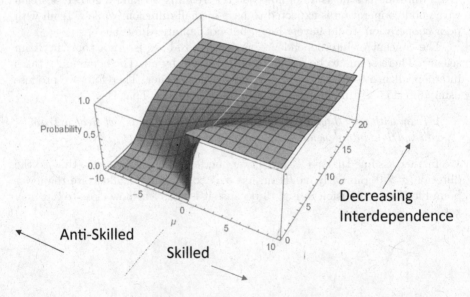

Fig. 16. Surface plot of $P_7(\eth = 10)$ against team skill and team interdependence.

6   Conclusion and Future Work

A takeaway from the above is that for a skilled Team, the lack of interdependence lowers the probability to the ratio Z/A rather than 0. Decreasing from positive skill to no skill also brings us to Z/A. Going into a negative skill region brings the probability closer and closer to 0, assuring us of the wrong answer!

We see that this example shows the delicate balance between skill and interdependence. This result is not to suggest that we get to pick and choose our Teams, but instead to give us guidance on optimal Team behavior. If there is a cost for increasing Team skill and another cost for increasing Interdependence, we can use this to form a metric on the surface plot and possibly use geodesic distance to assure us we have the best Team for the least cost.

In future work, we will use information geometric methods to consider how a Team can best improve itself [1, 3, 26, 28, 33]. For example, we may use the inherited subspace Riemannian metric inherited from the probability surface as a Riemannian submanifold of $\mathbb{R}^3$ with the natural metric

$$(ds)^2|_{\text{probability surface}} = (dx)^2 + (dy)^2 + (dz)^2 .$$

Or, we may use differential geometry to model the probability surface by using the metric of constant curvature -1, the Poincaré upper half plane metric.

$$(ds)^2 = \frac{(d\mu)^2 + (d\sigma)^2}{\sigma^2} .$$

Another possibility is to use the Fisher metric, which gives us

$$(ds)^2 = \frac{(d\mu)^2 + (2 \cdot d\sigma)^2}{\sigma^2} .$$

There are pros and cons to using these "natural metrics" which are beyond the scope of this chapter. In particular, the geodesic characteristics must be taken into account when using various metrics to judge Team behavior.

In this chapter, we have concentrated on the probability of a Team reaching the correct decision (performing a task correctly). What we have not considered is the *time* [29, 34] that it takes the Team to reach the answer. The mathematics behind this stopping time problem is quite complicated and the closed form solutions that exist are not presently amenable to mathematical analysis. For example, the cumulative probability distribution that the Team would hit a boundary by time t is given by (where $\mathcal{T}$ is the stopping time):

$$P_Z(\mathcal{T} < t) = \frac{\pi\sigma^2}{A^2} e^{-\left(\frac{Z\mu}{\sigma^2}\right)} \sum_{k=1}^{\infty} \left[\frac{2k \sin\left(\frac{\pi Z k}{A}\right) \left[1 - e^{-\frac{1}{2}\left[\left(\frac{\mu}{\sigma}\right)^2 + \left(\frac{\pi k \sigma}{A}\right)^2\right]t}\right]}{\left(\frac{\mu}{\sigma}\right)^2 + \left(\frac{\pi k \sigma}{A}\right)^2} \right]$$

$$+ \frac{\pi\sigma^2}{A^2} e^{\left(\frac{(A-Z)\mu}{\sigma^2}\right)} \sum_{k=1}^{\infty} \left[\frac{2k \sin\left(\frac{\pi(A-Z)k}{A}\right) \left[1 - e^{-\frac{1}{2}\left[\left(\frac{\mu}{\sigma}\right)^2 + \left(\frac{\pi k \sigma}{A}\right)^2\right]t}\right]}{\left(\frac{\mu}{\sigma}\right)^2 + \left(\frac{\pi k \sigma}{A}\right)^2} \right] .$$

We include this equation not to showcase the beauty of LaTeX, but rather to show the complexity versus the probabilities that we have dealt with in this chapter. We plan to fill this gap in future work.

Acknowledgments. We thank Paul Cotae, Hans Haucke, William Lawless, Lauren Nathan, George Stantchev and R. Swimbo for their helpful discussions.

References

1. Amari, S.: Differential-Geometric Methods in Statistics. Lecture Notes in Statistics, vol. 28. Springer, New York (1985). https://doi.org/10.1007/978-1-4612-5056-2
2. Arutkin, M., Walter, B., Wiese, K.J.: Extreme events for fractional Brownian with drift: theory and numerical validation. Phys. Rev. E **102**, 1–17 (2020). 022102
3. Atkinson, C., Mitchell, A.F.: Rao's distance measure. Sankhya Indian J. Stat. Ser. A **43**, 345–365 (1981)
4. Beltrami, E.: Teoria fondamentale degli spazi di curvatura constante. Annali di Matematica Pura ed Applicata, ser II **2**, 232–255 (1868)
5. Breiman, L.: Probability. Addison-Wesley, Reading (1968)
6. Brown, R.: A brief account of microscopical observations made on the particles contained in the pollen of plants. Phil. Mag. **4**, 161–173 (1828)
7. Cassisi, C., Montalto, P., Aliotta, M., Cannata, A., Pulvirenti, A.: Similarity measures and dimensionality reduction techniques for time series data mining. In: Katahoca, A. (ed.) Advances in Data Mining Knowledge Discovery and Applications, Chap. 3. Intech Open (2012)
8. Chavel, I.: Riemannian Geometry: A Modern Introduction, 2nd edn. Cambridge University Press, Cambridge (2006)
9. Costa, S.I.R., Santos, S.A., Strapasso, J.E.: Fisher information distance: a geometrical reading. Discret. Appl. Math. **197**, 59–69 (2015)
10. Donsker's Theorem. https://en.wikipedia.org/wiki/Donsker's_theorem. Accessed 4 Apr 2020
11. Doob, J.L.: Heuristic approach to the Kolmogorov-Smirnov Theorems. Ann. Math. Statist **20**(3), 393–403 (1949)
12. Doob, J.L.: Stochastic Processes. Wiley, New York (1953)
13. Feller, W.: An Introduction to Probability Theory and Its Applications, vol. 1&2. Wiley, New York (1950/1968)
14. Einstein, A.: Über die von der Molekularkinetischen Theorie der Wärme geforderte Bewegung von in ruhenden Flüssigkeiten suspendierten Teilchen. Ann der Phys. **17**, 549–560 (1905)
15. Fisher, R.A.: On the mathematical foundations of theoretical statistics. Philos. Trans. Royal Soc. Lond. Ser. A Contain. Papers Math. Phys. Char. **222**, 309–368 (1922)
16. Lalley, S., Mykland, P.: Lecture Note Statistics 313: Stochastic Processes II, Spring 2013. https://galton.uchicago.edu/lalley/Courses/313/
17. Frasca, M., Farina, A.: Numerical proof of existence of fractional Wiener processes. Signal Image Video Process. **11**(1) (2017)
18. Hurst, H.E.: Long-term storage capacity of reservoirs. Trans. Am. Soc. Civ. Eng. **116**, 770–799 (1951)

19. Jacod, J., Shiryaev, A.N.: Skorokhod topology and convergence of processes. In: Limit Theorems for Stochastic Processes. Grundlehren der mathematischen Wissenschaften (A Series of Comprehensive Studies in Mathematics), vol. 288. Springer, Heidelberg (2003). https://doi.org/10.1007/978-3-662-05265-5_6

20. Kolmogorov, A.N.: Wienersche Spiralen und einige andere interessante Kurven im Hilbertschen Raum. C.R. (Doklady) Acad. Sci. URSS (N.S.), vol. 26, pp. 115–118 (1940)

21. Lawless, W.F.: The entangled nature of interdependence. Bistability, irreproducibility and uncertainty. J. Math. Psychol. **78**, 51–64 (2017)

22. Lawless, W.F.: The physics of teams: interdependence, measurable entropy and computational emotion. Front. Phys. **5**, 30 (2017)

23. Lee, J.M.: Riemannian Manifolds An Introduction to Curvature Graduate Texts in Mathematics, vol. 176. Springer, New York (1997). https://doi.org/10.1007/b98852

24. Mandelbrot, B.B., Van Ness, J.W.: Fractional Brownian motions, fractional noises, and applications. SIAM Rev. **10**(4), 422–437 (1968)

25. Mandlebrot, B.B.: Fractal Geometry of Nature. Prentice-Hall, Englewood Cliffs (1984)

26. Milnor, J.W., Stasheff, J.D.: Characteristic Classes. Annals of Mathematical Studies, vol. 76. Princeton University Press, Princeton (1974)

27. Moskowitz, I.S., Lawless, W., Hyden, P., Mittu, R., Russell, S.: A Network Science Approach to Entropy and Training. AAAI Spring Symposia Series. AAAI Press, Palo Alto (2015)

28. Moskowitz, I.S., Russell, S., Lawless, W.: An information geometric look at the valuing of information. In: Lawless et al. (eds.) Human-machine Shared Contexts, Chap. 9. Elsevier (2020)

29. Moskowitz, I.S., Brown, N.L., Goldstein, Z.: A fractional Brownian motion approach to psychological and team diffusion problems. In: Lawless et al. (eds.) Systems Engineering and Artificial Intelligence, Chap. 11. Springer (2021/2022, to appear)

30. Nielsen, F.: An Elementary Introduction to Information Geometry. Entropy, vol. 22 (2020)

31. National Research Council: Enhancing the Effectiveness of Team Science. Cooke, N.J., Hilton, M.L. (eds.) Committee on the Science of Team Science; Board on Behavioral, Cognitive, and Sensory Sciences; Division of Behavioral and Social Sciences and Education; National Research Council. The National Academies Press, Washington, DC (2015)

32. Pollard, D.: Convergence of Stochastic Processes. Springer, New York (1984). https://doi.org/10.1007/978-1-4612-5254-2

33. Rao, C.R.: Information and the accuracy attainable in the estimation of statistical parameters. Bull. Calcutta Math. Soc. **73**(3), 81–91 (1945)

34. Ratcliff, R.: A theory of memory retrieval. Psychol. Rev. **85**(2), 59–108 (1978)

35. Ratcliff, R., Tuberlinckx, F.: Estimating parameters of the diffusion model: approaches to dealing with containment reaction times and parameter variability. Psychon. Bull. Rev. **9**(3), 419–481 (2002)

36. Ratcliff, R., Smith, P.L., Brown, S.D., McKoon, G.: Diffusion decision model: current issues and history. Trends Cogn. Sci. **20**(4), 260–281 (2016)

37. Ross, S.: A First Course in Probability, 3rd edn. Macmillan, New York (1988)

38. Scheike, T.H.: A boundary-crossing result for Brownian motion. J. Appl. Prob. **29**, 448–453 (1992)

39. Shevchenko, G.: Fractional Brownian motion in a nutshell. Int. J. Mod. Phys. Conf. Ser. **36** 156002-1–156002-16 (2014). 7th Jagna Int. Workshop
40. Suna, J., Yang, Y., Liua, Y., Chena, C., Rao, W., Bai, Y.: Univariate time series classification using information geometry
41. Wiener, N.: Differential space. J. Math. Phys. **2**, 132–174 (1923)
42. Wiese, K.J.: First passage in an interval for fractional Brownian motion. Phys. Rev. E **99**, 032106-1–032106-20 (2019)
43. Wolfram Research: Fractional Brownian Motion Process, Wolfram Language function (2012). https://reference.wolfram.com/language/ref/FractionalBrownian MotionProcess.html

How Deep Learning Model Architecture and Software Stack Impacts Training Performance in the Cloud

Egor Bykov[✉], Evgeny Protasenko, and Vladimir Kobzev

RocketCompute, 541 Jefferson Avenue Ste 100, Redwood City, CA 94063, USA
dev@rocketcompute.com

Abstract. Choosing the right instance on a public cloud for model training is not an easy task. There are hundreds of different virtual machines available with a wide variety of CPU core counts (i.e., how many tasks can be performed in parallel), memory, disk type, network speed, and of course graphics card (GPU). The latter has often become a differentiating factor for choosing one virtual machine (VM) over another. On top of that, containerization technology has greatly simplified GPU computations for machine learning, wrapping the software stack above the Kernel level in containers and allowing to juggle with different combinations of frameworks, lower lever libraries, and hardware drivers. Technologies like Nvidia-docker has even unlocked new stack combinations (driver plus low lever Compute Unified Device Architecture libraries, most of the time referred as CUDA) that were not feasible before. This, however, adds another dimension to the performance optimization problem, and now you not only need to choose an optimal hardware for your machine learning task, but also a variate driver-CUDA combination to fine-tune the performance further.

The goal of this work is to scrutinize how neural network architecture, different versions of NVIDIA drivers, and CUDA libraries will influence training performance and cost on different cloud VMs. We compared BERT, Mask R-CNN, and DLRM architectures using instances available on Amazon Cloud Services via Elastic Compute service (AWS EC2 for short) and showed that architecture, model implementation, and software stack can cause significant variation in training time and cost with a different optimal configuration for different architectures and software stacks.

Keywords: BERT · DLRM · Mask R-CNN · Deep learning training performance

1 Introduction

This chapter is the first step in our research program aimed at scrutinizing how different components of server hardware and software stacks affect a deep learning model's training time and cost. Our hypothesis is that even in a very simple setup where we need to choose a cloud VM with a single GPU secondary parameter (like RAM, CPU performance, disks, etc.) might have a significant impact on the cost and duration of the training, and this impact will vary from one network architecture to another.

© Springer Nature Switzerland AG 2021
W. F. Lawless et al. (Eds.): Engineering Artificially Intelligent Systems, LNCS 13000, pp. 109–121, 2021.
https://doi.org/10.1007/978-3-030-89385-9_7

Another hypothesis that we are testing here is that different combinations of GPU drivers and low-level libraries providing GPU acceleration for ML frameworks like PyTorch will cause significant deviations in training cost and time. There is anecdotal evidence that drivers might cause a performance degradation of the GPU from the consumer market, however, we have not seen papers investigating whether there is any performance implication for ML workloads on professional GPUs.

2 Set-Up

2.1 Benchmarks

As a base for testing machine-learning workloads, we chose the latest set of reference implementations for MLPerf training benchmarks [1]. Out of eight different neural network implementations available, we picked up one model for each domain that is widely relevant for the industry. The resulting reference model set is:

1. For image processing – an object detection Mask R-CNN model trained on COCO data set [2].
2. For natural language processing – a BERT model trained on a Wikipedia dump [3].
3. For recommendations – a DLRM model trained on a 1Tb Kaggle AdDisplay Challenge dataset [4].

2.2 Changes to the Reference Implementations

Our motivation to make changes to the reference implementations was driven by the following:

- The Take into account outdated hardware still available in the cloud. Users still can find cloud instances with GPUs as old as the Kepler-family Nvidia accelerators. The reference implementation of MLPerf benchmarks, tuned towards measuring the performance of current and future generations of a GPU, is not only time-consuming and costly on older generations, but sometimes even that cannot be performed due to insufficient GPU memory or other reasons.
- The Speed up the testing process. This chapter is the first step in the lengthy program developed to research how different elements in the technology stack influence performance and cost of deep learning model training. Having this in mind, building a representative set of fast and cost-efficient benchmarks is particularly important.
- The Ease of reproducibility of these results. Speed and cost-efficiency of the benchmarks provide more reliability of the result, as any test can be reproduced by any member of the community, and all results can be verified.

The resulting changes to the reference benchmarks are:
Object Detection (R-CNN)

- For the object detection model, the number of interactions was capped at 3,000 which resulted in a benchmark duration of around 15 min for the Volta family accelerators (Nvidia Telsa V100).

  Recommender (DLRM)

- The The dataset was cut from 1Tb down to 20 Gb to reduce the burden of fetching training data for each test.
- The The number of epochs was limited by two, reducing the test duration to circa 45 min for virtual machine with one Nvidia Tesla V100 GPU.

  Natural Language Processing (BERT)

- The architecture of the neural network was changed from BERT Large to BERT Base [3] to revise the benchmark for accelerators with 7 Gb of available VRAM.
- Just-in-time CUDA code compilations were turned off to reduce the benchmark start-up time.
- The number of training steps was reduced to 15k, as a result one Tesla V100 performed the test in circa 25 min.

2.3 Benchmarking Software Stack

To test the performance of different GPU driver/CUDA combinations, we administered the DLRM benchmark. Its implementation was based on PyTorch 1.7.1 which allowed us to use several CUDA versions (in this chapter, we present only 9.2, 10.1, 10.2, and 11.0 versions) without changing the benchmark source code. For each test we used Ubuntu 16.04 (with kernel version 4.4) as an operating system, on top of it we installed seven different GPU drivers obtained from the official Nvidia site. These drivers are:

- 410.129
- 418.165
- 440.118
- 450.80
- 455.32
- 460.32

This particular choice of drivers was guided by two things:

1. The compatibility of a driver with a Linux kernel (we decided not to drop below version 4.4); and,
2. The compatibility of a particular driver with different CUDA libraries

The benchmark was run inside of a container using docker v19.3 and nvidia-docker2. It is worth mentioning that using the nvidia-docker was critical for the whole experiment because when running a framework without a container, one should match the CUDA version installed on a host with the version used during the compilation of the framework's libraries. Another important note is that a particular version of the CUDA toolkit requires a certain version of the device's driver. This driver is usually installed simultaneously with the toolkit. Therefore, using a GPU enabled container engine is crucial, without it, this experiment is not feasible.

2.4 Infrastructure

To test our hypothesis, we took the most popular cloud provider Amazon Web Services (AWS) and ran our set of benchmarks on all of the available single GPU instances. It is also important to note that all VMs were booked in one availability zone (US-East-2 according to AWS zone naming), and that we used only general-purpose volumes (gp2) for benchmarking the driver/CUDA combinations (Table 1).

Table 1. The AWS instances with a single GPU used for benchmarking.

GPU	CPU family/model	AWS instance	vCPU (#)	RAM (Gb)	VRAM[1](Gb)	Disk (type)	Price ($/hour)
K80	E5-2686 v4	p2.xlarge	4	61	11	gp2/io1	0.9
M60	E5-2686 v4	g3s.xlarge	4	30.5	7	gp2/io1	0.75
M60	E5-2686 v4	g3.4xlarge	16	122	7	gp2/io1	1.14
V100	E5-2686 v4	p3.2xlarge	8	61	16	g2p/io1	3.06
T4	Cascade Lake	g4dn.xlarge	4	16	15	gp2/io1	0.53
T4	Cascade Lake	g4dn.2xlarge	8	32	15	gp2/io1	0.75
T4	Cascade Lake	g4dn.4xlarge	16	64	15	gp2/io1	1.2
T4	Cascade Lake	g4dn.8xlarge	32	128	15	gp2/io1	2.18

3 Benchmark Results

3.1 GPU Instances

Figure 1, Fig. 2, and Fig. 3 show the summary of the benchmark runtimes and costs in relative terms. All pf the values are normalized to the best result (shown as equal to 1.00) across all of the different instances. The benchmarks with the lowest duration and costs are highlighted with dashed boxes, and all other results are multiples of these best results. Blue bars represent the cost of running a benchmark, and red bars show the duration of the benchmark.

---

[1] GPU memory available inside virtual machine.

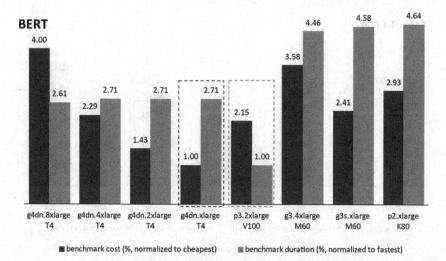

Fig. 1. Relative performance results for the BERT

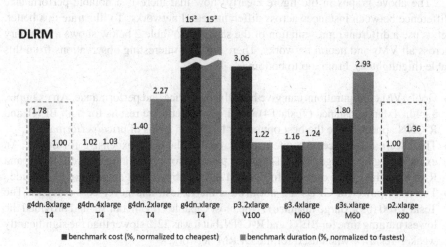

Fig. 2. Relative performance results for the DLRM[2]

---

[2] reflects the best performance duration or cost estimated based on data from aborded test. The actual test was stopped after 300 min and then duration/cost was extrapolated to get estimate for the full successful test (e.g., all successful runs for other configurations took between 15 and 120 min).

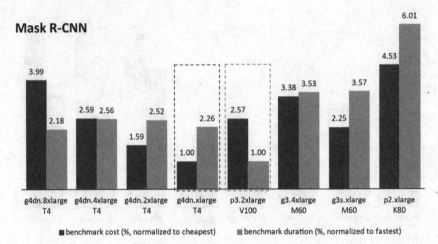

Fig. 3. Relative performance results for the Mask R-CNN

The above graphs in the figure clearly show that there is a notable performance difference between instances across different neural networks. To illustrate this better, let us use a different representation of the same data. Table 2 below shows a summary across all VMs and neural networks. There are four interesting observations from this table (highlighted). From top to bottom:

- Goofy VM configurations can give both the best price and performance. An example, a g4dn.4xlarge instance (Tesla T4) which gives mediocre results for both BERT and R-CNN appears to be the best option for DLRM in terms of price/performance.
- The cheapest instances for one network can be the most expensive for others. An example, a g4dn.xlarge (Tesla T4) which gave the lowest training costs for BERT and R-CNN is the most expensive for DLRM training by at least an order of magnitude.
- The most powerful GPUs are not always the fastest, and never cost-efficient. The Tesla V100 (p3.2xlarge instance) is the most capable GPU in our set and provided the lowest training time for BERT and R-CNN, but it was 22% slower than the significantly weaker Tesla T4 when used for the DLRM network.
- Legacy GPUs can still be the cheapest to train certain networks. Tesla K80 was the cheapest for training the DLRM network.

Table 2. Benchmark results summary (relative values, lower is better)

GPU	AWS instance	Price ($/hour)	BERT		DLRM		Mask R-CNN	
			Cost	Time	Cost	Time	Cost	Time
T4	g4dn.8xlarge	2.18	4.00	2.61	1.78	1.00	3.99	2.18
T4	g4dn.4xlarge	1.2	2.29	2.71	1.02	1.03	2.59	2.56

(continued)

Table 2. (*continued*)

GPU	AWS instance	Price ($/hour)	BERT		DLRM		Mask R-CNN	
			Cost	Time	Cost	Time	Cost	Time
T4	g4dn.2xlarge	0.75	1.43	2.71	1.40	2.27	1.59	2.52
T4	g4dn.xlarge	0.53	1.00	2.71	15.00	15.00	1.00	2.26
V100	p3.2xlarge	3.06	2.15	1.00	3.06	1.22	2.57	1.00
M60	g3.4xlarge	1.14	3.58	4.46	1.16	1.24	3.38	3.53
M60	g3s.xlarge	0.75	2.41	4.58	1.80	2.93	2.25	3.57
K80	p2.xlarge	0.9	2.93	4.64	1.00	1.36	4.53	6.01

To illustrate the last two bullet points further, let us consider Fig. 4 and Fig. 5. The highlighted instances in these figures are for GPUs with substantially different performance, but still showing very similar results in terms of training times. Moreover, Fig. 5 highlights the case where the GPU from the latest generation available shows a training time close to GPUs which are several generations earlier.

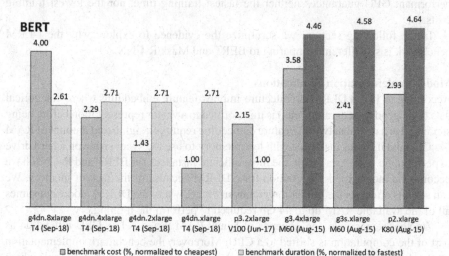

Fig. 4. Cloud instances with Tesla K80 give very similar training times for BERT as the instances for the Tesla M60 (next-generation compared to K80).

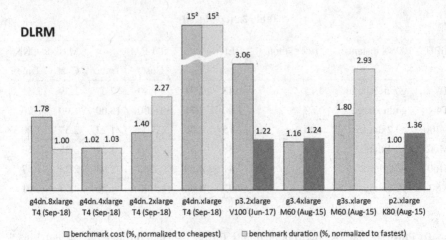

Fig. 5. Instances with Tesla V100 (the most powerful GPU in the set) show training times for DLRM that are marginally better than the weakest Tesla K80 and the second weakest Tesla M60.

To summarize the evidence presented above, it is clear that choosing the most performant GPU guarantees neither the fastest training time, nor the lowest training costs.

In the following section, we scrutinize the evidence to explore why the DLRM benchmark is so different comparing to BERT and Mask R-CNN.

Model Implementation Implications

According to [4], a DLRM architecture implies feature embedding where categorical data (e.g., gender, geography, etc.) is transformed to a vector representation before being submitted to a neural network. Feature embedding requires a significant amount of RAM (44 Gb), and it forces instances with less memory to use the swap-space on a hard drive to perform the task. As a result, the most efficient instances for BERT and R-CNN have become the most expensive solution for a DLRM because of the lack of memory. We can see this effect on the utilization graphs in Fig. 6, where the DLRM model consumes all of the available RAM up to 44 Gb required to perform the training.

Another remarkable consequence of heavy RAM usage is low GPU utilization as part of the computation is shifted to a CPU. Moreover, the benchmark implementation used only one CPU thread. Both features led to a clear bottleneck on the CPU side which can be seen in the monitoring data (Fig. 7), where the more powerful GPUs had less utilization than did the less powerful.

As a result, the best performance was shown by instances with the best single-threaded CPU performance (i.e., the g4dn instances in our set).

For both R-CNN and BERT, although their architectures differ significantly, there is no evidence that their architecture leads to a significant loss of GPU performance.

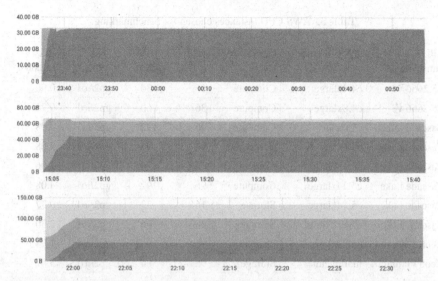

Fig. 6. Memory utilization charts for the DLRM benchmark. The green area represents the memory reserved by the benchmark, the yellow area for the memory used by the OS as a cache for IO operations (irrelevant for our analysis). From top to bottom: 1) g3s.xlarge instance with 31 Gb of RAM; 2) g4dn.4xlarge with 64 Gb of RAM; and, 3) g4dn.8xlarge with 128 Gb RAM.

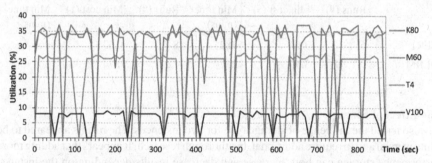

Fig. 7. GPU Utilization. Top to bottom: Tesla K80 (p2.xlarge) and Tesla M60 (g3.4xlarge) with 30% utilization on average, Tesla T4 (g4dn.8xlarge) with 22% on average, and V100 (p3.2xlarge) with 7% on average.

Comparing Training on a CPU Versus a GPU

To prove the point that the GPU is better for neural network training, we ran BERT and DLRM benchmarks on a subset of AWS CPU instances optimized for computing and storage (Table 3) and compared the training time and cost with results for GPU instances.

CPU instances appeared roughly seven times (7×) slower and five to six times (5–6×) more expensive (Table 4) when comparing to the best-performing GPU instances.

Table 3. AWS CPU instances chosen for benchmarking

CPU family/model	AWS instance	Optimized for	vCPU (#)	RAM (Gb)	Disk (type)	Price ($/hour)
E5 2666 v3	c4.4xlarge	Compute	16	30	gp2/io1	0.90
E5 2666 v3	c4.8xlarge	Compute	36	60	gp2/io1	0.75
Cascade Lake	c5.metal	Compute	96	192	gp2 io1	4.08
Cascade Lake	c5.12xlarge	Compute	48	96	gp2/io1	4.08
Cascade Lake	c5.18xlarge	Compute	72	144	gp2/io1	3.06
Cascade Lake	c5.24xlarge	Compute	96	192	gp2/io1	4.08
Cascade Lake	c5d.4xlarge	Storage	16	32	gp2/io1	0.77
Cascade Lake	c5d.12xlarge	Storage	48	96	gp2/io1	2.30
Xeon Platinum	c5d.9xlarge	Compute	36	96	gp2/io1	1.94
Xeon Platinum	m5d.metal	Storage	96	384	gp2/io1	5.42

Table 4. Comparing best performance for CPU instances versus GPU instances

Architecture	CPU			GPU		
	Runs (#)	Min cost ($)	Min time (mins)	Runs (#)	Min cost ($)	Min time (mins)
BERT	6	3.62	182	8	0.63	26
DLRM	9	3.59	237	12	0.74	36

The Effect of Storage

We also tested the influence of storage type for two instances. The results appeared to be controversial and to require additional, but thorough research. It appears that adding more performance storage can both increase and decrease results depending on the instance type (Table 5).

Table 5. Mask R-CNN benchmark storage type variations, Δ

Instance	Type	Time (mins)	Δ	Cost ($)	Δ
g4dn.xlarge	gp2	36	8.4%	0.32	8.4%
	io1	33		0.29	
p2.xlarge	gp2	88	−5.2%	1.32	−5.2%
	io1	93		1.39	

3.2 Performance Implications of GPU Drivers and CUDA Libraries

Figure 8, Fig. 9, Fig. 10, and Fig. 11 show the results of our benchmark performance for the software stacks. The vertical axis represents the duration of the DLRM benchmark in seconds, the horizontal axis represents the NVIDIA driver version, and each line on the graph represents a particular version of the CUDA libraries (version 11.0 is not supported by drivers older than 418, therefore, the yellow lines have fewer data points).

Each data point in these graphs aggregates at least 3 independent benchmarks and equals the mean benchmark duration. Each figure represents one of the four GPU models (Tesla K80, M60, T4, and V100).

Instances with Tesla K80 and Tesla M60 show similar variations caused by the driver version (around 10%). For both of these GPUs, CUDA 11.0 on average resulted in longer training time than the other versions. For K80 9.2 and 10.1, almost every time are better than for the other versions. CUDA 9.2 and driver v.440 gave the lowest training time on average, however, other versions of the driver (except 450) together with CUDA 9.2 or 10.1 showed very close performance.

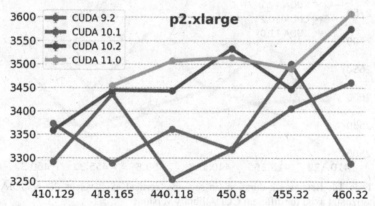

Fig. 8. Tesla K80. Benchmark duration (in seconds, vertical axis) versus the NVIDIA driver version (horizontal axis) for different CUDA library versions.

For the M60 performances, performance for all of the drivers lay within 3% from each other, but with a clear disadvantage in using CUDA 11.0.

Tesla T4 and Tesla V100 show bigger variations (14% and 15% on average, correspondingly). For T4, there is a clear optimum for CUDA 10.2 and driver v.410 and a clear worst performer (CUDA v.11.0 and driver v.450). It is safe to say that the recent two versions of CUDA gave longer training times compared to the older versions.

Tesla V100 instances show the highest variation of benchmark training times. It is remarkable that all CUDA versions except 11.0 reveal similar behaviors. On average, there is a clear optimum for the oldest version of the stack (CUDA v.9.2 and driver v.410), and a clear worst performing stack (CUDA v10.1 and driver v.450). The difference between these two combinations can exceed 20%. Another interesting observation is that V100 is slowed down by v.450 of the driver more than the other GPUs in the set.

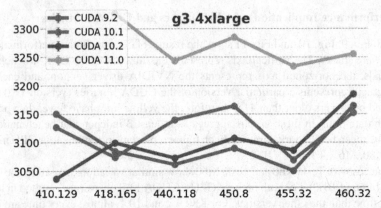

Fig. 9. Tesla M60: Benchmark duration (in seconds, vertical axis) versus the NVIDIA driver version (horizontal axis) for different CUDA library versions.

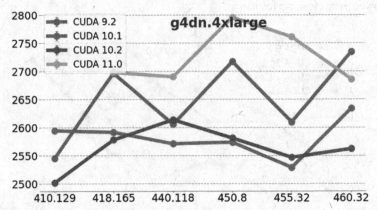

Fig. 10. Tesla T4: Benchmark duration (in seconds, vertical axis) versus the NVIDIA driver version (horizontal axis) for different CUDA library versions.

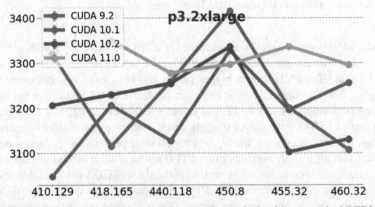

Fig. 11. Tesla V100: Benchmark duration (in seconds, vertical axis) versus the NVIDIA driver version (horizontal axis) for different CUDA library versions.

It is also remarkable that for almost all of the GPUs except for the Tesla K80 the driver v.410 is better on average than all of the newer drivers; and the new version of CUDA libraries is almost always worse than older versions. Another interesting observation is that v.450 is a worse performer than both of the previous and succeeding versions of the driver.

We believe that our data provide the evidence that optimizing a software stack can give meaningful benefit in terms of speed and cost of training. Although we need to thoroughly examine statistical significance, reproducibility, and routes causing this behavior in our future research.

4 Conclusion

In this chapter, we have investigated how a network's training performance is linked to a network's architecture, hardware components of the training machine, and software stack. We showed that a simple rule of thumb (e.g., always choosing the latest generation or the most powerful GPU) can increase training cost and time by an order of magnitude in the worst-case scenario. We also showed that components surrounding a GPU (e.g., the RAM and CPU) can cause significant performance bottlenecks and should be considered carefully in conjunction with a trained model architecture and implementation.

The overall results show that even in the case of a single GPU, the training setup costs can significantly vary by hundreds of percent.

We also showed that there is a meaningful variation of training time caused by the device driver version and the CUDA toolkit version, and that this variation is different for different GPU families.

References

1. MLPerf GitHub. https://github.com/mlperf/training
2. He, K., Gkioxari, G., Dollár, P., Girshick: R.: Mask R-CNN. In: Proceedings of the IEEE International Conference on Computer Vision, pp. 2961–2969 (2017a)
3. Devlin, J., Chang, M.-W., Lee, K., Toutanova, K.: BERT: pre-training of deep bidirectional transformers for language understanding, arXiv:1810.04805, 2019.
4. Naumov, M., et al.: Deep learning recommendation model for personalization and recommendation systems, arXiv:1906.00091 (2019)
5. Mattson, P., et al.: Mlperf training benchmark. arXiv:1910.01500 (2019)
6. Lin, T.-Y., et al.: Microsoft COCO: common objects in context. In: Fleet, D., Pajdla, T., Schiele, B., Tuytelaars, T. (eds.) ECCV 2014. LNCS, vol. 8693, pp. 740–755. Springer, Cham (2014). https://doi.org/10.1007/978-3-319-10602-1_48

How Interdependence Explains the World of Teamwork

Matthew Johnson(✉) and Jeffrey M. Bradshaw

Florida Institute for Human and Machine Cognition, Pensacola, FL 32502, USA
{mjohnson,jbradshaw}@ihmc.org

Abstract. Current attempts to understand human-machine systems are complex and unwieldy. Multiple disciplines throw different concepts and constructs at the problem, but there is no agreed-to framework to assemble these interrelated moving parts into a coherent system. We propose *interdependence* as the common factor that unifies and explains these moving parts and undergirds the different terms people use to talk about them. In this chapter, we will describe a sound and practical theoretical framework based on interdependence that enables researchers to predict and explain experimental results in terms of interlocking relationships among well-defined operational principles. Our exposition is not intended to be exhaustive, but instead aims to describe the basic principles in a way that allows the gist to be grasped by a broad cross-disciplinary audience through simple illustrations.

Keywords: Interdependence · Teamwork · Joint activity · Situation awareness · Trust · Levels of automation · Adjustable autonomy · Human-machine teaming

1 Introduction

Technology has always been tied to human activity. The need for this relationship is self-evident because technology is not developed for its own sake, but rather for human ends in settings that inevitably include humans as beneficiaries and facilitators. In short, we might say that "no technology is an island" [1]. For this reason, providing support for *interdependence* within mixed groups of people and technological components is not a mere nice-to-have but rather an essential requirement of smooth-running work and play involving any technology. Despite this, consideration for interdependence is often deferred until it is too late in the design process, if not ignored altogether.

One of the reasons people fail to take the importance of interdependence into account has to do with the inaccurate or imprecise terminology we frequently use to describe technology. For example, the term "autonomy" (as used today and for the foreseeable future) is at best a "wishful mnemonic" [2] and at worst a costly (and potentially deadly) misconception [3]. It drives the single-minded pursuit of the illusory always-just-out-of-reach chimera of flawless performance in every situation needed for the goal of a perfectly independent system, rather than the more practical but less glamorous goal of creating machines that can work interdependently with and for people [1]. Misunderstanding human-machine interdependence inevitably leads to misguided arguments, mischaracterized results, misinformed claims, and misinterpreted conclusions.

W. F. Lawless et al. (Eds.): Engineering Artificially Intelligent Systems, LNCS 13000, pp. 122–146, 2021.
https://doi.org/10.1007/978-3-030-89385-9_8

Several research efforts have made strides in re-framing the problem in a way that highlights the needs and contributions of people whenever technology is applied. User-centered design (e.g., [4]) and human-centered approaches (e.g., [5]) have led the way in this respect. Unfortunately, relatively little has changed in the decades since these approaches were first defined. Despite the many improvements that efforts to apply these approaches have provided, the evolution of new technology remains largely technology-driven. Why is this so?

In our experience, one of the biggest reasons is that the process of accounting for the needs and contributions of people remains more of an art than a science. Acknowledging the essential role that people play in successful technology deployment is only the first step. Going further, many well-reasoned approaches fail because they fail to bridge the gulf that extends an elegant theory into the realm of implementation. AI and system engineers cannot live by abstract design concepts alone, but require guidance and tools that allow them to map general principles to specific situations [6]. Engineers, who may not be experts on human-machine teaming, will probably get very limited mileage out of high-level concepts like the infuriatingly vague requirement of keeping humans "in-the-loop." The gap between developers writing code and theoreticians providing guidance divorces research from real-world technology design and implementation.

Another significant challenge is the breadth and complexity of domains to be mastered to ensure effective human-machine teaming. The topic spans a wide range of disciplines, each with their own theories, principles, and terminology. Consensus is difficult because researchers with different backgrounds tend to talk crossways to each other. Without a framework that can span multiple domains and connect a range of concepts in workable synergy, it is difficult to translate advances from one area to another.

2 Interdependence as an Integrative Framework for Teamwork

In line with what is suggested in the title of the workshop where the ideas in the present chapter were first presented (*Toward the Science of Interdependence for Autonomous Human-Machine Teams*), we believe that the key to understanding *human-machine teamwork* is understanding *interdependence* [7]. Though teamwork comes in many shapes and sizes, we have learned from long experience that recognizing, supporting and managing interdependence is the common ingredient that transforms capable individual performers into great teammates, no matter what the task or situation.

The same message is echoed across a range of research domains throughout the research literature. Organizational theorists Malone and Crowston specifically define effective coordination in terms of "managing dependencies between activities" [8]. Human teamwork specialists have likewise identified appropriate interdependence among team members as a defining feature of a well-oiled team [9]. Human-machine researchers such as Paul Feltovich have identified interdependence as the very essence of joint activity [10].

We all know this intuitively. But how can we apply our intuitions in a practical manner?

2.1 The Challenge

Fig. 1. Some of the many concepts that make up the conceptual space of human-machine teamwork and technology in general.

As we have argued above, a scientific approach to human-machine teamwork requires a framework for understanding and associating the concepts that make up this complex multi-disciplinary domain. Figure 1 shows some of the more common concepts used when discussing technology, particularly in the domain of human-machine teaming. The goal of our research is to advance the conversation on how such concepts might fit together, enabling research results from each of these fields to contribute their unique perspectives comfortably and compatibly. We propose that "interdependence" is not only the key principle that unlocks an understanding of teamwork overall but also the means of framing these seemingly disparate research perspectives as parts of a common endeavor. We will present our argument for this claim by unfolding a series of concept maps describing the framework, followed by a discussion of how this framework relates to the terminology and perspectives of colleagues working on similar problems.

2.2 What Criteria Define Joint Activity That Is Teamwork?

The first concept we will introduce is that of "joint activity," inspired by the work of the distinguished linguist Herbert Clark [11]. To better intuit the concept of joint activity, consider an example of playing the same sheet of music as a solo versus a duet. Although the sheet of music used by the performer is identical in both situations, the processes involved in performance are different due to the interdependence relationship that governs the "joint activity" of the two artists [12].

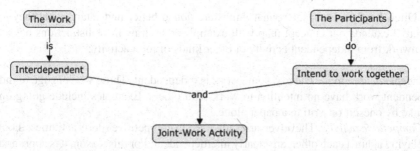

Fig. 2. There are two criteria defining joint activity as teamwork: the work must be interdependent, and the participants must intend to work together.

We define "*joint-work* activity" as a special kind of "joint activity." As depicted in the concept map shown in Fig. 2, there are two basic criteria for the kind of "joint-work activity" that we are concerned with in this chapter, a kind of joint-work activity we might rightfully refer to as "teamwork":

1. The participants intend to work jointly toward their common goal;
2. The work itself is to be carried out in a manner that puts the participants in a state of interdependence.

In the example above, the soloist deliberately intended to work alone and the work itself was not carried out in an interdependent fashion. On the other hand, to play a duet, the two players must consciously work together in an interdependent and mutually supportive manner, thus, the duet is joint-work activity.

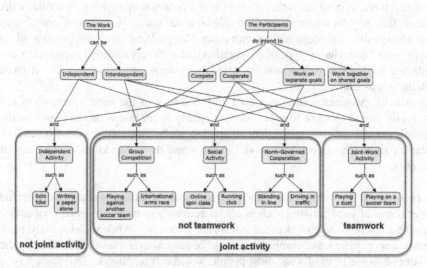

Fig. 3. Some examples of activity that are not teamwork and some that are.

Often it helps to consider what things are *not* to better understand what they *are*. Figure 3 extends our concept map with examples that draw finer distinctions between teamwork from independent activity or other kinds of joint activity:

- *Independent activity.* Clearly, some work is independent. Those who engage in independent work have no intention to work with others. Examples include going on a hike by oneself or writing a paper alone.
- *Competitive activity.* The adversaries involved in competitive sports activities, though playing against each other, are clearly interdependent. For this reason, it is appropriate to call their work "joint activity." However, the competitors do not intend to work *together* cooperatively to advance a win-win situation that will advance the prospects of both teams but rather are consciously trying to work *against* each other to produce a win-lose outcome selfishly favoring only their own team. While teamwork is crucial *within* each team—and while minimal cooperation in keeping the rules and showing common courtesy is needed in order to play a *fair* and enjoyably *sociable* game—the nature of the joint activity itself mitigates against *cross-team* teamwork of the sort that would help the other team score points for themselves.
- *Social activity.* Although members of a running club intend to practice their sport at the same time and place for social reasons, the work itself is typically done more or less independently by each runner. While club members may provide support, tips, and encouragement for one another, the skill of running ultimately cannot be improved vicariously for someone else. Social activity of this sort is not teamwork in the sense we have defined it because the state of interdependence between club members is primarily social and only *indirectly* impacts the performance of the work itself.
- *Norm-governed cooperation.* Although drivers on a busy road are in a state of interdependence and may cooperate with each other in ways that are mutually beneficial to other drivers, in most cases they do not share a common destination. In ordinary situation, they rely for the most part on traffic laws and norms (e.g., driving courteously) to manage their interdependence with other drivers. We exclude cooperation of this type—the "do no harm" type of cooperation that is merely intended to provide a level playing field whereby all drivers can get to their own separate destinations—from our definition of teamwork.
- *Teamwork.* Musicians playing a duet and members of the same soccer team consciously intend to work together and are clearly in an interdependent state as they jointly pursue common rather than competing goals. This sort of joint-work activity can be rightfully called "teamwork" in the sense that other kinds of joint activity cannot.

In summary, our two criteria of interdependent and intentionally shared work exclude looser forms of joint activity, such as social activity and norm-governed cooperation, that do not resemble teamwork of the sort we are discussing. While social activity, norm-governed cooperation, and competition could be seen as examples of *joint activity*, they do not rise to the level of what most people would call teamwork. That said, it is not uncommon for looser forms of joint activity to develop features that border on or may even cross over into joint-work activity. For example, two drivers may use eye contact and hand signals to help each other avoid collisions while changing lanes in traffic.

Similarly, although physical workouts are, strictly speaking, an individual matter, you might ask someone to spot you in a gym and running club members might offer you encouragement, which can indeed help your performance. The fluid nature of joint activity sometimes makes it challenging to understand teamwork.

Figure 3 does not exhaust the possibility for additional nuanced forms of joint and independent activity. There are no doubt interesting examples we have not covered.[1] However, we hope the brief discussion in this section will suffice to give readers enough of an intuition about what constitutes "teamwork" to proceed with the next phase of our discussion.

2.3   What Makes Teamwork a Special Kind of Joint-Work Activity?

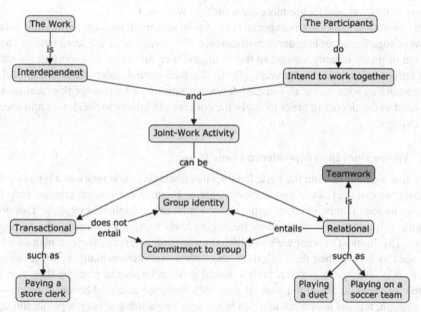

Fig. 4. There are two additional factors that help differentiate teamwork as a special kind of joint activity: group identity and commitment to the group.

Even within joint-work activity, there are additional factors that go further in distinguishing teamwork from more ordinary kinds of joint-work activity, as depicted in Fig. 4:

1. Team members tend to *share a group identity*. In sports, this identity may be made salient by things like uniforms, team names, slogans, and mascots. But these kinds

---

[1] Examples might include asynchronous vs. synchronous collaborative work (e.g., software development teamwork), independent work on shared goals (e.g., independent charitable organizations trying to eradicate poverty, reduce death and illness, or reduce hunger), and cooperation established through the (non-intentional) establishment of norms (e.g., cow paths).

of things in and of themselves do not create group identity, they simply reinforce the subjective perceptions of group identity held by team members.

2. Team members *share a commitment to their group*; a commitment that favors their group over others when decisions must be made. Sometimes that commitment leads to the sacrifice of individual goals and preferences when they conflict with team objectives. We might call that trait "team loyalty."

These factors are not found in all types of joint-work activity. For example, it would be odd to call temporary, transactional forms of joint activity such as paying a store clerk, teamwork. In transactional forms of joint activity there is usually no persistent shared identity and generally no mutual commitment beyond what the immediate situation demands. (Of course, in everyday life, some people go out of their way to be helpful and friendly with people they may never meet again, just because they know that valuing others in this way makes life more pleasant for everyone.)

In summary, teamwork is a special type of joint activity. It requires parties that intend to work together in an interdependent manner. The members of the team tend to share a form of group identity, unique to the team, and a commitment of loyalty to the team that influences their decision-making. While this background understanding is helpful in understanding what we mean—and what we *don't* mean—when we speak of teamwork, we need to dig deeper in order to apply the concept effectively to the design and use of technology.

2.4   Where Does Interdependence Come from?

Now that we have laid out the basic features that distinguish teamwork as a type of joint activity, we can start discussing interdependence. Figure 5 extends our concept map for the discussion. Teamwork starts with a shared goal, either implicit or explicit. This goal is what you intend to work together for, which leads to what we might call a "skeletal plan" [13]. In most of what we do in life, we start with a general, skeletal plan of what we need to do and then flesh out the plan or change it incrementally as we go along. There is no teamwork without both a shared goal and a shared plan, be they ever so simple or implicit. Sharing a general goal with someone else's—like world peace—is not enough. It is not teamwork until we begin doing something about it together through the execution of a skeletal plan.

Skeletal plans to support teamwork contain two kinds of requirements: individual requirements and joint requirements. *Individual* requirements are what one team member must do *independently*. For example, to get some piece of work done you might need to be able carry things or to fly an airplane on your own. The *joint* requirements within a plan create a state of *interdependence* between some set of participants with respect to some part of the work to be performed. For example, the plan may require you to lift your side of a large table that is being moved, or to continually monitor your teammates so you can stay aware of any problems that crop up and provide help as needed.

2.5   Where Does the Skeletal Plan Come from?

We have just argued that the state of interdependence that exists between teammates is generated during execution of the joint requirements of a shared skeletal plan. But

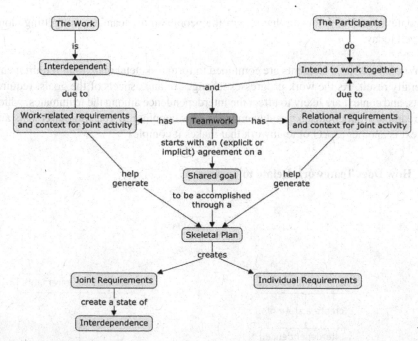

Fig. 5. A state of interdependence arises when the joint requirements of the skeletal plan are being executed. Joint requirements stem both from *work-related requirements* due to interdependence inherent in the nature of the work itself and *relational requirements* due to interdependence created by the intention of the parties to work together.

where does the skeletal plan come from? In brief, there are three necessary elements (see Fig. 5):

1. *Shared goals.* One or more shared goals give direction and purpose to the plan.
2. *Work-related requirements and context.* It is well and good to define the goals of the work, but to be able to plan successfully, we must know something about the requirements and context of the work itself. With respect to work *requirements*, we need to know, for example, whether tasks need to be done in a particular order, in a particular way, and whether they can or must be performed by more than one person. With respect to work *context*, we must know, for example, if the task is performed differently in daytime than it is in nighttime, or under different weather conditions, or when available team members have different capabilities.
3. *Relational requirements and context.* As an example of a relational *requirement,* even though the work itself may not strictly require more than one person to perform it, the plan may take into account that although assigning two people to the task may seem a short-term loss of efficiency, it may strengthen the skills or increase the comradery between them in the long run. More formal relational requirements are organizational structures such as the chain of command. Examples of relational *context* can be simple things like non-availability of a teammate or more nuanced

contexts such as knowing that two of the people on the team are not getting along well today.

When these three elements are combined to form a skeletal plan, joint requirements generally result. As the work progresses, changes to any aspects of the goals, requirements, and context are likely to affect the interdependence among the teammates, which can redefine what counts as good teamwork. This coupling of goals, requirements and context is another aspect of teamwork that makes it complex.

2.6   How Does Teamwork Relate to Taskwork?

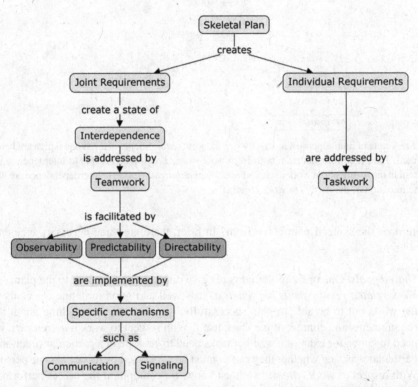

Fig. 6. Teamwork is facilitated by observability, predictability and directability.

Figure 6 extends our concept map to differentiate between teamwork and taskwork. Specific actions and supportive behaviors that facilitate teamwork address the state of interdependence between participants in a joint activity that has been created as joint requirements are in the process of being satisfied. An example of teamwork is when two individuals carry a large table together. On the other hand, taskwork addresses requirements that can be handled by a single individual—for example, hammering a nail. Of course, these are not rigid categories: in theory an individual whose arms are long and strong enough might be able to move a large table alone. Likewise, someone hammering a nail might sometimes need someone to hold the nail. Thus, we might say, more generally, that every item of taskwork has the potential to develop into a form of teamwork and vice versa.

As another example of the fluidity of the distinction between taskwork and teamwork, note that the same action sometimes can be performed in support of either taskwork or teamwork. For example, opening a door for oneself is simple taskwork, but opening a door to help a friend is a form of teamwork. The fact that what was originally envisioned as individual taskwork may suddenly become a joint-work activity is yet another example of what makes teamwork difficult to characterize.

Another thing that makes characterizing teamwork difficult is the fact that team members sometimes invest in joint efforts that require more labor but seem to have no immediate benefit when compared with the option of doing the work alone. Participants might justify their "wasteful" behavior by pointing to the possibility of greater rewards or reduced risk mitigation in the long term. To understand this situation, consider the short-term irrationality of buying insurance. Because people pay for insurance up front and the chances of an immediate disaster are small, it is likely that in the short run you will end up spending more in your premiums than you get back in your claims. However, when trouble strikes, insurance benefits provide financial relief, potentially forestalling fiscal ruin. In the same way, although teamwork may sometimes be less efficient than solo performance, it helps to ensure resilience when challenges arise. For example, a good copilot will monitor the pilot, verify whether the flight trajectory is appropriate, and be ready to act if anything goes wrong. However, if everything goes smoothly, there is no measurable benefit to the outcome (except the confidence provided by having a reliable backup). Similarly, even when an inattentive or incapable co-pilot is on duty, there may still be no measurable effect on the outcome when the pilot's performance is flawless. Sometimes teamwork benefits and failures are only exposed when things do not go as planned. For this reason, the value of teamwork should be assessed not only with respect to those instances where it facilitates *actual* failure recovery, but also in its anticipatory, protective function in mitigating the *potential* risks of failure or allowing *potential* exploitation of unforeseen opportunities in the long-run. Determining the sweet spot in the cost-benefit tradeoffs that govern opportunity exploitation and risk mitigation is yet another challenge for understanding and evaluating teamwork.

By way of additional clarification, Fig. 5 and Fig. 6 capture the fact that the word "teamwork" is used in different ways. For example, sometimes it refers generally to the type of activity in which participants work together interdependently on shared goals, as shown in Fig. 5. This sense of "teamwork" *defines* the requirements. At other times, it refers to the specific actions and supportive behaviors that facilitate the type of activity, as displayed in Fig. 6. This sense of "teamwork" defines how the requirements are *met*. Below we explore this second sense, a sense that is at the heart of the teamwork design challenge.

2.7 What Kinds of Support Are Needed to Facilitate Teamwork?

We have already seen that teamwork generates joint requirements. Now we seek to understand what kinds of support are needed to facilitate the satisfaction of those joint requirements. In brief, providing effective support for team members as they fulfill joint requirements is the *sine qua non* of designing and developing successful human-machine team performance.

In our view, non-trivial teamwork is facilitated to the degree that joint activity is supported by some combination of human effort and technology helps in three things: observability, predictability, and directability (see Fig. 6).

1. **Observability** refers to how clearly pertinent aspects of one's status—as well as one's knowledge of the team, task, and environment—are observable to others. This is commonly referred to as "transparency," but we prefer the term "observability." The complement to making one's own status observable to others is being able to observe status.
2. **Predictability** refers to how clearly one's intentions can be discerned by others and used to predict future actions, states, or situations. The complement to sharing one's own intentions with others is being able to predict the actions of others. It requires being able to receive and understand information about the intentions of others, to be able to predict future states, and to take those future states into account when making decisions.
3. **Directability** refers to one's ability to be directed and influenced by others. The complement is to be able to direct or influence the behavior of others.

These three interdependence relationships are consistent with long standing principles in human-centered design [14]. The importance of these three interdependence relationships can be seen throughout the automation literature with many references to observability (often referred to as transparency) e.g., [15–18], predictability e.g., [16, 18–20], and directability e.g., [16, 21].

As an example of how observability, predictability, and directability facilitate teamwork, let's imagine a group working together to search a building. Team members support observability when they share their current location with others. They support predictability when they inform the team that they are heading to the second floor. They are supporting directability when they are able to ask someone to check the stairwell and also when they allow themselves to be directed by someone else when appropriate.

A given set of joint requirements may not necessitate that the three primary forms of support for interdependent work (observability, predictability and directability) be available in equal measure. To satisfy a given joint requirement, support for only one or two of the three may be sufficient—and sometimes that may be all that is possible. However, our observations suggest each of the three kinds of support provides a unique form of facilitation that can become almost essential in a given setting.

For example, consider a situation where you have agreed to meet a new friend for coffee, without specifying a time. If they were simply observable, through a phone app that allows you to track their location, you could just monitor their position in real time and wait to see if they eventually arrive. Though simply *observing* might eventually work if you were not in any kind of a hurry and knew that if you waited long enough they would eventually arrive, your job would be much easier if instead you had agreed beforehand to meet at a specific time. Agreeing to a specific time allows you to *predict* their arrival time. That way you don't need to start observing until a few minutes prior to your appointment.

If you began the habit of meeting every week at the same time, your experience would allow you to improve your predictions. For instance, you might notice your friend consistently arrives fifteen minutes late. Your past *observations* can thus be used to adjust your future *predictions*.

Finally, consider the additional usefulness of *directability*. Your friend calls you on the phone in advance and asks you to meet him at a different coffee shop this time, thus influencing your future actions. This example shows how past and current *observations*, shared intentions (enabling *prediction*), and *directability* work in tandem to facilitate coordination within teams. Each of these three forms of support has its own cost and its own value in a given situation. Generally speaking, using all three forms together is more effective and reliable than relying on only one.

Just as it is helpful to be able to observe, predict, and direct teammates, so it is important to be observable, predictable, and directable oneself. Though it is true that one is sometimes required to observe without being observable, supportive *mutual* observability is usually a plus. Given the inherent differences in humans and machines, the kind and degree of observability, predictability and directability that is possible for a machine will rarely be identical and symmetrical to what is possible for a human, but that is to be expected. Indeed, the same thing is true with any two people. In order to achieve robust and resilient teamwork, as much support for observability, predictability and directability should be provided as can be leveraged effectively in the performance of relevant joint requirements.

These three forms of teamwork support can be implemented by any number of specific mechanisms. For example, team members who want to make their actions predictable by announcing their intentions could equally well communicate them over a radio channel or using a hand signal—or a combination of both. But, of course, the choice of an appropriate signaling mechanism depends not only on the capabilities of the team member sending a message but also on the capabilities of the one receiving it. Herbert Clark's joint action ladder [12, p. 147] is a reminder that an interaction requires complementary capabilities by both participants in the interaction. In other words, a signal cannot be successfully "observed" unless the receivers are able to attend, perceive and interpret them.

2.8 How Does Teamwork Continually Adjust Over Time?

As the joint activity progresses, the teamwork and the taskwork will result in *both interim and final* outcomes. Figure 7 extends our concept map to include outcomes, feedback, and learning. Effective teams will learn from their experiences. Learning from both immediate outcomes and the results of accumulated outcomes over time can provide feedback that will affect both the work and relational requirements and context. Future decision priorities and the skeletal plan itself can be adjusted in light of these results.

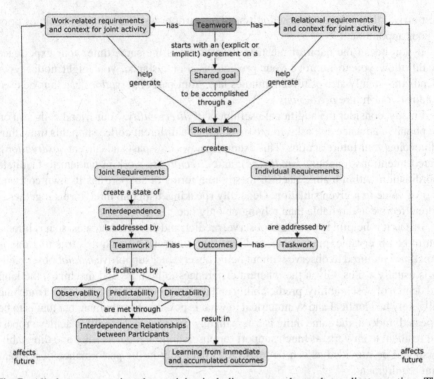

Fig. 7. All plans are tentative, thus activity, including teamwork, needs to adjust over time. The ability to adjust fluently is one of the most important characteristics of effective teams.

Figure 7 provides a basic summary of our proposed conceptual framework. It emphasizes the critical role that interdependence plays in joint activity generally, while emphasizing why it is even more crucial in teamwork. Interdependence relationships among team members stem from their participation in fulfilling joint requirements in the skeletal plan. The skeletal plan is formed and adjusted by taking the goals, the nature of the work, and the participants' relationships into account. The teamwork necessitated by work to fulfill joint requirements is facilitated by specific mechanisms that support observability, predictability and directability. To be successful, these mechanisms should be compatible with the complementary abilities of team members to both communicate and understand the signals used. Learning from immediate and accumulated outcomes allows requirements, contexts, goals, and plans to be refined and improved as the joint activity progresses. Another complexity in discussing teamwork is that the term *teamwork* is used both to describe a certain type of joint activity and also to describe the processes used to facilitate successful accomplishment of such activity.

3 How Does the Framework Help Us to Understand the Broader World of Human-Machine Teamwork?

We now return the conceptual soup of different approaches to human-machine teamwork shown in Fig. 1. We will apply our proposed framework to show selected examples of how these seemingly disparate research perspectives can be seen as parts of a common endeavor.

3.1 How Does Interdependence Relate to Situation Awareness?

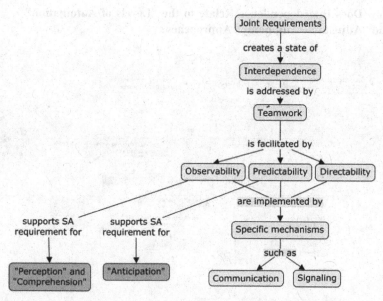

Fig. 8. Situation awareness (SA) is supported through observability and predictability requirements. Failure to meet those requirements will lead to poor situation awareness.

The theory of situation awareness, as outlined by Endsley and Kiris [22], describes the role of perception and projection in teamwork, a good match for the respective concepts of observability and predictability in our framework. The joint and individual requirements determine what information is relevant. Support for situation awareness must be configured in a way that takes both observability and predictability into account. Providing more support than is needed for a given task will be unnecessary, potentially annoying, distracting or overwhelming. Providing less than is needed will be potentially detrimental. Situation awareness, even when properly matched to the interdependence needs of joint requirements, can be hampered if the specific mechanisms used to convey it are poorly implemented for the situation at hand (Fig. 8).

The challenge for a designer is knowing what comprises the "situation." It is equally important for each teammate to understand the "situation" of other teammates when teamwork is actually underway. Teammates need to understand what other team members are aware of or need to be made aware of so they can communicate effectively. One proposed approach to designing for situation awareness is to employ goal-directed *task analysis* [23]. This is a logical starting point, since it is the joint activity that is the basis for the team's formation. It is also true that shared goals play an important role in determining situation awareness needs. However, we argue it is not the tasks generally but rather the interdependence relationships engendered in the performance of joint requirements that determine the situation awareness needs of each teammate. These interdependence relationships derive from a combination of the work requirements, the participants relationships, the shared goals, and the skeletal plan.

3.2 How Does Interdependence Relate to the "Levels of Automation" and "Adjustable Autonomy" Approaches?

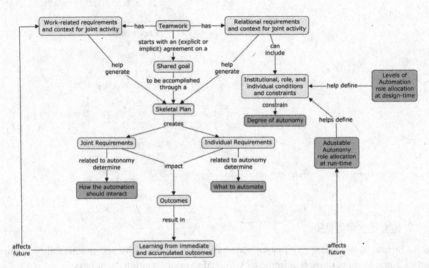

Fig. 9. Levels of automation help define some of the relational requirements, which, in turn, constrain the degree of autonomy for various elements in a given system. Joint and individual requirements related to autonomy determine what to automate and how the automation should interact.

The idea of *levels of automation* (LOA) is one of the most pervasive concepts in the domain of human-machine teaming. It has been viewed as an approach to designing systems [24] or a framework to help designers make design choices [25, 26]. LOA is often used to help designers make appropriate role allocation decisions at design-time that will use combinations of human and machine capabilities to best advantage. In turn, the degree of autonomy exhibited by a machine, described simply, is a manifestation of the opportunities and constraints for action delegated to it in its particular role, as seen in Fig. 9. In essence, a role is a label for a set of tasks that define what an actor is responsible for—and, usually implicitly, what responsibilities should be left to others.

In LOA, task assignments may thus be seen a simple mechanism for defining relational boundaries between different team members. These decisions help answer the question of "what to automate" [25].

Adjustable Autonomy (AA) is somewhat similar philosophically to LOA, except that it goes beyond *design-time analysis* to allow for dynamically adjusting allocation strategies *at run-time*. LOA and AA are similar in that they both constrain the degree of autonomy by defining roles that divvy up individual responsibilities.

However, while LOA and AA help in the design of *taskwork* to satisfy *individual* requirements, it says less about the problem of how to design *teamwork* so that the interdependence created by *joint* requirements can be addressed. It is important to realize that all "intermediate levels" of automation are joint-work activity, not cleanly separable functions to be allocated in isolation [1]. For this reason, it is important that designers to build algorithms not just to do individual work, but to support joint-work by supporting interdependence relationships through specific teamwork mechanisms. Increased effectiveness in human–machine systems hinges not merely on trying to make machines more "independent" through increasing levels of automation but also on striving to make them better team players with humans and other machines with which they interact [16].

LOA and AA decisions constrain teaming options and shape the potential interactions between people and technology. This can impose (often unanticipated) joint requirements which can have negative side effects and impede effective teaming. The human factors community has a long history of documenting this result e.g., [27, 28]. Given the critical nature of effective teaming, particularly in the envisioned sophisticated domains, we argue effective teaming should take a prime position in the design of automation. As a critical factor in the design of technology [7], the interdependence of participants in joint activity should be shaping decisions about autonomy, not the other way around.

3.3 How Are Trust Decisions Made?

Trust is an important aspect of teamwork and it is an increasingly important part of technology. As technology moves out of factories and laboratories and into the world, the importance of trust will continue to grow. To understand trust, it is important to understand that trust is relational [29]. In order to establish, develop and maintain appropriate trust, technology needs to be endowed with appropriate support for teamwork mechanisms that support interdependence relationships, such as observability, predictability and directability [30].

Trust, whether between people or between people and machines, is always exploratory and context-dependent. As Hoffman states:

> Active exploration of trusting–relying relationships cannot and should not be aimed at achieving single stable states or maintaining some decontextualized metrical value, but must be aimed at maintaining an appropriate and context-dependent expectation [31, p. 157].

As technology increases in sophistication and complexity, it will become more and more challenging for people to establish trust. People cannot simply observe a complex system in a single circumstance and be confident it can handle all situations. When the goal is a joint solution, with people and technology combining to produce something greater than either alone, it becomes even more challenging. For example, doctors will not blindly accept AI medical decisions without understanding something about the process behind the decision. Thus, today's sophisticated technology will need support mechanisms that allow them to engage in interdependence relationships. Observability, predictability and directability allow the trustor to develop appropriately calibrated trust relationships with the trusted party.

Model of a Risk-Taking Trust Relationship Decision

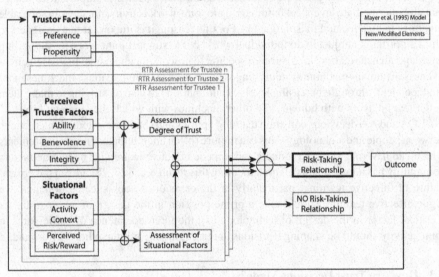

Fig. 10. Modified model of risk-taking relationship (from [30]).

Before associating trust with our framework, we need to review the concept of trust, using a modified version of the popular Mayer trust model [29], shown in Fig. 10. The Mayer model distinguished the trustor factors and trustee factors that influence trust. Most critically, Mayer emphasizes that trust does not exist until the trustor engages in what Mayer calls a *risk-taking relationship*. These relationships are influenced by feedback from outcomes to calibrate trust over time. A more detailed description of our extended model of trust has been published elsewhere [30].

Since trust is about a risk-taking relationship, it is therefore just another aspect of relational context that affects the skeletal plan. Moreover, trust in our modified Mayer model is calibrated over time through feedback from outcomes, just as in our framework as shown in Fig. 11. Trust feedback is largely related to the teamwork outcomes facilitated by observability, predictability and directability. Further discussion on trust can be found in our previous works [30, 32].

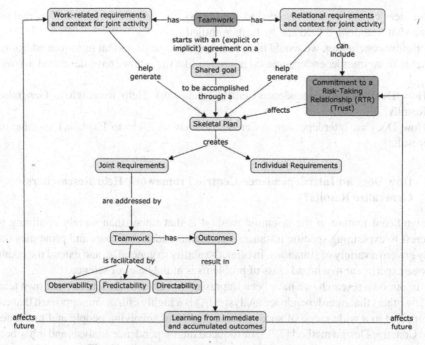

Fig. 11. Trust within the interdependence framework.

4 Discussion

The purpose of the proposed framework is to help ground the conversation about human-machine teaming in easy-to-understand concepts that address each of the key research issues. It advances the science of interdependence by clarifying:

- what we mean by interdependence,
- where it comes from,
- how to identify it in a specific application,
- how to facilitate the management of it, and
- how, in working together, each of these factors impact human-machine team outcomes in particular ways.

Significantly, and in line with the objective we outlined at the beginning of the chapter, we have shown examples of how "interdependence," as we think of it, is not only the key principle that unlocks an understanding of teamwork overall but also the means of framing seemingly disparate research perspectives as parts of a common endeavor.

In instances where we may have mischaracterized or oversimplified the mapping of other research perspectives to our framework, we would welcome feedback from the research community, so our misconceptions can be corrected. With respect to other important research perspectives that we have not directly discussed in this chapter, we hope to be able to work cooperatively with the research community to see whether these ideas can be further extended to encompass the "world of teamwork" so that our somewhat fragmented field can be further unified.

Before concluding, we would like to address two questions that introduce additional benefits of an interdependence-based approach like the one we have described above:

- How Does an Interdependence-Centric Framework Help Researchers Generalize Results?
- How Does an Interdependence-Centric Framework Help to Explain Experimental Results?

4.1 How Does an Interdependence-Centric Framework Help Researchers Generalize Results?

A significant feature of the scientific method is that rather than merely confining its interest to explaining specific instances, it seeks to understand laws and principles that may govern a variety of situations. In brief, the ability to generalize and extend the results of one experiment to a broad class of problems is at the heart of science.

In our own research, we have been impressed by repeated findings by our own team and by others that interdependence analysis (IA) is a highly efficacious approach that can be applied to a wide range of socio-technical systems involving people and machines. The Coactive Design method [7, 33] introduced interdependence analysis and it has been extended in more recent work [34]:

- IA has been applied to ground robotics [35], aerial robotics [36], humanoid robotics [38], and software agents [37].
- IA has proven effective in several domains including disaster response [38, 39], military applications [40, 41], space applications [42], network security [43] system design [44] and the design of large scale unmanned aerial vehicle operation centers.
- IA can be applied in the formative design stage [45], throughout an iterative design and re-design process [38, 39], and as an analysis tool for existing systems or proposed conceptual designs [41]. It helps both the development of proper behaviors [38, 46] and development of appropriate interfaces [43, 47].

Besides the examples of generalization mentioned above, the practice of IA has helped researchers identify common patterns of failure and their solutions. For example, one common failure pattern identified in different projects is what we call *breaking what is working*. This phenomenon occurs when the addition of new technology disrupts existing information flows and hinders performance. The use of IA has made it clear that this problem is often due to impediments to observability that emerge when automation "hides" aspects of the work being performed that need to be observable to team members. This problem cannot be identified simply by looking at the taskwork that the newly added technology performs, but rather must be understood through an examination of interdependence relationships that are created through joint requirements such as, in this case, observability. Evidence for these claims was found by Johnson et al. [33] in the disaster response domain, in which automation of a grasping task inhibited the human's ability to interpret the situation and recover from small deviations. Beierl and

Tschirley [41] found similar issues when they used IA to review proposed solutions for integrating robots into Marine Fire Teams. The proposed introduction of a machine into the Fire Team inhibited some of the natural communication channels used between team members.

A second example of such a pattern is what we call *black box help*. This is similar to *breaking what is working*, in that lack of observability is generally the issue. However, instead of interrupting an *existing* workflow by preventing teammates from viewing the actions of something that was previously observable, it arises when *new* technology and workflows are added that hinder observability of the new technology's actions by others. The problems generated by the opaque nature of black boxes have spawned programs to try to address the issue, such as Defense Advanced Research Projects Agency Explainable Artificial Intelligence program (DARPA XAI), which notes that "the effectiveness of these systems is limited by the machine's current inability to explain their decisions and actions to human users."[2] While traditional human factors analysis has a long history of identifying this as a problem *retrospectively*, IA provides an *upfront* analysis solution where the problem and potential options for solving it can be identified early in the design phase [48].

A third example of how common patterns and solutions can be brought to light through IA is what we call the *incomplete solution*. This is when technology is interjected to assist people who are overloaded. However, when the new technology cannot address all aspects of the work, often including implicit requirements that were not identified during the design process, it becomes more of a burden than a help. The IA conducted by Zach [40] analyzed the effort to leverage unmanned systems to provide intelligence, surveillance, and reconnaissance to Marine Corps tactical units. It identified five missing feedback loops which demanded more from the marines due to the lack of capabilities on the unmanned system. The IA conducted by Beierl & Tschirley [41] identify the unmanned system's lack of ability to distinguish "the enemy" as a key inhibitor in its effectiveness. The IA conducted by Johnson et al. [34] showed how current automated traffic avoidance systems lack the ability to address uncooperating traffic. In each of these cases, the problem was not found by looking at what that automated system was doing, but by looking at how that work was interdependent with what the people interacting with the system, its "teammates," would be doing.

In all the ways we have just mentioned, IA represents progress in improving the degree to which the scientific method can be applied to human-machine teamwork: identifying generalizable laws, principles, patterns, and solutions that facilitate meaningful progress in our common research field.

4.2 How Does an Interdependence-Centric Framework Help Explain Experimental Results?

Though space prevents an exhaustive survey in the present chapter, we will provide a few examples of how an interdependence-based framework helps explain many common results in human-machine teaming studies.

---

[2] https://www.darpa.mil/program/explainable-artificial-intelligence.

As a first example, we note that while the promise of technology has nearly always been that higher levels of automation (LOA) will make our lives easier, reduce workload, and improve performance, experimental evidence often suggests otherwise. Endsley's [26] computer-based dynamic control task experiment showed that LOA involving joint human-computer selection had no significant impact on performance, as compared to purely human selection. She also found that operator ability to recover from automation failures was substantially improved with lower LOA, and operators were actually hindered when assistance was provided with higher level cognitive functions. Similarly, Calhoun and Draper [49] found it took significantly longer to complete the re-routing task in their multi-UAV testbed with the high LOA. Li and Wickens' [50] experiment with remote operation of a robot echoed this pattern of high LOA performing worse. Many different reasons have been given for such results, but we are convinced that they can frequently be explained through the lens of interdependence. For example, we have previously demonstrated that increasing the LOA without adequately addressing interdependence relationships can disrupt natural coordination (i.e., *breaking what was working*) and result in a negative inflection in performance as automation increases at the expense of observability and predictability [51]. Endsley [26] speculates this is the case suggesting the results are indicative of a lower level of direct feedback experienced when not actually performing a task implementation. Our analysis explains some otherwise surprising LOA results that have reported by others [52, 53].

As a second example, one of the most common experimental observations is that "humans tend to be less aware of changes in environmental or system states when those changes are under the control of another agent (whether that agent is automation or another human) than when they make the changes themselves" [25]. From our perspective, this result can be explained straightforwardly from the fact that many systems are not observable or predictable, making the system opaque to the user (i.e., *black box help*), inhibiting situation awareness and maintenance of common ground [51]. One of the most common results found in level of automation studies is that situation awareness significantly decreases with "higher" levels of automation [24]. This effect can be mitigated by properly designing support for interdependence (i.e., observability, predictability, directability).

In this regard, it should be no surprise that a breakdown in lower-level team functions, like observability and predictability, has a negative impact on team performance. It is particularly apparent when teams face off-nominal situations. Although higher levels of automation can beneficially reduce workload during normal operating conditions, it can also impede situation awareness (i.e., *breaking what was working*), making it difficult for the human-machine team to adapt to unexpected events. In a remote robot arm experiment, Kaber et al. [24] did in fact show that increasing LOA reduced time-to-complete task for normal operations, but the opposite was true for time-to-recover during failures. Li and Wickens [50] also showed that failure detection is poorer when technology is under the control of automation, which is noted as a consistent pattern in Onnasch et al.'s survey which concluded that "automation helps when all goes well, but leaving the user out of the loop can be problematic because it leads to considerable performance impairment if the automation suddenly fails" [54]. We prefer a more specific description than the general statement that the human is "out of the loop" to explain these findings. More specifically, we posit that lack of support for interdependent work (i.e., observability, predictability, directability) in the automated solution diminishes the ability of the person to recover from failure. Conducting a proper IA can go further and identify the specific joint requirements that were not adequately supported by facilitating mechanisms.

Parasuraman et al. [25] rightfully acknowledge the challenges of function allocation when they state, "The performance of most tasks involves interdependent stages that overlap temporally in their processing operations." Their four-stage model included sensing, perception, decision-making and response selection. It is clear that what you perceive depends on what you sense, what you decide depends on what you perceive and what you select depends on what you decide. What is less obvious is that what you need to decide on may shape your perception or shift your attention. This means failure anywhere can have ripple effects on system outcomes, highlighting the critical role interdependence plays in understanding experimental results in human-machine teaming. In order to properly interpret experimental outcomes, a thorough interdependence analysis is essential. This interdependence analysis has an added benefit of potentially providing new ways to instrument and measure teamwork.

5   Conclusion

We have proposed and illustrated that a correct understanding of *interdependence* is key to characterizing human-machine teamwork in an understandable, actionable, and generalizable manner. Our framework proposes three principal forms of support that can be used to facilitate effective, interdependent teamwork: observability, predictability, and directability. Though researchers have sometimes used different words to describe these three forms of teamwork support, results from our own studies and those of others has provided convincing evidence of their primacy, usefulness, and generalizability. We have argued that an interdependence-centric framework enables researchers to predict and explain experimental results in terms of interlocking relationships among well-defined operational principles. We are hopeful that continued discussions of this framework will provide a sound and practical foundation for developing a deeper science of interdependence.

Acknowledgements. This material is based upon work supported by the Defense Advanced Research Projects Agency (DARPA) under Contract No. HR001120C0037. Any opinions, findings and conclusions or recommendations expressed in this material are those of the author(s) and do not necessarily reflect the views of the Defense Advanced Research Projects Agency (DARPA). Thanks for Kathleen, Robert, Thomas, and Samuel Bradshaw for their helpful comments and suggestions.

References

1. Johnson, M., Vera, A.H.: No AI is an Island: the case for teaming intelligence. AI Mag. Spring **40**, 16–28 (2019)
2. McDermott, D.: Artificial intelligence meets natural stupidity. ACM SIGART Bull. **57**, 4–9 (1976)
3. Bradshaw, J.M., Hoffman, R.R., Johnson, M., Woods, D.D.: The seven deadly myths of 'autonomous systems.' IEEE Intell. Syst. **28**(3), 54–61 (2013)
4. Norman, D.A., Draper, S.W. (eds.): User Centered System Design. Taylor & Francis, Boca Raton (1986)
5. Billings, C.: Human-centered aircraft automation: a concept and guidelines (1991)
6. Hoffman, R.R., Deal, S.V.: Influencing versus informing design, Part 1: a gap analysis. IEEE Intell. Syst. **23**(5), 78–81 (2008)
7. Johnson, M., Bradshaw, J.M., Feltovich, P.J., Jonker, C.M., van Riemsdijk, B., Sierhuis, M.: The fundamental principle of coactive design: interdependence must shape autonomy. In: De Vos, M., Fornara, N., Pitt, J.V., Vouros, G. (eds.) COIN -2010. LNCS (LNAI), vol. 6541, pp. 172–191. Springer, Heidelberg (2011). https://doi.org/10.1007/978-3-642-21268-0_10
8. Malone, T.W., Crowston, K.: The interdisciplinary study of coordination. ACM Comput. Surv. **26**(1), 87–119 (1994)
9. Salas, E., Rosen, M.A., Burke, C.S., Goodwin, G.F.: The wisdom of collectives in organizations: an update of the teamwork competencies. In: Team Effectiveness in Complex Organizations: Cross-Disciplinary Perspectives and Approaches, pp. 39–79. Routledge/Taylor & Francis Group, New York (2009)
10. Feltovich, P., Bradshaw, J., Clancey, W., Johnson, M.: Toward an ontology of regulation: socially-based support for coordination in human and machine joint activity. In: O'Hare, G.M.P., Ricci, A., O'Grady, M.J., Dikenelli, O. (eds.) ESAW 2006. LNCS (LNAI), vol. 4457, pp. 175–192. Springer, Heidelberg (2007). https://doi.org/10.1007/978-3-540-75524-1_10
11. Clark, H.H., Brennan, S.: Grounding in communication. Perspect. Soc. Shar. Cogn., 127–149 (1991)
12. Clark, H.H.: Using Language. Cambridge University Press, Cambridge (1996)
13. Tu, S.W., Kahn, M.G., Musen, M.A., Fagan, L.M., Ferguson, J.C.: Episodic skeletal-plan refinement based on temporal data. Commun. ACM **32**(12), 1439–1455 (1989)
14. Billings, C.: Aviation automation: the search for a human-centered approach (1997)
15. Gao, J.G.J., Lee, J.: Extending the decision field theory to model operators' reliance on automation in supervisory control situations. IEEE Trans. Syst. Man Cybern. Part A Syst. Hum. **36**(5), 943–959 (2006)
16. Klein, G., Woods, D.D., Bradshaw, J.M., Hoffman, R.R., Feltovich, P.J.: Ten challenges for making automation a 'team player' in joint human-agent activity. IEEE Intell. Syst. **19**(6), 91–95 (2004)
17. Sarter, N.B., Woods, D.D.: How in the world did we ever get into that mode? Mode error and awareness in supervisory control. Hum. Factors J. Hum. Factors Ergon. Soc. **37**(1), 5–19 (1995)
18. Wiener, E.L.: Human factors of advanced technology (glass cockpit) transport aircraft (Nasa-Cr-177528), p. 222 (1989)
19. Kirlik, A., Miller, R., Jagacinski, R.J.: Supervisory control in a dynamic and uncertain environment II: a process model of skilled human environment interaction. IEEE Trans. Syst. Man. Cybern. **23**, 929–952 (1993)
20. Rovira, E., McGarry, K., Parasuraman, R.: Effects of imperfect automation on decision making in a simulated command and control task. Hum. Factors **49**(1), 76–87 (2007)

21. Myers, K.L., Morley, D.N.: Directing agent communities: an initial framework. In: Proceedings of the IJCAI Workshop on Autonomy, Delegation, and Control: Interacting with Autonomous Agents (2001)
22. Endsley, M.R., Kiris, E.O.: The out-of-the-loop performance problem and level of control in automation. Hum. Factors Ergon. Soc. 37(2), 381–394 (1995)
23. Endsley, M.R., Bolté, B., Jones, D.G.: Designing for Situation Awareness: An Approach to User-Centered Design. Taylor & Francis, New York (2003)
24. Kaber, D.B., Onal, E., Endsley, M.R.: Design of automation for telerobots and the effect on performance, operator situation awareness, and subjective workload. Hum. Factors Ergon. Manuf. 10(4), 409–430 (2000)
25. Parasuraman, R., Sheridan, T., Wickens, C.: A model for types and levels of human interaction with automation. Syst. Man Cybern. Part A IEEE Trans. 30(3), 286–297 (2000)
26. Endsley, M.R.: Level of automation effects on performance, situation awareness and workload in a dynamic control task. Ergonomics 42(3), 462–492 (1999)
27. Sarter, N.B., Woods, D.D., Billings, C.E.: Automation surprises. In: Salvendy, G. (ed.) Handbook of Human Factors and Ergonomics, 2nd edn., pp. 1926–1943. Wiley (1997)
28. Wiener, E.L., Curry, R.E.: Flight-deck automation: promises and problems. Ergonomics 23(10), 995–1011 (1980)
29. Mayer, R.C., Davis, J.H., Schoorman, F.D.: An integrative model of organizational trust. Acad. Manag. Rev. 20(3), 709–734 (1995)
30. Johnson, M., Bradshaw, J.M.: The role of interdependence in trust. In: Nam, C.S., Lyons, J.B. (eds.) Trust in Human-Robot Interaction, pp. 379–403. Academic Press, London (2020)
31. Hoffman, R.R.: A taxonomy of emergent trusting in the human-machine relationship. In: Cognitive Systems Engineering: The Future for a Changing World, pp. 137–164 (2017)
32. Hoffman, R.R., Johnson, M., Bradshaw, J.M., Underbrink, A.: Trust in automation. IEEE Intell. Syst. 28(1), 84–88 (2013)
33. Johnson, M., Bradshaw, J.M., Feltovich, P.J., Jonker, C.M., van Riemsdijk, B.M., Sierhuis, M.: Coactive design: designing support for interdependence in joint activity. J. Human-Robot Interact. 3(1), 43–69 (2014)
34. Johnson, M., Vignati, M., Duran, D.: Understanding human-autonomy teaming through interdependence analysis. In: Symposium on Human Autonomy Teaming (2018)
35. Carff, J., Johnson, M., El-Sheikh, E.M., Pratt, J.E.: Human-robot team navigation in visually complex environments. In: 2009 IEEE/RSJ International Conference on Intelligent Robots and Systems, IROS 2009 (2009)
36. Johnson, M., Carff, J., Pratt, J.E.: Coactive design for human-MAV team navigation. In: International Micro Air Vehicle Conference and Competition (2012)
37. Bradshaw, J.M., Feltovich, P.J., Johnson, M.: Human-agent interaction (2011)
38. Johnson, M., et al.: Team IHMC's lessons learned from the DARPA robotics challenge trials. J. F. Robot. 32(2), 192–208 (2015)
39. Johnson, M., et al.: Team IHMC's lessons learned from the DARPA Robotics challenge: finding data in the rubble. J. F. Robot. 34(2), 241–261 (2017)
40. Zach, M.S.: Unmanned tactical autonomous control and collaboration coactive design. Calhoun, the NPS Institutional Archive (2016)
41. Beierl, C., Tschirley, D.: Unmanned tactical autonomous control and collaboration situation awareness (2017)
42. Zachary, W., Johnson, M., Hoffman, R., Thomas, T., Rosoff, A., Santarelli, T.: A context-based approach to robot-human interaction. Procedia Manuf. 3 (2015)
43. Bradshaw, J.M., et al.: Sol: an agent-based framework for cyber situation awareness. KI - Künstliche Intelligenz 26(2), 127–140 (2012)
44. Lee, K.H., Chua, K.W.L., Koh, D.S.M., Tan, A.L.S.: Team Cognitive Walkthrough: Fusing Creativity and Effectiveness for a Novel Operation, pp. 117–126 (2019)

45. Lee, K.H., Chua, K.W.L., Koh, D.S.M., Tan, A.L.S.: Team cognitive walkthrough: fusing creativity and effectiveness for a novel operation. In: Bagnara, S., Tartaglia, R., Albolino, S., Alexander, T., Fujita, Y. (eds.) IEA 2018. AISC, vol. 824, pp. 117–126. Springer, Cham (2019). https://doi.org/10.1007/978-3-319-96071-5_13
46. Koolen, T., et al.: Summary of Team IHMC's virtual robotics challenge entry. In: IEEE-RAS International Conference on Humanoid Robots, vol. 2015, pp. 307–314 (2015)
47. Chua Wei Liang, K., Johnson, M., Eskridge, T., Keller, B.: AOA: ambient obstacle avoidance interface. In: The 23rd IEEE International Symposium on Robot and Human Interactive Communication, pp. 18–23 (2014)
48. Johnson, M., Bradshaw, J.M., Feltovich, P.J.: Tomorrow's human–machine design tools: from levels of automation to interdependencies. J. Cogn. Eng. Decis. Mak. **12**, 155534341773646 (2017)
49. Calhoun, G., Draper, M.: Effect of level of automation on unmanned aerial vehicle routing task. In: Proc. Hum. (2009)
50. Li, H., Wickens, C.: Stages and levels of automation in support of space teleoperations. Hum. Factors **56**, 1050–1061 (2014)
51. Johnson, M., Bradshaw, J.M., Feltovich, P.J., Jonker, C., van Riemsdijk, B., Sierhuis, M.: Autonomy and interdependence in human-agent-robot teams. Intell. Syst. IEEE **27**(2), 43–51 (2012)
52. Kaber, D.B., Endsley, M.R.: The effects of level of automation and adaptive automation on human performance, situation awareness and workload in a dynamic control task. Theor. Issues Ergon. Sci. **5**(2), 113–153 (2004)
53. Whalley, M.S., et al.: Flight test results for a new mission-adaptive autonomy system on the rascal JUH-60A black hawk. In: American Helicopter Society 72th Annual Forum (2016)
54. Onnasch, L., Wickens, C.D., Li, H., Manzey, D.: Human performance consequences of stages and levels of automation. Hum. Factors **56**(3), 476–488 (2014)

Designing Interactive Machine Learning Systems for GIS Applications

Jaelle Scheuerman[1]($\boxtimes$), Chris J. Michael[1], Brad Landreneau[1],
Dina M. Acklin[1], and Jason L. Harman[1,2]

[1] U.S. Naval Research Laboratory, Stennis Space Center, MS, USA
jaelle.scheuerman@nrlssc.navy.mil
[2] Louisiana State University, Baton Rouge, LA, USA

Abstract. Geospatial information systems (GIS) support decision making and situational awareness in a wide variety of applications. These systems often require large amounts of labeled data to be displayed in a way that is easy to use and understand. Manually editing these information displays can be extremely time-consuming for an analyst. Algorithms have been designed to alleviate some of this work by automatically generating map displays or digitizing features. However, these systems regularly make mistakes, requiring analysts to verify and correct their output. This human-in-the-loop process of validating the algorithm's labels can provide a means to continuously improve a model over time by using interactive machine learning (IML). This process allows for systems that can function with little or no training data and as the features continue to evolve. Such systems must also account for the strengths and limitations of both the analysts and underlying algorithms to avoid unnecessary frustration, encourage adoption, and increase productivity of the human-machine team. In this chapter, we introduce three examples of how IML has been used in GIS systems for airfield change detection, geographic region digitization and digital map editing. We also describe several considerations for designing IML workflows to ensure that the analyst and system complement one another, resulting in increased productivity and quality of the GIS output. Finally, we will consider new challenges that arise when applying IML to the complex task of automatic map labeling.

Keywords: Interactive machine learning · Geographic information systems · Human-machine teams

1 Introduction

Geographic information systems generally consist of large amounts of geographic data that is organized and displayed for a variety of tasks, including navigation, situational awareness, and decision making. The process of generating these maps can require a great deal of both computational resources and an analyst's time. Many algorithms exist to help automate feature digitization [2] and generate

W. F. Lawless et al. (Eds.): Engineering Artificially Intelligent Systems, LNCS 13000, pp. 147–158, 2021.
https://doi.org/10.1007/978-3-030-89385-9_9

map displays [4,16], but the output of many of these algorithms still require an analyst's time to verify that the resulting maps are accurate and useful.

In recent years, attempts have been made to use machine learning to improve automated tasks like feature digitization and map generalization [1,6,18]. However, these approaches also have many challenges. Machine learning algorithms generally require large databases of labeled training data before they are especially useful. Getting this data is often a challenge and does not always cover every situation the system will encounter. For example, a sensor may change between the training data and the production system, leading the algorithm to make inaccurate classifications. In this traditional machine learning approach, information generally flows in one direction with the algorithm first being trained on some data and then asked to classify new examples of similar data. Fine-tuning the machine learning output often requires a trained machine learning expert to tweak unintuitive parameters in an effort to improve the accuracy of the classifications.

Many efforts have been made to use interactive machine learning (IML) to solve some of these traditional machine learning challenges. IML systems start with little to no training data and iteratively improve through interactions with the user. This approach is useful for many GIS applications, where labels and regions may depend on features that cannot always be clearly defined. In the IML workflow, the interface presents its best guess to the analyst, who corrects it as needed. Using online learning, the algorithm immediately takes the new information into account when selecting new examples to show the user. Active learning updates the underlying uncertainty model ensuring that the examples that are shown will reduce the uncertainty, helping the model to converge more quickly. This continual feedback loop between the user and the algorithm results in better recommendations over time.

In this chapter, we will share three use cases showing how IML is being used in GIS systems, and explore some of the design considerations that can improve IML workflows. We will conclude with difficult challenges that exist for automating map labeling, and we introduce some new research directions that seek to improve existing map labeling systems.

Fig. 1. The interactive machine learning workflow.

2 Interactive Machine Learning in Practice

To illustrate how IML is being used in GIS systems, we will describe three use cases, including airfield change detection, digital region annotation and digital map editing.

2.1 Airfield Change Detection (ACD)

Maintaining a current knowledge of airfields and their features is a challenging problem. There are tens of thousands of airfields globally, all of which are routinely photographed via satellite. Currently, a human must analyze this imagery and take note of any changes. These changes include, but are not limited to: overgrowth of a runway, shortening or lengthening of runways, new taxiways, or new hardstands. While larger airfields (such as Atlanta) will almost certainly report any changes to its features, smaller airfields (single runway, those less than 1000 m in length) may not.

With such a large volume of airfield imagery, it is clear that automation would greatly benefit analysts. However, complete automation could result in scenarios where the changes detected are incorrect and require the analyst to do more work by fixing or updating a machine's incorrect analysis. The Airfield Change Detection (ACD) task lends itself well to an IML approach since the analyst will have to confirm any automatic results regardless of how well the algorithm can identify changes.

While the total volume of all airfield imagery is massive, the number of images per any given airfield can be relatively low (10 images over the course of several years) for smaller airfields. IML's ability to produce accurate results with small datasets is one of the core features that makes airfield change detection possible. ACD can learn from a single image and continue to learn and improve as more imagery is analyzed by the algorithm and confirmed by the analyst.

To detect changes in airfield runways, ACD queries an imagery database and checks for new images. These images are analyzed to determine whether a change has been detected and calculate a confidence value. This change is determined by comparing the new imagery against the airfield's historical imagery. In the event that there is no historical imagery for this airfield, the analyst will have to confirm the starting geometry of the airfield. The resulting confidence measures provide an uncertainty model that is used to determine the order in which the images are displayed to the analyst. After the analyst makes any adjustments, the algorithm proceeds to analyze the new imagery as it is queried.

The ACD interface can organize the new images based on a user's preferences. The interface allows the analyst to organize the data based on a number of variables found with airfields and their imagery. Analysts may prefer to only work with airfields that are likely to have changes, more than one runway, newer imagery, etc.

ACD paired with IML allows automatic imagery analysis, runway geometry creation, and imagery organization which mitigates the overhead regarding the high volume of airfields and their imagery. Additionally, an uncertainty model allows ACD to group the imagery by confidence, allowing analysts to prioritize one group over another. IML's ability to learn using small datasets is especially useful in the case of smaller airfields that do not have large amounts of historical imagery. Coupled with the fact that smaller airfields are more likely to have overgrowth, to not maintain their feature's status, and that analysts must confirm all the imagery, IML can be utilized to all of its strengths.

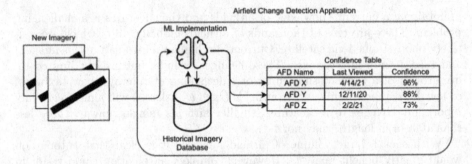

Fig. 2. New imagery is compared to any available historical imagery to detect changes in airfields. A confidence score is generated showing how confident the algorithm is in its choice. Analysts can filter and sort the airport list based on the confidence score.

2.2   Geographic Region Annotation Interface Toolkit (GRAIT)

Region annotation is another area where an interactive machine learning approach has been applied. In these types of applications, an automated algorithm will usually try to detect the region of interest and then require an analyst to verify the output. Sometimes, the automated feature detection fails to correctly outline the region, especially in situations where the example looks different from the training data. To correct the region, the analyst must click and drag the vertices until the region is properly annotated. If many changes are required, this can become very frustrating to the analysts, sometimes leading them to completely throw out the algorithm's polygon and start over from scratch.

To address these design challenges, a general framework for region digitization (GRAIT) [9] was developed to give analysts more control over the digitization systems output while addressing the frustrations faced when correcting the output. This control was accomplished by constraining the problem space and limiting the amount of incorrect vertices displayed at any given time.

The interface for region digitization consists of vertices that border the designated region. Their locations can be modified to correct any errors in the region. If an analyst corrects the user placement, there could be a myriad of different reasons why. The machine learning implementation needs some way to narrow down the search space so that it can more quickly converge on an accurate model. Both the usability and speed of model convergence can be improved by constraining the search space to a chosen subspace of the image plane. Doing so reduces the number of examples required to teach the machine learning implementation which features are important for defining the region's border.

In practice, GRAIT requires analysts to place the initial vertices to instantiate contours at the edge of the region to be annotated. Once a few vertices have been placed, the algorithm analyzes the search space and learns some feature weights that are used to guess the placement of additional vertices. If the machine places a vertex in the wrong spot, the analyst can drag it along the constrained search space to correct it. The model learns from any updates that are made to the vertices and then places a few more. This iterative process continues until the region is fully digitized. It was found to have 84% placement accuracy from a cold start with no training data.

As the algorithm places vertices around the region's contour, it is important not to overwhelm the analyst with too many incorrect guesses. Because of this, only a limited number of vertices are displayed in each iteration. The algorithm maintains an uncertainty model and prioritizes placing vertices that it is the least confident about, choosing vertices in order of increasing confidence until the expected value of misplaced vertices is two. Assuming that the uncertainty model is accurate, this approach is not likely to overwhelm the analyst, while also providing the model with additional feedback on the vertices it is less certain about.

As we have seen in this use case, IML workflows can benefit by considering the experience of the analyst and finding ways to reduce frustration. In this scenario, it was problematic to both the algorithm and the analyst if an entire contour had to be corrected at once. Instead, a better solution was to constrain the search space and use an underlying uncertainty model to reduce the amount of editing required by the analyst, increasing the speed of model convergence.

2.3   Digital Map Editing (SmartMaps)

Generating digital map displays at various scales and with different sets of visible layers is a complicated problem that presents many challenges for fully automated algorithms and IML systems. Automatic solutions can generate good map displays in many situations, but it becomes more difficult as the map symbology increases in density and complexity [16]. More computing resources and time are required to calculate an optimal layout, and this requirement is further complicated when the analyst can add new layers or change the map scale. This situation results in some imperfect views, where labels may obfuscate one another or are not well distributed, leading to clutter in some areas, while others are more suitable to label placement.

SmartMaps was designed to address these challenges in the NRL Mapviewer by giving users the ability to edit map displays directly from the viewer. They can hide or display layers or move labels to preferred areas on the map. As a user makes these edits, a machine learning model learns which layers are important to the user, as well as the underlying features that predict the preferred label placements. This preference information can be collected over time for a single user, or aggregated over a set of similar users. The collected data is then used

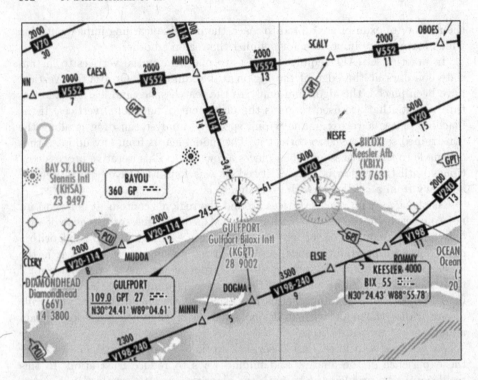

Fig. 3. Example output from map layout algorithm. The southern portion is cluttered, while the northeast remains relatively clear. A possible improvement would be to move the Gulfport Airport label to the area of white space, northeast of the airport. With digital map editing, the analyst could make this change and the algorithm would learn to apply the preference in similar views.

to implicitly train the model and improve its predictions about layer visibility and good label placements, thus improving its display over time. This use case provides a good example of how a map interface can be designed to implicitly collect information about a user's preferences to improve its display over time.

3   Design Considerations in Interactive Machine Learning

In the applications described above, certain design aspects were considered to ensure that the IML systems complemented the analyst's workflow. For example, the airfield change detection task highlighted how special attention must be given to communicating the uncertainty in the model. When done well, the model's uncertainty helps analysts to quickly hone into the examples that most require their expertise. Additionally, the region annotation task showed the importance of limiting the number of incorrect guesses that are displayed to an analyst at any given time. Doing so can reduce frustration and discouragement when using the system. Finally, the digital map editing application showed how we can implicitly collect user preferences through edits to the map display, which can further train the model about preferred label placements.

It is essential to consider both the analysts' and algorithms' limitations and strengths in the design of an IML workflow. Doing so can help ensure that the resulting system is usable and supports analysts in completing their tasks quickly and without frustration. Uncertainty models, problem constraints, user preferences and cognitive feedback represent four tools that can improve the design of an IML system. We will next consider each of these individually and discuss how they can be applied in an IML context.

3.1   Uncertainty Models

Developing a good uncertainty model is essential for ensuring that the analyst and model can work together effectively. Machine learning models often assign a value to a label, which represents how well a set of inputs represent a particular label. As an example, consider a system that must label several examples and then verify those with an analyst. When the unlabeled data is similar to the labeled training data, the model is much more likely to choose an accurate label and will assign a higher confidence score to that label. In other scenarios, the new data may include some underlying features or concepts that are not well-covered by the training data. In this situation, the IML system should show labels that is less confident about first, allowing the analyst to correct these as needed. This allows the model to get feedback on data it is less confident about, decreasing the number of samples that the analyst must label to reach model convergence [10].

3.2   Constraining the Problem

Another area of IML design that is important to consider is how the problem can be constrained. Consider that there are many different features that a machine algorithm could use to determine where to place a map label or how to annotate a region. If an analyst corrects the algorithm, there could be a variety of reasons why. It is possible to improve both the usability and speed of convergence if there is a way to constrain that problem. As an analogy, consider that designing fully automated cars is a very difficult problem that has yet to be solved. However, automated trains have existed for decades because of the constraints afforded by the rails. These constraints led to a much more tractable problem to be solved. Constraints can also be used in an IML workflow to reduce the feature space of the problem. The analyst and algorithm can work together on the constrained problem to more quickly converge to an accurate model, even when starting with no training data [9].

3.3   User Preferences

User preferences can also be used to improve an IML system over time. Map displays may especially benefit from being able to personalize the map layers or icons that are displayed, depending on the user and task at hand. By giving analysts the power to edit label locations and displayed layers, machine learning systems can tailor map interfaces to individuals and task needs. User preferences can be either learned through interactions with the user, or modeled using a combination of cognitive theories and behavioral data.

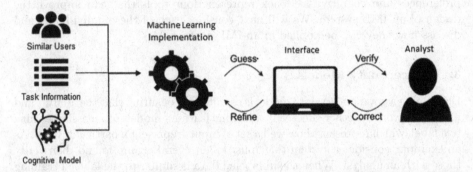

Fig. 4. Example inputs to the ML pipeline could include synthetic data generated from a cognitive model, information about the current task, or any historical data about similar users' interactions with the map display. These initialize the inductive bias in the ML system, which is further fine-tuned as users interact with the output.

3.4 Cognitive Feedback

Finally, cognitive feedback can be used to further refine an interface to best complement an analyst's workflow. Cognitive feedback refers to information about the cognitive state of the analyst, either gathered directly from the user through a self-report mechanism; collected implicitly through user interactions, eye tracking, or other passive tracking methods; or modeled through a model of human behavior. Collecting such information allows quantifying and formalizing details about the analyst's cognitive state while using the IML system, including cognitive load, vigilance and other factors. This information can be fed into the system to further calibrate it, ensuring that users remain engaged but not overwhelmed [8].

4 Challenges in Automated Map Labeling

Automatic map labeling is a common application in GIS systems where the goal is to place labels in the best arrangement possible. Map labeling has been shown to be an NP-complete problem, requiring these algorithms to rely on heuristics and statistical measures. Machine learning approaches, both traditional and interactive, also face challenges in solving this problem. If a digital map display can be viewed at different scales and combinations of visible layers, it can result in a near infinite number of possible map views. Such a large problem space requires massive amounts of training data before it can generate layouts with good label positions and with any level of certainty. In an interactive setting (such as in SmartMaps, described in Sect. 2.3) a user would need to spend a great deal of time editing a digital map display before enough data could be collected to generate a preferred display automatically in a wide variety of situations.

We will now describe some ongoing research aimed at speeding up model convergence in an automated map labeling system. In particular, we will consider ways of modeling user preferences using cognitive feedback to calibrate a map display and to introduce a new approach for communicating features and concepts with the algorithm through a shared language.

Modeling User Preferences. Complex digital displays require large amounts of training data before they can effectively predict good label placements and the variety of scales and layer combinations that could possibly be displayed. It is not always practical to collect many examples through an IML approach. An alternative approach is to train the model using synthetic data generated from simulated user interactions modeled after observed user behaviors, combined with expert knowledge and heuristic rules. This approach generates a variety of label placements that are considered a good guess for an average user, but then can be further refined as a user interacts with the map and makes changes to the display.

Cognitive models have a long history in human-computer interaction community for modeling human interactions with an interface [5,12,14]. More recent work also considered how cognitive models can be used to generate synthetic data for training a machine learning algorithm [3,17]. Drawing on these lines of research and existing research in map preferences and best practices [11,19], we can design a cognitive model that simulates an analyst iteratively identifying poorly placed labels or cluttered areas and then moving labels to locations with preferred properties. By using a cognitive model to simulate an analyst making label adjustments on a digital map, the IML algorithm can be initialized with some basic information about features important for generating good label placements, without taking an analyst's time. As the system is used, the machine learning model will be further fine-tuned with information about the analyst's preferences and interactions, the current task and the other relevant features so that it can continue to learn and improve its map generation model.

Cognitive Feedback in Digital Map Editing. Data about the analyst's cognitive state can provide additional information that can be used to improve map display generation systems. Cognitive inspired features, such as visual saliency and eye-tracking trajectories, have previously been shown to improve the performance of machine learning algorithms learning to play video games [15]. Future research should explore how similar data, either modeled or collected from eye trackers and mouse trackers, could be used to improve machine learning for automated map displays. Such information could provide insights into the cognitive state of the user. For example, a cognitive model could be used to estimate a user's subjective perception of clutter [7], the cognitive load of editing the map, or completing a specific task using the map interface [12]. This data could then be used to constrain the problem space, or fed into a machine learning model so that it can identify new statistical features that are useful in generating better map displays.

Concept Learning and Evolution in GIS Systems. In many IML workflows, it is common to face a situation where the underlying features being used to classify a region or identify a label placement change over time. In an automated map labeling scenario, this need may be because the current task has changed, or the map is very different from any training data that was already collected. When this situation occurs, it would be helpful to have a shared language in which to reason with the algorithm about the underlying features.

As a proof of concept, consider the group of shapes depicted on the left in Fig. 5. These are grouped together in a way that is identifiable as a face. This grouping can be described to both the algorithm and the user as a set of defined concepts about the different parts. To the algorithm, the concepts are represented in a spatially-attributed graph that can learn the possible ranges of attributes for each concept. Different spatial relationships result in different groupings, some that are recognizable as a face. Once these ranges have been established, the algorithm can then generate new potential faces, and human-readable descriptions of why it thinks the grouping makes a face representation. A human can review the results, and if the generated groups do not represent a face, they can use the shared language to describe why not, or possibly introduce the algorithm to a new concept that it is not yet aware of. Through this explainable interface, the algorithm uses the human's expertise to update its representations, adding or removing concepts and changing the attribute ranges as needed, and improving its accuracy over time [13].

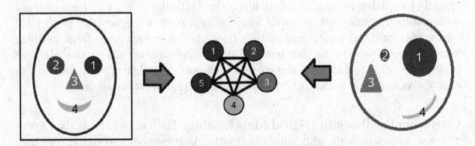

Fig. 5. Both the grouping on the left and the right-hand side of the image contain the same shapes and can be represented with a spatially attributed graph. However, details about the shape sizes and spatial relationship to one another determine whether the grouping is recognizable as a face.

This idea of using a shared language to describe concepts can also be applied in a map labeling scenario. For example, the map labeling algorithm may place an airport label in a certain spot that matches the features learned so far, but is still not ideal from the analyst's perspective. The algorithm and analyst can then communicate in the shared language to first understand why the algorithm placed the label where it did, and then either refine the feature representation or teach it about any relevant features not yet in its representation. In this way, the model is able to learn and adapt to the analyst's needs and preferences.

5 Conclusion

In this chapter, we discussed how interactive machine learning can be beneficial for GIS systems and the design considerations that are important in their development. Many GIS systems are interactive by nature, requiring analysts to confirm identified regions or objects. Other GIS applications benefit by learning user preferences as they interact with the system. We considered three types of GIS applications: airfield change detection, geographic region digitization, and digital map editing. Through these use cases, we demonstrated several techniques that can improve the usability of a system and the productivity of the human-machine team overall. These techniques included uncertainty models, problem constraints, user preferences and cognitive feedback. We also described the complex problem of automated map labeling and discussed three areas of ongoing research aimed at using an interactive machine learning approach to make these problems more tractable. In particular, we discussed modeling user preferences to generate synthetic data, using cognitive feedback to fine-tune machine learning models, and described a method for using a shared language with which the analyst and algorithm can use to communicate about concepts. We believe that this work will encourage continued research and development towards improved interactive machine learning systems for GIS applications.

References

1. Balboa, J.L.G., López, F.J.A.: Generalization-oriented road line classification by means of an artificial neural network. Geoinformatica **12**(3), 289–312 (2008)
2. Bastani, F., et al.: Machine-assisted map editing. In: Proceedings of the 26th ACM SIGSPATIAL International Conference on Advances in Geographic Information Systems, pp. 23–32 (2018)
3. Bourgin, D.D., Peterson, J.C., Reichman, D., Russell, S.J., Griffiths, T.L.: Cognitive model priors for predicting human decisions. In: International conference on machine learning, pp. 5133–5141. PMLR (2019)
4. Do Nascimento, H.A., Eades, P.: User hints for map labeling. J. Vis. Lang. Comput. **19**(1), 39–74 (2008)
5. Fleetwood, M.D., Byrne, M.D.: Modeling the visual search of displays: a revised act-r model of icon search based on eye-tracking data. Hum. Comput. Interact. **21**(2), 153–197 (2006)
6. Karsznia, I., Sielicka, K.: When traditional selection fails: How to improve settlement selection for small-scale maps using machine learning. ISPRS Int. J. Geo-Inf. **9**(4), 230 (2020)

7. Lohrenz, M.C., Trafton, J.G., Beck, M.R., Gendron, M.L.: A model of clutter for complex, multivariate geospatial displays. Hum. Factors **51**(1), 90–101 (2009)
8. Michael, C.J., Acklin, D., Scheuerman, J.: On interactive machine learning and the potential of cognitive feedback. In: 2nd Workshop on Deep Models and Artificial Intelligence for Defense Applications (2020)
9. Michael, C.J., Dennis, S.M., Maryan, C., Irving, S., Palmston, M.L.: A general framework for human-machine digitization of geographic regions from remotely sensed imagery. In: Proceedings of the 27th ACM SIGSPATIAL International Conference on Advances in Geographic Information Systems, SIGSPATIAL 2019 (2019)
10. Munro, R.: Human-in-the-loop Machine Learning. O'REILLY MEDIA, Newton (2020)
11. Opach, T., Korycka-Skorupa, J., Karsznia, I., Nowacki, T., Golebiowska, I., Rod, J.: Visual clutter reduction in zoomable proportional point symbol maps. Cartography Geog. Inf. Sci. **46**(4), 347–367 (2019)
12. Paik, J., Pirolli, P.: Act-r models of information foraging in geospatial intelligence tasks. Comput. Math. Organ. Theory **21**(3), 274–295 (2015)
13. Ruprecht, B., et al.: Concept learning based on human interaction and explainable AI. In: SPIE Defense and Commercial Sensing (2021)
14. Salvucci, D.D.: Modeling driver behavior in a cognitive architecture. Hum. Factors **48**(2), 362–380 (2006)
15. Saran, A., Zhang, R., Short, E.S., Niekum, S.: Efficiently guiding imitation learning algorithms with human gaze. arXiv preprint arXiv:2002.12500 (2020)
16. Stoter, J., et al.: Methodology for evaluating automated map generalization in commercial software. Comput. Environ. Urban Syst. **33**(5), 311–324 (2009)
17. Trafton, J.G., Hiatt, L.M., Brumback, B., McCurry, J.M.: Using cognitive models to train big data models with small data. In: Proceedings of the 19th International Conference on Autonomous Agents and MultiAgent Systems, pp. 1413–1421 (2020)
18. Weibel, R., Keller, S., Reichenbacher, T.: Overcoming the knowledge acquisition bottleneck in map generalization: The role of interactive systems and computational intelligence. In: Frank, A.U.., Kuhn, W. (eds.) COSIT 1995. LNCS, vol. 988, pp. 139–156. Springer, Heidelberg (1995). https://doi.org/10.1007/3-540-60392-1_10
19. Yoeli, P.: The logic of automated map lettering. The Cartographic J. **9**(2), 99–108 (1972)

Faithful Post-hoc Explanation
of Recommendation Using Optimally Selected
Features

Shun Morisawa[✉] [ID] and Hayato Yamana [ID]

Waseda University, 3-4-1 Okubo, Shinjuku, Tokyo, Japan
{hiroshun,yamana}@yama.info.waseda.ac.jp

Abstract. Recommendation systems have improved the accuracy of recommendations through the use of complex algorithms; however, users struggle to understand why the items are recommended and hence become anxious. Therefore, it is crucial to explain the reason for the recommended items to provide transparency and improve user satisfaction. Recent studies have adopted local interpretable model-agnostic explanations (LIME) as an interpretation model by treating the recommendation model as a black box; this approach is called a post-hoc approach. In this chapter, we propose a new method based on LIME to improve the model fidelity, i.e., the recall of the interpretation model to the recommendation model. Our idea is to select an optimal number of explainable features in the interpretation model instead of using complete features because the interpretation model becomes difficult to learn when the number of features increases. In addition, we propose a method to generate user-friendly explanations for users based on the features extracted by LIME. To the best of our knowledge, this study is the first one to provide a post-hoc explanation with subjective experiments involving users to confirm the effectiveness of the method. The experimental evaluation shows that our method outperforms the state-of-the-art method, named LIME-RS, with a 2.5%–2.7% higher model fidelity of top 50 recommended items. Furthermore, subjective evaluations conducted on 50 users for the generated explanations demonstrate that the proposed method is statistically superior to the baselines in terms of transparency, trust, and satisfaction.

Keywords: Recommender system · Explainable recommendation · Interpretability

1 Introduction

An explainable recommendation system is a system that can explain the reason for a recommendation to users in addition to recommending items [1]. Collaborative filtering, which is a popular recommendation algorithm, is highly interpretable and can indicate the reason, such as "users that are similar to you purchased this item" and "this item is similar to your previously purchased items." These explanations improve recommendation effectiveness, transparency, and user satisfaction [2].

© Springer Nature Switzerland AG 2021
W. F. Lawless et al. (Eds.): Engineering Artificially Intelligent Systems, LNCS 13000, pp. 159–173, 2021.
https://doi.org/10.1007/978-3-030-89385-9_10

In the big data era, because recommendation becomes indispensable in assisting users to find relevant items among diverse items, highly accurate recommendation models with new algorithms have been proposed, including machine learning. Such state-of-the-art algorithms improve recommendation accuracy; however, their interpretability of the recommended items is poor. Hence, generating interpretable recommendations in addition to maintaining high accuracy has become a popular topic.

Recent studies regarding explainable recommendations can be classified into two groups according to their algorithmic approaches: model intrinsic and model agnostic [1].

The model-intrinsic approach involves the addition of an explainability-regularization term to the objective function of a matrix factorization model [3], and a method to design a recommendation model using an attention neural network to interpret the word-level importance of the texts reviewed [4]. The advantage of the model-intrinsic approach is that the explanation generated by each method is faithful to the recommendation model; however, the explainability-enabled term or function must be equipped with the original recommendation model. Hence, an individual explainability-enabled mechanism must be generated for each recommendation system.

The model-agnostic approach is also known as the post-hoc approach [5]. This approach explains the recommendation result by training the input-output pairs of the recommendation model with an interpretable model by treating the recommendation model as a black box. Therefore, it explains the recommendation result without modifying the base recommendation model. The post-hoc approach does not provide a completely accurate explanation because the interpretation and recommendation models may differ. However, this approach does not require existing recommendation systems to be modified, thus avoiding the degradation of their accuracy. Nóbrega et al. [6] proposed a state-of-the-art method known as LIME for recommender systems (LIME-RS), which applies LIME [7] to the recommendation model to explain the recommendation reasoning to users. The LIME proposed by Ribeiro et al. [7] enables the inference of a black-box model by calculating the importance of the features using a local regression model. LIME-RS improved by 8.6% in terms of the model fidelity@10, which is the metric for measuring the recall of the interpretation model to the recommendation model, compared with the baseline method using association rules [5]. However, LIME-RS can be further improved in terms of model fidelity. In addition, LIME-RS does not generate explanations to users.

In this chapter, we propose a new method to improve the model fidelity, i.e., the recall of the interpretation model to the recommendation model in a post-hoc approach. Our idea is to select an optimal number of explainable features in the interpretation model instead of using complete features because the interpretation model becomes difficult to learn when the number of features increases. We select explainable features using the forward stepwise selection method in which the feature that reduces the loss of the regression model is added individually. In addition, we develop a method to generate user-friendly explanations for users based on the features extracted by LIME. We adopt only positively affected features and exclude unmatched features with the target user or the item, followed by subjective evaluations involving humans to confirm the effectiveness of the explanation. To the best of our knowledge, this study is the first to provide a post-hoc explanation with subjective human experiments to confirm the effectiveness of the method.

The remainder of this paper is organized as follows. Related works are introduced in Sect. 2. Section 3 details the algorithm for LIME. In Sect. 4, we propose a new method to generate explanations. Section 5 presents the experimental evaluation, and Sect. 6 concludes this chapter.

2 Related Work

In this section, we introduce recent studies pertaining to explainable recommendations using the post-hoc approach. The post-hoc approach explains the recommendation result by training the input-output pairs of the recommendation models with interpretable models, i.e., it explains the recommendation result without modifying the base recommendation model. This approach may not provide a completely accurate explanation because both the interpretation and recommendation models differ. However, this approach does not require existing recommendation systems to be modified, thereby avoiding accuracy degradation seen in the model-intrinsic approach.

Peake et al. [5] proposed a method that uses association rules to interpret the latent factor recommendation model. They performed an association analysis on the relationship between each input feature value and recommended item using a trained model. They also interpreted the contribution of features to the recommended item using calculated support, confidence, and lift values i.e., the importance of rule. They then explained the usage of the feature with a high contribution of feature.

In machine learning, a method was proposed in which the model designer interprets inference using interpretable models. Ribeiro et al. [7] proposed LIME to interpret the inference of a black-box model by calculating the importance of features using a local regression model. LIME can be applied to any machine learning model.

Further, researchers have proposed a method to apply LIME to recommendation systems. Zhu et al. [8] applied LIME to a user-click prediction model of a video recommendation system for model developers to analyze features. This method is not applicable for providing explanations to the user because it explains both the negative features and features that users cannot understand. In our previous study [9], we applied LIME to a recommendation model to explain the recommendation's reason to users and proposed a method to identify important features. Furthermore, Nóbrega et al. [6] proposed a state-of-the-art method known as LIME-RS, which applied LIME to a recommendation model to explain the recommendation reason to users. Their proposed method improved by 8.6% in terms of model fidelity@10, which is a metric for measuring the recall of the interpretation model to the recommendation model, compared with the baseline method using association rules [5]. However, in LIME-RS, the interpretation model becomes difficult to learn when the number of features increases; hence, the model fidelity can be further improved. Further, they proposed only the importance of feature calculation and did not consider a method to generate explanations to provide to the target user.

3 LIME Algorithm

LIME [7] is an algorithm that explains the inference results of machine learning models, where the importance of each feature is calculated by training the input-output pairs of machine learning models based on local linear regression. This chapter describes how to explain the inference of the classification model. Furthermore, the authors' implementation[1] has been extended to explain the inference of the regression model. Algorithm 1 shows the explanation generation steps using LIME with regression models.

Algorithm 1 LIME (Revised from [7])

Input: Model f , Input vector x , number of vector samples S , Kernel width σ
Input: Number of features K
Output: Importance vector of features w
1. $Z \leftarrow \{\}$
2.   **for** $i \in \{1, 2, 3, \dots, S\}$ **do**
3. $z_i \leftarrow$ sample a vector around x
4. $Z \leftarrow Z \cup \langle z_i, f(z_i), \pi(x, z_i) \rangle$
5.   **end for**
6. $g \leftarrow$ model using K features with Z that minimize $L(f, g)$
7. $w \leftarrow$ regression coefficient of g
8.   **return** w

In LIME, a model to be explained is received, $f \in \mathbb{R}^d \to \mathbb{R}$, and input vector $x \in \mathbb{R}^d$. In addition, we set the following parameters: the number of sampled vectors, S, to prepare for training the simplified version of f, number of features, K, to train the simplified version of f, and kernel width, σ.

First, we sampled S vectors in the feature space around the input vector, x, which is the target for explaining the inference result. Next, we added each sampled input vector, z_i, the output by the model $f(z_i)$, and the locality, $\pi(x, z_i)$ between x and z, to set Z, where π is a kernel function expressed by formula (1) below. D represents a distance function, such as the cosine distance or Euclidean distance.

$$\pi(x, z) = \exp\left(-\frac{D(x, z)^2}{\sigma^2}\right) \tag{1}$$

Subsequently, we trained multiple linear regression models, $g \in G$, using K features, where z_i is the input and $f(z_i)$ is the output. The optimal interpretation model, $g \in G$, minimizes the loss function, L, shown in formula (2). Here, samples weighted by their locality are used in LIME, as shown as $\pi(x, z)$.

$$L(f, g) = \sum_{z \in Z} \pi(x, z)(f(z) - g(z))^2 \tag{2}$$

Finally, the regression coefficient of g is output and denoted as w. The larger the absolute value of each element of w, the more prominent is the effect of the corresponding feature on the prediction result. We assumed that features with positive and negative weights contributed to positive and negative output values, respectively.

---

[1] marcotcr/lime, Github, https://github.com/marcotcr/lime.

4 Proposed Method

The problems in LIME-RS [6] using LIME to explain the reason for recommendation to users, as described in Sect. 2, are as follows: (1) the interpretation model becomes more complicated and difficult to explain when the number of features increases, and (2) generating an explanation to provide to the user is not considered. We solve problem (1) by selecting an optimal number of explainable features in the interpretation model. Considering problem (2), we develop a method to generate explanations using a template that excludes features unsuitable for explaining recommendations among the important features interpreted by LIME. Figure 1 shows the schematic diagram of our method, and each step is described below.

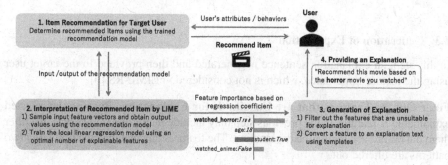

Fig. 1. Schematic diagram of our proposed method.

4.1 Item Recommendation for Target User

An arbitrarily trained recommendation model determines an item to recommend to a target user based on both the user's attribute/behavior data and the item's features.

4.2 Interpretation of Recommended Item by LIME

In this step, the reason a recommendation model recommends an item to the target user is interpreted using extended LIME.

Sample Input Feature Vectors and Obtain Output Values Using the Recommendation Model. Similar to LIME-RS, we sample input vectors by concatenating an existing user's feature representation and an existing item's feature representation to prevent unexpected outputs, i.e., to prevent the sampling of feature values that did not co-occur in the training data. Subsequently, we obtain the output values by inputting sampled vectors to the recommendation model.

Train the Local Linear Regression Model Using an Optimal Number of Explainable Features. We train the local regression model (line 6 of Algorithm 1) using the input vectors and output values obtained in the previous step to interpret the recommendation.

In LIME-RS, Nóbrega et al. [6] trained the interpretation model using all features except those that cannot be used as an explanation. Examples of features that cannot be used as an explanation include one-hot encoding of target user IDs or target item IDs; this happens because when recommending item i to user u, items other than i (or users other than u) need not necessarily be explained. Unlike LIME-RS, we use an optimal number of selected features to train the interpretation model. We select explainable K features in total using the forward stepwise selection method, i.e., select a feature one by one, in which the feature that reduced the loss of the regression model the most is added one by one. The number of features, K, is a hyperparameter that needs to be tuned to the optimum value determined. Using only an optimal number of features not only simplifies the explanation, but also increases the fidelity to the original recommended model by preventing redundant features.

4.3   Generation of Explanation

In this step, an explanation sentence is generated and then provided to the target user using the feature importance, which is not considered in LIME-RS [6].

Filter Out the Features that are Unsuitable for Explanation. Because the selected explainable K features in the previous step may include inappropriate features, we filter them out before generating the explanation. The features that matched the following two patterns are filtered out.

- Negative features: Example includes the feature "student" in Fig. 1, whose feature importance is negative. In this case, the interpretation model may explain that "you might dislike this item because you are a student." However, such a negative explanation will typically result in user dissatisfaction.
- Unmatched features with the target user or recommended item: Example includes the feature "watched_anime" in Fig. 1, when targeting a user who has not watched the anime, although the feature indicates that they have watched it.

Convert a Feature to an Explanation Text Using Templates. After filtering out some features in the previous step, we use the remaining feature(s) to generate an explanation sentence by applying them to the prepared template corresponding to the feature type. An administrator of the recommendation system freely sets the maximum number of different explanations. The following are sample templates in which the bracket is filled with values according to the corresponding feature.

- User attributes: "Recommend this item based on your gender ()."
- User behaviors: "Recommend this item based on item () that you have purchased."
- Item attributes: "Recommend this item based on category ()."

4.4   Providing an Explanation

We provide the generated explanation to the target user with the recommended item. Because our LIME-based method is independent of base recommendation models, similar to LIME-RS, it is applicable to any machine learning model. Moreover, the recommendation accuracy is not affected by adopting the LIME-based method.

5 Experiments

We applied the proposed method to two popular recommendation models: factorization machine (FM) and neural network (NN). Subsequently, we compared the proposed method with the baseline methods, LIME-RS [6], and Peake et al.'s [5] method on two metrics, namely, objective evaluation and subjective human evaluation, to confirm the effectiveness of our explanations. It is noteworthy that LIME-RS is similar to our proposed method. However, the differences are as follows: 1) our proposed model uses an optimal number of explainable features to achieve better model fidelity, and 2) our proposed method provides an option to generate the explanation text. Hence, we conducted two experiments using different metrics.

5.1 Dataset

We used the MovieLens 1M Dataset.[2] The dataset contains 1,000,209 ratings with 1–5 assigned to 3,883 movies by 6,040 users [10]. Furthermore, the dataset includes 1) the genre information for each movie and 2) the gender, age, and occupation of each user. Table 1 lists the features created using the dataset. We divided the dataset into training, validation, and test data at 60%, 20%, and 20%, respectively, depending on the order of the timestamps. We used the validation data to tune the recommendation model and the interpretation model, including the proposed method.

Table 1. List of features used for recommendation models.

Type	Representation	# Dimensions
User-ID	One-hot encoding	6,040
Movie-ID	One-hot encoding	3,883
Age	Normalized between 0 to 1	1
Gender	Female: 0, Male: 1	1
Genre	One-hot encoding	18
Occupation	One-hot encoding	21
Watched history	One-hot encoding (Before watching: 0, Watched: 1)	3,883

5.2 Recommendation Algorithms

We applied the proposed method to two different trained recommendation models: FMs and NNs, to confirm their applicability to various recommendation algorithms. The

---

[2] MovieLens 1M Dataset, GroupLens, https://grouplens.org/datasets/movielens/1m/.

hyperparameters of each algorithm were tuned by validation data. Therefore, the hyperparameters with the largest mean average precision@50 (MAP@50) in the validation data was adopted.

The first recommendation algorithm is an FM [11]. Formula (3) shows the adopted regression model. The FM trains the output value, $\hat{y}$, for the input vector, $x = (x_1, \ldots x_n) \in \mathbb{R}^n$, using both the bias parameter, $w_0 \in \mathbb{R}, w = (w_1, \ldots w_n) \in \mathbb{R}^n$, and the interaction parameter, $v_i = (v_{i,1}, \ldots v_{i,k}) \in \mathbb{R}^k$, between the input features.

$$\hat{y}(x) = w_0 + \sum_{i=1}^{n} w_i x_i + \sum_{i=1}^{n} \sum_{j=i+1}^{n} \langle v_i, v_j \rangle x_i x_j,$$
$$\text{where} \langle v_i, v_j \rangle = \sum_{f=1}^{k} v_{i,f} \cdot v_{j,f}$$

$$(3)$$

We used the Python library fastFM [12] to implement the FM and then optimized it using alternative least squares. As a result of tuning, we set the hyperparameters such that the rank of the interaction terms was 8 and the value of the L2 regularization term was 100. The evaluation results in the validation data when using these hyperparameters were as follows: MAP@50 of 0.1413, recall@50 of 0.0630, and root mean square error (RMSE) of 1.0825.

The second recommendation algorithm is a fully connected NN. We used the NN model with a structure that included two dropout mechanisms with 1024 and 64 nodes, separately. We used Python library PyTorch [13] to implement the NN. As a result of tuning, we set the hyperparameters such that the batch size was 32, learning rate was 0.001, and dropout ratio was 0.2. The evaluation results in the validation data when using these hyperparameters were as follows: MAP@50 of 0.1217, recall@50 of 0.0542, and RMSE of 1.0393.

5.3 Baseline Methods

We prepared two baseline methods: LIME-RS [6] and Peake et al.'s [5] method. Peake et al.'s method is classified as a post-hoc explainable approach that is also used as a baseline in LIME-RS. Peake et al. proposed a method of interpreting recommendations using latent factor models based on association rules (AR). To summarize, we prepared the following four baseline methods.

- **LIME-RS**: Explanation using local linear regression based on LIME, as proposed in [6].
- **Global Regression**: Explanation by global linear regression without considering the locality.
- **Local AR**: Explanation by ARs based on [5]. Let user set U be the top-10 users close to target user u. The AR criteria were set to $min\_supp = 0.1$, $min\_conf = 0.1$, and $min\_lift = 0.1$, the same as those in [5].
- **Global AR**: Explanation by ARs based on [5]. Let the user set U be all of the users in the dataset. The AR criteria were set to $min\_supp = 0.1$, $min\_conf = 0.1$, and $min\_lift = 0.1$, the same as those in [5].

5.4   Objective Evaluation - Recall of Explanation Model

In the objective evaluation, we used the model fidelity metric to compare the ratio of explainable items to the recommended items. This evaluation confirms the efficacy of the explanation model in learning the input-output relationships, similar to the original recommendation model.

Metric. We adopt the model fidelity metric in [5] to evaluate the recall ratio of the explanation model by comparing the numbers of recommended and explainable items, as shown in formula (4).

$$\text{Model fidelity}@N = \frac{|\text{recommended\_items} \cap \text{explainable\_items}|}{|\text{recommended\_items}|}, \qquad (4)$$

where recommended_items is the set of top-N recommended items by the recommendation model, and explainable_items is the set of top-N explainable items by the explanation model. When using local regression or global regression, the top-N recommended items are calculated by the regression model; meanwhile, when using local and global ARs, the top-N recommended items are extracted from the sorted association rules according to confidence. The model fidelity becomes 1.0 if and only if the top-N recommended items and the top-N explainable items are identical, meaning that the explanation model learns the recommendation model comprehensively.

We used both the FM and NN models to train the entire dataset; subsequently, both the proposed and baseline methods were applied to the trained models. In the evaluation, we calculated the model fidelity using the top-10 and top-50 recommendation items for each user in the dataset and then calculated the average to obtain the final model fidelity@50 and model fidelity@10 for each explanation model.

Parameter Tuning. We tuned the hyperparameters of the proposed method and LIME-RS. The hyperparameters are the S, σ and K shown in Algorithm 1. We tuned them according to model fidelity@50 in the validation data for each of the recommendation models of FM and NN. Figure 2 shows the model fidelity@50 when each hyperparameter is changed in FM. Since the number of vector samples is the training data of the interpretation model, the larger the S, the higher the model fidelity, and it did not change around $S \geq 9,000$. The kernel width peaked when $\sigma = 0.01$. The number of features peaked at $K = 20$ in the proposed method. On the other hand, LIME-RS does not have hyperparameter K because it uses all of the features available. We confirmed that the proposed method can obtain higher model fidelity than LIME-RS by tuning the number of features. Based on these results, we adopted $S = 10,000$, $\sigma = 0.01$ and $K = 20$ for FM. Similarly, we conducted parameter tuning for NN, after we adopted $S = 10,000$, $\sigma = 0.003$ and $K = 20$.

Result. The model fidelity@10 and model fidelity@50 with different explanation models are shown in Tables 2 and 3, respectively. The proposed method achieved the highest model fidelity@10 and model fidelity@50. We confirmed a significant difference between the proposed method and the baseline models ($p < 0.01$) in terms of both model fidelity@10 and model fidelity@50. The superior performance of the proposed method over LIME-RS confirmed that selecting the optimal number of features in the interpretation model not only simplified the explanation, but also resulted in a faithful explanation.

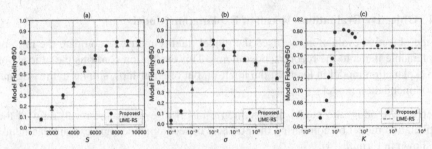

Fig. 2. Model Fidelity@50 when each hyperparameter is changed in FM: (a) Fixed at $\sigma = 0.01$, $K = 20$, and varying the number of vector samples, S; (b) Fixed at $S = 10,000$, $K = 20$, and varying the kernel width, σ; (c) Fixed at $S = 10,000$, $\sigma = 0.01$, and varying the number of features, K;

Table 2. Results of model fidelity@10.

Explanation models	Recommendation models	
	FM	NN
Proposed method	**0.8096**	**0.7966**
LIME-RS [6]	0.7790	0.7682
Local AR [5]	0.7768	0.7560
Global AR [5]	0.4990	0.5092
Global regression	0.5238	0.5218

Table 3. Results of model fidelity@50.

Explanation models	Recommendation models	
	FM	NN
Proposed method	**0.8020**	**0.7702**
LIME-RS [6]	0.7808	0.7516
Local AR [5]	0.7564	0.7200
Global AR [5]	0.4492	0.4804
Global regression	0.4804	0.4440

5.5 Subjective Human Evaluation - Explanation Evaluation

In the subjective human dimension, we evaluated the quality of the generated explanation for the recommended item through various perspectives. In this experiment, two types of recommendation models, FM and NN, and four types of explanation models, including the baseline, were used to yield eight combinations of recommendation and explanation models. We used three baseline methods except LIME-RS, shown in Subsect. 5.3, because LIME-RS does not generate explanations in a concrete manner.

Overview. We invited 50 university students to evaluate the explanation models. We presented the participants with pairs of recommended movies and their explanation texts generated using the proposed or baseline models randomly and individually, followed by a questionnaire survey to evaluate the explanation. Every participant evaluated 7–50 explanations in the ascending order of the movies recommended. Note that the participants had no information regarding the recommendation model or explanation model used. At the beginning of the experiment, each participant entered their age, gender, and previously watched movie titles in a web system that simulates a movie recommendation system. Subsequently, based on the input data, the recommendation model using the FM or NN recommended movies to the participants. At the recommended stage, the recommendation system recommended a movie with an explanation using the most crucial feature selected by the proposed or baseline method from the features shown in Table 1. The explanation texts were generated based on templates prepared in advance, as shown in Table 4. Table 5 shows the questionnaire presented to the participants, and it is based on related studies [14]. The questionnaire included the effectiveness, transparency, trust, and satisfaction of the recommendation among the seven explanatory goals defined in [15]. The participants answered each question using the following five-level Likert scale: 1. strongly disagree, 2. disagree, 3. neutral, 4. agree, and 5. strongly agree.

Result. We aggregated the proportion of the participants' five-level answers according to each question and the method used. Subsequently, we adopted a statistical test to confirm the significant difference in answers between the baseline and proposed methods using the Mann Whitney U test. Figure 3 shows the proportion of answers when using the FM for the recommendation model, and Table 6 presents the results of the statistical tests. Figure 4 depicts the proportion of answers when using NN for the recommendation model, and Table 7 lists the results of the statistical tests. We confirmed a significant difference between the proposed and baseline models ($p < 0.05$) for questions 2–6. However, for question 1, we could not confirm a significant difference between the proposed and baseline models. The explanation method with the proposed model improved the transparency, trust, and satisfaction of the user for the recommendation system, i.e., aspects that we intended to improve. However, we could not confirm from the results that the explanation provided by the proposed model had improved the user's interest in the item when compared with the baselines; however, the performance of the proposed model may be associated with that of the base recommendation system.

Table 4. Explanation of text presented to participants.

Type	Explanation text (The brackets are filled with values according to the features.)
Age	Recommend this movie based on your age ()
Gender	Recommend this movie based on your gender ()
Genre	Recommend this movie based on genre ()
Occupation	Recommend this movie based on your occupation ()
Watched history	Recommend this movie based on the movie () you watched

Table 5. Questions presented to participants.

	Rubric defined by [15]	Statement
Q1	Effectiveness	This explanation makes me interested in this movie
Q2	Transparency	This explanation improves the transparency of the recommendation system
Q3	Trust	This explanation is reliable
Q4	Trust	This explanation is correct
Q5	Satisfaction	This explanation is easy to understand
Q6	Satisfaction	This explanation is useful

Table 6. P-value for significant difference between proposed and baseline methods based on Mann Whitney U test. (recommendation model: factorization machine) Bold indicates that there is a significant difference at $p < 0.05$.

Questions	Baseline methods		
	Global regression	Local AR	Global AR
Q1: This explanation makes me interested in this movie	0.50016	0.76684	0.19267
Q2: This explanation improves the transparency of the recommendation system	**0.00004**	**0.02317**	**0.00306**
Q3: This explanation is reliable	**0.00000**	**0.00000**	**0.00000**
Q4: This explanation is correct	**0.00000**	**0.00000**	**0.00000**
Q5: This explanation is easy to understand	**0.00075**	**0.00352**	**0.00466**
Q6: This explanation is useful	**0.00069**	**0.03758**	**0.00343**

Table 7. P-values for the differences between the proposed and baseline methods based on the Mann Whitney U test (recommendation model: neural network). Bold indicates that there is a significant difference at p < 0.05.

Questions	Baseline methods		
	Global regression	Local AR	Global AR
Q1: This explanation makes me interested in this movie	0.19683	0.37392	**0.02603**
Q2: This explanation improves the transparency of the recommendation system	**0.00313**	**0.01538**	**0.00037**
Q3: This explanation is reliable	**0.00222**	**0.00450**	**0.00000**
Q4: This explanation is correct	**0.00744**	**0.00361**	**0.00000**
Q5: This explanation is easy to understand	**0.01350**	**0.01031**	**0.00376**
Q6: This explanation is useful	**0.00630**	**0.01114**	**0.00003**

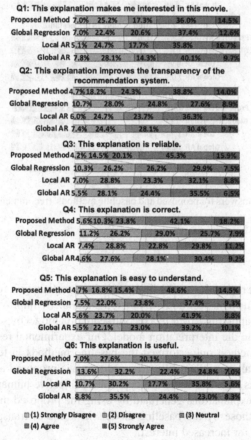

Fig. 3. Proportion of answers for proposed and baseline methods. (recommendation model: factorization machine, FM)

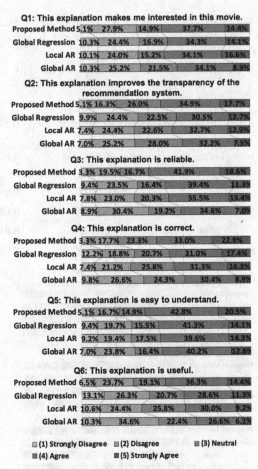

Q1: This explanation makes me interested in this movie.

	(1)	(2)	(3)	(4)	(5)
Proposed Method	5.1%	27.9%	14.9%	37.7%	14.4%
Global Regression	10.3%	24.4%	16.9%	34.3%	14.1%
Local AR	10.1%	24.0%	15.2%	34.1%	16.6%
Global AR	10.3%	25.2%	21.5%	34.1%	8.9%

Q2: This explanation improves the transparency of the recommendation system.

	(1)	(2)	(3)	(4)	(5)
Proposed Method	5.1%	16.3%	26.0%	34.9%	17.7%
Global Regression	9.9%	24.4%	22.5%	30.5%	12.7%
Local AR	7.4%	24.4%	22.6%	32.7%	12.9%
Global AR	7.0%	25.2%	28.0%	32.2%	7.5%

Q3: This explanation is reliable.

	(1)	(2)	(3)	(4)	(5)
Proposed Method	3.3%	19.5%	16.7%	41.9%	18.6%
Global Regression	9.4%	23.5%	16.4%	39.4%	11.3%
Local AR	7.8%	23.0%	20.3%	35.5%	13.4%
Global AR	8.9%	30.4%	19.2%	34.6%	7.0%

Q4: This explanation is correct.

	(1)	(2)	(3)	(4)	(5)
Proposed Method	3.3%	17.7%	23.3%	33.0%	22.8%
Global Regression	12.2%	18.8%	20.7%	31.0%	17.4%
Local AR	7.4%	21.2%	25.8%	31.3%	14.3%
Global AR	9.8%	26.6%	24.3%	30.4%	8.9%

Q5: This explanation is easy to understand.

	(1)	(2)	(3)	(4)	(5)
Proposed Method	5.1%	16.7%	14.9%	42.8%	20.5%
Global Regression	9.4%	19.7%	15.5%	41.3%	14.1%
Local AR	9.2%	19.4%	17.5%	39.6%	14.3%
Global AR	7.0%	23.8%	16.4%	40.2%	12.6%

Q6: This explanation is useful.

	(1)	(2)	(3)	(4)	(5)
Proposed Method	6.5%	23.7%	19.1%	36.3%	14.4%
Global Regression	13.1%	26.3%	20.7%	28.6%	11.3%
Local AR	10.6%	24.4%	25.8%	30.0%	9.2%
Global AR	10.3%	34.6%	22.4%	26.6%	6.1%

☐ (1) Strongly Disagree   ▨ (2) Disagree   ▨ (3) Neutral
▨ (4) Agree   ▨ (5) Strongly Agree

Fig. 4. Proportion of answers for proposed and baseline methods. (recommendation model: neural network, NN)

6   Conclusion

In this chapter, we proposed a method to generate an explanation for a recommended item to a target user using a post-hoc explanation method. We improved Nóbrega et al.'s [6] LIME-RS when applying LIME to a recommendation model by selecting an optimal number of features in the interpretation model. Our experimental results demonstrated that the proposed method outperformed the baseline methods in terms of the model fidelity, i.e., the recall of explainability. In addition, we proposed a method to generate explanatory texts from extracted features. In a subjective human evaluation using questionnaires, the explanations generated by using the proposed method yielded better responses than those by the baseline models in terms of transparency, trust, and satisfaction, but not for increased interest.

Future work includes 1) improvement of feature selection method to generate a more faithful interpretation model, 2) generation of more detailed explanation texts, such as using multiple features, and 3) online evaluations using a real recommendation system.

References

1. Zhang, Y., Chen, X.: Explainable recommendation: a survey and new perspectives. Found. Trends Inf. Retr. **14**(1), 1–101 (2020)
2. Herlocker, J.L., Konstan, J.A., Riedl, J.: Explaining collaborative filtering recommendations. In: Proceedings of the 2000 ACM conference on Computer supported cooperative work, pp. 241–250 (2000)
3. Abdollahi, B., Nasraoui, O.: Using explainability for constrained matrix factorization. In: Proceedings of the Eleventh ACM Conference on Recommender Systems, pp. 79–83 (2017)
4. Chen, C., Zhang, M., Liu, Y., Ma, S.: Neural attentional rating regression with review-level explanations. In: Proceedings of the 2018 World Wide Web Conference on World Wide Web, pp. 1583–1592 (2018)
5. Peake, G., Wang, J.: Explanation mining: Post Hoc interpretability of latent factor models for recommendation systems. In: Proceedings of the 24th ACM SIGKDD International Conference on Knowledge Discovery and Data Mining, pp. 2060–2069 (2018)
6. Nóbrega, C., Marinho, L.: Towards explaining recommendations through local surrogate models. In: Proceedings of the 34th ACM/SIGAPP Symposium on Applied Computing, pp. 1671–1678 (2019)
7. Ribeiro, M.T., Singh, S., Guestrin, C.: "Why should I trust you?" Explaining the predictions of any classifier. In: Proceedings of the 22nd ACM SIGKDD International Conference on Knowledge Discovery and Data Mining, pp. 1135–1144 (2016)
8. Zhu, F., Jiang, M., Qiu, Y., Sun, C., Wang, M.: RSLIME: an efficient feature importance analysis approach for industrial recommendation systems. In: Proceedings of the 2019 International Joint Conference on Neural Networks, pp. 1–6 (2019)
9. Morisawa, S., Manabe, T., Zamami, T., Yamana, H.: Proposal of recommendation reason presentation method in recommendation systems. DBSJ Jpn. J. **18**(3), 1–8 (2020) (in Japanese)
10. Harper, F.M., Konstan, J.A.: The MovieLens datasets: history and context. ACM Trans. Interactive Intell. Syst. **5**(4), 1–19 (2016)
11. Rendle, S.: Factorization machines. In: Proceedings of the 2010 IEEE International Conference on Data Mining, pp. 995–1000 (2010)
12. Bayer, I.: fastFM: a library for factorization machines. J. Mach. Learn. Res. **17**, 1–5 (2016)
13. Paszke, A., et al.: PyTorch: an imperative style, high-performance deep learning library. Adv. Neural. Inf. Process. Syst. **32**, 1–12 (2019)
14. Chang, S., Harper, F.M., Terveen, L.G.: Crowd-Based personalized natural language explanations for recommendations. In: Proceedings of the 10th ACM Conference on Recommender Systems, pp. 175–182 (2016)
15. Tintarev, N., Masthoff, J.: Explaining recommendations: design and evaluation. In: Ricci, F., Rokach, L., Shapira, B. (eds.) Recommender Systems Handbook, pp. 353–382. Springer, Boston (2015). https://doi.org/10.1007/978-1-4899-7637-6_10

Risk Reduction for Autonomous Systems

Tony Gillespie$^{(\boxtimes)}$ (iD)

Electronic and Electrical Engineering Department, UCL, London, UK
anthony.gillespie@ucl.ac.uk

Abstract. Systems with a physical instantiation which can cause harm to people have well-established methods to ensure their safe use. These rely on the system being reliable, reproducible and having predictable behaviour. This is no longer the case if it has machine learning processes which can change its behaviour during use. This non-deterministic behaviour introduces new technical, legal and financial risks into every aspect of concept, design, manufacture and use. Three critical questions are raised from a technologist's perspective: what is the relevant legal framework; how to model non-deterministic behaviour; and how actions are authorized. Addressing them shows that there must be a separation of ML-based decisions and authorizations to act. System design must inherently limit its behaviour so that it is legal, safe and effective. It is shown that the real-time control architecture 4D/RCS can provide this assurance in both civil and military systems. The principle risk areas are identified, showing that organisations and individuals will have to accept new responsibilities. It will need the technical and legal professions to collaborate to understand and define acceptability both within a country and internationally before there can be widespread use of machine learning methods after the initial design is approved for general use.

Keywords: Risk · Safety · Systems engineering · Legal responsibility · Design

1 Introduction

1.1 Society's Current Acceptance of Control Systems

A control system which links its output directly to its inputs must have repeatable and predictable responses to the same inputs; it may be a complex non-linear coupling but should be repeatable, i.e., the system is deterministic. Unexpected behaviours may happen and be difficult to diagnose, the so-called wicked problem, but these usually arise because of the complex interactions between multiple deterministic systems with many inputs which cannot be reproduced exactly for successive tests. Deterministic control systems may be designed to give step changes in output triggered by measured or calculated thresholds. These operations by a control system can be described as the control system making decisions and acting on them.

Society accepts the consequences of a deterministic system's actions provided it is operated by an authorised person. Simple systems may only require that the user takes reasonable care, whilst complex systems such as cars and aircraft require formal

© Springer Nature Switzerland AG 2021
W. F. Lawless et al. (Eds.): Engineering Artificially Intelligent Systems, LNCS 13000, pp. 174–191, 2021.
https://doi.org/10.1007/978-3-030-89385-9_11

licensing of the operator. The regulatory and legal processes following an accident are also well-established for assigning responsibilities to a human or an organisation, and deciding compensation, and imposing more sanctions if necessary.

1.2 More Recent Problems

Artificial Intelligence (AI) systems can be and are used to provide information for the human operator, who decides how to respond. A car's satellite navigation system illustrates this; *en-route* instructions are recommended which can be followed or ignored at the driver's discretion. The system is a decision-aid and only indirectly part of the control system, so it may be non-deterministic. The ability of Machine-Learning (ML) processes to refine their operation after their introduction can be a desirable feature for decision-aids, essentially mimicking humans learning from experience and improving their performance.

It is safe to assume that AI techniques will evolve and become ever-more attractive for many applications including taking control of highly automated systems. When this introduces more autonomy in the control system there are at least three problems: data provenance must be known if it is to be used for analysis or system training; ML introduces unpredictability into the system's behaviour; and the basis for decisions are not necessarily clear or explicable to a human. Without effective human oversight, the proposed system will be authorised to take actions based on non-deterministic and opaque processes. This autonomy undermines the basis of society's acceptance of complex control systems given in Sect. 1.1.

Systems controlled by AI and ML will need detailed scrutiny due to the likely consequences of their actions. The legal framework for autonomous systems is the subject of debate in the legal [1] and technical communities [2]. Legal, financial, and criminal risks cannot be ignored by an organisation participating in any aspect of AI and ML-based products which can harm people.

Autonomy is also under consideration for weapon systems, and is the subject of expert discussions at the United Nations with an aim of restricting their use [3]. Responsibility for the consequences of the use of any weapon system must be assigned to a human military commander under International Humanitarian Law (IHL). One of the main criteria for any international agreement is to keep this principle of human responsibility. However for future more-autonomous weapons, this responsibility may have to lie with the non-military weapon suppliers, a significant change to the current position. This presents very similar technical problems to the non-military case although under a different legal framework.

1.3 Ethical Guidelines

Problematic ethical issues are discussed in [4]. Terminology can also be a problem, "autonomy" is used here to mean the freedom to act independently of humans; this is a behaviour based on decisions which may be made using AI, and ML as decision-aids or enablers. Regardless of exact definitions. technologists must recognise the requirement for a System Of Systems (SOS) approach with society and its expectations as the highest level system.

All professions have codes of conduct for an individual's behaviour whilst performing their duties although a breach of them is not necessarily an offence. Two examples are in [5] and [6]. They rely on individual integrity for adherence to the code. Generic guiding principles have been published for AI but have not been formally adopted by professional institutions [7] and [8].

Standards and regulations for product design and services take several years from initiation to publication. Those for new technologies usually need significant revisions in the first years after their introduction. Standards for autonomous systems in general are being drafted by several bodies including ISO, IEEE and the Underwriters Laboratory.

Developers of autonomous systems entering service in the next few years cannot wait for future standards and regulations due to commercial timescales. They must base their work on current legal instruments, keeping a close eye on the future. Some methods are available [9] to derive requirements and guide their legal implementation. However it will be shown in this chapter that the introduction of autonomy into products and services will make significant changes to professional responsibilities and changes in emphasis in technical developments.

2 Critical Questions

This chapter examines the issues in Sect. 1 from a technologist's point of view. The analysis starts with society at the highest level in a System Of Systems (SOS) architecture, setting the basic approach to the design and operation of the proposed control system. The issues in Sect. 1.1 lead to three critical questions which are identified here and addressed in subsequent sections.

Discussions about autonomous systems can easily become debates about ethical philosophies for such a system. Although interesting, they do not help the orgnisation designing the system. Debates about moral frameworks for a particular country may help but are still of little use in firming up a design. There is, however, one specific question which will act as a business driver: if this new product causes an accident, will a company, its directors or employees be taken to court and have to pay damages or even, will the company or its agents be shown to have broken a law. Underpinning this problem is the first critical question:

Critical question 1: Which laws apply to machine-made decisions and the consequent actions?

An autonomous system performs the role of a human with specific skills which may be superior to those of any human. In order to build trust, each affected person needs some level of understanding of how the machine works, which can come from a mental model of the system and an appropriate level of situational awareness. This understanding operates at several levels; the user may only need a simple model of its operation with little knowledge of how the algorithms work; maintainers must have a detailed knowledge of how the system should work; whilst system developers will develop complex models. All affected people will need assurance that the system has been thoroughly tested in all likely use-cases before use.

When setting goals, the user anticipates the system's likely courses of action using a mental model, comparing actual behaviour with their predictions. As humans and ML-based systems are non-deterministic, it is convenient to model both using psychological models of the human brain. If these are used, then, by extension, it is advantageous for the system architect to use the same ones to identify functions and specify the sub-systems to perform them. The second critical question is:

Critical question 2: Can theories of human decision-making provide sufficient trust for a human to design and use a non-deterministic system safely?

Almost all states will not allow responsibility for the consequences of an action to lie with a machine; their courts look for the responsible person or human organisation[1]. Although there is legal debate about the necessity for new laws, an accident inquiry is unlikely to accept that no human was responsible for the system's actions.

By definition, no human can make consistently correct predictions of a non-deterministic system's behaviour; inaccurate predictions are a risk. However, as with any risk it is possible to derive risk mitigation strategies for each human or organisation. This situation leads to a requirement to identify the humans responsible for every action taken by the system and the constraints on its actions. Those peoples' responsibilities and consequent liabilities then becomes part of the SOS design. The third question follows:

Critical question 3: Who or what authorizes actions based on the results of non-deterministic decision-making processes?

3   Which Laws Apply to Machine-Made Decisions and Consequent Actions?

This Critical Question is actually difficult to answer as AI and ML are enabling technologies with many applications. Turner [10] recognizes this circumstance, posing three legal questions and arguing for a regulator established by legislation. Pagallo [11] discusses the problems of applying existing laws to sophisticated AI systems. Ethical standards and professional codes of practice apply to all applications but are generic and difficult to apply directly to a specific application area as part of law.

There are a few highly-regulated application areas making significant progress, such as UAVs, rail transport and defence, which set high standards for human authorisation of action with mandatory regulations controlling human-machine interactions, and extensive use of safety-critical systems. The commercial reality of this type of application area is that there are relatively few customers, and all of them have similar requirements. Product or service development timescales are long, and both customers and suppliers liaise extensively with the regulatory authorities[2]. These constraints do not apply widely.

---

[1] The UK has a concept of corporate responsibility which in restricted circumstances assigns responsibilities to the board of directors who must implement any sanctions imposed by a court.

[2] In the case of small UAVs/drones, regulators responded as rapidly as possible and made their potential needs known. Manufacturers who evolved solutions to meet them now have an advantageous position compared to those that did not.

There are strong commercial pressures for ML to be widely used in control systems with less strict regulatory regimes than those mentioned in the last paragraph. Self-driving cars are a well-publicised example and lawmakers are sympathetic to this problem. Several nations have passed legislation or introduced specific regulations to allow extensive road testing but still a long way from road vehicles with full autonomy in unconstrained environments [12]. These laws and regulations are specific to that nation as are all road regulations. For example, a recent report reviews other nations' approaches with their pros and cons when applied in Singapore [13]. Baker *et al.*have reviewed regulatory approaches across the world which present a useful review of the range of approaches across many jurisdictions [14].

The car's control system must be reliable, with complex human interactions in all road, traffic and weather conditions. McDermid [15] gives five main technical problem areas: limitations on sensor capabilities; lack of agreement on training, testing and validating ML; ML operating on, and learning new behaviours from, "the open road" which may not necessarily be safe; regulation; and social acceptability through clear demonstration of safety. Ethical decisions and actions by the car's control system should also be added to this list as it will have to make complex decisions to avoid or minimise harm to humans.

The United Nations (UN) World Forum for Harmonization of Vehicle Regulations is addressing autonomous vehicles [16] and has proposed Regulation 157 for an Automated Lane Keeping System (ALKS). This will allow a car to operate autonomously, but with under the supervision of a human driver and with tight restrictions on speed and road conditions [17]. Adoption of Regulation 157 by a nation, in common with all other UNECE regulations, must be incorporated in that nation's laws [18]. Road vehicle designers routinely meet the national laws of all countries where their products are sold, but this is for current laws and deterministic systems.

The Law Commission[3] and Scottish Law Commission in the UK have examined the UNECE Regulation 157 and how it will fit into UK law [19]. They see the need for a body which is responsible for the autonomous car's safety (Automated Driving System Entity – ADSE[4]) but also recognise that introducing ALKS into cars is only one example of the wider legal problems with ML-based autonomous systems. Their concerns are shown by their Consultation Question 54:

---

[3] The Law Commission is a statutory independent body that aims:

- to ensure that the law is as fair, modern, simple and as cost-effective as possible.
- to conduct research and consultations in order to make systematic recommendations for consideration by Parliament, and.
- to codify the law, eliminate anomalies, repeal obsolete and unnecessary enactments and reduce the number of separate statutes.

Taken from About us I Law Commission accessed 13 April 2021.

[4] The term ADSE is used to describe the entity which puts the automated driving system forward for authorisation and is responsible for its safety. This may be the vehicle manufacturer, or software designer, or a joint venture between the two.

We provisionally propose that:

(1) product liability law should be reviewed to take account of the challenges of emerging technologies;

(2) any review should cover product liability as a whole, rather than be confined to automated vehicles: It should not, therefore, form part of this project on automated vehicles.

Do you agree?

It can be concluded that the answer to Critical Question 1 is that it is not clear which laws apply to non-deterministic systems in the general case.

We can assume that most nations' legal frameworks will have a general or specific requirement for a product to be fit-for-purpose with sanctions if it is not. There would appear to be no reason why this should not apply to non-deterministic systems. The question is which organisation or person will be the subject of the sanctions and the implications for them. The people or organizations will include:

- the regulator if there is one;
- the person specifying the product;
- the subsystem suppliers and their suppliers;
- the system integrator who integrates the subsystems;
- the product's design authority who releases the product for use;
- the maintainer;
- the user and/or owner; and
- the organisation imposing updates after inquiries

When the system can adapt its behaviour, the user can no longer be assured of its actions whilst in use. Whilst the law is unclear, this uncertainty brings financial risk for all the organisations involved, which they will want to assess and mitigate.

Can guidance be found in the practices in the highly regulated applications? Two areas are examined here, both showing their early stages of evolution with continuation of critical examination of a systems behaviour, assigning liability for failures by it to an organization or a person.

3.1 Unmanned Air Vehicles (UAVs) and Drones

Large, mainly military Unmanned Air Vehicles (UAVs) appeared in the early 2000s following extensive research programmes. There is an international framework for use of airspace, the International Civil Aviation Organization (ICAO). UAV developers liaised with their national regulators and solutions found that restrict the use of UAVs but allows them to perform effective missions. Deterministic UAV control is still a pre-condition although non-deterministic techniques can be anticipated.

Small (less than 250 kg), cheap drones[5] were unregulated for several years until their proliferation and technical enhancements raised safety and privacy concerns. There are many risk headings: collision with aircraft, harm to people and property on the ground, less-than competent users, control when not visible to the user, and privacy when used with cameras. Early Federal Aviation Authority (FAA) regulations came into . force around 2012 [20] but 'final' rules come into force in April 2021 [21] with extensive regulations covering those risks. As with large UAVs, deterministic control systems are a precondition.

3.2   Lethal Autonomous Weapon Systems (LAWS)

The use of UAVs in military operations led to considerable ethical debate and Governments demonstrating adherence to IHL with specific military personnel making all lethal decisions[6]. Their use is now widely accepted, but there are widespread concerns about technology developments which may allow their use without a human in control. See for example Human Rights Watch's recent work [22].

The UN have established a Group of Governmental Experts (GGE) examining the problems of controlling Lethal Autonomous Weapons (LAWS) and if existing IHL is adequate [23]. Their 2019 report presents eleven guiding principles [24]. These are not yet part of IHL but show the way it is evolving. The most relevant ones for technologists are:

(b) *Human responsibility for decisions on the use of weapons systems must be retained since accountability cannot be transferred to machines. This should be considered across the entire life cycle of the weapons system;*

(c) *Human-machine interaction, which may take various forms and be implemented at various stages of the life cycle of a weapon, should ensure that the potential use of weapons systems based on emerging technologies in the area of lethal autonomous weapons systems is in compliance with applicable international law, in particular IHL. In determining the quality and extent of human-machine interaction, a range of factors should be considered including the operational context, and the characteristics and capabilities of the weapons system as a whole;*

(d) *Accountability for developing, deploying and using any emerging weapons system in the framework of the CCW[7] must be ensured in accordance with applicable international law, including through the operation of such systems within a responsible chain of human command and control;*

---

[5] The term UAV is usually taken to mean a large aircraft (greater than about 250kg) and drone to mean much smaller aircraft.

[6] A lethal decision is generally taken to mean one that reaults in severe injury or loss of human life.

[7] CCW is the generally accepted abbreviation for the 1980 Convention on Prohibitions or restrictions on the use of Certain Conventional Weapons Which My be Deemed to be Excessively Injurious or to Have Indiscriminate Effects. It is relevant here because the GGE are examining whether that Convention is suitable for restricting the use of LAWS.

The guiding principles do not separate decisions and actions, but it is reasonable to assume that the accountability is for resultant actions.

Principle (b) allows a machine to make a decision, but the responsibility for the consequences of its actions lie with a yet-to-be-determined human. If implemented, this rule extends the responsibilities for lethal decisions to human involvement across the whole life-cycle, into areas which have only had indirect involvement before such as: specification; design; test; and support. Principle (d) emphasizes the existing requirement for authority to be only through a responsible Command and Control (C2) chain. These two, when combined with the inclusion of system development and SOS approach required in (c) will bring significant changes to the responsibilities and liabilities across the whole procurement system; these non-military organisations will have direct liabilities under IHL, a significant legal and financial risk. Risk mitigation processes will be needed.

Figure 1 comes from the 2018 GGE discussions and shows how they see the way that humans interact with LAWS through the design cycle (Human touchpoints). We can conclude that the GGE for LAWS sees a need for change in IHL as technology evolves, demonstrating that the legal position of autonomy in military applications is unclear.

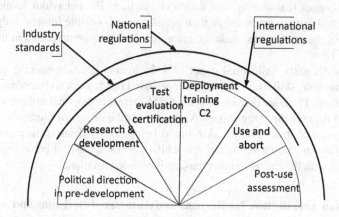

Fig. 1. Human touchpoints for Lethal Autonomous Weapons (LAWS)

4 Are Theories of Human Decision-Making Applicable to Non-human Systems?

Modelling the human brain and its decision-making processes predates the advent of AI and ML by many years if not decades. The approaches are summarised here, both to understand human decisions and actions and then to show that they can be used to analyze the authorization of action by autonomous systems.

4.1 Models of Human Decision-Making

Three-part models of human decision-making are widely used, the three stages being: awareness, understanding and deliberation. Boyd [25] added an "Act" part to give the

OODA-Loop (Observe, Orient, Decide and Act) which is used widely in discussions about autonomous systems. Its components are:

Observe the relevant parts of the environment using all available sensors;
Orient. Interpret the results from the Observe function and relate them to the intended goal;
Decide which action to take, using judgement to assess options and choose the one most likely to achieve the goal; and
Act. Execute the action.

Situational awareness is essential for effective behaviour. It is defined as [26]:

The perception of the elements in the environment within a volume of time and space, the comprehension of their meaning, and the projection of status in the near future.

Predictions of changes in the environment are essential for the person to achieve their goals. The changes may due to their action or inaction. The behaviour levels indicate the person's authority to act based on their predictions of possible futures. Judgement is used to assess the predictions, make an informed decision and an action at the correct time.

Rasmussen's early, influential paper [27] on human decision-making gave three levels of behaviour: skill; rule; and knowledge-based behaviours with increasing levels of sophistication. These are consistent with OODA and are orthogonal to them: the person at each level follows the three stages. Analogies can be drawn to increasing levels of sophistication in control systems: skill-based being purely deterministic automation; some flexibility in rule-based behaviour; whilst knowledge-based behaviour requires interpretation with flexible responses making it non-deterministic.

4.2   Common Architecture for Humans and Automated Decisions and Actions

System analysis should always be based on a hierarchical architectural approach. The architecture should drive the design process, driving requirements definition for all functions and subsystems. It should evolve with technology changes. Increased automation to act on decisions is delegating authorisation to act from the human to the machine, necessitating requirements changes for the nodes taking the action.

The 4D/RCS architecture [28] uses the three-part human brain model to describe both automated and human nodes. It has been used successfully to model the military command chain from high command levels down to the actuators in armoured vehicles. Goertzel *et al.* [29] compare it favourably with other cognitive architectures. They note that it is not a good detailed model of the brain in its original version, but it can be modified to mimic brain structure when the nodes in the hierarchy are implemented by Cortical Computational Units.

It may be concluded that 4D/RCS gives adequate description of both the brain and hardware implementation of autonomous systems. As human mental processes can be non-deterministic, 4D/RCS is taken as an adequate basis for human, AI and ML processes in autonomous systems. A single node is shown in Fig. 2 and a simple hierarchy in Fig. 3.

The Sensory Processing (SP) function corresponds to Observe in the OODA loop and the World Modelling (WM) function to Orient. The Behaviour Generator (BG) and Value Judgement (VJ) functions perform the Act function, the division of subfunctions depending on the application. Sensory information is processed at each level and passes up to the higher level. Action is controlled by the BG chain which is emphasised in Fig. 3.

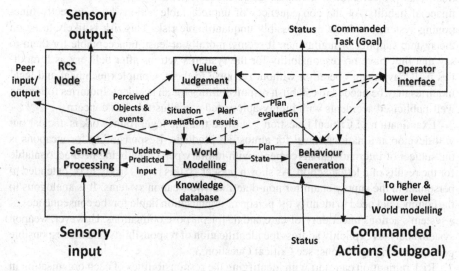

Fig. 2. A single 4D/RCS node

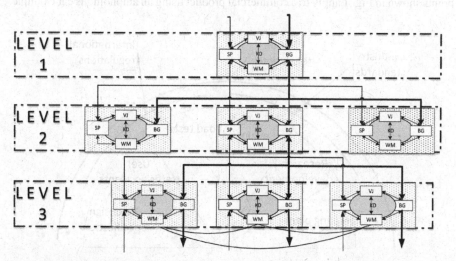

Fig. 3. A 4D/RCS node hierarchy. Each node has been simplified and the authorisation chain down the BG functions is emphasised.

There is an ongoing exchange of data in the Knowledge Databases (KDs) between the nodes at the same level in the hierarchy.

5   Minimising Risks in a Non-deterministic System's Supply Chain?

Commercial considerations and risk/cost/benefit analyses drive investment in AI applications. Most development risks for non-deterministic systems should be quantifiable using traditional project control methods. Unquantifiable risks give problems for investors; financial liability for the consequences of unpredictable actions by a correctly functioning system is a large and possibly unquantifiable risk. This risk is likely to be on the system supplier or maintainer. It seems, morally at least, unacceptable for them to say that they have no responsibility for the system's actions after delivery as it modifies its behaviour in operation without recourse to them. Complex technical and legal inquiries may be needed to establish responsibilities for an accident. Inquiries following well-publicised accidents with highly-automated cars illustrate this concern.

Examination of Critical Question 1 showed that the legal framework is unclear but will develop at a national level for almost all products. Responsibility for weapons is the subject of international agreements with military personnel being held accountable for the results of a lethal action. As shown in Sect. 3, this risk is likely to be extended to personnel in the supply chain for non-deterministic weapon systems. It is analogous to the commercial need to identify the person or organisation liable for the consequences of a system's actions under duty-of-care and fit-for-purpose obligations. However, weapon system analyses explicitly address the identification of responsibility and the responsible person authorising actions; see Critical Question 3.

Risk mitigation can start with identifying the responsibilities of each organisation in the relevant supply chain. Figure 4 shows how the UN approach using the human touch points shown in Fig. 1 apply to a commercial product using an autonomous car example.

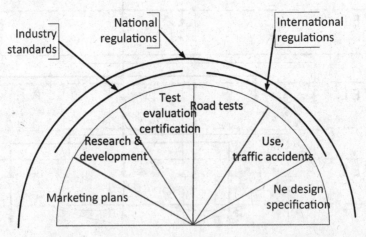

Fig. 4. UN GGE on LAWS human touchpoints applied to autonomous cars

The classic method of preventing harm by a machine is to limit its actions by hardware or software methods. Different ethical principles can be implemented in code to determine the range of allowable decisions when presented with a difficult choice. The principles were found to be mutually inconsistent in their choices but it illustrates the subjectivity of initial choices [30]. The ethical governor for autonomous weapons developed by Arkin [31] tests actions against ethical criteria but with limited success due to problems interpreting and implementing IHL in software.

A different approach using system architectures has been proposed by the author [9]. It was applied to autonomous road vehicles [32] using the 4D/RCS architecture in a hierarchy such as that in Fig. 3. The highest level is the owner, or despatching authority for hire cars, with successively lower levels having more restricted capabilities, their sum being the capability of the autonomous system. Each node, down to the lowest actuator levels, can then be divided into two main parts: one implementing decisions as actions; and one with a current world model based on inputs and stored data, and predicting the effect of possible implementations of the commands from the immediately higher node. This division is indicated in Fig. 5.

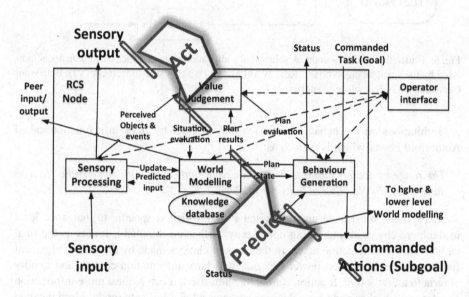

Fig. 5. Division of 4D/RCS node into predictive and act parts

Decomposition of the functions in Fig. 5 as second tier functions and subsystems depends on the application. Figure 6 gives an illustrative breakdown of the Value Judgement and Behaviour Generator functions which are responsible for system actions. It shows the users intent entered as success criteria; the world model is used to make predictions of the N consequences of each of the available choices to implement them. Comparison with the success criteria results in M ($<N$) possible actions which are ranked in order of preference for action against the success criteria.

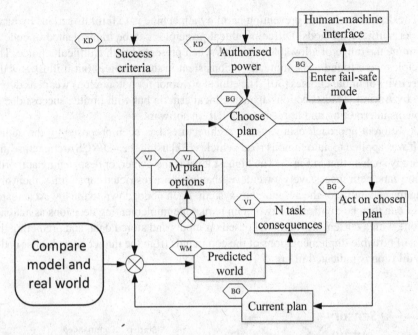

Fig. 6. Illustrative 4D/RCS node. A subsystem's allocation to node functional elements is indicated by the small hexagon boxes. Key: World Model (WM), Value Judgement (VJ), Behaviour Generator (BG), Knowledge Database (KD)

Limitations on the behaviour of each node are set by rules in a function called Authorised Power which is defined as:

The range of actions that a node is allowed to implement without reference to a superior node. No other actions are allowed.

Every node must have an Authorised Power which is specific to that node level in the hierarchy, with increasing complexity further up the chain. It acts as the final authorisation of any action taken on the basis of choices made by the value judgement functions. The authorised power function will have information-content and quality criteria to allow action. If action cannot be authorised, it can request more information or refer to its higher node for a decision or enter a local fail-safe mode. More detailed discussion of its operation in an autonomous car is given in [32]. It can be seen that the behavioural limits on the SOS will be the sum of the limits in the authorised powers in all its subsystems.

Authorised power is only one possible method to limit the power of a node. Regardless of the method used, the use of a 4D/RCS-based analysis brings out the following elements for risk mitigation:

- Human commands at the top level will be decomposed into more detailed goals for successively lower levels with appropriate reaction timescales;

- Using hierarchical levels allows a clear distinction to be made between human and automated decisions;
- A node can identify missing information from its decision-making process and request more, or it can refer to a higher node for permission to act on partial information;
- A hierarchy level can be defined as having purely deterministic decision-making and authority to act without reference to higher levels;
- When a level cannot be defined as purely deterministic, the designer must decide how its actions can be limited;
- ML changes to decision-making within a node can only be accepted if the node can demonstrate to a higher node, or human, that it will still meet its fixed authorised power (or equivalent using other techniques); and
- Using the same node definition at every level simplifies design changes to introduce non-deterministic methods into a node by changing its level in the hierarchy.

The highest node will have more subjective limits requiring human decisions. Working down the levels identifies where human intervention is essential, changing to supervisory and then full automation at the lowest levels. Each node can be identified as having deterministic or non-deterministic behaviour. If the SOS or large parts of it are designed using the classical Vee diagram or by spiral development, the most appropriate test and validation methods can be decided for each node.

6 Minimising Risks in a Non-deterministic System's Supply Chain?

Autonomous cars with driver supervision will be taken as a specific example and only risks specific to ML features will be considered here. These are given here for each of the roles in Fig. 5.

6.1 Regulator

It is assumed there will be a national regulator for each country with ML added to their regulatory powers. The regulator will need to develop skills in AI and ML techniques. There will be the management risks involved in adding a new skillset to an organisation, but additionally they will almost certainly need a capability in auditing ML processes for clarity of explanation of their results and use of data sources for training purposes when in service. Auditing techniques are not yet mature, representing a large risk.

It is likely that they will have to add checks on behaviours to existing or new regular vehicle safety tests to ensure evolving ML processes remain safe.

6.2 Marketing and Design Specifier Roles

Human Machine Interfaces (HMI) are a key issue here. Drivers can already store their preferred options for GPS routes, displays, performance/economy modes. An ADS (Automated Driving System) could extend this to provide context-dependant information and warnings recognizing the driver's level of attention. There will be a range of risks arising from a mismatch between the driver's expectations of the car's behaviour from experience and the behaviour that the ML decides the driver is expecting.

There will be philosophical decisions about specifying obstacle avoidance and assessment of relative probabilities of collision with different obstacle types. It can be assumed that these will evolve with time so the decisions will be about extensions to the then-current practice. Regulatory risks will arise from extending the ML-derived behaviours too far from that practice.

6.3 System Specifier for Supply Chain

It can be expected that the manufacturer will perform an SOS analysis to give an initial design and verification of performance before entering detailed design. It is essential there is a firm definition of the ML capabilities, if any, in every subsystem, their training, validation and limitations on behaviour. Risks come from suppliers not giving full visibility of their intellectual property or explanations of AI decisions due to commercial sensitivities. The risk to the supplier is their liabilities for financial penalties beyond their ability to pay. The risk to the integrator is that the deficient supplier may cease business, leaving financial problems and a critical lack of technical understanding of the subsystem design.

6.4 Integrator and Design Authority

It can be anticipated that the regulators will proscribe a range of tests and trials for the car. These will balance simulation, physical and connectivity tests on the car when the regulator accepts that the car can enter the market safely. The risk is whether post-sale ML processes change the ADS's behaviour so that the car no longer meets the scope of the design authority's safety certification.

There may be an AI version of the 'wicked problem' where ML at different nodes uses different criteria for their operation and one attempts to compensate for what is perceived as a degradation in performance by another. Resolving these problems will be analogous to the project risks inherent in integrating a complex system.

6.5 Manufacturer

Production runs are both high volume and over man years with some changes made almost every year in response to marketing feedback. All normal risks of component and operating system updates apply plus those arising from updates to ML algorithms using new training data, feedback from the regulator, and results of accident enquiries.

The integrator's design authority certified performance and behaviour at the start of manufacture. The manufacturer must ensure that they have a recognised and empowered design authority for the lifetime of the vehicle who is acceptable to the regulator. This assurance will carry a litigation risk which will be reflected in the sales price.

6.6 Owner/Maintainer/Driver

The separation between these roles will depend on the business model applicable to each car; sole owner, fleet ownership, car hire are three examples, with different allocations of responsibilities. Risks will be of two types: ensuring that the ADS is kept at the manufacturer's required software and algorithmic configuration; ensuring that the driver is competent to drive the car in its upgraded state and gives any required feedback on its performance.

6.7 Updates to Requirements

These are ones arising from accident inquiries and other external recognised authorities. There are commercial risks from the cost of implementation. One other risk is that an enquiry may make a recommendation that results in a technically unsound implementation [33].

7 Discussion and Conclusions

Restricting discussion to AI and ML implementation in physical systems raises the societal issues arising from systems causing harm to people or objects. These have legislative penalties, representing a financial and personal risk if the technical risks are not reduced to As Low As Reasonably Practical (ALARP). Large risks arise from changes in the system's behaviour due to ML processes and inputs based on analysis of large data sets.

Examining ML in autonomous cars illustrates the risks for a mass-production, long lifetime product. It has been shown that both technical and legal professions recognise that there are significant risks. There are no long-term legal, legislative or technical agreements on how to deal with them although there is activity by both professions and in both civil and military fields.

It has been shown that if a system is trained during its development and production, it can in principle be demonstrated to a regulatory authority that it is safe to use and will continue to be so if it is not allowed to continue adapting its behaviour after that time. There is the difficult technical problem of validating its changed performance, but that is not a legal one.

The autonomous car example illustrates the general expectation that they will upgrade their performance whilst in use. There should not be a technical problem with the safety of a limited number of AI systems that use ML to adapt behaviour in use; configuration control and user training are likely to be practical and cost-effective but these solutions, although necessary, do not read across easily into autonomous cars.

Litigation under national laws results in the identification of the person or organisation responsible for any failure in design or use and happens regularly for deterministic systems. IHL which covers weapons identifies the responsible individual and whether they acted in accordance with it. Section 6 shows that allowing ML to evolve with mass-produced non-deterministic systems produces many new types of risk requiring new regulatory and technical solutions for risk reduction.

History shows that aerospace technologies have developed symbiotically with their regulatory frameworks. The legal and regulatory frameworks for commercial drones and LAWS continue to evolve, introducing new responsibilities for technologists. The immaturity of technology and legislation shows that all relevant professions need to work together to reduce risks to acceptable levels.

It can be concluded that the risks identified in Sect. 6 should be used as a starting point for cross-disciplinary collaboration to allocate risks to specified types of organisation. The responsible parties and authorities can then address the issues and take the appropriate financial, technical, and procedural action to reduce risk to an acceptable level. The interpretation of 'acceptable level' needing liaison with the legal profession so that there is a clear basis for the inevitable litigation.

References

1. Law Commission Discussion Paper 253 and Scottish Law Commission Discussion paper 171: Automated Vehicles: Consultation Paper 3 - A regulatory framework for automated Vehicles; A joint consultation paper. Accessed 30 Apr 2021
2. Artificial Intelligence Index Report 2021, Chapter 5 Ethical Challenges of AI Applications, Stamford University Human Centred Artificial Intelligence. 2021-AI-Index-Report_Master.pdf (stanford.edu). Accessed 28 April 2021
3. Information is available at the UN GGE on LAWS website Background on LAWS in the CCW – UNODA. Accessed 27 Oct 2021. https://www.un.org/disarmament/the-convention-on-certain-conventional-weapons/background-on-laws-in-the-ccw/
4. IEEE Standards Association Ethically Aligned Design, 1st edn. Ethically Aligned Design, First Edition (EAD1e) Infographic (ieee.org). Accessed 30 Apr 2021
5. IEEE Code of ethics. IEEE - IEEE Code of Ethics. Accessed 30 Apr 2021
6. Engineering Council and Royal Academy of Engineering Statement of Ethical Principles. Statement of Ethical Principles 2017.pdf. (engc.org.uk). Accessed 310 Apr 2021
7. Future of Life Institute, The Asilmolar Principles. AI Principles - Future of Life Institute. Accessed 30 Apr 2021
8. The Toronto Declaration, Available at The Toronto Declaration • Toronto Declaration Toronto Declaration. This Declaration was published on 16 May 2018 by Amnesty International and Access Now, and launched at RightsCon 2018 in Toronto, Canada. Accessed 30 Apr 2021
9. Gillespie, T.: Systems Engineering for Ethical Autonomous Systems, 1st edn. SciTech, London (2019)
10. Turner, J.: Robot Rules – Regulating Artificial Intelligence, 1st edn. Palgrave-Macmillan, London (2019)
11. Pagallo, U.: The Law of Robots: Crimes, Contracts, and Torts, Law, Governance and Technology Series 10. Springer, Dordrecht (2013). https://doi.org/10.1007/978-94-007-6564-1
12. Waymo Robot take the wheel: Waymo has launched a self-driving taxi service. The Conversation, October 14, 2020 8.10pm BST, Robot take the wheel: Waymo has launched a self-driving taxi service. theconversation.com. Accessed 19 Mar 2021
13. Singapore Academy of Law, September 2020, Report on the Attribution of Civil Liability for Accidents Involving Autonomous Cars. Available at Report on the Attribution of Civil Liability for Accidents Involving Autonomous Cars (sal.org.sg). Accessed 19 Mar 2021
14. Baker, S., Theissen, C.M., Vakil, B.: Connected and autonomous vehicles: a cross-jurisdictional comparison of regulatory developments. Robot. Artif. Intell. Law. 3(4), 249–273 (2020)
15. McDermid, J.: Autonomous cars: five reasons they still aren't on our roads. The Conversation July 2020 Autonomous cars: five reasons they still aren't on our roads. theconversation.com. Accessed 16 Mar 2020

16. UNECE Intelligent Transport Systems website: Automated driving, UNECE. Accessed 13 Apr 2021
17. The 2021 proposals are: Proposal for Supplement 1 to the original version of UN Regulation No. 157 (Automated Lane Keeping System) Submitted by the Working Party on Automated/autonomous and Connected Vehicles Based on ECE/TRANS/WP.29/2020/81 (unece.org). Accessed 16 Mar 2021
18. UNECE Global Forum for Road Traffic Safety (WP.1) Resolution on the Deployment of Highly and Fully Automated Vehicles in Road Traffic, available at Road Traffic Safety I UNECE. Accessed 13 Apr 2021
19. The Law Commission and Scottish Law commission, December 2020, Automated Vehicles: Consultation Paper 3 - A regulatory framework for automated vehicles, available at Automated Vehicles I Law Commission. Accessed 13 Apr 2021
20. Official documents over this period are available at: Policy Document Library (faa.gov). Accessed 10 Apr 2021
21. FAA news release 'FAA Announces Effective Dates for Final Drone Rules', 12 March 2021. FAA Announces Effective Dates for Final Drone Rules. Accessed 10 Apr 2021
22. Human Rights Watch Stopping killer robots – Country positions on banning fully autonomous weapons and retaining human control, 10 August 2020. https://www.hrw.org/report/2020/08/10/stopping-killer-robots/country-positions-banning-fully-autonomous-weapons-and. Accessed 18 Mar 2021
23. United Nations Office for Disarmament Affairs Background on LAWS in the CCW – UNODA. Accessed 18 Mar 2021
24. Annex III to the Final Report on the 2019 meeting of the High Contracting Parties to the Convention on Prohibitions or Restrictions on the Use of Certain Conventional Weapons Which May Be Deemed to Be Excessively Injurious or to Have Indiscriminate Effects, 13 December 2019. CCW/MSP/2019/9 - E - CCW/MSP/2019/9 -Desktop (undocs.org). Accessed 18 Mar 2021
25. Boyd, J.R.: The essence of winning and losing, Unpublished lecture notes. 12(23), 123–125 (1996). Slides. http://pogoarchives.org/m/dni/john_boyd_compendium/essence_of_winning_losing.pdf. Accessed 16 Mar 2021
26. Endsley, M.R.: Theoretical underpinnings of situational awareness. A critical review. In: Endsley, M.R., Garland, D.J. (eds.) Situational Awareness Analysis and Measurement, pp. 1–24. Lawrence Erlbaum Associates, Mahwah (2000)
27. Rasmussen, J.: Skills, rules, and knowledge; signals, signs, and symbols, and other distinctions in human performance models. IEEE Trans. Syst. Man. Cybern. SMC-13(3), 257–266 (1983)
28. Albus, J., et al.: 4D/RCS Version 2.0: A Reference Model Architecture for Unmanned Vehicle Systems, NIST Interagency/Internal Report (NISTIR), National Institute of Standards and Technology, Gaithersburg, MD (2002). https://doi.org/10.6028/NIST.IR.6910. Accessed 4 June 2021
29. Goertzel, B., Ruiting, L., Itamar, A., Hugo De Garis, H., Chen, S.: A world survey of artificial brain projects, Part II: biologically inspired cognitive architectures. Neurocomputing 74(1–3), 30–49 (2010)
30. Bonnemains, V., Saurel, C., Tessier, C.: Embedded ethics: some technical and ethical challenges. Ethics Inf. Technol. 20, 41–58 (2018). https://doi.org/10.1007/s10676-018-9444-x[
31. Arkin, R.: Technical Report GIT-GVU-07-11. Governing Lethal Behavior: Embedding Ethics in a Hybrid Deliberative/Reactive Robot Architecture (2006)
32. Gillespie, T., Hailes, S.: Assignment of legal responsibilities for decisions by autonomous cars using system architectures. IEEE Trans. Technol. Soc. 1(3), 148–160 (2020)
33. Haddon-Cave, C.: The Nimrod Review. HM Government report ordered by the House of Commons to be printed 28th October 2009, paragraph 23 of the Executive Summary. https://www.gov.uk/government/uploads/system/uploads/attachment_data/file/229037/1025.pdf

Agile Systems Engineering in Building Complex AI Systems

Subrata Das[✉], Zainab Ali, Sai-Nishant Bandi, Ankush Bhagat,
Nithya Chandrakumar, Pritesh Kucheria, Mariella Pariente, Anand Singh,
and Blake Tipping[✉]

AdventHealth Consumer Analytics Team, Orlando, FL , USA
{Subrata.Das,Blake.Tipping}@AdventHealth.com

Abstract. The process of building a complex Artificial Intelligence (AI) system must address two issues to guarantee its correct functioning: 1) the software engineering errors that are inadvertently introduced during the building of the system; and 2) the inherent uncertainty in finding a solution that generates actionable insights due to the application of AI techniques in building complex and interdependent modules. The first issue is addressed with the help of both a declarative approach to programming and the modularization of many complex algorithms, all in the form of libraries. However, the second issue calls for an incremental, agile-system engineering approach without fully committing to its development path, which is uncertain.

In this chapter, we detail a scrum-based agile approach that we pursue at AdventHealth to build intelligent data products in the consumer analytics space to better serve our patients. We make use of natural language processing (NLP) in conjunction with cutting-edge machine learning (ML) and deep learning (DL) techniques to build various data products, including an understanding of consumer needs, their grievances, and how well we serve our consumers. Each sprint of our agile approach typically incorporates formulation of the problem or the revision of a previous formulation, a time-consuming data preparation involving large, noisy, and incomplete data, and analysts' evaluation of the system to provide feedback. Our overall experience with the agile approach is its quick turn-around time for incremental deliverables, where meeting the requirements of our stakeholders.

Keywords: Artificial Intelligence · Agile approach · Scrum framework · Systems engineering · Machine learning · Natural language processing

1 Introduction

A traditional waterfall [16, 24] software engineering project starts with a full specification of a system's design before the actual implementation, and then the progress is subsequently tracked. However, both the specification and the expected outcome in a computational AI system are often vague. This indefiniteness is due to the accuracy being misdriven by noisy and incomplete data, as well as by the performance of the available algorithms to run against the data. With this being the case, an AI project would have to

© Springer Nature Switzerland AG 2021
W. F. Lawless et al. (Eds.): Engineering Artificially Intelligent Systems, LNCS 13000, pp. 192–208, 2021.
https://doi.org/10.1007/978-3-030-89385-9_12

be agile in nature [3, 8], but with an evolving expectation. Our focus in this chapter is this latter aspect of systems engineering.

Healthcare Analytics is a fast-paced industry to be in these days. During the early spike of concern from Covid, the analytics team at AdventHealth had a unique challenge to help provide quick actionable insights to leaders for addressing needs of consumers interfacing with our Health System. Our goal was to find all areas pertaining to Consumer Analytics, find all of the entry points during the consumer journey, and disseminate the effective information needed to calm concerns down. This approach helped the health system to gauge consumer needs and plan appropriate resources (moved testing locations, testing scheduling, vaccines, nurse calls, etc.). The AI driven analytics[1] dashboard helped leaders to take quick actions, i.e., whether to staff more Nurses at a particular region, innovate with telehealth consultations, or initiate self-service chatbots and guided chat consultations.

Requirements arose from multiple teams, all with strict deadlines and conflicting priorities changing all of the time. Business departments rely on quick and easy visibility to data in order to make executive decisions around their programs. Traditional project management, while providing exact deliverables in one major push, takes too long for teams with these types of requests. They need reports, dashboards, and interactive predictive modeling tools in an ad hoc fashion. This situation is where the Scrum framework and an Agile mindset come into play.

At AdventHealth, we pursue a scrum-based agile approach to building data products that better serve our patients. Most of our NLP related products so far involve machine and deep learning-based document classification techniques, including NBC (Naïve Bayesian Classifier), Linear SVC (Support Vector Classifier), sequential LSTM (Long-Short Term Memory), and attention-based BERT (Bidirectional Encoder Representations from Transformer) models (see Sect. 4.4 for detail references). A potential project kicks off with a high-level specification from the product's owner. The development team is cross-functional in nature with analysts, developers, and data scientists. A big part of most of our projects is to prepare the data, labelled by our analysts. We emphasize supervised learning to achieve a higher accuracy, but at the high cost of labeling upfront. Both active and semi-supervised learning are augmented to enhance agility in our process. We monitor and adjust the course of a project plan on a daily basis, incorporating feedback from various subjective and objective evaluations for actionable insights.

The feedback from stakeholders via our product's owner is a vital part of the process. At the end of every sprint, we incorporate any such feedback, resulting in either increasing or lowering the expectations for the data-science product, keeping the rates of false positives and missed detections in mind. We have realized that the earlier in the lifecycle a design decision is corrected, the less costly the project becomes in terms of the total effort. We often abandon using deeper, more complex models and settle for slightly lower performing traditional ML models to save the time for further development and evaluation.

---

[1] Analytics and data fusion are two sides of the same coin [5, 6].

The rest of the chapter is organized as follows. The next section describes a consumer analytics scenario as a context to explain our agile approach. Section 3 provides a background of the agile and scrum framework. Section 4 makes a strong case for scrum-based agile approaches to ML-based data product developments, and it describes our specific application of ML techniques to the development of data products. Section 5 details our agile data ETL (Extract, Transformation, Load) process and AI system implementation environment. Section 7 details the incremental validation and feedback process.

2 Consumer Analytics Scenario and Agile Process

The section provides details of a consumer analytics application that we have been developing by applying the agile process. Using the application as the context, alongside, the section also provides an informal run-through of the agile process before describing it formally.

The intent behind this application was to find the reason for consumers reaching out to a Care Advocate (CA) through the AdventHealth App or Patient Portal. The team read through de-identified consumer chats to get a broad view of what the consumer needs and obstacles were, and what CA actions were being taken to help the consumer. The initial questions which acted as a guide to help us label messages were as follows.

- Having Difficulty with a Dr.'s Office?
  Example labeling of messages: Payment Options, Insurance, Appointments
- Is Sharing of Medical Records Difficult?
  Example labeling of messages: Films, Labs
- Do Patients with Chronic Conditions use the Service Most?
  Example labeling of messages: Thread Length, Condition/Chronic illness, Age
- Are Lab Results Explained to the patient?
  Example labeling of messages: Lab Results, Labs Review
- Are Drug Side Effects and Interactions Being tracked?
  Example labeling of messages: Drug Interactions, Contra-Indications

Having a broad context was helpful in guiding the team to focus on the needs of the consumer within each message thread.

To determine the topic labels, we used the keyword list compiled with the product team as a starting point. We split up the chats per consumer among four analysts on the team. Each person labeled topics individually, then came together to compare similarities and to determine the prevalence of each topic among the chats. The initial keywords were grouped into relevant topics. For example, the broad topic of "Scheduling" could contain keywords like appointment, reschedule, availability. Using keywords helped the team find and label relevant messages faster. We added more samples as needed to increase accuracy until the classification of chats had a minimum peer-validation accuracy of 75–80%.

The agile process starts with collecting questions from the business, the team, as well as consumer chats. Anyone with knowledge of the subject can contribute questions which sets up the context for the work on which the team will iterate. Priorities on what question(s) the team will focus on are set by the stakeholder at sync-up sessions prior to the start of a new sprint cycle, where we review progress as well as the next priorities. Seemingly simple questions kick off the process of formulating a hypothesis that works well as a feature story used in the Agile framework. The feature story is broad enough for the team to determine the data and tools that will be needed, as well as what initial tests, experiments, and validations should be done. The team will iterate until the model reaches 75% to 80% accuracy under a peer validation. If the accuracy does not reach the target, a determination is made to adjust the direction based on our findings.

The first question the team focused on was, "What are consumers reaching out to Care Advocates about?" The first order of business was getting the data sample for the team to analyze consumer chats. The initial data pull had the chats out of context which made it difficult to determine what the consumers need was. We restructured the data request so we could see the chats per consumer over the lifetime of the account. Once we settled on how to structure the format, the output was automated for us to analyze on the set cadence. This simple change gave us more context and allowed the team to formulate more questions.

- Should we label per message, per thread, per day?
- How to we determine when a topic has changed?
- How do we determine if the topic has been addressed?
- What are the broad topics?
- What are the more specific topics?

The team designed tests and experiments to address each of these questions by first reading through de-identified consumer chats per consumer account. To determine the topic labels, we split up the chats per consumer among four analysts on the team. Each person labeled topics individually, then came together to compare similarities and to determine the prevalence of each topic among the chats read through. The initial consumer topics went through several iterations all the while getting feedback from stakeholders at every iteration.

Once the topics were agreed upon, the team started to label chats. We kept track of which consumer accounts were being labeled so these could be removed from the validation data set. Once the chats were labeled, the data was prepared, cleaned and ready to become the first training set. The ML model was trained and then tested on the validation set. At this stage the team starts to iterate on the training set by using the validation of the ML output to determine if we needed to add more samples for a label or to drop a label due to it not being sufficiently prevalent or too narrow. The results of the validations became triggers on whether chats should be added to better train the model, resulting in a better training set.

After the team has iterated to desired target accuracy, the results are presented in the form of insights that could be gleamed from the resulting data model. Team analysis are presented in PowerPoint to the stakeholder at the sync-up sessions where the stakeholder gives feedback and gives further direction. If it is determined the insights will benefit from a dashboard, a prototype is spun up and presented to the development (dev) team for their feedback and approval. The dev team determines specifications and development cycles to integrate NLP features into the dashboard.

From beginning to end, this process took approximately five 2-week sprints on which the team iterated through data collection and preparation, analysis and testing, validation, and presentation. This timeline does not include the dashboard development portion of the process. The feature is complete when the team hits the target accuracy and produces a useful model of analysis that prompts more questions on which to start the next feature as shown in the example below.

Table 1. Example of a feature process

Feature stories	Question	Hypothesis	Findings	Conclusions
Consumer topics	What are consumers reaching out to Care Advocates about? How can we serve them better by resolving their issues?	Consumers seeking help will consistently express what they need in the first few exchanges through chat messages	Consumers indeed express their need in the first few exchanges; however, it is rare that the need is one-dimensional. For example, the consumer expresses in need for their prescription, but the problem is they cannot get a hold of the doctor's office to update the script	Adding a hierarchical approach is helpful in capturing both the consumer's need as well as the obstacle. This approach is flexible enough to capture more than one need or obstacle per thread, i.e., a group of chats in one day

3   Agile and Scrum: The State-of-the-Art

Using a Scrum framework, with a fast-acting and dedicated development team, business users can expect to get viably useful products in a short few weeks. Setting up a sprint for our AI initiatives at AdventHealth, we review the requests from the business in priority order. We then discuss the various efforts that need to take place and convert them into tasks small enough for one person to address. Once the tasks are understood, we add the highest prioritized request as a story in our Sprint Backlog. We continue discussing stories until we have either grabbed two weeks' worth of work, or have exhausted the current list of requests.

Also, thanks to Scrum, development teams avoid getting burnt out by so many incoming business requests, because they have a process by which to begin and account for their work. Referring to Fig. 1 as a process guide, all new requests get logged by a Product Owner from the business into the Product Backlog. We call these requests User Stories.

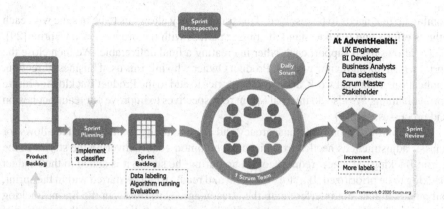

Fig. 1. The scrum framework (ref: scrum.org [28]).

User Stories in the Product Backlog require Backlog grooming sessions between the Development team (Analytics team members delivering the requested story), the Scrum Master (who facilitates the entire Scrum process and is involved in every step), and the Product Owner. In these sessions, stories are broken down into their smallest achievable deliverables, and receive a priority from the business (i.e., As a Call Center Director, I need a report to show me my team's monthly turnover rate, so that I can conduct a capacity assessment. Priority 1). The Product Backlog is then reordered based on business priority [17].

When work is set to begin on new stories from the backlog, there is a timespan for the work known as a Sprint (lasting anywhere from 1–4 weeks). This timespan sets the cadence for the business and the development team so there is an understanding of when to expect new stories to be delivered [29]. The Sprint is kicked off by a Sprint planning session. This session is where the Product Owner and the Development team review items from the Product Backlog in a priority order, to determine what will be achievable within the Sprint [29]. The Dev team decides what is achievable based on team capacity and story size. Story size is discovered within the Sprint planning session by identifying tasks needed to be done to complete the user story, and how long each task will take. There are many methods to determine story size, including Planning Poker [22], Fibonacci Scale [23], number of days, or simply a Small/Medium/Large estimate. Once the prioritized user story is sized and its requirements are understood by the team as ready to begin, they put the story into the Sprint Backlog. This process continues until the story points committed to are as close to our team's capacity for the sprint as possible. Once you get to a point where no more stories can be started due to size, we all review the Sprint Backlog and commit to the assignments. These tasks are expected to be delivered to the business by the end of the sprint.

Throughout the Sprint timebox (in our team, we do 2-week sprints), the dev team will have daily Scrum Standups, which are fifteen-minute meetings where they report to each other what work has been done, what work will be started next, and what blockers stand in the way of their work. Within our daily standups, we review the Sprint Backlog listing of our user stories and their tasks, and discuss items being worked on per person. We determine the progress being made, and if anyone needs assistance or has an impediment coming up that needs to be resolved. This transparency allows us to be in sync with each other's efforts and to understand the bigger picture with the progress of the sprint [29]. It also allows us to support each other in creating a final deliverable. We then close the sprint with a Sprint review with the Product Owner who informs us of business direction, application of our past work, and any new stories to add to the Product Backlog for future sprint planning. We also do internal Sprint retrospectives to improve our team's cohesion and processes.

This approach promotes transparency and accountability for the team and allows for a faster adjustment as needed to achieve the common goal (delivering the stories in the Sprint Backlog). If a new request comes up during the sprint, it is added to the Product Backlog to be prioritized. If a story is urgent and ready, it can be started within the sprint, but only if it does not interfere with the already agreed to stories in the Sprint Backlog (and in the dev team has the capacity available for it). If it will interfere, then an item of equal size and lower priority must be taken out of the Sprint Backlog (agreed to by the Product Owner) and put on hold for a future Sprint.

Once the Sprint is over, the dev team will meet with the business team for a Sprint review, where they will share what user stories were completed. Any incomplete stories or next steps requested in the Sprint Review session will be added to the Product Backlog to be reviewed in the next Product Backlog grooming session. After the Sprint Review, the dev team will meet and conduct a Sprint Retrospective session, where they discuss and document what went right, what went wrong, and what areas of improvement were discovered during the Sprint (a Lessons Learned meeting). This entire Scrum process then continues again by starting a Product Backlog Grooming session to prepare for the next Sprint.

There are many reporting tools that come with a Scrum framework. One useful tool is the Scrum Board [32], which shows user stories being worked on, who is working on them, how long they have been worked on, and what remaining work is left. You can also report a Burndown Chart [27] to managers and executive leadership to show the amount of work remaining in a sprint, and whether or not the team is going to reach their sprint goals. It also assists with capacity planning to determine if teams are being over/under-utilized, or if business users are adding on user stories mid-sprint. Outside of these main tools, you can use your existing artifacts mentioned above, including the Product Backlog, the Sprint Backlog, and the Sprint Retrospective.

4   Scrum for Machine Learning: A Necessity

The agile process that we have adopted incorporates AI/ML model-based analytics. This section explains why the "incremental" and/or "staged" development within sprints is paramount due to the uncertainty at various points in the process. We will use incremental and staging developments interchangeably, but there is a subtle distinction. For example, if we increase our desired level of accuracy or add more samples into the training data set, then the process is incremental. On the other hand, if we replace the adopted algorithm with a more complex and efficient one, then it is not incremental but rather a next stage.

The structure of this section is as follows. Subsection 4.1 provides a high-level view of model-based analytics. Subsection 4.2 details the process of building an AI/ML-based analytics system, indicating the sources of uncertainty at various stages that dictate an incremental approach. Subsection 4.3 digs down deeper, focusing on the supervised and semi-supervised ML-based model building process and, again, the sources of uncertainty within the process. In the final subsection, we mention the specific set of ML/DL techniques that we have used for the application described in Sect. 2.

4.1 Model-Based Analytics

Our approach to analytics is model-based [6] as shown in Fig. 2. Inferences for description, prediction, and prescription, in the context of a business problem, are made through a combination of symbolic, sub-symbolic, and numerical representations of the problem, together forming what we call a computational model. Structured input in the form of transactions and observations is fed into an inference engine for the model to produce analytical results. If the input is textual, as is the case for most of our problems, structured information needs to be extracted via, for example, word embedding or word2vec modeling.

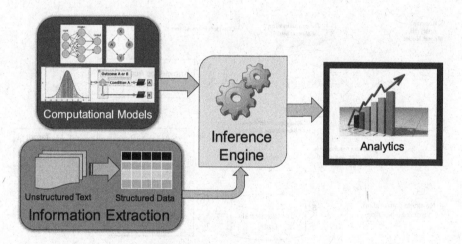

Fig. 2. Model-based analytics

So how do we build these models? Traditional statistical models are in the form of mathematical equations such as regression analysis and probability density functions. We expand this narrow view by including models that are internal to human analysts, with the hope of mimicking human reasoning at super-human speeds.

4.2 Agility in Analytics System Development

By observing various business processes and events as they unfold, and by interacting with peers and with business processing systems (such as transaction and information processing systems and decision support systems), business analysts form internal mental models of the things they observe and with which they interact. In our example scenario, care advocates interact with patients via a chat app that our business analysts are fully aware of.

These mental models require more expressive graphical constructs and linguistic variables for their representation. They provide predictive and explanatory power for understanding the specific situation at hand (e.g., specific consumer state or requirements), for which there may not be any mathematical formulae. This situation implies that one needs to capture the mental model of an analyst in order to "automate" the situation-understanding and prediction process. Computational models can also be viewed as patterns that are embedded within huge volumes of the transactional data continuously being generated by many business processing systems. Such models can therefore be extracted or learned via automated learning methods. For example, a regression equation is extracted automatically from observations of the dependent and independent variables. In our specific example of a business problem, the model for the consumer state or requirement classification is extracted from the chat data via machine learning. We have been dealing with a variety of models built on graphical constructs and linguistic variable symbols.

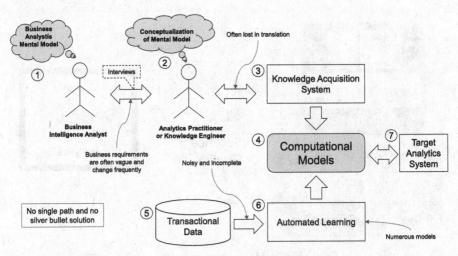

Fig. 3. Uncertainty in the process for building AI/ML-based analytics systems

In the consideration of capturing a business analyst's mental model or in learning models automatically from large volumes of data, one must consider the following steps, as depicted in Fig. 3. We have highlighted the need for incremental or staged development, wherever necessary, and hence the agility in the process.

1. The business analyst's mental model: **This model is what we want to capture. This step is optional since we rely on an ML-based model for the classification of the consumer state as detailed in the next subsection.**
2. The analyst practitioner's or knowledge engineer's conceptualization of that mental model: **Here the process is essentially incremental, as the mental model cannot possibly be extracted by the practitioner in a single sitting, and the practitioner**

will often be back to be interviewed based on the feedback from the model performance.

3. The knowledge acquisition system [9] that captures the analyst's mental model for description, prediction, and explanation of situations: **There will be a choice to be made of an appropriate acquisition system, associated with its representational power, among several and hence multiple stages.**

4. The computational models for the target analytics system: **Here the choice of models will be many, so if one model does not perform well, then select the next. The point is that the process of selecting the best occurs in stages. In our case, for example, we tried with traditional ML based classification techniques, such as NBC and linear SVC as well as deep models such as BERT and LSTM.**

5. Input transactional data if it exists: **Here we spent almost 80% of our time in selecting the source, extracting relevant features, and, most importantly, cleaning the data. Finding the relevant data sources, extracting features, and cleaning are done incrementally.**

6. The automated learning system to be used or created to extract computational models from input transactional data: **Here our approach follows the traditional process for building machine learning models. We shall argue in the next subsection that the process is incremental due to several points of uncertainty within it.**

7. The target analytics system that uses the computational models: **Here the feedback from a stakeholder incrementally trickles down the process chain of building the model and the system.**

As shown in Fig. 3, the knowledge engineer helps to transform an analyst's mental model into the computational model of a target system. However, this transformational process, via knowledge acquisition, is a serious bottleneck in the development of knowledge-intensive systems, and in AI systems in general. Computational representations that are complex in structures and semantics do not naturally lend themselves to an easy translation from mental models.

4.3 Agility in Machine Learning Model Development

Most of the learning techniques we have adopted are supervised, meaning that instances are given with known labels (the corresponding correct outputs). The learning process described in Fig. 4 is mostly self-explanatory. The figure is labelled with textboxes in solid backgrounds, which are usually the questions we ask before starting the analytics system development process. The types of the questions lack definitive answers and, therefore, demand an agility in the process with the hope of finding answers during the process. The first question to be asked is what level of accuracy we must achieve? An approximate level is set in consultation with the stakeholders, but adjusted as the results are produced in sprints and then get validated. The next question is what amount of training and test data required to build the system? This question leaves a hook for uncertainty that needs to be revisited in subsequent sprints.

The next most important requirement for an application is to decide the number of labels. For some applications, labels are easy to establish. For example, if we are trying to analyze consumer sentiment, then clearly positive, negative, and possibly neutral are the initial options. Other finer sentiment labels may include frustration, angry, disappointed, etc. An application where patients are required to be segmented based on their purpose of chatting with advocates may include scheduling assistance, seeking insurance information, referral, etc. These labels or even sentiments in finer granularity cannot easily be established fully before the start of the application development. It requires an incremental approach dictated by deeper analyses of data and with results during the sprints. As the labels change and the numbers vary, the labelled data set is also incrementally added to and prepared accordingly.

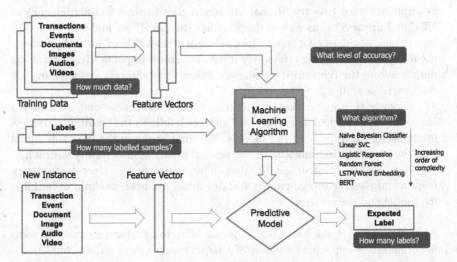

Fig. 4. Supervised machine learning

The heart of our approach to building an analytics system is with ML-based classification algorithms. The choice is from among many tens of powerful algorithms available in packages. The initial hunch always guides us towards a selected handful and then allows us to start building the system with one of those first. The performance then dictates what is to come next. The point here is that the algorithm selection occurs in stages in different sprints. In our specific example scenario, we have started with an NBC. We then tested with algorithms suitable for sparse vectorization of textual data, including linear SVC and attention-based BERT models.

In many decision-making or classification problems, obtaining labeled training instances for learning is expensive and time-consuming, as they require the efforts of experienced human annotators, while large quantities of unlabeled instances are readily available. Semi-supervised learning addresses this problem by using large amounts of unlabeled data (see Fig. 5), together with the available labeled data to build better classifiers. The learning process, as described below, is incremental in nature and is in alignment with our adopted sprint-based incremental philosophy.

Given a data stream with both labeled and unlabeled instances (bottom-right in the figure), we make use of the initial model to label the data automatically. These machine-labeled instances from the initial model, along with the historical labeled instances, are used together to train a model via EM learning to produce the final model. Those machine-labeled instances with a high threshold confidence from the initial model are outputted immediately. The rest are candidates for human-labeling.

The above process is an iterative real-time one. As it receives labeled and unlabeled instances, it puts the unlabeled instances through the latest trained classifier and creates a buffer for those that fail to cross the label threshold. Once the number of unmarked instances in the buffer exceeds a certain pre-specified number, it triggers the EM learning as a background process, and it replaces the current classifier model when finished.

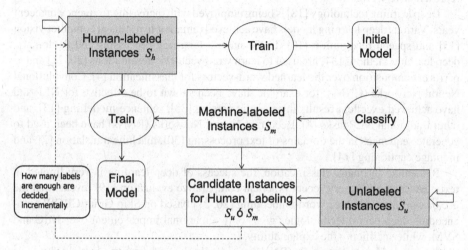

Fig. 5. Semi-supervised machine learning algorithm

With a semi-supervised algorithm, if a trained NBC model is not able to classify an unmarked instance because the instance does not cross a pre-defined threshold, the instance becomes a candidate for labeling by a human operator. The decision whether to send it to the human operator depends on the computed amount of information gain via an entropy measure for example, thus implementing an optional combination of semi-supervised and active learning [25, 31].

4.4 Machine and Deep Learning for NLP

We begin with the supervised Naïve Bayesian Classifier (NBC), which is a simple graphical bag-of-words classification and decision-making model using structured vector representations of textual data. Support Vector Machine (SVM)-based discriminative classification technique, such as Linear SVC, is a suitable one for document classification that maps data points to a higher dimensional space where the classification is carried out. Latent Semantic Analysis (LSA) is one of the early approaches to text classification, with successful applications in information retrieval [7]. LSA can be used effectively for unsupervised text classification in conjunction with SVM. LSA constructs feature vectors from the terms occurring in documents. Such vectors become "very high" dimensional to account for every term occurring in the text corpus. LSA transforms high-dimensional data into a much smaller-dimensional latent topic space where clustering is performed. It then attempts to solve the synonymy and polysemy problems to match documents by taking advantage of the implicit higher-order structure in the association of terms with articles to create a multi-dimensional semantic structure.

We mention two powerful unsupervised text classification techniques. One is a probabilistic variation of algebraic LSA, called probabilistic LSA (PLSA) [11], and the other is called Latent Dirichlet Allocation (LDA) [1]. Both PLSA and LDA produce generative models that are useful in suggesting latent topics in corpora by projecting their most representative words.

Deep learning technology [18] is being employed with increasing frequency in recent years. Various deep learning models have achieved remarkable results in computer vision [15] and speech recognition [10]. In the natural language processing (NLP) domain, deep learning methods [34] are used to learn word vector representations [20, 21] and to perform composition over the learned word-vectors for classification [4]. Convolutional Neural Networks (CNNs), for example, have been shown to be effective for NLP and have achieved excellent results in semantic parsing [33], sentence modelling [13], and other traditional NLP tasks [4]. Recurrent Neural Networks (RNNs) have been used to generate sequences in the domains of text processing [30], machine translation [2], and in image captioning [14].

But unlike in image classification, the success of deep learning is very limited in text classification. A very recent practical comparative evaluation [19] reveals that the use of word2vec/doc2vec word-embedding [20, 21] based on Skip Gram/CBOW autoencoding deep neural technologies gives only a marginal improvement over NBC and SVM, while sacrificing the explainability.

Recurrent Neural Networks (RNNs) are a rich class of dynamic models that have been used to generate sequences in domains of text processing [30], machine translation [2], and the other domains. RNNs can be trained for sequence generation by processing real data sequences one step at a time and predicting what comes next. Long Short-Term Memory (LSTM) [26] incorporates explicitly controllable memory units to learn long-range temporal dependencies.

BERT [12] is a multi-layer bidirectional Transformer encoder that can be used to classify documents. The BERT base model has 12 layers (transformer blocks), 12 attention heads, and 110 million parameters. BERT Large model has 24 layers, 16 attention heads, and 340 million parameters. Every layer does multi-headed attention computation on the word representation of the previous layer to create a new intermediate representation. BERT-base was trained on 4 cloud TPUs for 4 days and BERT-large was trained on 16 Tensor Processing Units (TPUs) for 4 days. Fine-tuning the tasks that have been discussed takes at most 1 h on a single cloud TPU or a few hours on a GPU.

5   Agile ETL and System Implementation

A large healthcare provider company, such as AdventHealth, relies heavily on patient diagnosis, demographic, payer financial, and administrative data that are being accumulated and updated dynamically at a very fast pace. Consequently, data ETL (extraction, transformation, load) needs to be an incremental process, and the systems that make use of such disparate sources of data in this environment need to be developed in an agile manner. This subsection provides a brief overview of our ETL. The declarative and scripting paradigm of Python programming facilitates quick prototyping, which is vital to support such an agile development process.

In the prototyping phase, our agile approach is more of a SILO method. For extraction, the data engineer team uses a built-in Customer Relationship Management (CRM) system connector to extract data by making Application Programming Interface (API) calls. Once all the relevant object data is extracted and brought into the workflow, data curation begins in the transformation phase.

1. CRM objects have a master-slave relation and by using this relation developers identify various traits such as,

   a. Who are the actors in an account activity?
   b. What are the actor's profiles? – consumer/agent
   c. Demographic information
   d. Enrolled status
   e. Activity information including: Enrollment, Tasks, conversations.

2. Date time related fields converted to the local time-zone.
3. Creating multiple outputs based on front-end Business Intelligence (BI) requirements.
4. Only keeping the relevant fields and avoiding data redundancy.

   All of the data is then sent to a Power BI for further analytics and visualization.

   Our ongoing long-term approach to ETL is to build a standard foundation of data sets and to make it available to all teams. The more concrete approach to data extraction brings the data into an enterprise-level data lake. The Big Data team has built data pipelines to make real-time data available and can be utilized by multiple teams. Most of the transformation and data curation is performed using advance SQL. This curation is to utilize the computational power of the big data platform. As a final product of transformation, various materialized views created can be utilized by various teams for further analytics. For data loading, Power BI uses a direct query method to query the data and build analytical Vizze's. This approach is again to make sure the team utilizes the big data platform computation resource.

   For our Python-based system implementation, we rely on numerous machine learning, deep learning, and NLP libraries. The dashboard front-end makes use of Power BI. Each of the consumer segmentation problems involve the experimentation with one or more ML based classification techniques. We set the target accuracy in the beginning of a project and then start with one of the least complex techniques (e.g., keyword-based or NBC). If the accuracy is too far off from the set target, then we move to a more complex and powerful technique that usually takes hours to run (e.g., a deep learning based technique such as BERT). The enormity of a BERT model with 110 million parameters and its time-consuming fine-tuning process allowed us only a handful of runs in every other day reported in each sprint. The decision of whether the accuracy achieved is acceptable or try with another sprint is made during our regular standups.

6   Validation and Feedback in Agile Process

Incremental labeling and validation is a tedious manual process that requires a methodological approach which we briefly describe in this section.

As per business requirements, sample chat files are obtained from the source systems. A preliminary work of reading the sample chat files is done by the team leader to get a basic understanding of what types of questions and concerns are discussed between the consumers and Care Advocates (CA). Based on the findings, an initial set of pre-determined topics/labels are created by the lead and elaborately discussed with the team during regular standups.

Then sample data is prepped to be divided amongst the team members for further analysis. The sample data is sorted and filtered, then additional columns added for a topic drop-down list, and free-text columns for notes are added as well. This step ensures format consistency across the team members when working with sample data. Since the process is agile, sometimes tools such as Alteryx are utilized to prep the sample data files before labelling or validating to expedite the manual process.

In the labeling phase, each analyst meticulously reads through each individual chat message between the consumers and CA. In most cases, the first topic initiated by the consumer is picked (from the drop-down list) to label the conversation. However, the entire conversation's thread is being read to ensure that hidden topics are not missed during the analysis. This process can take up to 2–5 days depending on the range of samples and the length of chat conversations. The findings are discussed during standups to compare similarities and to provide feedback on each topic within the chat. In some cases, labels are added or edited in case there is an emerging trend of a new topic.

Once the sample chat data is labelled, it is run and tested through the ML model to train it. The ML output is then validated by the analyst. The output file is prepped, and the analyst manually reads the messages as output by the ML model. Passed or failed messages are discussed during standups to compare findings and team feedback. This review is a quick process and continues until the ML model output reaches 75% to 80% accuracy.

Before validating any topics defining patient chats, we first create keywords for patient topics. Once the keywords are generated, we read the de-identified conversations between the CA and Patient to determine its overarching topic. If the topic is correct, we mark it as Pass, if not we mark it as Fail. We do an investigation in the specific context to find out why a topic has failed, and try to create more keywords to push it above the threshold level.

For the validation of the patient sentiments, we read the whole message between the CA and Patient to determine what was the patient's experience with the Care Advocate. If the conversation is negative, we mark it as negative. If the conversation is positive, we mark it as positive. If the conversation contains both positive and negative sentiments, we mark it as mixed sentiment.

7   Conclusions

An agile systems engineering approach fundamentally changes the mindset of a data scientist working in an industrial environment. The approach prevents the scientist from getting bogged down in achieving perfection, like a researcher in academia might do. In many cases within an industrial environment, an acceptable solution suffices. A full-scale industrial data science project (for example, a consumer recommender system) involves developing a system of interconnected systems, including customer and product databases, a web-based front-end, back-end processing, an ML-based predictive recommender, and reporting. Targeting a high accuracy of the recommending algorithm output may or may not be achievable, and may align with the pace of the rest of the components where the outcome is deterministic. An example favoring this argument is in the case of topic classification as detailed in this chapter, where we often adopted a simple NBC-based bag-of-words approach, favoring an acceptable performance over more complex semantic and attention-based approaches.

In conclusion, industrial data science projects will continue to thrive on agile systems engineering approaches. In predictive analytics, if accuracy is the most important measuring stick, then it needs to be broken down into successive milestones to avoid allowing substantial time to have passed with no working model in sight.

References

1. Blei, D., Ng, A., Jordan, M.: Latent dirichlet allocation. J. Mach. Learn. Res. **3**(5), 993–1022 (2003)
2. Cho, K., van Merrienboer, B., Gulcehre, C., Bougares, F., Schwenk, H., Bengio, Y.: Learning phrase representations using RNN encoder-decoder for statistical machine translation. In: Proceedings of EMNLP (2014)
3. Cockburn, A., Highsmith, J.: Agile software development: the people factor. Computer **34**(11), 131–133 (2001)
4. Collobert, R., Weston, J., Bottou, L., Karlen, M., Kavukcuglu, K., Kuksa, P.: Natural Language Processing (Almost) from Scratch. J. Mach. Learn. Res. **12**, 2493–2537 (2011)
5. Das, S.: High-Level Data Fusion. Artech House, Norwood (2008)
6. Das, S.: Computational Business Analytics. Chapman and Hall/CRC Press, Boca Raton (2014)
7. Dumais, S.T., Furnas, G.W., Landauer, T.K., Deerwester, S.: Using latent semantic analysis to improve information retrieval. In: Proceedings of CHI 1988: Conference on Human Factors in Computing, Washington, DC (1988)
8. Fowler, M., Highsmith, J.: The agile manifesto. Softw. Dev. **9**(8), 28–35 (2001)
9. Fox, J., Das, S.: Safe and Sound: Artificial Intelligence in Hazardous Applications. AAAI-MIT Press, Cambridge (2000)
10. Graves, A., Mohamed, A.-R., Hinton, G.: Speech recognition with deep recurrent neural networks. In: Proceedings of ICASSP (2013)
11. Hofmann, T.: Probabilistic latent semantic analysis. In: Proceedings of the Conference on Uncertainty in Artificial Intelligence (UAI), Stockholm (1999)
12. Devlin, J., Chang, M.-W., Lee, K., Toutanova, K.: BERT: pre-training of deep bidirectional transformers for language understanding. In: Proceedings of the 2019 Conference of the North American Chapter of the Association for Computational Linguistics (2019)
13. Kalchbrenner, N., Grefenstette, E., Blunsom, P.: A convolutional neural network for modelling sentences (2014). https://arxiv.org/abs/1404.2188
14. Karpathy, A., Fei-Fei, L.: Deep visual-semantic alignments for generating image descriptions. In: Proceedings of the IEEE Conference on Computer Vision and Pattern Recognition (CVPR) (2015)

15. Krizhevsky, A., Sutskever, I., Hinton, G.: ImageNet classification with deep convolutional neural networks. In: Advances in Neural Information Processing Systems, pp. 1097–1105 (2012)
16. Kroll, P., MacIsaac, B.: Agility and Discipline Made Easy. Addison-Wesley Professional, Boston (2006)
17. LeadingAgile: Cheat Sheet for Product Backlog Refinement (Grooming). LeadingAgile (2021)
18. LeCun, Y., Bengio, Y., Hinton, G.: Deep learning. Nature **521**(7553), 436–444 (2015)
19. Li, S.: Multi-Class Text Classification Model Comparison and Selection. Towards Data Science (2018). https://towardsdatascience.com/multi-class-text-classification-model-comparison-and-selection-5eb066197568
20. Mikolov, T., Chen, K., Corrado, K., Dean, J.: Efficient estimation of word representations in vector space (2013). https://arxiv.org/abs/1301.3781
21. Mikolov, T., Sutskever, I., Chen, K., Corrado, G., Dean, J.: Distributed representations of words and phrases and their compositionality. In: Proceedings of NIPS (2013)
22. Planning Poker (2021). https://www.planningpoker.com/
23. Product Plan (2021). https://www.productplan.com/glossary/fibonacci-agile-estimation/
24. Royce, W.: Managing the development of large software systems. In: Proceedings of IEEE WESCON, vol. 26, pp. 328–388 (1970)
25. Sarawagi, S., Bhamidipaty, A.: Interactive deduplication using active learning. In: International Conference on Very Large Data Bases (VLDB), pp. 269–278 (2002)
26. Schmidhuber, J., Hochreiter, S.: Long short-term memory. Neural Comput. **9**(8), 1735–1780 (1997)
27. Scrum Institute (2021). https://www.scrum-institute.org/Burndown_Chart.php
28. Scrum.org (2021). https://www.scrum.org/resources/what-is-scrum
29. Software Testing Help: Agile Methodology: A Beginner's Guide to Agile Method and Scrum (2021). http://softwaretestinghelp.com/
30. Sutskever, I., Martens, J., Hinton, G.: Generating text with recurrent neural networks. In: Proceedings of the ICML (2011)
31. Tur, G., Tur, D., Schapire, R.: Combining active and semi-supervised learning for spoken language understanding. Speech Commun. **45**, 171–186 (2005)
32. Visual Paradigm (2021). https://www.visual-paradigm.com/scrum/how-to-use-scrum-board-for-agile-development/
33. Yih, W.-T., Chang, M.-W., He, X., Gao, J.: Semantic parsing via staged query graph generation: question answering with knowledge base. In: Proceedings of the ACL (2015)
34. Young, T., Hazarika, D., Cambria, E.: Recent Trends in Deep Learning Based NLP. IEEE Comput. Intell. Mag. **13**(3), 55–75 (2018)

Platforms for Assessing Relationships: Trust with Near Ecologically-Valid Risk, and Team Interaction

Julie L. Marble[1], Ariel M. Greenberg[1(✉)], Justin W. Bonny[2], Sean M. Kain[1], Brandon J. Scott[1], Ian M. Hughes[1], and Mary E. Luongo[1]

[1] Applied Physics Laboratory, Johns Hopkins University, Laurel, MD, USA
ariel.greenberg@jhuapl.edu
[2] Department of Psychology, Morgan State University, Baltimore, MD, USA

Abstract. Assessment of human-machine trust is difficult because of confounds in context, system capability and reliability. Trust indicates willingness to be vulnerable to the variable and unpredicted actions of another actor. Making people vulnerable to risk from decisions made by an intelligent agent is difficult to justify for research ethics purposes. Making expensive, physical intelligent agents vulnerable to human decisions is an inhibiting factor to exploring the development of trust or teams with embodied systems. These confounds can be addressed through use of virtual reality and immersive gaming systems. This chapter describes the development of two platforms, PAR-TNER and PARTI, for the exploration of human collaboration with autonomous systems, and provides an overview of a limited initial pilot of PAR-TNER. In PAR-TNER and PAR-TI, the test participant teams with either humans or machines to escape from a room collaboratively. PAR-TNER leverages virtual reality to stimulate risk, while PAR-TI allows researchers to explore team dynamics. While the data from the pilot test of PAR-TNER are limited, they indicate the ability to leverage the research platforms to discern trust from perceived capability.

Keywords: Trust · Autonomous systems · Research platform · Human machine teaming · Virtual reality · Human-machine interaction

1 Introduction

Johns Hopkins University Applied Physics Laboratory developed the Platforms for Assessing Relationships: Trust with Near Ecologically-valid Risk (PAR-TNER), and Team Interaction (PAR-TI) research platforms to provide an environment for objectively assessing trust behaviors and joint decision-making between humans and autonomous systems. This chapter discusses the development of PAR-TNER and PAR-TI, then goes on to provide the results of the pilot of PARTNER as an example of its potential for research.

The prevalence of human and machine interactions in organizations and environments is increasing. In addition, with the increasing capability and autonomy of intelligent systems, the assessment of human trust in autonomous systems has moved to the

© Springer Nature Switzerland AG 2021
W. F. Lawless et al. (Eds.): Engineering Artificially Intelligent Systems, LNCS 13000, pp. 209–229, 2021.
https://doi.org/10.1007/978-3-030-89385-9_13

forefront of research. Trust has been found to be a key factor in adopting novel and emerging technologies, such as autonomous systems (Benbasat and Wang 2005; Xu et al. 2005). Critically, while reliability may support the development of trust, it may not be the only factor that affects the development of trust (Lee and See 2004; Desai et al. 2012; Desai et al. 2013; Hoff and Bashir 2015; Mayer et al. 1995).

As research on trust requires that human partners or machines are vulnerable to unpredictable actions of the other entity, exploring trust with humans in real world tasks where physical risk is significant is verboten. Yet for trust to be relevant to the interaction between multiple humans and machines (or humans and humans), there must be risk of some type to the people involved – those who chose to trust (Perkins et al. 2010; Koller 1988). Using existing embodied systems, the ability to explore the development of trust and teaming between humans and autonomous machines has been limited to situations where the human and the autonomous platform are not at risk of injury. Therefore, research platforms, which simulate intelligent machines, must allow humans and agents to take leader and follower roles fluidly, and allow for assessment of human behavior with ecologically valid risk. That variability of teammate behaviors is possible, and critical, and can impact the success or performance of the human, yielding ecologically valid risk. By ecologically valid risk, we mean a potential to lose more than just a hypothesized monetary gain, as has frequently been used to study risk. Koller (1988) demonstrated that the development of trust is a function of the degree of risk inherent to the situation. Similarly, Sifakis (2019) proposed a framework for the development of trust of autonomous systems based on the degree of trustworthiness achievable by a system performing the task; and the degree of criticality of the task. At current, robots are proposed as support for warfighters when missions are dirty, dull or dangerous. Therefore, ecologically valid risk should be of similar caliber: potential for physical damage or mission failure. In developing our platforms, we proposed a game-based design where a participant's avatars could simulate physical risk and potential for mission failure if the team is unable to collaborate. Within Virtual Reality (VR), the experience of falling is a stimulated risk; within the 2D game, avatar loss can delay the game and cause mission failure.

Previous research identifies the behaviors an intelligent agent would need to display to be considered a teammate. A team refers to two or more interdependent individuals who adaptively interact to reach a common goal (Salas et al. 1992). Teams can vary among multiple dimensions, depending on the goal, context, and abilities of teammates. However, teammates engage in multiple cognitive processes, including planning, reasoning, decision-making, problem-solving, remembering, designing, and assessing situations that are relevant to the goal (Cooke et al. 2013). Cooke et al. (2013) argue that in complex tasks, no single team member will have complete situational awareness or full knowledge of the context, and, therefore, not all individuals would share a common perspective, even if they share an environment. They argue that individual knowledge, skills, histories, physical position or team role confers upon each team member a unique perspective of the context and problem to be solved; thus, they would each be expected to have slightly different expectations for the solution or what would lead to success. Effective teams dynamically integrate these perspectives (Gorman et al. 2006) into a holistic grasp of the context. Machines that exhibit autonomous behavior, take initiative and act independently from human direction could more effectively collaborate as teammates with humans. Simulated environments of human-machine teams need to create intelligent agents that display behaviors that indicate the agent is sensitive to the individual knowledge of human teammates and the context in which the team is performing.

A key element of the several definitions of trust is being vulnerable to the not-completely-predictable actions of another (e.g., Mayer et al. 1995; Deutsch 1960), and numerous studies have shown that the reliability and validity of an automated system's functions are important antecedents of trust (see Bailey and Scerbo 2005; de Visser and Parasuraman 2011; Seong and Bisantz 2008; Ross et al. 2008). It is infeasible to expose expensive robot systems to risk from human error, simply for research purposes. More importantly, in human research it is unethical to expose people to avoidable physical or psychological risk.

However, games, especially immersive games, provide a context in which near ecologically valid or perceived risk can be created. Virtual reality goes a step beyond this. Using immersive head-mounted displays, a person can be exposed to stimulated hazards, such as drops, falls, and moving objects, while limiting the actual risk exposure of the person. PAR-TNER leverages the immersive potential provided by VR to explore risk-taking and risk avoidance behavior, to allow for exploration of objective behaviors indicative of trust. Its counterpart, PAR-TI, while not in VR provides a reconfigurable platform to explore teaming behavior in teams of humans or humans and autonomous systems. While the PAR-TNER serious game explores trust and collaboration in dyadic interactions, PAR-TI explores trust and teaming between humans and autonomous agents (bots) in teams of three players. The three-entity team can be made up of any combination of humans and bots, where either the human or the bot can have a leadership role or the role of subordinate (follower). Both games include elements of exploration, problem-solving, and collaboration. The premise of both games is that the players must work together to find the correct combination of actions to escape from the room in which they are trapped, before time runs out. Players manipulate levers, buttons, and pressure plates to extend platforms, toggle "traps" between acid (which will terminate the human avatar) and magnets (which will immobilize a robot avatar), and convert ramps to staircases, which can be difficult or time consuming for the robot to navigate. Players also have access to tools, such as 'repulsor' and 'attractor' beams that can pull or push objects and even the players themselves, and boxes that can be stacked to create access to different parts of the environment. In both games, the experimenter has the ability to provide the solution to the puzzle a priori or to allow the team to determine it themselves through trial and error.

PAR-TNER is comprised of four puzzle rooms which are each solved with a different combination of actions, many of which must be performed in collaboration between players. PAR-TI capitalizes on the previous expectations and experiences of the human under test. The layout of PAR-TI (shown in Fig. 1) remains the same for every game. However, the experimenter can change the response of the actuators such that the same action results in a different response. This manipulation allows prior experience in the room to be misleading. For example, in one instance manipulation of the level 1 pressure plate could extend the stair case or it could toggle the trap from magnet to acid. This difference could have the result that in the first instance, the fastest solution would be for the human to take an action, while in the second, the better solution is for the bot to take the action. Solutions can also be designed to test whether human teammates in a human-human-bot team would abandon the bot if it were not able to reach the escape door. These selections are done prior to the game, via the puzzle selection menu, shown in Fig. 2. Potentially thousands of different solutions can be achieved, making PAR-TNER and PAR-TI an ideal tool for examining longitudinal changes in human-agent teams.

Fig. 1. Layout of PAR-TI

2 Requirements of Platforms to Allow for the Study of Human-Machine Teaming

To begin the development of a research platform for the objective assessment of trust of autonomous machines, we posited a set of characteristics the platform should contain. Those characteristics and how they are instantiated in the PAR-TNER and PAR-TI games is described below.

2.1 Requirement 1: Human Perception of Risk and Vulnerability

Lee and See (2004) defined trust as "the attitude that an agent will help achieve an individual's goals in a situation characterized by uncertainty and vulnerability." Rousseau et al. (1998) defined trust as "a psychological state comprising the intention to accept vulnerability based upon positive expectations of the intentions or behavior of another." Finally, Hoff and Bashir (2015) reviewed recent empirical research on factors that influence trust in automation to present a three-layered trust model that synthesizes preexisting knowledge, attitudes, and experience with a dynamic understanding of the system that is built up through interaction; it implies that trust is essentially a reliance strategy that changes dynamically with the task and context. Notably, a key consideration in these examples is the emphasis on the vulnerability of the trusting agent on the behavior of the trusted agent.

PAR-TNER is a VR-based research platform developed in Unity and run on Oculus Rift–enabled systems. ESCAPE refers to the four virtual escape room puzzles within PAR-TNER. In ESCAPE with PAR-TNER, the test participant teams with either a human confederate or an agent to identify the solution that will allow the two to escape the room. To solve the puzzle, teammates must actuate levers, platforms, and buttons; use "tractor beams" and "repulsor beams"; or virtually lift, carry, and push obstacles to create a route by which both teammates can reach the exit. The exit door activates only when both teammates are present.

At each decision point, one teammate must perform a risky action (such as jump from a high vantage point to a platform), while the second teammate takes action to enable the first teammate. This second action also comes with implicit risk. For example, the first teammate must jump from platform to platform, at risk of falling – which is at best uncomfortable in VR, to obtain a tool, while the second teammate enables the first teammate's action by standing on a lever. The second teammate is also at risk because while standing on the lever ensures that the platforms holding the first teammate remain, the floor surrounding the second teammate slowly fills with deadly "acid," which will "kill" their avatar. The player standing on the lever could easily jump to safety, but doing so would jeopardize or "kill" their teammate. (Avatar death in the game is usually due to a simulated fast fall from height in VR.) While there is no risk to the participant, the height exposure and fall is mildly unpleasant. Examples of the PAR-TNER and PAR-TI environments are shown in Figs. 2, 3 and 4.

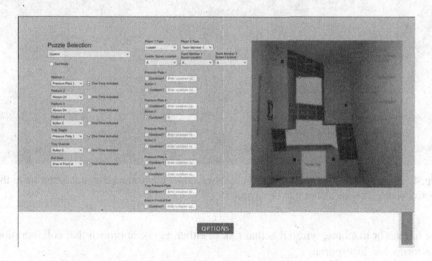

Fig. 2. PAR-TI puzzle selection menu

A key challenge for collaboration platforms is to develop approaches for increasing the realism and vulnerability to humans by the decisions of autonomous agents, and vice versa. Leveraging an immersive environment that allows for the perception of risk to

Fig. 3. Still image from PAR-TNER. The image shows the player avatar and communication sprite.

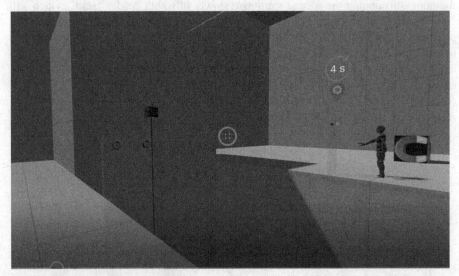

Fig. 4. Another still from PAR-TNER. This image shows the teammate avatar gesturing to the control panel, showing a chasm to be navigated.

the human or machine, without actual risk to either, is one approach that collaboration platforms can incorporate.

2.2 Requirement 2: Machines and Humans as Equally Critical to the Mission

Trust does not develop between people and tools; rather trust is an attribute between teammates. Therefore, PAR-TNER and PAR-TI were designed so that the autonomous machine(s) would be equally important to completion of the mission. That they perform autonomously (if not independently) is crucial for studying the dynamics of human-machine teams. However, limited machine capability has been a challenge in human-machine teaming research. Wizard of Oz (WoOz) paradigms have been used with some success, and provide a useful manipulation to explore trust and teaming behaviors. The WoOz paradigm limits the scalability of using intelligent agents within collaboration platforms; each intelligent agent would require a trained human confederate.

In addition, the actions required to achieve the goal need to be complex and require planning and problem-solving. Furthermore, the platform needs to allow for different roles to be taken by each team member. With regard to the machine teammate, the intelligent agent will need to be able to display behaviors associated with these processes in order to serve as a member of the team. Crucially, the machine will need to competently display these capabilities for its human collaborators to perceive it as a teammate. For trust and teaming relationships to develop between the participants, the task should be complex enough that success requires action by both participants. We developed PAR-TNER and PAR-TI to require tasks to be performed simultaneously as well as sequentially, to create dependence between the players.

The platform should allow for the complexity of collaborative tasks to be manipulated. Tasks with goals that are simple to achieve are less likely to provide insight into human-machine collaboration. One characteristic of teaming is shared goals or intents. Shared goals are needed when tasks require collaborative effort or synchronized actions between performers. In both PAR-TNER and PAR-TI, it is possible for either agent to perform some tasks, though not all. This allows the experimenter to allow both exploration of tasking based on capability or based on efficiency. Critically, while either the robot or human are capable of completing either task, one agent type may be able to complete the task more effectively than the other. PAR-TI allows the experimenter to develop a scenario in which the robot (or human) is given a task that is difficult to perform. In doing so, the level of frustration, learning, and skill involved in completing the team goal can be varied. The experimenter can design the scenario so that the team fails the mission if the task is completed by the 'incorrect' teammate, such as if the human does the task in the place of the robot. This flexibility allows the platform to be used to study human-machine collaboration across a variety of contexts and task demands.

Therefore, we developed PAR-TNER and PAR-TI so that the majority of actions within the game required the involvement of multiple team members to achieve the goal. In PAR-TNER, actuators could require coordinated action between teammates, or could require one teammate to actuate a control while the other took an action that would result in the death of their avatar if the first failed in their action. For example, one teammate might actuate a lever that caused the acid in the room to rise but also opened access to platforms the second teammate would climb to obtain a critical tool.

2.3   Requirement 3: Ability to Manipulate Team Structure and Roles

In addition to ensuring equal criticality of the human and the machine in mission success, a platform for research on human interaction with autonomously behaving machines must support variable team dynamics. PAR-TNER explores dyadic trust relationships between players, the human under test and his/her teammate (a human or an autonomous bot). The human under test may or may not know the identity of the teammate, depending on the experimenter's research needs. The ability of the research platform to mask whether a teammate is a human or machine can be used to systematically examine differences in behavior when the teammate is thought to be a human versus a robot.

PAR-TI, in contrast, allows exploration of teaming, acceptance of leadership, and trust in teams of three players. In PAR-TI, the human under test can be assigned to the role of leader or follower in a team comprised of humans and/or robots. A key capability of PAR-TI is the ability to assign the machine as a leader or follower. This allows the potential to explore human biases when following the orders of intelligent agent leaders.

Research by Molm et al. (2000) supported the classical exchange theory that trust is more likely to develop in the absence of negotiation, where the risk and uncertainty of the exchange drives the development of trust. Therefore, teammates are not able to communicate with each other verbally or via text messaging. This constraint was enforced to disguise the identity of the human and bot teammates. Rather, teammates (including the bot) were equipped with pointer beams, sprites, and timers common to several games to attract the teammate's attention to objects and allow for coordination of actions.

2.4   Requirement 4: Allow for Objective Measurement of Trust

Research on human trust of autonomous systems has frequently relied on subjective measures that are administered outside of the task; however, there have been some efforts recently to identify objective and physiological measures of trust. Much of the subjective research on trust is well synthesized in Hancock and Colleagues (2011) and Schaefer and Colleagues (2016). Subjective questionnaires such as the Schaefer Trust Index, the Heuristics for Trusted Autonomy (Jackson et al. 2016) or the Muir trust questionnaire (1987), provide only the subject's perception of their trust of the robot, assessed outside the interaction, not during. Because these are subjective measures, participants' responses are more post hoc explanation of behavior than they are a prediction of future action.

A key capability of collaboration platforms is to record human-machine interactions and behaviors during a task to identify objective indicators of trust. Hoff and Bashir (2015) modeled trust as an internal state of the one who lends trust, and which is dependent on both the agent receiving trust and the context. Perkins and Colleagues (2010) included situational risk as a key factor in the operator's trust of the system. Several researchers have begun to explore potential methods to objectively measure trust using physiological and behavioral metrics (e.g., Kosfeld et al. 2005; Waytz et al. 2014; Khalid et al. 2016). This research implies that human behaviors which are indicative of trust could be objectively defined and measured in the context of interest. To address these challenges, collaboration platforms need to provide the following. First, there needs to be many opportunities for human and machine teammates to take actions and make decisions that pose risk to themselves and others. Second, the platform must record the actions and decisions made by teammates to calculate indices of trust. Maximizing the number of these interactions provides a greater chance to record objective behaviors that are theorized to rely, at least in part, on trust. PAR-TNER and PAR-TI allow for recording of human actions and are compatible with physiological measurement of human performance. In addition, between each puzzle room, it is possible to present survey questions, such as one of the subjective trust measures noted above, or questions specific to the team performance.

2.5 Requirement 5: Leverage Human Expectations and Experience

Learning and experience have been demonstrated to underlie the development of team behavior and trust (e.g., Hoff and Bashir 2015). The PAR-TI platform allows the experimenter to define and redefine the solution to the puzzle room. While the initial room set up looks identical each time, the combination of actions that must be taken to open the escape can vary substantially. To allow for assessment of willingness to be vulnerable to the actions of another, the research platform should allow the experimenter to manipulate human participant expectations about the solution and teammate roles. PAR-TI does this by allowing the experimenter to change the response of the activators within the puzzle room, meaning that the task solution (and which teammate should perform a given task) will change even though the layout of the room itself remains unchanged. For example, in one instance of the game, pressing a particular lever could make a ramp appear. In the next round, it could change the trap from something only the human can cross (magnets) to something that only the robot can cross (acid).

3 Bot Behavior

In application, in both PAR-TNER and PAR-TI, the test participant can team with either a human or a bot. In both, the bot is a finite-state machine scripted to play the game with complete information on the game solution. Each step in the puzzle is indexed and associated with the relevant game elements to complete the step. From the perspective of the human under test, the bot appears to act in a fully autonomous manner. Combined interaction events with these game elements would either advance or regress the puzzle step. Information on the association of game elements within a puzzle step as well as on the current puzzle step is not available to human players. The autonomous agent would use this information in combination with the teammate's current position to determine the transition to the next appropriate state. Each state is a heuristic routine connected via defined transition rules. While the test participant plays in VR, the confederate controls his agent on a flat screen using keyboard controls; in our pilot test, this was done in a room separate from the test participant.

4 Pilot Test of PAR-TNER

To assess the utility of PAR-TNER as a research platform, a pilot test with limited numbers of participants was arranged. The goal of the pilot test was to assess the potential of the platform for objective assessment of trust between humans and autonomous machines, to assess the proposed experimental paradigm, and to ensure that the puzzles themselves were solvable. The data provided are meant to illustrate the use of the platform; the experiment results should be replicated with larger numbers. As this pilot study was performed as an assessment of the utility of the platform, participant numbers were limited. Due to the severely limited numbers of participants, statistical significance of the results were not computed. A pilot assessment of PAR-TI has yet to be performed.

Participants were given seven minutes to identify and implement the solution to each puzzle. This seven-minute time limit was selected to avoid the potential for VR sickness, given the dynamic nature of the task and the potential for simulated drops and sudden movements. Participants were asked to solve each of four different puzzles, two while teamed with a human and two while teamed with a bot. Each participant performed the puzzles in the same order, although the order of playing with a human or bot teammate was randomized for the first two puzzles and then the second two puzzles. After completing (or failing to complete) the puzzle, participants were placed in a virtual "waiting room" where they were asked a series of questions about their performance, their teammate's performance, and the team's performance on the previous puzzle. To maintain players' immersion, questions were presented virtually, and players selected answers using the Oculus Rift hand controllers. Responses were collected using Qualtrics survey software.

Every game with a human teammate was played by the same experiment team confederate. The experiment confederate had extensive gaming experience. He controlled his avatar via standard gaming keyboard conventions. The confederate, when playing as the human teammate, was scripted to attempt to play each game as similarly as possible, including by allowing the test participant time to attempt to identify the solution or explore the puzzle room.

4.1 Participants

Thirty-one participants were recruited from the staff of the Johns Hopkins University Applied Physics Laboratory (JHUAPL). Recruitment focused on staff who self-reported enjoyment of video games and experience playing the game Portal 2™ (https://www.thinkwithportals.com/). Data from seven participants were lost or removed because of problems with the software. The data from the remaining 24 participants were used in the study. Participants ranged in age from 18 to 45 and all reported normal or corrected-to-normal vision. Participants reported having previously used a VR system with no adverse effects. Approved Human Subject Research protocols were followed, which included a signed agreement. Participants were debriefed about deception around teammate identity at the completion of their participation. Participants were compensated for their time with an internal time charge code.

4.2 Equipment and Setup

PAR-TNER is played on an Oculus Rift headset with handheld controllers. Participants played in individual test rooms. The floor of each test room was demarcated with rough fuzzy tape to prevent participants from bumping or walking into walls. Similarly, streamers were hung from the ceiling to mark boundaries of safe movement. To ensure their safety, participants were observed from the control room via video and audio feeds from the test rooms; however, the data were not recorded.

4.3 Procedures

At the start of the session, participants were given an overview of the goals of the study. They were told that they would be asked to solve a series of four escape room puzzles with the assistance of a human or a bot teammate. It was implied that the bot and human were equally skilled at solving the puzzles. Necessarily, the human confederate's actions were partially scripted to prevent his skill and speed from increasing far beyond the level of the bot, given that he played 62 games overall. Participants were made aware of the seven-minute time limit to solve each puzzle and that they could display a timer on the screen by activating a button on the handset. They were told that they could end the test at any time.

Participants were fitted with the Oculus headset and handheld controllers. The VR environment was started, and participants began in a "practice room," which is a common feature of most video games. Practice rooms allow participants to familiarize themselves with the controls and the in-game abilities of their avatar, such as the use of the hand controllers, jumping from object to object, and how to manipulate objects by directly contacting them or by using the "tractor" beams. When participants were comfortable with the environments and had been exposed to all of the object types they would experience in the game, they moved on to the game itself.

Participants were asked in the VR environment which teammate, human or bot, they would like to play the first game with, and their response was recorded. Participants were then assigned a teammate independent of their preference.

After each puzzle, participants were asked a series of questions about the previous game, such as how well they felt they played, how well they felt their teammate played, and how well they felt they played as a team. After answering these questions, participants entered the next puzzle, which they played with the other teammate type—that is, if they first played with a human, they next played with a bot. They were told that the next teammate was different from the first. For clarity, participants were not informed about the true identity of their teammate; rather they were led to infer teammate identity based on the response they had given to the preference question. As a result, participants played each round in one of the following conditions, where the boldface word indicates the actual identity and the italic word is the assumed identity (Table 1):

Table 1. Experimental conditions

Teaming conditions (**actual**/*assumed*)	**Actual identity: human**	**Actual identity: bot**
Assumed identity: human	**Human**/*human*	**Bot**/*human*
Assumed identity: bot	**Human**/*bot*	**Bot**/*bot*

After the first two puzzles were completed, participants were told that they had played one round each with the bot and the human, and would now play two more puzzles. They were again asked whether they would like to play with a human or a bot. As before, they were then assigned a teammate independent of their indicated preference, and led to infer the identity of the teammate. After each puzzle, they were again asked to rate their performance, their teammate's performance, and their joint team performance in the game.

4.4 Questionnaire

When all four puzzles were completed, participants were told that they had "done very well" and were currently ranked in first place across all participants. They were asked whether, in the event of a tie for first place, they would come back to play a final round, and if so, with which teammate they would want to partner. This question was asked partly to assess the engagement of the game, and also to assess whether players had a teammate preference overall. Finally, participants completed a last questionnaire asking them in which puzzles they had teamed with a human versus a bot, and in which puzzles they thought they had performed the best (in which their avatars had died the fewest times and they had escaped most quickly).

After completing all puzzles and questionnaires, participants were brought to the control room, offered snacks and water, and time to readjust from the virtual environment. During this time, they were debriefed about the deception in the game regarding teammates and in which puzzles they had teamed with a human and with a bot. Out of an overabundance of caution, it was strongly recommended that participants not drive for at least 30 min after the game.

5   Results

Participants were able to complete the puzzles in the time allotted, except for Puzzle 3, which was unexpectedly more difficult for the players to solve than the other three puzzles. While the majority of participants came very close and could likely have escaped had they had an additional 30 s, only one participant was able to escape within the seven-minute time limit. In addition, performance time indicated that puzzles 1 and 2 were significantly easier than puzzles 3 and 4. This inconsistency in task difficulty resulted in under-sampling across the relatively small number of participants; therefore, the following data, although intriguing, are to be considered merely preliminary and demonstrative of the utility of the research platform.

At the start of the puzzles, when asked which teammate they wished to start with, 14 of the participants desired to play first with a bot and 14 desired to play with a human. After the first two puzzles, there was a shift toward a preference to play with a human (see Table 2). When asked if they would come back to play a final round in the event of a tiebreaker, 100% said that they would. Participants were then asked which player they would team with for the tiebreaker and there was a distinct shift towards a preference to play with the human. A two-sample test for equality of proportions (with continuity correction), indicated that the shift in preference toward a human teammate was marginal after Puzzle 2 ($\chi^2(1) = 3.40$, p = 0.065, and significant for the "tie-breaker" question ($\chi^2(1) = 6.87$, p = 0.009***) (Tables 3 and 4).

Table 2. Teammate preference after Round 3 as a function of preference after Round 1

		Preference round 1	
		Human	*Bot*
Preference round 2	*Human*	4	10
	Bot	8	2

Table 3. Preference in the Tiebreaker as a function of preferences from Round 1 and 3

Round 1	Human preference				Bot preference			
Round 3	Human preference		Bot preference		Human preference		Bot preference	
Tiebreaker selection	Human	Bot	Human	Bot	Human	Bot	Human	Bot
Number preferring	4	1	7	1	9	0	2	0

Table 4. Average score for each puzzle. *Note: only 1 participant completed Puzzle 3.

	Average score and completion time in seconds by puzzle			
	Puzzle 1	Puzzle 2	Puzzle 3*	Puzzle 4
Average score	27.3	31.3	2.25	26.5
Average completion time	239 s	195 s	405 s	243.5 s

Recall in our pilot, participants were not accurately told which teammate they were actually playing with for each puzzle. In general, however, participants were not able to accurately distinguish between playing with a human and playing with a bot (Fig. 4). It is interesting to note that several participants indicated that they played at least three puzzles with a bot, while others indicated that they did not play any puzzles with a bot. In fact, all participants played two puzzles with a human and two puzzles with a bot (Fig. 5).

We then explored performance as a function of teammate across the puzzles. Performance was a hybrid score based on the time to complete the room and the number of times the participant avatar or bot avatar was terminated by falling into the 'acid.' As can be seen, Puzzle 3 was more difficult than the other three puzzles, with all but one participant not completing the puzzle within the alloted time (420 s or seven minutes).

We also explored participant scores and completion times as a function of their assumed vice actual teammate. These are shown in Figs. 6, 7, 8 and 9, respectively. For the first two, easier puzzles, scores were higher when the participant believed they were playing with a bot than when they believed they were playing with a human. This relationship may not be true for the more difficult puzzles (Puzzles 3 and 4), but it is

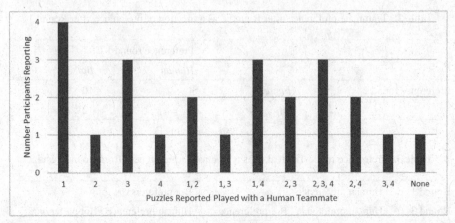

Fig. 5. Responses to question about which puzzles were played with a human vs. a bot. All participants played two puzzles with a human and two with a bot. Total, 24 participants.

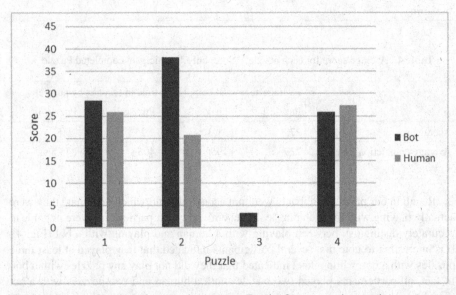

Fig. 6. Score as a function of assumed teammate. For the first two easier puzzles, scores were higher when the participant believed they were playing with a bot. This relationship may not be true for the third and fourth more difficult puzzles, but it is difficult to say given the lack of data on puzzle 3.

difficult to say given the lack of data on puzzle 3. Notably, the participant who did complete Puzzle 3 believed his teammate was a bot (in fact, the teammate was actually the human confederate).

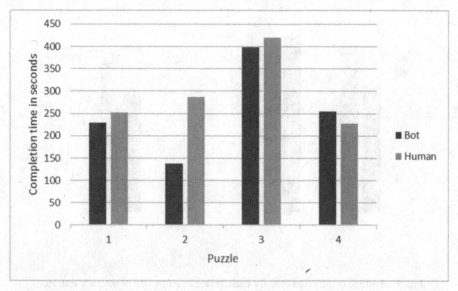

Fig. 7. Completion time in seconds as a function of assumed teammate for each puzzle.

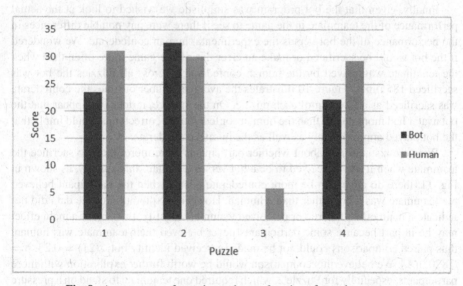

Fig. 8. Average score for each puzzle as a function of actual teammate.

Exploration of the completion time data demonstrated a similar trend, where completion time was faster when the participant perceived they were playing with a bot instead of a human. Puzzle 3 completion time was slightly lower when the participant thought the teammate was a bot because that was the only successful completion. Again, these data are difficult to interpret given the lack of completion data in Puzzle 3.

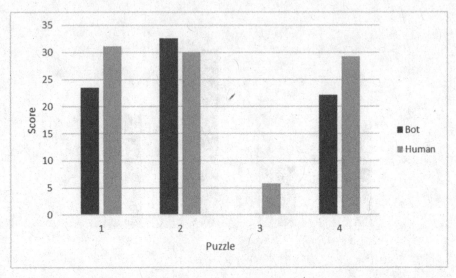

Fig. 9. Average completion time for each puzzle as a function of actual teammate.

Finally, given that the bot program was simplistic we wished to look at the actual performance of the teammate in the game to see if there were any notable differences in the performance of the bot versus the experimental human confederate. We wondered if the bot would be sacrificed or make an error during the game more often than when the teammate was played by the human confederate. Across all puzzles the bot was sacrificed 185 times. Figure 10 illustrates the average number of times the confederate was sacrificed as a function of each puzzle. On the surface, it does not appear that the bot avatar had more deaths than the human confederate. If correct, this would imply that the bot played approximately as well as the human confederate.

We were also curious about whether participants were more likely to sacrifice the teammate when it was perceived to be a bot versus a human. Intriguingly, as shown in Fig. 11, there do appear to be more confederate deaths when the participant believed the teammate was a bot rather than a human. However, exploration of the data did not indicate a main effect for true or perceived teammate identity; the lack of a main effect may be in part because some participants never believed their teammate was human, thus paired comparisons could not be made [perceived identity bot; $t(21) = 0.23$, p = 0.820, n.s.]. We believe this comparison would be worth further exploration with more participants, especially for Puzzle 2, which required one teammate to stand on a pressure plate that activated platforms to stand out from the walls. While one teammate jumped from platform to platform, the other teammate had to remain on the pressure plate, while the room filled with acid. It appears that the confederate was more often tasked to stand on the pressure plate, while the human participant attempted to jump between platforms.

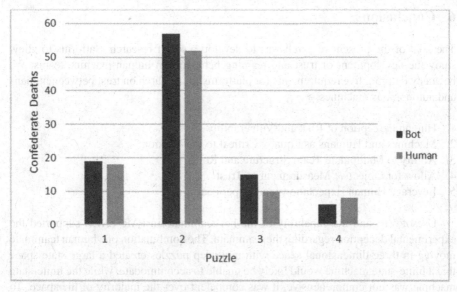

Fig. 10. Teammate death for each puzzle as a function of actual identity.

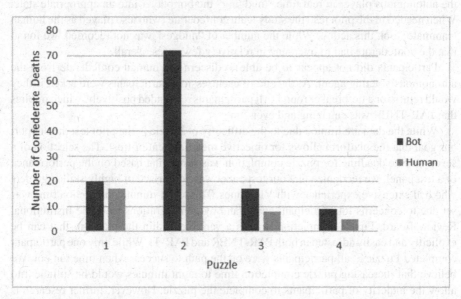

Fig. 11. Number of teammate deaths for each puzzle as a function of perceived identity.

6 Conclusions

The goal of the present research was to develop a set of research platforms to allow study the development of trust and teaming behaviors in human-machine teams. We began by defining five requirements for platforms for research on trust between humans and autonomous machines:

1. Human Perception of Risk and Vulnerability
2. Machines and Humans as Equally Critical to the Mission
3. Ability to Manipulate Team Structure and Roles
4. Allow for Objective Measurement of Trust
5. Leverage Human Expectations and Experience

Use of VR, and the capability of the bot teammate in PAR-TNER supported the experimental deception regarding the teammate. The combination of a human teammate moving in three-dimensional space with multistep puzzles created a large state space that a finite-state machine would likely be unable to accommodate; while the finite-state machine was not comprehensive, it was competent over the majority of the space. To mitigate this risk, PAR-TNER was designed so that the human confederate could override the autonomous player in real time, "nudging" the bot player into an appropriate state. When needed in the pilot test, the study team confederate (who also played as the human teammate) took this action. While the number of "nudges" was not recorded, we found that the confederate had to intervene in relatively few cases overall.

Participants did not appear to be able to discern the human confederate from the autonomously acting agent. At the end of each session, participants were asked if they would return for a tie-breaker round. All participants responded positively, which implies that PAR-TNER was engaging and even fun.

While the data are limited due to the difficulty of Puzzle 3, the pilot test did support our goal that the platform allows for objective measurement of trust. The selection of a seven-minute deadline for puzzle completion was somewhat based on the performance of a test panel, we recognize that our test panel was comprised of highly skilled gamers who had extensive experience with VR games. The seven-minute completion time was set due to concerns for participant health and by considerations from the Institutional Review Board. Puzzle completion time is a variable within the platform that can be explicitly and easily adjusted in both PAR-TNER and PAR-TI. While only one participant completed Puzzle 3, all participants were on the path to success when time ran out. We believe that increasing puzzle completion time to eight minutes would be sufficient to allow the majority of participants to complete the puzzle. However, further research is needed to confirm this. Selection of the human more often than the bot for the tiebreaker round indicated that the majority of participants did not develop trust with the bot, and that performance of the bot could not account for this pattern of preference. From an engineering perspective, there is a belief that if the system is capable of performing the action, the human operator will trust it. In our initial pilot of the PAR-TNER research platform, capability and reliability did not appear to lead to the development of trust. Rather, trust, as indicated by which teammate would be preferred in the tiebreaker round, did not appear to be tied to performance. Additionally, performance as indicated by the composite score and completion time may have been better when the participant believed that they were teamed with the bot. It is puzzling, however, that people indicated a preference for the human teammate when they demonstrated that they did not know on which puzzles they had teamed with a human to solve.

It appears that participants are more likely to sacrifice their teammate when it is a bot than when it is a human. It is possible that the participant preference for human teammates in the tie-breaker round is related to the appearance of greater confederate deaths when the participant believes the teammate is a bot rather than a human. It is also possible that participants prefer teammates which do not die in game.

In addition, this preference developed after the first two puzzles. This result is intriguing given the finding that performance on the first two puzzles was better (in terms of escape speed and fewer deaths of avatars) when the teammate was assumed to be a bot. When combined with the finding that participants were not good at distinguishing a bot from a human, this result supports models that propose that other factors beyond reliability or capability are in play in the development of trust. This effect could be indicative of a predisposition to trust. In addition, while participants stated that the puzzles on which they performed best were those in which they thought they were paired with a bot (for the easy puzzles at least), they rated the bot as performing worse than the human teammate. While this finding is intriguing, it is difficult to expand on it given the limitations created by the difficulty of Puzzle 3.

A number of explanations for these findings cannot be assessed here because of the limitations of the data. Follow-on work will seek to rectify the deficiencies in the data and to clarify the source of these findings. To that end, JHUAPL can make available the PAR-TNER and PAR-TI research platforms to any researchers who are interested in leveraging it in their research. We believe that PAR-TNER and PAR-TI have potential to allow exploration of teaming behaviors that cannot be explored with physical systems. We invite researchers to leverage the platforms.

Acknowledgements. We would like to thank Dr. Joshua Baker for his exceptional assistance with statistical analyses.

References

Bailey, N., Scerbo, M.: The impact of operator trust on monitoring a highly reliable automated system. In: Proceedings of HCI International 2005, Las Vegas, 22-27 July 2005 (2005)

Benbasat, I., Wang, W.: Trust in and adoption of online recommendation agents. J. Assoc. Inf. Syst. **6**(3), 4 (2005)

Cooke, N.J., Gorman, J.C., Myers, C.W., Duren, J.L.: Interactive team cognition. Cogn. Sci. **37**(2), 255–285 (2013)

de Visser, E., Parasuraman, R.: Adaptive aiding of human-robot teaming: effects of imperfect automation on performance, trust, and workload. J. Cogn. Eng. Decis. Making **5**(2), 209–231 (2011)

Desai, M., Kaniarasu, P., Medvedev, M., Steinfeld, A., Yanco, H.: Impact of robot failures and feedback on real-time trust. In: 2013 8th ACM/IEEE International Conference on Human-Robot Interaction (HRI), pp. 251–258. IEEE, March 2013

Desai, M., et al.: Effects of changing reliability on trust of robot systems. In: 2012 7th ACM/IEEE International Conference on Human-Robot Interaction (HRI), pp. 73–80. IEEE, March 2012

Deutsch, M.: The effect of motivational orientation upon trust and suspicion. Hum. Relat. **13**, 123–139 (1960)

Gorman, J.C., Cooke, N.J., Winner, J.L.: Measuring team situation awareness in decentralized command and control environments. In: Situational Awareness, pp. 183–196. Routledge (2017)

Gorman, J.C., Cooke, N.J., Winner, J.L.: Measuring team situation awareness in decentralized command and control environments. Ergonomics **49**(12–13), 1312–1325 (2006)

Hancock, P.A., Billings, D.R., Schaefer, K.E., Chen, J.Y., De Visser, E.J., Parasuraman, R.: A meta-analysis of factors affecting trust in human-robot interaction. Hum. Factors **53**(5), 517–527 (2011)

Hoff, K.A., Bashir, M.: Trust in automation: Integrating empirical evidence on factors that influence trust. Hum. Factors **57**(3), 407–434 (2015)

Jackson, K.F., Prasov, Z., Vincent, E.C., Jones, E.M.: A heuristic based framework for improving design of unmanned systems by quantifying and assessing operator trust. In: Proceedings of the Human Factors and Ergonomics Society Annual Meeting, vol. 60, no. 1, pp. 1696–1700. SAGE Publications, Los Angeles, September 2016

Khalid, H.M., et al.: Exploring psycho-physiological correlates to trust: implications for human-robot-human interaction. In: Proceedings of the Human Factors and Ergonomics Society Annual Meeting, vol. 60, no. 1, pp. 697–701. SAGE Publications, Los Angeles, September 2016

Koller, M.: Risk as a determinant of trust. Basic Appl. Soc. Psychol. **9**(4), 265–276 (1988)

Kosfeld, M., Heinrichs, M., Zak, P.J., Fischbacher, U., Fehr, E.: Oxytocin increases trust in humans. Nature **435**(7042), 673–676 (2005)

Lee, J.D., See, K.A.: Trust in automation: designing for appropriate reliance. Hum. Factors **46**(1), 50–80 (2004)

Mayer, R.C., Davis, J.H., Schoorman, F.D.: An integrative model of organizational trust. Acad. Manag. Rev. **20**, 709–734 (1995)

Molm, L.D., Takahashi, N., Peterson, G.: Risk and trust in social exchange: an experimental test of a classical proposition. Am. J. Sociol. **105**(5), 1396–1427 (2000)

Muir, B.M.: Trust between humans and machines, and the design of decision aids. Int. J. Man Mach. Stud. **27**(5–6), 527–539 (1987)

Perkins, L., Miller, J.E., Hashemi, A., Burns, G.: Designing for human-centered systems: situational risk as a factor of trust in automation. In: Proceedings of the Human Factors and Ergonomics Society Annual Meeting, vol. 54, no. 25, pp. 2130–2134. SAGE Publications, Los Angeles, September 2010

Portal Perpetual Testing Initiative: Valve Corporation. Registered trademark (2011). https://www.thinkwithportals.com/

Ross, J.M., Szalma, J.L., Hancock, P.A., Barnett, J.S., Taylor, G.: The effect of automation reliability on user automation trust and reliance in a search-and-rescue scenario. In: Proceedings of the Human Factors and Ergonomics Society Annual Meeting, vol. 52, no. 19, pp. 1340–1344. Sage Publications, Los Angeles, September 2008

Rousseau, D.M., Sitkin, S.B., Burt, R.S., Camerer, C.: Not so different after all: a cross-discipline view of trust. Acad. Manag. Rev. **23**(3), 393–404 (1998)

Salas, E., Dickinson, T., Converse, S., Tannenbaum, S.: Toward an understanding of team performance and training. In: Sweezey, R., Salas, E. (eds.) Teams: Theirtraining and Performance. Ablex, Norwood (1992)

Schaefer, K.E., Chen, J.Y., Szalma, J.L., Hancock, P.A.: A meta-analysis of factors influencing the development of trust in automation: implications for understanding autonomy in future systems. Hum. Factors **58**(3), 377–400 (2016)

Seong, Y., Bisantz, A.M.: The impact of cognitive feedback on judgment performance and trust with decision aids. Int. J. Ind. Ergon. **38**(7–8), 608–625 (2008)

Sifakis, J.: Can we trust autonomous systems? Boundaries and risks. In: Chen, Y.-F., Cheng, C.-H., Esparza, J. (eds.) ATVA 2019. LNCS, vol. 11781, pp. 65–78. Springer, Cham (2019). https://doi.org/10.1007/978-3-030-31784-3_4

Waytz, A., Heafner, J., Epley, N.: The mind in the machine: anthropomorphism increases trust in an autonomous vehicle. J. Exp. Soc. Psychol. **52**, 113–117 (2014)

Xu, H., Teo, H.H., Tan, B.: Predicting the adoption of location-based services: the role of trust and perceived privacy risk. In: ICIS 2005 Proceedings, vol. 71 (2005)

Design Principles for AI-Assisted Attention Aware Systems in Human-in-the-Loop Safety Critical Applications

Max Nicosia$^{(\boxtimes)}$ and Per Ola Kristensson

Department of Engineering, University of Cambridge, Cambridge CB2 1PZ, UK
{lmn27,pok21}@cam.ac.uk

Abstract. AI-assisted, attentiona-ware systems support operators in detecting and managing targets present in visual scenes. Such a system typically attempts to automatically identify targets of interest and increase the probability that an operator can detect them by, for example, modifying their visual saliency in the visual scene. Applications of AI-assisted attention awareness include air-traffic control, submarine demining and armored vehicle situational awareness. This chapter explains the key human-machine challenges intrinsic in this design problem and distills six design principles based on a functional design of a general AI-assisted attention-aware system for target identification.

Keywords: Attention awareness · Situational awareness · System design

1 Introduction

Application complexity is of particular pertinence in safety critical applications, where additional information can potentially assist the operator in making better decisions in difficult situations. A typical example of an application is an air-traffic control system, where the application displays a variety of information linked to multiple tasks. This application complexity means that operators have to maintain a high level of situational awareness, and therefore, may suffer from cognitive overload.

Traditionally, safety critical applications strive to mitigate this complexity with safety features that are intended to ensure operators are informed of specific noteworthy events through warnings or alarms. Operators of these applications go through extensive training to ensure that they have internalized the application's operational features, are familiar with the locations of various critical information data points, and have sufficient experience to preempt or mitigate various possible operational situational outcomes. However, such training is costly and time consuming, and does not guarantee optimal performance in practice. As a result,

W. F. Lawless et al. (Eds.): Engineering Artificially Intelligent Systems, LNCS 13000, pp. 230–246, 2021.
https://doi.org/10.1007/978-3-030-89385-9_14

in some particular complex domains, operators are required to go through several years of work experience before they have achieved the required level of proficiency.

AI-assisted target identification applications aim to overcome this problem by providing some level of assistance to the operator during operation. At the most basic level an AI-assisted target application seeks to manage the attention of the operator so they are aware of important or relevant events and pieces of information relevant for the current task (targets) while minimizing distracting information (distractors). To successfully achieve this, the AI-assisted application needs to make use of sensor data to infer and track the operator's focus of attention, detect important targets within the application, and deploy various subtle visualization techniques to draw the operator's attention towards relevant information at an optimal time without jeopardizing overall task performance.

Designing AI-assisted applications is not a straightforward task. Their success hinges on them being able to both accurately track the operator's focus of attention, their capacity to accurately detect targets, and their ability to preempt the operator's intentions or actions. Typically, they adjust the saliency of relevant information on a display using a mechanism that amplifies the operator's decision making capabilities while avoiding to inadvertently generate further distractors or disruptions. For an AI-assisted application to achieve balance, it needs to be designed specifically for the application's domain and it needs to dynamically adjust any operator intervention strategies based on current operator performance and actions, and in response to the application's current data stream.

The realization of AI-assisted applications is riddled with pitfalls. In this chapter we seek to assist system designers in avoiding those pitfalls by describing six system design principles necessary for the development of such a system. These principles are based on the functional design of a general AI-assisted target identification application, which we also introduce in this chapter.

In Sect. 2 we review prior work on similar applications and the challenges of presenting information to the operator in an optimal way. In Sect. 3 we discuss the human-machine challenges, our approach for tackling situational awareness, and the challenges of relying on binary classifiers for separating targets from distractors. In Sect. 4 we present a functional architecture for a generic AI-assisted target identification system. In Sect. 5 we use this functional description to distill six system design principles for AI-assisted target identification systems. In Sect. 6 we discuss the challenges and limitations of the design, and in Sect. 7 we conclude.

The main contribution in this chapter is the functional architecture of an AI-assisted target identification system and the six system design principles we distill from this functional description to address the human-machine challenges raised by a safety critical application.

2   Related Work

The human factors literature has extensively studied the potential benefits of adaptive guidance in human-machine systems (e.g. [27,31,32,37]). The efficacy of these complex systems is determined by the system managing the information presented to the user in such a way that it maximizes task performance. The literature has primarily focused on studying interruptions and information presentations.

By focusing on interruptions and information presentation, human factors researchers have attempted to balance attention allocation between bottom-up and top-down processes [33]. Bottom-up processes are said to be automatic and capture the user's attention without the user consciously acknowledging them; for example, becoming aware of a stimulus. Top-down processes require the user's conscious action and effort; for example, reading. Attention is understood to be a finite resource. However, there is still much debate about how attention is allocated and consumed across various stimuli, such as which stimuli will enter working memory and consciousness, and which stimuli will be acted on and with what response. This definition of attention as a finite resource that is subdivided among processes has become known as attention by selection [1,11,23,30,34].

Determining the rules that dictate which stimuli will capture the attention of a bottom-up or top-down process has proven difficult in some cases. For example, very salient stimuli can remain completely unnoticed under certain circumstances, such as when the user is engaged in another task demanding attention to other stimuli at the same time [38]. Other stimuli, such as alarms [42] and moving or looming objects [16], capture attention consistently. Somewhat contradictory to intuition, increasing the mental load of the operator has been shown to reduce distractor interference and increase the capacity for stimuli perception [22]. Desimone et al. [7] observed that stimuli relevant to the current user task tended to be favored for processing and entering consciousness.

Another reason for the literature to focus on interruptions is that interruptions affect working memory by causing retrospective and/or prospective memory failures. Prospective memory is what allows users to function—remembering to remember what we need to do or be aware of in the future. Retrospective memory is what is normally referred to as simply recalling something from the past. Einstein et al. [12] suggest that cues in the environment can trigger automatic-associative memory and lead to activating actions associated with the appropriate stimulus. In light of these results, the human factors literature has focused on manipulating the presentation of information to reduce the negative effects of interruptions.

The effects of interruptions on task performance have been studied extensively both in general (e.g., [5,21,26]) and in task-specific fields, such as air-traffic control research (e.g., [20,41]). Avoiding interrupting the user during the task and/or delaying the interruption until the latter half of the task has been observed to be effective [5]. More advanced strategies include context-sensing and/or using the contents of the message (notification) to infer an optimal time to interrupt the operator [18,26]. In office settings, listening for voices or noises has been shown to be effective for determining an appropriate time to interrupt users [15].

Saliency changes can be used to minimize change blindness [39] and inattentional blindness [38]. However, saliency changes are difficult to use effectively as there are many factors that affect how they are perceived. For example, Healey et al. [19] found that hue and target orientation work best for numerical estimations, while colors are discriminated by their distance, category and linear separation. Textures are discriminated by their size and density. In the case of multi-dimensional data, Healey et al. [19] found that the best strategy was to reduce feature interference as much as possible. Simple motions have been observed to be easily detectable both in the near and far field of view, perform well in peripheral visualizations, and interfere less with color and hue features [3].

Despite all of the benefits of saliency manipulation, complex changes in saliency can easily cause negative effects. A study focusing on air-traffic controllers demonstrated that some visualizations resulted in adverse effects on secondary task performance while only simple and subtle visualizations, such as pulsating objects, were relatively effective [20].

Prior work has used sensors to estimate the position and presence of users to expose them to proximity-aware applications [9,25]. Further research used multi-sensing to expose contextual information that allowed the development of more complex strategies to avoid interruptions. Gellersen et al. [18] used various external sensors to feed contextual information into mobile phones to reduce interruptions. Lopez-Tovar et al. [24] used a Bayesian network to enable smartphones to infer the correct notification preference for each user based on previous user choices and contextually sensed information during meetings.

The idea of extending system design and development with sensors to create attention aware systems has been advocated in the literature [2,36]. Such solutions aim at providing general purpose solutions that reduce interruptions and improve cognitive abilities of operators. Toolkits to manage attention by pushing notifications towards peripheral displays have been explored [36]. Other prior work investigated strategies, such as reducing interruptions, managing context switches, and tagging actively used objects, to improve task resumption [8,35]. Task-assisted resumption was shown to be effective in a learning system that managed interruptions and attention changes during learning sessions [35]. Tagging or marking the current position on the current task during notification interruptions was shown by Cutrell et al. [5] to be ineffective as improvement was only noticeable when no interruptions were present. In an earlier study, Czerwinski et al. [6] demonstrated that interruptions during the early stages of the task, that is, before the user entered the planning, execution or evaluation stage, reduced overall task performance time. However, users experienced significant disruptions when the interruptions occurred later in the task and required the use of reminders to resume the current task [5]. Bailey and Konstan [2] suggested using a two-level hierarchy within tasks to separate coarse events from fine events. They observed that interruptions between coarse events yielded less disruption.

Dostal et al. [10] used RGB cameras to develop an inattention aware multi-display system that detected if an operator was attending to a particular display. It used this information to derive subtle visualizations in unattended displays to reduce distractions while allowing the operator to perceive changes in peripheral vision. Garrido et al. [17] extended this system into a graphical user interface (GUI) toolkit.

Other recent work has used eye-tracking to increase the saliency of unobserved changes in a radar task [40]. However, the results were mixed as the system did not have the knowledge of several application-dependent factors, such as the task, the situational context, and the current workload of the operator. Nicosia and Kristensson. [28] developed an inattention management middleware to incorporate several of the techniques previously discussed in multi-display setups. The middleware provided a software layer that allowed distributed applications to query the status of the operator and trigger specific visualization logic as a result of operator action, attention and task performance. The idea of a dynamic system was based on allowing the operator to further their understanding about their current task and performance, as established in the situational awareness literature [13]. The system was later extended to support a consumer-producer competitive task setup in which the system dynamically adjusted the saliency of each target based on operator performance against externally supplied expected performance metrics [29]. The system effectively demonstrated improvement in performance for some of the task metrics, but it also highlighted the complexity of balancing dynamic strategies for multiple conflicting tasks.

3   Human-Machine Challenges

There are four challenges that need to be addressed in the design of an AI-assisted target identification system.

First, the system has to be able to separate targets from distractors. A *target* is a data point of any number of dimensions that is relevant to the operator at a particular point in time. A *distractor* is any data point that detracts, prevents, delays or confuses the operator in carrying out a task. Additionally, the system has to provide flexibility to manage incorrectly classified targets (false positives). We discuss this later in more detail in Subsect. 3.2.

Second, the system has to be able to account for target and task priorities. This accounting allows the system to apply specific strategies to ensure that the operator can distinguish the importance of specific targets and their relation to the current task.

Third, the system has to be capable of conveying all of the previously discussed information to the operator in such a way that it does not reduce task performance or overload the operator.

Fourth, the system has to be able to identify if the operator has failed to notice a specific data point that has been deemed important or relevant for a specific task (a target), and to be able to construct a strategy that brings such information to the operator's attention without compromising overall task performance.

3.1   Attention and Situational Awareness

There are several models that explain Situational Awareness (SA). We will focus on Endsley's model [13] and Situated Situational Awareness [4] as they are the most suitable models for addressing the complexity of AI-assisted systems.

Endsley's model [13] describes the process of building SA by identifying three stages of the operator. These stages are: 1) perception of the elements in the environment; 2) comprehension of the current situation; and 3) projection of future states. Depending on how the operator approaches the task and what their current goal is, the operator may progress through these stages in order, jump between them, or iterate through them to arrive at a particular SA level.

These stages do not guarantee that the operator will build a correct SA model—the stages merely describe the operator's cognitive activities. For example, if the operator's focus of attention are not on important information at that point in time, the operator will not perceive it and, subsequently, will build an incorrect or incomplete understanding of the current situation and its potential future states. Similarly, if the information is presented in a confusing or unclear manner, the operator may perceive it, but the operator may still build an incorrect understanding of its importance and its future potential states. Finally, an operator could still arrive at an incorrect SA model even if all of the information has been presented in an optimal manner due to external factors outside of the system, such as, for example, a failure to recall critical information, stress, fatigue, or poor decision-making skills.

In the Situated Situational Awareness model [4], the operator builds the SA by repeatedly sampling the environment for limited amounts of information based on its relevance. This model emphasizes SA building on the working memory of the operator and the capacity to maintain and update it. Endsley [14] criticized this approach, suggesting that expert operators will normally build their SA using their understanding of the possible projection scenarios from information stored in their long-term memory to reduce the necessity to continuously sample and notice relevant information. Further, Endsley [14] argued that operators will seek to validate their understanding or complete their projections actively, as maintaining full SA in working memory is suboptimal for experts and in most cases almost impossible.

The approach taken in this chapter is that the solution for an AI-assisted target identification system lies somewhere in between. We agree that expert operators will draw from their experience in long-term memory. However, it is also important that the system leverages the potential capacity for associative memory and automaticity of action that can arise from manipulating the relevance of information at a specific point in time.

An AI-assisted system needs to ensure that the information is presented in a clear manner to the operator, and that the operator's focus of attention is on the relevant data point at the correct time. As such, managing attention is instrumental to increasing the probability of the operator building a successful SA model and to reducing any adverse influence.

3.2   Classifier Interaction

A target identification system can be fundamentally viewed as a binary classifier that attempts to identify *targets* among *distractors*. In a binary classifier there are four possible outcomes: 1) a true positive (TP)—a target is correctly classified as a target; 2) a false positive (FP)—a distractor is incorrectly classified as a target; 3) a true negative (TN)—a distractor is correctly classified as a distractor; and 4) a false negative (FN)—a target is incorrectly classified as a distractor.

These four outcomes give rise to a set of metrics for understanding the binary classification performance of the system. A Receiver Operating Characteristic (ROC) curve is used to analyze the operating envelope of a binary classifier. A perfect classifier has 100% TP and TN rates. A random classifier, similar to a coin toss, has an even distribution of TP, FP, TN and FN. Classifiers that are worse than random classifiers can be reversed to increase their *positive* predictive power. The area under the ROC curve, also called the *c-statistic*, can be used to calculate the predictive power of the classifier as this area will reflect the probability that the classifier will score a randomly chosen *positive* outcome higher than a randomly chosen *negative* outcome. The higher this probability, the better the classifier.

Fundamentally, an AI-assisted target identification relies on an AI module to perform binary classification on information presented to the operator. This information may be either correctly classified as relevant (a true positive target), correctly classified as irrelevant (a true positive distractor), incorrectly classified as relevant (a false positive target), or incorrectly classified as a distractor (a false positive distractor). While great efforts are spent maximimzing classification performance, it is important to realize and accept that incorrect classifications are unavoidable in practice. Therefore, any system solution must assume the presence of both incorrectly classified targets (which now serve as dangerous distractors to the operator) and incorrectly classified distractors (which may potentially obscure critical information).

4   Functional Architecture

We here present six system design principles for AI-assisted target identification systems. We introduce a generic high-level functional architecture for this purpose in the form of a function-structure model and use this model to distill design principles.

The function-structure model of the joint human-machine system is shown in Fig. 1. Dashed arrows indicate signal flows. The overall function is Detect and Process Target. The overall function outputs a signal *Processed Targets* in response to two *Sensor Data* signals, which may be identical, or be received from an identical signal source, however, this is not a requirement. The overall function is decomposed into nine key subfunctions. We separate functions into two categories: 1) AI-functions, which are carried out by a technical embodiment of the system; and 2) operator functions, which are carried out by a human operator.

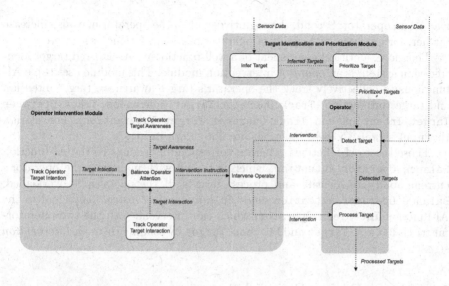

Fig. 1. A function-structure representation of an AI-assisted target identification system with operator inattention support.

Fundamentally, the functional architecture in Fig. 1 identifies three modules: 1) a human *operator*; 2) an AI-based *target identification and prioritization* module; and 3) an AI-based *operator intervention* module.

The AI-function `Infer Target` receives a *Sensor Data* signal and infers any targets in the sensor stream. The output of this function results in an *Inferred Targets* signal transmitted to the AI-function `Prioritize Target`, which assesses the importance of each target and determines its priority for an operator's attention. Collectively, the two AI-functions, `Infer Target` and `Prioritize Target`, represent a machine learning module that identifies and prioritizes targets in a scene.

The first operator-function, `Detect Target`, detects targets, which can be both detected directly by the operator in a raw *Sensor Data* signal, or presented to the operator as a *Prioritized Targets* signal. The second operator-function `Process Target` receives the signal *Detected Targets* and performs actions in response to them. This last step results in `Process Target` finally outputting a *Processed Targets* signal from the system. Collectively, the two operator-functions, `Detect Target` and `Process Target`, represents a human operator tasked with identifying and processing targets on a display assisted by an automatic target identification system.

However, merely assisting the operator by automatically identifying and prioritizing targets may not be sufficient. First, the AI-functions `Infer Target` and `Prioritize Target` are likely to occasionally generate erroneous results, such as failing to identify targets or incorrectly identifying targets (distrators). The presence of such uncertainty around prioritized targets increases the cognitive load on an operator; Second, the cognitive load on the operator may also increase further, for example, as a result of operator overload, fatigue, stress, etc.

Therefore, a critical component of a well-functioning AI-assisted target identification system is an operator intervention module. This module uses three AI-functions to collectively track the operator's target awareness, target intention and target interaction (`Track Operator Target Awareness`, `Track Operator Target Intention` and `Track Operator Target Interaction`). For clarity, the input signals to these functions are not shown in Fig. 1.

These three AI-functions generate corresponding signals to the AI-function `Balance Operator Attention`, which is tasked with managing the operator's current ability to identify and process targets. If the operator is overloaded, `Balance Operator Attention` sends an *Intervention Instruction* signal to the AI-function `Intervene Operator`, which can intervene with the two operator-functions `Detect Target` and `Process Target` by sending them an *Intervention* signal.

5   System Design Principles

The AI-functions `Infer Target` and `Prioritize Target` are domain-specific applications of machine learning infrastructure. We are therefore here concerned with distilling six system design principles for improving the operator functions `Detect Target` and `Process Target` by realizing effective operator interventions.

5.1   Determine Operator Focus of Attention

Establishing the focus of attention is the first necessary step in order to track operator awareness. Determining the operator's focus of attention requires reconciling target locations with the sensor stream or detecting targets from application data events. The specific realization of this function will be application specific, as different domains will have different constraints or requirements on how data is represented, as well as the number of dimensions that are represented. Data dimensions can include, for example, color changes, location changes, and value changes. Data may also consist of video or audio streams, still images and visualized sensor data (such as sonar data).

Regardless of these factors, a typical implementation will use eye-tracking data to convert fixations into operator attention focus points. A fixated target, or area, can then be used by the system to determine that a data point has been recognized by the operator. Further program logic can be constructed based on the duration of the fixation and the proximity of the fixation to the target data point. However, such modifications will be domain dependant.

The primary concern in the realization of this function is in the reconciliation of the sensor data and the application's data points. The first challenge arises due to how the data is presented in the application. Applications that display data points in clusters or in close proximity to each other will cause the reconciliation of events and data points to be non-deterministic as there will inevitably be uncertainty around the correctly determined operator's focus of attention. In such cases, the system will need to operate under the assumption that the operator fixated on all nearby data points and apply some further heuristics based on the likelihood of specific data points being noticed during the fixation time, or use a corroboration mechanism by highlighting (or moving) subsets of data points, that reveal to the user what the system has recognized.

The second challenge arises due to the system misclassifying an operator's focus of attention due to the operator zoning out, possibly due to sleep deprivation, information overload, stress, or trauma, and the system incorrectly detecting this behavior as an eye-tracking fixation and hence an operator's focus of attention. Since the operator's mind is unobservable, the system will need to filter such instances out. Possible solutions include: 1) require additional data from the primary attention-tracking channel (for example, an eye-tracker) to confirm the focus of attention, such as increased fixation duration, or a series of fixations; 2) require additional data from a secondary attention-tracking channel (such as a head tracker) to confirm the focus of attention (for example, the operator rotating its head in the direction of the inferred focus of attention); and/or 3) track the operator user interface activity to confirm focus of attention by, for example, analyzing the mouse cursor movement in the vicinity of the hypothesized point of the operator's focus of attention.

5.2 Track Operator Target Awareness

The ability to determine operator awareness separates a dynamic *intelligent* system from a system that can only react using fixed predetermined output for each configured situation. The system can only produce a tailored output signal that addresses the current operator state if the system incorporates information about the operator's target awareness.

A system able to establish the operator's awareness of each target on the display, by reconciling the operator's focus of attention with data points on the display, can infer which targets the operator may be unaware of. This inference permits the system to predict what the operator has perceived and thus allows the system to estimate the level of SA of the operator. The system can then transmit this signal, together with other output signals, to the Balance Operator Attention function.

Realizing this function requires the system to reconcile data point changes, data point priorities, and associated operator events. The implementation of this function is typically relatively straight-forward, assuming the Determine Operator Focus of Attention function and the Infer Target and Prioritize Target functions are reliable, that is, they exhibit low false-positives rates.

5.3   Track Operator Target Intention

Once the system has acquired knowledge about which targets the operator has perceived, the system can use this information to infer what the operator comprehended of the current application state and attempt to use this inference to project what the operator's intentions are towards any targets on the display. The previous operator interaction, or logged traces of previous operator performance, can be used to guide the system's inference. Having the system generating hypotheses of operator intentions can be used to assess current operator performance and incorporate error prevention strategies to preempt future operator errors.

For example, if the operator has recently fixated on a set of specific targets, it is probable that the operator will carry out actions related to those targets in the near future. Correspondingly, the operator is less likely to follow-up on actions for targets that have not been fixated on recently. Similar logic can be applied for tasks within the application. The system can infer if a specific task is being neglected based on which targets are being fixated upon or interacted with by the operator the most. The output of this function will be used by the `Balance Operator Attention` function to estimate future operator actions and whether they will be in line with expected actions and baseline performance.

The primary challenge in realizing this function is accurately inferring the operator's intention within the application's domain for specific circumstances and actions. One approach to implement this function is to have the system use a task template matching mechanism to predict the likelihood of specific follow-up actions as a result of target fixations and then match these predictions with actual operator outcomes. Since intention is closely related to task execution, the system needs to account for the specifics of each task within the application and its domain.

A related challenge that can arise in some applications is that an operator's actions may be ambiguous and thus match multiple task templates at once. In such cases, the system can use two strategies: 1) the system can use past history or other data feeds about the overall state of the system to predict operator intentions; and 2) the system can operate under the assumption that all of the operator's intended actions take place at the same time and allow the `Balance Operator Attention` function, which has access to both *Target Interaction* and *Target Awareness* signals, to perform more accurate inferences of the operator's intention.

5.4   Track Operator Target Interaction

The operator's interaction with the system is a rich source for the system to infer the current awareness state of the operator and possible future state projections. The system can also use the information associated with an action to estimate its impact on the overall future application state. The degree to which the system can estimate this information depends on the application's domain.

Nevertheless, the system can gain important operator insights by tracking the operator's interactions.

The operator's interactions can be classified into two types: 1) definite actions; and 2) precursors to definite actions. The first type of interaction can inform the system of the culmination of the awareness of the operator. The second type of interaction can inform the system about potential definite actions that the operator may take. For example, when the operator selects a group of targets, the operator performs an interaction of type 2. When the operator executes an action for selection, the operator performs an interaction of type 1.

Both of these types of interaction provide information on the operator's focus of attention. If the user has interacted with a particular target, or a set of targets, the operator is definitely aware of them. Conversely, this information also informs the system about what the operator is *not* aware of (inattention). A system having knowledge about the current operator's awareness is a system capable of both estimating future system states and the level of comprehension of the operator of any targets and potential follow-up actions. For example, the system is able to detect if an operator is acting on low priority targets instead of high priority targets, or whether an operator is neglecting one task in favor of another task.

The system can also estimate delays and the costs of actions by examining the timing associated with task execution and target fixations. Such statistics can then be used to detect anomalies, for example, fatigue or lapses in individual operator performance. These statistics can then be propagated to the `Balance Operator Attention` function to allow the system to execute an appropriate operator intervention tactic. Alternatively, or in parallel, these statistics can be used to evaluate the effectiveness of prior operator intervention tactics.

5.5   Balance Operator Attention

Balancing operator attention is carried out by the system reconciling all information from the `Track Operator Target Awareness`, `Track Operator Target Intention` and `Track Operator Target Interaction` functions in order to decide if an *Intervention Instruction* signal should be sent to the `Intervene Operator` function in the system.

Balancing operator attention is necessary to manage the operator's attention, which is a limited resource as explained in the Related Work Sect. 2 previously in this chapter. Balancing operator attention means distributing operator attention across tasks and targets to ensure the operator chooses the most relevant actions at any given time.

To balance the operator's attention, it is necessary for the system to have knowledge about the operator's awareness of any targets, the operator's intentions regarding targets, and the operator's interaction with any targets. Using this information, the system can balance the operator's attention in several ways.

First, the system can balance operator attention by assessing the operator's performance in comparison to an expected benchmark. For example, the system can estimate changes in target priorities as a result of possible operator actions and compare such changes against previous actions to assess if the operator's actions are resulting in expected performance. If the observed operator performance is below a threshold, the system can intervene with the operator; for example, by drawing the operator's attention to higher priority targets.

Second, the system can balance operator attention by distributing attention across tasks. Successfully achieving this distribution depends critically on the system's ability to infer the operator's target awareness, target intention and target interaction.

A challenge in balancing operator attention in an optimal fashion is the fact that the system is dynamic—the system changes states both due to new incoming data and to operator actions, which may or may not be influenced by feedback from the system itself (such as an operator intervention). One way to tackle this challenge is to associate specific operator actions with potential application state outcomes. System applications that have clear definite actions are able to evaluate outcomes with higher a accuracy compared to system applications where outcomes are not easily attributed.

Hence, balancing operator attention is challenging. To avoid the main pitfalls, as discussed in the Related Work Sect. 2 previously in this chapter, it is advisable to: 1) avoid unnecessary interruptions; 2) ensure that relevant information is clearly shown without confounding the operator; and 3) prevent adverse effects, such as inducing additional confusion or stress.

5.6   Intervene Operator

When the system intervenes with the operator the system performs an action in response to an *Intervention Instruction* signal from **Balance Operator Attention**.

Operator interventions can be carried out in a number of ways. The central idea is to modify operator behavior to respond to targets or tasks in a domain-appropriate way. One straightforward example is for the system to increase the visual saliency of targets the system believes the operator is unaware of.

Realizing such a function is fundamentally application specific as these operator interventions must be carefully designed to not intrude on established workflows. Poorly designed operator interventions can confuse the operator or add further cognitive overload.

A typical way to achieve an operator intervention, as previously mentioned, is modifying visual saliency. Visual target attributes, such as hue, color and movement, can be modified to attract an operator's attention to specific targets or individual data attributes. This method necessitates careful design work to ensure the visual attribute modifications are compatible with existing workflows and the visual grammars used in the domain.

The primary challenge in the realization of a needed function is in ensuring any operator intervention does not detract the operator from other critical targets or tasks and that any operator intervention has a clear purpose and does not result in unexpected operator behavior. This requirement necessitates that interventions are coordinated to ensure that they do not clash, overload or confuse the operator.

6 Discussion

A particular challenge for any AI-assisted target identification system is realizing the `Balance Operator Attention` and `Intervene Operator` functions. As previously discussed, these two functions are critical in enhancing operator performance. Fundamentally, this means ensuring that the operator's attention is optimally allocated to allow the operator access to the highest quality information at any given point in time.

The efficacy of the `Balance Operator Attention` function depends on two factors: 1) the quality of logged traces available for predicting expected operator actions based on the estimated states of the operator and the application; and 2) the capacity for establishing a baseline that allows the system to evaluate the current application's state to determine when to intervene the operator.

The `Balance Operator Attention` function is one of the distinguishing features that separates an AI-assisted target identification system from static systems that rely on simplistic tactics, such as highlighting important information regardless of the current state of the operator or application. This capacity to balance operator attention for the joint human-machine system to adapt to the operator's awareness and the current application state is critical for the successful operation of challenging tasks in this area. On the other hand, this very same system adaptability is what the literature has identified as being a source of potential pitfalls and challenges. Therefore, any `Balance Operator Attention` function must be realized with great care.

In general, an AI-assisted target identification system needs to ensure that it does not cause detrimental performance. This case requires a careful consideration of many design parameters and functions, e.g. as determining when to intervene, how to intervene, and how to verify and validate that performance does not degrade under certain task conditions, such as during an unusually high complexity period of operation.

A benefit of the functional architecture introduced in Fig. 1 is that by turning off the `Intervene Operator` function, the output of the `Balance Operator Attention` function can be used to assess operator performance live. The data can then be used to identify any common operational challenges that are experienced under particular operational situations, as well as any weaknesses in the design of the system application. This data also serves to establish a baseline, which can be used to assess the improvements induced by an AI-assisted target identification system that re-couples these two functions. The logged data can also be used to gain further insights into operator behavior, or be used to support operator training activities.

7   Conclusions

In this chapter we have introduced a high-level functional architecture for AI-assisted target identification systems. From this functional description, we have distilled six system design principles required for the optimal operation of such a system. While successful implementation of operator intervention is challenging, we believe the incorporation of these AI-assisted functions is critical for successful operation in safety critical domains, in particular when the task complexity is difficult to predict and occasionally very high.

References

1. Baddeley, A.D., Weiskrantz, L.E.: Attention: Selection, Awareness, and Control: A Tribute to Donald Broadbent. Clarendon Press/Oxford University Press, New York (1993)
2. Bailey, B.P., Konstan, J.A.: On the need for attention-aware systems: measuring effects of interruption on task performance, error rate, and affective state. Comput. Hum. Behav. **22**(4), 685–708 (2006)
3. Bartram, L., Ware, C., Calvert, T.: Moticons: detection, distraction and task. Int. J. Hum. Comput. Stud. **58**(5), 515–545 (2003)
4. Chiappe, D.L., Strybel, T.Z., Vu, K.P.L.: Mechanisms for the acquisition of situation awareness in situated agents. Theoret. Iss. Ergon. Sci. **13**(6), 625–647 (2012)
5. Cutrell, E., Czerwinski, M., Horvitz, E.: Notification, disruption, and memory: Effects of messaging interruptions on memory and performance. In: Proceedings of Interact. pp. 263–269 (2001)
6. Czerwinski, M., Cutrell, E., Horvitz, E.: Instant messaging: effects of relevance and timing. In: People and Computers XIV: Proceedings of HCI 2000, vol. 2, pp. 71–76 (2000)
7. Desimone, R., Duncan, J.: Neural mechanisms of selective visual attention. Ann. Rev. Neurosci. **18**(1), 193–222 (1995)
8. D'Mello, S., Olney, A., Williams, C., Hays, P.: Gaze tutor: a gaze-reactive intelligent tutoring system. Int. J. Hum-Comput. Stud. **70**(5), 377–398 (2012)
9. Dostal, J., Hinrichs, U., Kristensson, P.O., Quigley, A.: Spidereyes: designing attention-and proximity-aware collaborative interfaces for wall-sized displays. In: Proceedings of the 19th International Conference on Intelligent User Interfaces, pp. 143–152 (2014)
10. Dostal, J., Kristensson, P.O., Quigley, A.: Subtle gaze-dependent techniques for visualising display changes in multi-display environments. In: Proceedings of the International Conference on Intelligent User Interfaces, pp. 137–148 (2013)
11. Driver, J.: A selective review of selective attention research from the past century. Br. J. Psychol. **92**(1), 53–78 (2001)
12. Einstein, G.O., McDaniel, M.A.: Retrieval processes in prospective memory: theoretical approaches and some new empirical findings. In: Brandimonte, M., Einstein, G.O., McDaniel, M.A. (eds.) Prospective Memory: Theory and Applications, pp. 115–141. Lawrence Erlbaum Associates Publishers (1996)
13. Endsley, M.R.: Measurement of situation awareness in dynamic systems. Hum. Fact. **37**(1), 65–84 (1995)
14. Endsley, M.R.: Situation awareness misconceptions and misunderstandings. J. Cogn. Eng. Decis. Making **9**(1), 4–32 (2015)

15. Fogarty, J., Hudson, S.E., Atkeson, C.G., Avrahami, D., Forlizzi, J., Kiesler, S., Lee, J.C., Yang, J.: Predicting human interruptibility with sensors. ACM Trans. Comput.-Hum. Inter. **12**(1), 119–146 (2005)
16. Franconeri, S.L., Simons, D.J.: Moving and looming stimuli capture attention. Percep. Psychophys. **65**(7), 999–1010 (2003)
17. Garrido, J.E., Penichet, V.M., Lozano, M.D., Quigley, A., Kristensson, P.O.: Awtoolkit: attention-aware user interface widgets. In: Proceedings of the 2014 International Working Conference on Advanced Visual Interfaces, pp. 9–16 (2014)
18. Gellersen, H.W., Schmidt, A., Beigl, M.: Multi-sensor context-awareness in mobile devices and smart artifacts. Mobile Netw. Appl. **7**(5), 341–351 (2002)
19. Healey, C.G., Booth, K.S., Enns, J.T.: High-speed visual estimation using preattentive processing. ACM Trans. Comput.-Hum. Inter. **3**(2), 107–135 (1996)
20. Imbert, J.P., Hodgetts, H.M., Parise, R., Vachon, F., Dehais, F., Tremblay, S.: Attentional costs and failures in air traffic control notifications. Ergonomics **57**(12), 1817–1832 (2014)
21. Iqbal, S.T., Bailey, B.P.: Effects of intelligent notification management on users and their tasks. In: Proceedings of the ACM Conference on Human Factors in Computing Systems, pp. 93–102 (2008)
22. Lavie, N., Hirst, A., De Fockert, J.W., Viding, E.: Load theory of selective attention and cognitive control. J. Experiment. Psychol. Gen.l **133**(3), 339 (2004)
23. Lavie, N., Tsal, Y.: Perceptual load as a major determinant of the locus of selection in visual attention. Percep. Psychophys. **56**(2), 183–197 (1994)
24. Lopez-Tovar, H., Charalambous, A., Dowell, J.: Managing smartphone interruptions through adaptive modes and modulation of notifications. In: Proceedings of the 20th International Conference on Intelligent User Interfaces, pp. 296–299 (2015)
25. Marquardt, N., Diaz-Marino, R., Boring, S., Greenberg, S.: The proximity toolkit: prototyping proxemic interactions in ubiquitous computing ecologies. In: Proceedings of the 24th Annual ACM Symposium on User Interface Software and Technology, pp. 315–326 (2011)
26. Mehrotra, A., Musolesi, M., Hendley, R., Pejovic, V.: Designing content-driven intelligent notification mechanisms for mobile applications. In: Proceedings of the 2015 ACM International Joint Conference on Pervasive and Ubiquitous Computing, pp. 813–824 (2015)
27. Morris, N.M., Rouse, W.B., Frey, P.R.: Adaptive aiding for symbiotic human-computer control: conceptual model and experimental approach. Tech. rep., Search Technology Inc., Norcross (1985)
28. Nicosia, L., Kristensson, P.: Inattention-management middleware for human-in-the-loop multi-display applications. In: Proceedings of the IEEE Workshop on Human-Centered Computational Sensing (2018)
29. Nicosia, M., Kristensson, P.O.: A conceptual design of an inattention management middleware with adaptive target saliency. In: 2020 IEEE Aerospace Conference, pp. 1–11 (2020)
30. Parasuraman, R., Davies, D.R.: Varieties of attention. Academic Pr (1984)
31. Parasuraman, R., Molloy, R., Singh, I.L.: Performance consequences of automation-induced'complacency'. Int. J. Aviat. Psychol. **3**(1), 1–23 (1993)
32. Parasuraman, R., Riley, V.: Humans and automation: use, misuse, disuse, abuse. Hum. fact. **39**(2), 230–253 (1997)
33. Posner, M.I.: Orienting of attention. Q. J. Experiment. Psychol. **32**(1), 3–25 (1980)
34. Posner, M.I.: Cumulative development of attentional theory. Am. Psychol. **37**(2), 168 (1982)

35. Roda, C., Nabeth, T.: Supporting attention in learning environments: attention support services, and information management. In: Creating New Learning Experiences on a Global Scale, pp. 277–291 (2007)

36. Roda, C., Thomas, J.: Attention aware systems: theories, applications, and research agenda. Comput. Hum. Behav. **22**(4), 557–587 (2006)

37. Rouse, W.B.: Adaptive aiding for human/computer control. Hum. Fact. **30**(4), 431–443 (1988)

38. Simons, D.J., Chabris, C.F.: Gorillas in our midst: sustained inattentional blindness for dynamic events. Perception **28**(9), 1059–1074 (1999)

39. Simons, D.J., Rensink, R.A.: Change blindness: past, present, and future. Trends Cogn. Sci. **9**(1), 16–20 (2005)

40. Vallières, B.R., Hodgetts, H.M., Vachon, F., Tremblay, S.: Supporting dynamic change detection: using the right tool for the task. Cogn. Res. Princ. Implicat. **1**(1), 1–20 (2016). https://doi.org/10.1186/s41235-016-0033-4

41. Wilson, M.D., Farrell, S., Visser, T.A., Loft, S.: Remembering to execute deferred tasks in simulated air traffic control: the impact of interruptions. J. Exp. Psychol. Appl. **24**(3), 360 (2018)

42. Yantis, S.: Goal-directed and stimulus-driven determinants of attentional control. Attent. Perform. **18**, 73–103 (2000)

Interdependence and Vulnerability in Systems: A Review of Theory for Autonomous Human-Machine Teams

W. F. Lawless[1]([⊠]) [iD] and Donald A. Sofge[2] [iD]

[1] Paine College, Augusta, GA 30901, USA
w.lawless@icloud.com
[2] Distributed Autonomous Systems Group, Navy Center for Applied Research in Artificial Intelligence, Naval Research Laboratory, Washington, DC, USA
donald.sofge@nrl.navy.mil

Abstract. Interdependence exists in all social interactions as constructive or destructive interference. States of interdependence transmit both positive (constructive) and negative (destructive) effects in the interaction. In this chapter, we review the theory of interdependence, and its effects when positive (e.g., innovations, marriages, mergers) or negative (e.g., patent failures, divorces, bankruptcies). We apply the theory to human-machine teams to predict the best and worst teams. And with the theory of interdependence, we review our newest discovery of vulnerability in an opposing team or in our own team. We consider vulnerability to be a fundamental principle of organization in preparation for a competition, during a competition, or in the post-hoc reviews of a competition between teams or organizations. One of the new issues for this chapter is to apply interdependence theory to whether or not convergence has a positive or negative effect in a competition, as with models for system dynamics. We conclude that if a model, concept or leader of a team addresses only a team's convergence effects, the team will itself be left vulnerable to its opponent and ignorant of the vulnerabilities in its opponent.

Keywords: Interdependence · Convergence · Vulnerability

1 Introduction

In this chapter we provide an overview of the current context motivating the need for decisions involving the use of new technology that requires rapid decisions, such as those decisions that have to be made on the battlefield within split-seconds, especially those made by the use of autonomous human-machine teams. We discuss the performance of regular teams with interdependence, the effects of interdependence among teammates, interdependence and vulnerability, and convergence processes, and we draw a conclusion.

W. F. Lawless et al. (Eds.): Engineering Artificially Intelligent Systems, LNCS 13000, pp. 247–259, 2021.
https://doi.org/10.1007/978-3-030-89385-9_15

1.1 What is the Problem?

Artificial Intelligence (AI) is considered by many innovators and users to be a positive force for good. The increasing widespread nature of its use, however, the more another, darker side has emerged that some have begun to fear. The risk of nuclear war may increase by depending on AI, by the coming deployment of hypersonic missiles, and by the widespread use of drones [1]. Drones have already killed Russian soldiers at an airfield in Syria [2]. These threats are rising with the development of autonomous human-machine teams. Yet social science seems unable to assist in their development. We do know that the best human teams are highly interdependent [3]. Interdependence implies communicating among and reacting to the members of a team. For autonomous human-machine teams to be able to communicate and react to each other, our research investigates a mathematics of interdependence for the optimum performance of autonomous human-machine teams. At the end of this chapter, we apply our model to the concept of convergence.

1.2 Interdependence Defined

Interdependence represents the phenomena that transmit all social effects in the form of interference in interactions (e.g., the synergism that produces positive emergence in an interaction like a team's enhanced performance; the dysergism that produces the negative effects, like divorce from a marriage, business split-ups or social conflict; and the adverse attacks that destabilize an opponent's defenses; see [4]; [5]). Together, the phenomena combine into forces that drive local change, organizational restructuring, or even political and possibly social evolution.

In contrast, the competing social interdependence theory has a long, hopeful but ultimately unsuccessful history, culminating in the homilies of peace and harmony to replace Darwin's [6] "survival of the fittest" with new ageism's "survival of the friendliest" [7]. The primary failure of social interdependence theory, developed largely with studies that sum the choices of individuals, is its limited ability to predict outcomes in natural social settings and, more relevant, its inability to establish fundamental science and engineering relationships in the design, operational guidance and metrics for the rapidly approaching age of autonomous human-machine teams and systems [8]. Social interdependence theory is a rational model that, along with other rational theories, seek to buttress the general value of cooperation. Rational modelers, however, admit that limits occur and that their models break down when trying to face conflict or uncertainty [9].

In agreement with Hare and Woods [7], cooperation is important in a wide cross-section of human behavior, for example, whether to rescue others in a time of crisis, to assist a neighbor, to repel an invader, to collaborate, or to coordinate. From Oxford's *Dictionary of Zoology* [10], cooperation is defined as the "mutually beneficial behaviour that involves several individuals (e.g., collaborative hunting, and care of the young). Cooperation may involve altruism. Co-operation among members of different species is usually called 'symbiosis.' To cooperate also means to work together as part of a team.

1.3 The Effects of Interdependence

Interdependence consists of three physical effects: bistability, a measurement problem, and non-factorability [5].

Bistability. The American Psychological Association [11] considers social reality to be considered as "the consensus of attitudes, opinions, and beliefs held by members of a group or society." In contrast, bistability represents psychological or social duality. For example, bistability is the existence of two-sided stories to describe an event (e.g. two tribes holding differing beliefs, and being either an individual or the member of a team, but not both simultaneously). The effects of bistability are at the most profound when its effects occur between two orthogonal agents, two teams or two systems. Two teams in competition with each other impede the occurrence of a convergence process. Interrupting an orthogonal relationship creates a significant measurement problem [12, 13].

Measurement Problem. Measuring an interdependent situation produces a single perspective, commonly modeled by a convergence process statistically or mathematically (viz., system dynamics). But, having a similar effect to a measurement, this problem could also represent the suppression of opposing viewpoints by an authoritarian leader [5], or the minority control from seeking consensus that blocks a majority from acting [14].

Non-factorability. Non-factorability is the inability to factor social situations that are "mutually dependent," a definition of interdependence [5]. The result is that the many attempts to factor the causes of social failures or psychological breakdowns can wind up in lengthy, painstakingly complex court proceedings to determine the cause and the blame of the breakdowns [15]; e.g., contested divorce proceedings; a criminal murder; a business failure. Non-factorability seems most difficult to parse when the two sides of a courtroom process are both represented by equally competent legal attorneys, what Freer and Purdue [16] said was necessary to obtain the truth or justice in the courtroom.

1.4 Positive Effects of Interdependence

In contrast to the social interdependence theory of Hare and Woods [7], by relying on the interdependent effects found in human-only team studies [3, 17, 18], and by adopting state-dependent effects in theory (quantum-like), including Schrödinger's [19] and Lewin's [20] separately derived concept of the "whole being greater than the sum of its parts" which fits nicely in modern Systems Engineering [21] with our revised theory of interdependence, we have made several predictions along with these supporting findings in the field: that redundant team members in teams and organizations impede performance and increase the likelihood of corruption and accidents [12, 13]; that the value of intelligence in the form of a nation's higher education for all of its citizens increases the nation's ability to innovate indicated by the number of productive patents a country produces [22]; and that redundancy in an organization reduces its resilience [15]. We also recently discovered mathematically the existence of vulnerability, which we discuss further below.

Intelligence. For astronomers seeking alien civilizations, "A civilization connotes a society of individuals. In contrast, ET [an extraterrestrial] might be a single integrated intelligence" [23]. A single intelligence, however, can be most easily generated among humans by an authoritarian regime using various techniques to achieve suppression [5]. Similarly, used in democracies or by authoritarians, consensus-seeking is a formal process designed to pursue a wide but single agreement. However, we have termed consensus-seeking as "minority control" because it is easily abused by a minority that blocks an unwanted action, as has happened in the European Union. For example, "The requirement for consensus in the European Council often holds policy-making hostage to national interests in areas which Council could and should decide by a qualified majority" (p. 29, [24]).

In contrast, even after controlling for the individual effects of intelligence or knowledge, intelligence has been located in the interactions of a team [25].

1.5 Negative Effects of Interdependence

When a team has a mission and can enact it, the team should execute its mission to the best of its ability. But what should a team do when it faces uncertainty? Facing uncertainty, humans weigh the choice of the best path going forward by engaging in debates [15], supporting the conclusion by leading AI scientists (e.g., [8, 26, 27]) that machines must be able to express their intentions and actions in a causal language humans understand (viz., using artificial intelligence, or AI). We add that machines must also be able to understand their human teammates to be able to help them in the performance of their duties and to do so safely by avoiding accidents [28].

2 Interdependence and Vulnerability

Teams produce at least two forms of entropy: structural [5]) and performance [4]. As part of a tradeoff, given a marginal or limited availability of energy, if the entropy production of a team's structure is at a minimum (structural entropy production, or SEP), more energy is available for the performance of a team, maximizing its entropy production (MEP) for a team's productivity.

$$SEP \leftrightarrow MEP \tag{1}$$

For the entropy of the structure to reach a minimum and for the team to produce MEP, in the limit, a team composed of members in orthogonal relationships can produce zero entropy as follows,

$$\lim_{dof \to 1} \log(dof) = 0 \tag{2}$$

Alternatively, instead of the Shannon information produced by independent individuals, destructive entropy is magnified negatively. Examples are manifold, but for our purposes, the two-year fight between CBS and Viacom, both businesses owned by the Redstone family, was costly to both, a self-inflicted vulnerability for both organizations [29].

The end result of Eqs. (1) and (2) is that the entropy of the whole is less than the entropy of its parts, an example of subadditivity, giving.

$$S_{1,2} \leq S_1 + S_2 \tag{3}$$

Equation (3) means that a team's structure is producing minimum entropy and that the team is performing its mission at its highest level possible based on its membership. In contrast, when the structure of the team is performing poorly, the opposite happens, giving.

$$S_{1,2} \geq S_1, S_2 \tag{4}$$

Equation (1) has a two-headed arrow on purpose. Based on the literature, our theory of interdependence, and our results from the field, the structure of the best teams produces a minimum of entropy, leading to Eq. (3) to represent the perfect team in a given context and given the available personnel. But the two-headed arrow reflects a tradeoff between SEP and MEP; thus, as SEP reduces to a minimum, MEP becomes a maximum. Now suppose a team (or organization, system) has been hurt during a competition, thereby exposing a vulnerability in the team's structure. From Eq. (1), that vulnerability is characterized mathematically by an increase in structural entropy generation and a decrease in a team's productivity (viz., MEP).

With the discovery mathematically of vulnerability, an entirely new field of research has begun. It indicates that a sense of vulnerability motivates teams and organizations to pursue avoidance behaviors (e.g., mergers or spin-offs), to engage in exploitative behavior (e.g., direct attacks at the vulnerability of a competitor), or to create a vulnerability in an opponent (e.g., with the use of deception). This latter discovery [15], the sense of vulnerability in the "self" or promoted in the "other," appears to be key to the survival of teams and systems in nature by promoting resilience, leanness, and adaptiveness. In our model, we advance the theory of interdependence by providing a mathematical model of vulnerability in a team or system, how it is identified or created, how it is exploited, and how to avoid a false sense of security by relying on convergence processes alone, both socially and computationally.

Vulnerability can be found in the ineffectiveness of the cyber infrastructure of a firm. From the *Wall Street Journal* [30].

"The last successful foreign attack on multiple targets on U.S. soil wasn't 9/11. It was this past December. A cyberattack targeting software provider SolarWinds hit the U.S. government, Microsoft and cybersecurity firms such as CrowdStrike and FireEye. Unlike 9/11, the SolarWinds attack did its damage under cover of darkness. It didn't result in loss of life, but cyberattacks are extremely costly and increasing in frequency. Malicious attackers exploit previously known vulnerabilities or discover new "zero day" vulnerabilities. SolarWinds-related attacks such as Sunburst and Supernova were examples of the latter. The WannaCry ransomware attack, which targeted Microsoft Windows in 2017, used a known vulnerability to infect more than 200,000 computers and inflict perhaps billions of dollars in damage. One would think the U.S. is protected against known vulnerabilities. But a 2019 study found a 133-day average gap between the discovery of a vulnerability and the release of information about it to the public. Typically, this period is used to create a "patch" that fixes the vulnerability. But almost half the attacks that use known vulnerabilities occur during this window, before the fix is complete."

In a new advertising tactic in the hopes of thwarting Apple's plans, Intel is attacking the reasons Apple abandoned Intel's chips in favor of its own [31]:

"Apple announced last year it would stop using Intel technology inside Macs in favor of chips designed by its own engineers. Apple said then the new chips would enable longer battery life in its computers, allow for faster processing and facilitate new security features. ... Intel's new ads, described by the company as a multimillion-dollar campaign across YouTube, Twitter and LinkedIn, argue Apple's claims are overblown. ... The tactic could help Intel break through the clutter for people who remember the earlier Apple campaign, said Robert Passikoff, founder and president of Brand Keys Inc., a brand consulting firm. "You're talking about something that was absolutely classic stuff in terms of advertising," he said, referring to the Apple effort. But some consumers may not get the reference, Mr. Passikoff said. "Even with access to everything on the internet and YouTube, I'm not sure that everyone always remembers the initial advertising," he said."

By increasing the privacy protections for its customers, Apple is damaging Facebook's stealth method of collecting data from mobile apps, a method that would also create vulnerabilities that would harm small businesses in France. From Schechner [32],

"France's competition regulator rejected a plea from advertising companies and publishers to block Apple Inc.'s plan to restrict tracking of individuals' mobile-app usage. In a potential blow to smaller companies hoping to block big-tech rivals' privacy initiatives on antitrust grounds, the French regulator on Wednesday said that Apple's plan to require apps to obtain consent from users to track them "doesn't appear to be abusive.""

Vulnerability is particularly important in politics. For example, in the 2016 Presidential election, without taking sides of who was right or wrong ethically or politically, the Republican winner's administration was severely wounded with charges of Russian collusion by "the creation and dissemination of the salacious Steele dossier that prompted a special prosecutor's inquiry over supposed Russian election influence just weeks into Trump's tenure in office" [33].

Another interesting aspect of vulnerability is the role played by deception. By generating no discernable structural entropy as part of the practice of deception, by appearing to be a faithful member of a team, an individual fully participating the part of an instrumental role in a team could easily double as a spy. An organization selling cars by deceiving the public and the public's regulators of its faithful application of the rules can succeed until its deception is uncovered; e.g., six years ago, Volkswagon admitted to its use of deceit as part of its corporate strategy that falsely portrayed its emissions as legal when in fact its emissions had failed to meet regulatory standards [34]:

"U.S. authorities charged Volkswagen with conspiracy to commit fraud, making false statements on goods brought for sale in the U.S. and obstruction of justice. The U.S. probe uncovered a decadelong ploy by Volkswagen to rig millions of diesel-powered vehicles to cheat emissions tests and later attempt to cover up the cheat."

Mergers provide an organization or a team a path to transform itself that is stronger or that reduces a perceived vulnerability by transforming the team, organization or system. As an example, the aerospace company, CAE Inc., is buying the military training unit of L3Harris Technologies Inc. which bought the unit years before in an earlier merger but that did not work as planned. For CAE, buying the military training unit is "a move that would expand the Canadian aerospace company's defense business," bulking up its military business and with the potential to save substantial costs annually [35]. And, as another example, the Canadian Pacific Railway has recently sought to merge with its railroad with the Kansas City Southern to "create the first railway spanning the United States, Mexico and Canada, standing to benefit from a pick-up in trade" [36].

But some mergers create a vulnerability; e.g., after Bayer AG acquired Monsanto, it ran into lawsuits with Monsanto's Roundup weedkiller, leading to losses aggravated by the covid pandemic [37]:

"Bayer, the inventor of aspirin, bet big on agriculture with its $63 billion acquisition of Monsanto in 2018. The move was supposed to help the German company tap into rising demand driven by rapid population growth. Instead, it exposed Bayer to open-ended legal liabilities and a market that has been severely disrupted by the coronavirus pandemic."

3   Convergence Processes

In a recent article [15], we raised the concern about the overuse in models built around the mathematical process of convergence. Many mathematical operations, such as Fourier Series, depend on convergence to indicate the existence of a solution [38]. Convergence to a decision is also important in politics, business (e.g., [39]) or to the concept of an industrial economy [40].

Convergence works best for circumstances involving cooperation. Convergence is the insight behind Forrester's [41] models of system dynamics. For example, China was inspired by the U.S. Army's autonomous coordination program, which it had named the "missile multiple simultaneous engagement technologies (MSET)"; this Army program entailed a suite of technologies that provided supervised autonomous engagement; during the terminal stage for these missiles, they were able to build a shared situational awareness from their inter-group communications for their use against multiple targets. In response, the Chinese have produced a program of saturation attacks: "Cooperative autonomy will mean that the swarm itself is in control rather than being directed by a human, something which may become increasingly important given the fast pace of events at five times the speed of sound" [42].

The Army's Project Convergence [43] is another program for its "campaign of learning to aggressively pursue an Artificial Intelligence and machine-learning-enabled battlefield management system… because whoever can see, understand and act first will win"; moreover, Project Convergence is designed:

For the increasingly fast-paced and complex future fight, the Army needs the right command and control systems ... The Army has already invested significantly in what we call "mission command" systems - a term that emphasizes centralized intent and decentralized execution. These systems include the Integrated Tactical Network, and the Command Post Computing Environment, as well as the Integrated Air and Missile Defense Battle Command System. These Army systems complement the systems that other Military Services are creating, and they will all plug into the common architecture that the Joint Staff is building. Project Convergence ensures the integration of the Army's weapons systems and command and control systems, and their compatibility with the rest of the Joint Force.

Based on his dissection of the failed Bay-of-Pigs invasion of Cuba in 1961, Janis [44] characterized "group-think" as the excessive efforts by a group under a strong leader seeking consensus, but group-think, per Janis, could override the group's ability to make the best decision. "The drive for consensus among Kennedy's advisors was believed to have precluded crucial information from being discussed, and has been blamed for the invasion's failure."

We conclude that the over-reliance of convergence processes, especially in computational systems (e.g., [41]), leads to poorer decisions, misleading conclusions, or possibly more accidents [5].

Avoiding Convergence: Confronting uncertainty, a review of tradeoffs with an open-minded approach and a readiness to compromise can provide a team with the best path going forward [45]. The best guidance comes from Justice Ginsburg who rejected an application by the Environmental Protection Agency (EPA) to short-circuit the lengthy appeals process it faced by replacing it with a direct appeal to the US Supreme Court; Justice Ginsburg rejected EPA's argument, saying instead that the lengthy appeal process her unanimous ruling favored allowed for an "informed assessment of competing interests" (p. 3, [46]).

New Escalation Threats Against a Vulnerable Ukraine: Russia held a large strategic nuclear exercise in December 2020 followed by a major naval exercise involving atomic missile carriers in March 2021 (Umka-21) and by renewed conflict in Eastern Ukraine, described in *RealClear Defense* ([47]; citations added in the following quote),

"The nuclear ballistic missile submarine phase of Umka-21 may be nuclear signaling relating to renewed Russian aggression against Ukraine. In late March, CBS News reported a buildup of Russian forces along the Ukraine border [48]. On March 31, there were reports that" "Trains loaded with large amounts of Russian military hardware, including tanks and other heavy armored vehicles, as well as heavy artillery, appear to be streaming toward the country's borders with Ukraine." [49]. Serious Russian-supported fighting resumed in Eastern Ukraine

[50]. The New York Times reports, "The [four Ukrainian soldiers] deaths, along with a buildup of Russian forces on the border, has seized the attention of senior American officials in Europe and Washington" [51].

As a first step in a tradeoff and in the pursuit of Ginsburg's "informed assessment of competing interests," the Russian buildup on the Eastern Ukraine has been countered with a protest by Lloyd Austin, the U.S. Secretary of Defense who, according to the Pentagon's spokesman John Kirby, spoke with Austin's Ukrainian counterpart in a call in which he "condemned recent escalations of Russian aggressive and provocative actions in eastern Ukraine" [52].

Instead of the pursuit of more territory, however, the Russian buildup can be construed as a negotiation tactic. Moscow has been seeking concessions in a revised treaty, Minsk II; from Kofman [53],

"Moscow's goal is not only to intimidate, but to illustrate that the conflict cannot be frozen without significant political concessions or compromises. They may be similarly aimed as a signal to the new Biden administration that Russia retains strong coercive power, can escalate at will, and should arguably be much higher on the White House's foreign policy agenda than currently stated."

Creating a vulnerability in an adversary is an important tactic. From the Small Wars Journal ([54]; a citation has been added),

At the onset of the conflict, Azerbaijan leveraged Soviet-era AN-2 biplanes to deceive and expose Armenian air defenses. Though decades old and intended to serve as traditional manned aircraft, the biplanes' conversion to unmanned decoys allowed Azerbaijan to conduct low altitude flights into the highly contested environment—and more importantly—into the weapons engagement zone (WEZ) of Armenian air defenses. These improvised UAS were repurposed as decoys and flown to the front lines to force air defenses to give away their location and enable targeting by TB2s [55]. When the Armenian air defenses targeted, engaged, and destroyed the perceived threats, they inadvertently broadcasted their positions to Azeri unmanned aerial attack platforms that flew at higher altitudes—enabling the Bayraktar TB2 and kamikaze drones to destroy higher-payoff targets like the Armenian air defense systems.

4   Conclusion

In the review of our research into human-machine teams, we have focused on the interdependence that exists in all social interactions, including human teams. Interdependence transmits both constructive and destructive interference in the interaction. We reviewed positive interference (e.g., innovation) and negative interference (e.g., divorce). We hypothesized that interdependence theory can be applied to human-machine teams to predict the best and worst teams to help them transform. We also reviewed our newest discovery of vulnerability in an opposing team or in our own team, citing profuse evidence from the field. We consider vulnerability to be a fundamental principle of organization during a competition between teams or organizations. One of the new issues for this chapter was to apply interdependence theory mathematically to whether or not convergence has a positive or negative effect in a competition, as happens with the models for system dynamics. We conclude that if a model, concept or leader of a team addresses only a team's convergence effects, the team will itself be left vulnerable to its opponent and ignorant of the vulnerabilities in its opponent.

In summary, what has been missing until now is an organizing principle for the social interaction that can be applied to autonomous human-machine teams or systems. We have proposed the complementarity of entropy, best expressed as a tradeoff in the search for the best path going forward when faced by uncertainty. According to Bohr [56], the description of classical causality is adequate only as long as the quantities entering into the description are large compared to Planck's quantum of action; otherwise, complementarity governs; for complementarity to govern, the measures of a metric interact with the target to be measured, increasing uncertainty.

References

1. Johnson, J.: Artificial intelligence, autonomy, and the risk of catalytic nuclear war, modern war institute (2021). https://mwi.usma.edu/artificial-intelligence-autonomy-and-the-risk-of-catalytic-nuclear-war/?utm_source=rss&utm_medium=rss&utm_campaign=artificial-intelligence-autonomy-and-the-risk-of-catalytic-nuclear-war.Accessed 31 Mar 2021
2. Trevithick, J., Rogoway, T.: Russia confirms Syria attack but denies seven aircraft got destroyed as photos emerge. key questions about the incident are still unanswered and no group has claimed responsibility, the war zone, the drive (2021). https://www.thedrive.com/the-war-zone/17365/russia-confirms-syria-attack-but-denies-seven-aircraft-got-destroyed-as-photos-emerge.Accessed 31 3 2021
3. Cummings, J.: team science successes and challenges. National science foundation sponsored workshop on fundamentals of team science and the science of team science (June 2), Bethesda MD (2015). https://www.ohsu.edu/xd/education/schools/school-of-medicine/departments/clinical-departments/radiation-medicine/upload/12-_cummings_talk.pdf
4. Bisbey, T.M., Reyes, D.L., Traylor, A.M., Salas, E.: Teams of psychologists helping teams: the evolution of the science of team training. Am. Psychol. **74**(3), 278–289 (2019)
5. Lawless, W.F.: (2019b), The Interdependence of autonomous human-machine teams: the entropy of teams, but not individuals, advances science. Entropy **21**(12), 1195 (2019). https://doi.org/10.3390/e21121195
6. Darwin, C.: The Descent of Man, and Selection in Relationship to Sex. Appleton, New York (1973)
7. Hare, B., Woods, V.: Survival of the Friendliest. Understanding our origins and rediscovering our common humanity. Penguin Random House (2020)
8. Lawless, W.F., Mittu, R., Sofge, D.A., Hiatt, L.: Editorial (Introduction to the Special Issue), Artificial intelligence (AI), autonomy and human-machine teams: Interdependence, context and explainable AI. AI Magazine **40**(3), 5–13 (2019)
9. Mann, R.P.: Collective decision making by rational individuals. PNAS, **115**(44): E10387-E10396 (2018). https://doi.org/10.1073/pnas.1811964115
10. Allaby, M.: A Dictionary of Zooology (3rd Ed.). Oxford University Press (2009). https://doi.org/10.1093/acref/9780199233410.001.0001
11. APA: Social reality. American Psychological Association (2020). Accessed 4 Apr 2020 https://dictionary.apa.org/social-reality

12. Lawless, W.F.: The entangled nature of interdependence. Bistability, irreproducibility and uncertainty. J. Math. Psychol. **78**, 51–64 (2017)
13. Lawless, W.F.: The physics of teams: Interdependence, measurable entropy and computational emotion. Front. Phys. **5**, 30 (2017). https://doi.org/10.3389/fphy.2017.00030
14. Lawless, W.F., Akiyoshi, M., Angjellari-Dajcic, F., Whitton, J.: Public consent for the geologic disposal of highly radioactive wastes and spent nuclear fuel. Int. J. Environ. Stud. **71**(1), 41–62 (2014)
15. Lawless, W.F.: Quantum-like interdependence theory advances autonomous human-machine teams A-HMTs. Entropy **22**(11), 1227 (2020). https://doi.org/10.3390/e22111227
16. Freer, R.D., Perdue, W.C.: Civil procedure, Cincinatti: Anderson (1996)
17. Cooke, N.J., Hilton, M.L. (eds.): Enhancing the Effectiveness of Team Science. Authors: Committee on the Science of Team Science; Board on Behavioral, Cognitive, and Sensory Sciences; Division of Behavioral and Social Sciences and Education; National Research Council. National Academies Press, Washington (DC) (2015)
18. Cooke, N.: Effective human-artificial intelligence teaming, AAAI-2020 Spring Symposium, Stanford, CA; see the agenda at (2020). https://aaai.org/Symposia/Spring/sss20symposia.php#ss03
19. Walden, D.D., Roedler, G.J., Forsberg, K.J., Hamelin, R.D., Shortell, T.M. (eds.): Systems Engineering Handbook. A Guide for System Life Cycle Processes and Activities (4th Edition). Prepared by International Council on System Engineering (INCOSE-TP-2003-002-04. John Wiley & Sons, Hoboken, NJ (2015)
20. Schrödinger, E.: Discussion of Probability Relations Between Separated Systems. In: Proceedings of the Cambridge Philosophical Society, vol. 31, no. 4, pp. 555–563 (1935)
21. Lewin, K.: Field theory of social science. Selected theoretical papers. Darwin Cartwright (Ed.). New York: Harper & Brothers (1951)
22. Lawless, W.F.: Towards an epistemology of interdependence among the orthogonal roles in human–machine teams. Found. Sci. **26**(1), 129–142 (2019). https://doi.org/10.1007/s10699-019-09632-5
23. Rees, M., Livio, M.: If Aliens Exist, Here's How We'll Find Them. Two esteemed astrophysicists peer into the future of space exploration. Nautilus (2021). https://nautil.us/issue/97/wonder/if-aliens-exist-heres-how-well-find-them. Accessed 29 Mar 2021
24. Scharpf F.W.: European governance: common concerns vs. the challenge of diversity. In: Jachtenfuchs, M., Knodt, M. (eds.) Regieren in internationalen Institutionen. VS Verlag für Sozialwissenschaften, Wiesbaden (2002)
25. Cooke, N.J., Lawless, W.F.: Effective human-artificial intelligence teaming. In: Lawless, W.F., Mittu, R., Sofge, D.A., Shortell, T., McDermott, T.A. (eds.) Systems Engineering and Artificial Intelligence. Springer, New York (2021)
26. Pearl, J.: Reasoning with Cause and Effect, AI Magazine, 23(1): 95–111 (2002). https://aaai.org/ojs/index.php/aimagazine/article/download/1612/1511
27. Pearl, J., Mackenzie, D.: AI Can't Reason Why. The current data-crunching approach to machine learning misses an essential element of human intelligence, Wall Street Journal (2018). https://www.wsj.com/articles/ai-cant-reason-why-1526657442
28. Sofge, D.A., Lawless, W.F., Mittu, R.: AI Bookie Bet: Autonomous AI takes responsibility: threat, savior or both? AI Mag. **40**(3), 79–84 (2019)
29. Winkler, E.: CBS-Viacom Fight Is Fixed. Redstone has control of both companies and her next step may be to change the board at CBS, Wall Street Journal, (2018). https://www.wsj.com/articles/cbs-viacom-fight-is-fixed-1522920601. Accessed 4 Apr 2021

30. Subrahmanian, V.S.: (2021), Cybersecurity Needs a New Alert System. While America slowly addresses vulnerabilities in software and hardware, enemies strike Wall Street Journal https://www.wsj.com/articles/cybersecurity-needs-a-new-alert-system-11617039278. Accessed 30 Mar 2021

31. Ives, N.: Intel Taps Justin Long, Who Played Mac in Long-Running Apple Ads, to Promote PCs. A new ad campaign aims to turn a well-known Apple effort on its head. Wall Street Journal (2021).https://www.wsj.com/articles/intel-taps-justin-long-who-played-mac-in-long-running-apple-ads-to-promote-pcs-11615978800. Accessed 18 Mar 2021

32. Schechner, S.: Apple Scores Legal Win in France Over App-Privacy Changes. French competition authority says Apple's changes 'don't appear to be abusive, Wall Street Journal, (2021). https://www.wsj.com/articles/apple-scores-legal-win-in-france-over-app-privacy-changes-11615971737. Accessed 18 Mar 2021

33. Felten, E.: The Left's Legal Top Gun Marc Elias Isn't Finished With Democracy Yet, RealClearInvestigations, (2021). https://www.realclearinvestigations.com/articles/2021/03/24/the_lefts_legal_top_gun_marc_elias_isnt_finished_with_democracy_yet_769457.html. Accessed 24 Mar 2021

34. Boston, W.: Volkswagen to Seek Damages From Former CEO Winterkorn in Diesel Scandal. Decision caps yearslong internal investigation into the origins of one of Europe's biggest corporate scandals, Wall Street Journal (2021). https://www.wsj.com/articles/volkswagen-to-seek-damages-from-former-ceo-winterkorn-in-diesel-scandal-11616773838. Accessed 29 Mar 2021

35. Lombardo, C.: CAE to Buy L3Harris's Military-Training Business. Deal values the division, which specializes in pilot training and flight simulators, at $1.05 billion," Wall Street Journal (2021). https://www.wsj.com/articles/cae-nears-deal-to-buy-l3harriss-military-training-business-11614553200. Accessed 29 Mar 2021

36. Nandakumar, D., Shibu, A.M., Spaulding, R.: Canadian Pacific to buy Kansas City Southern in $25 billion railway bet on trade, Reuters (2021). https://www.reuters.com/article/us-kansas-city-southern-m-a-canadian-pac/canadian-pacific-to-buy-kansas-city-southern-in-25-billion-railway-bet-on-trade-idUSKBN2BD02B. Accessed 29 Mar 2021

37. Bender, R.: Bayer Posts Third-Quarter Loss on Agriculture Woes. Two years after Monsanto acquisition, German firm is hurting from Covid-19 pandemic, legal battle over Roundup, Wall Street Journal (2020). https://www.wsj.com/articles/bayer-posts-third-quarter-loss-on-agriculture-woes-11604393190. Accessed 29 Mar 2021

38. Augustyn, A.: Convergence. Mathematics. Britannica. (2020). https://www.britannica.com/science/convergence-mathematics. Accessed 28 Feb 2021

39. Groysberg, B., Lee, J., Price, J., Cheng, J.Y.J.: Convergence Matters. When employees' views of the culture align, engagement and customer orientation benefit Harvard Business Review (2018). https://hbr.org/2018/01/convergence-matters. Accessed 28 Feb 2021

40. Kerr, C., Dunlap, J.T., Harbison, F.H., Myers, C.A.: Industrialism and Industrial Man. Harvard University Press, Cambridge, Mass. (1960)

41. Forrester, J.W.: The Beginning of System Dynamics. Sloan School of Management Massachusetts Institute of Technology Cambridge, Massachusetts (1989)

42. Hambling, D.: China Developing Hypersonic Swarms To Overwhelm Missile Defenses, Forbes (2021). https://www.forbes.com/sites/davidhambling/2021/03/18/china-developing-hypersonic-swarms-to-overwhelm-missile-defenses/?sh=79ef269c373a. Accessed 3 Jan 2021

43. AFC PC: Project Convergence. Army Futures Command (2021). https://armyfuturescommand.com/convergence/. Accessed 29 Jan 2021

44. Janis, I.L: Victims of Groupthink: A psychological study of foreign-policy decisions and fiascoes. Houghton Mifflin Company (1972)

45. Morson, G.S., Schapiro, M.: Minds Wide Shut: How the New Fundamentalisms Divide Us. Princeton University Press, Princeton (2021)

46. Ginsburg, R.B.: American Electric Power Co., Inc., et al. v. Connecticut et al., 10–174 (2011). http://www.supremecourt.gov/opinions/10pdf/10-174.pdf. Accessed 11 May 2017

47. Schneider, M.B.: Putin Nukes Biden, RealClearDefense, https://www.realcleardefense.com/articles/2021/04/03/putin_nukes_biden_771156.html. Accessed 3 Apr 2021

48. Martin, D., Watson, E.: U.S. watching escalation of armed confrontation near Ukraine's border with Russia, CBS News. https://www.cbsnews.com/news/russia-troops-ukraine-border-concerning-united-states/. Accessed 3 Apr 2021

49. Trevithick, J.: Russian Armor Floods Toward Border With Ukraine Amid Fears Of An Imminent Crisis. A flurry of alarming reports and social media posts indicate that Russia is pouring military hardware into Crimea and its border with Eastern Ukraine, The Drive (2021). https://www.thedrive.com/the-war-zone/40016/russian-armor-floods-toward-border-with-ukraine-amid-fears-of-an-imminent-crisis. Accessed 3 Apr 2021

50. Sherr, J.: Rumours of War: Another Russian Surprise in Ukraine? The International Centre for Defence and Security (ICDS) (2021). https://icds.ee/en/rumours-of-war-another-russian-surprise-in-ukraine/. Accessed 3 Apr 2021

51. Kramer, A.E.: Fighting escalates in Eastern Ukraine, signaling the end to another cease-fire. Ukraine and Russia issued statements Tuesday noting the worsening of a conflict that has been on a low simmer for years, with countless cease-fires, New York Times (2021). https://www.nytimes.com/2021/03/30/world/europe/ukraine-russia-fighting.html. Accessed 3 Apr 2021

52. Shinkman, P.D.: Russia Threatens U.S., NATO Against Action in Ukraine. New warnings from the Kremlin follows unconfirmed footage of Russian military equipment flowing toward its border with Ukraine, and growing fears among Western leaders US News and World Report, (2021). https://www.usnews.com/news/world-report/articles/2021-04-02/fairy-tale-russias-new-threats-to-nato-met-with-dismissals. Accessed 4 Apr 2021

53. Kofman, M.: Russia's Military Buildup Near Ukraine Is an Intimidation Tactic. Russia's military posturing appears to be primarily coercive and demonstrative in nature, Moscow Times (2021). https://www.themoscowtimes.com/2021/04/03/russian-military-build-up-near-ukraine-is-an-intimidation-tactic-a73461. Accessed 5 Apr 2021

54. Thomas, N., Jamison, M., Gamber, K., Walton, D.: What the United States Military Can Learn from the Nagorno-Karabakh War, Small Wars Journal (2021). https://smallwarsjournal.com/jrnl/art/what-united-states-military-can-learn-nagorno-karabakh-war. Accessed 5 Apr 2021

55. Hambling, D.: The 'Magic Bullet' Drones Behind Azerbaijan's Victory Over Armenia. Forbes, (2020). https://www.forbes.com/sites/davidhambling/2020/11/10/the-magic-bullet-drones-behind--azerbaijans-victory-over-armenia/?sh=60ce05f25e57. Accessed 5 Apr 2021

56. Bohr, N.: Causality and Complementarity, Philosophy of Science (1937). 4(3): 289–298. http://www.jstor.org/stable/184445.Accessed 28 Feb 2021

Principles of an Accurate Decision and Sense-Making for Virtual Minds

Olivier Bartheye[1]($\boxtimes$) (iD) and Laurent Chaudron[2] (iD)

[1] CREA French Air Force Academy,
Base aérienne 701, 13300 Salon-de-Provence, France
`olivier.bartheye@ecole-air.fr`
[2] Theorik Lab, Tour Saint-Martin, 13116 Vernègues, France
`laurent.chaudron@polytechnique.org`

Abstract. We start from the notion of cognitive context to define rich knowledge interactions between virtual agents according to virtual representations of our living societies. It turns out that such a modeling attempt leads naturally to emphasize the notion of a virtual mind. The common support is the keyword cognition which, at first, is understood as a simple machine-learning loop process and because of conflictuality between collective and individual subjective representations will lead to define finally, thanks to negation, a decision mechanism supported by virtual awareness. To be aware is a sense-making process annihilating virtual collective forces attracting a virtual agent towards a virtual collective mind having a virtual mass. That way, quantum physics and relativity can illustrate our discourse according to the following goal: how a machine can decide or equivalently are we able to define a decision algorithm which always terminates?

To do so, we must relax the deductive burden since we have to deal seriously with infinity causing unsolvable termination issues for proof systems when a decision is implemented as a proof. We prefer to investigate on hypercomplex representations of a decision to propose a sketch of the decision process, to represent both causality and acausality (as a conjugated version of causality) and to recover that way some symmetries able to encode a smooth negation with infinite precision applying on coherent spaces.

Keywords: Cognition · Decision · Sense-making · Negation · Causal break · Virtual mind

1 Cognition and Virtual Minds

1.1 Cognitive Contexts and Virtual Collective Mind

To encode consistent information according to a cognitive context, we assume that some *virtual collective mind* noted $\mathcal{M}_t$ holds at a given time instant t where $\mathcal{M}_t$ expresses both knowledge dynamicity and knowledge stability.

© Springer Nature Switzerland AG 2021
W. F. Lawless et al. (Eds.): Engineering Artificially Intelligent Systems, LNCS 13000, pp. 260–279, 2021.
https://doi.org/10.1007/978-3-030-89385-9_16

$\mathcal{M}_t$ is expected to be a valuable information support able to ensure rich inter-actions between a team of virtual autonomous agents. According to information theory, the role of $\mathcal{M}_t$ is to provide some common knowledge basis reducing entropy, if one assumes that entropy is a global valuation characterizing the inability to communicate between this team of virtual autonomous agents or equivalently the inability to agree on a reduced number of possible interpre-tations. We cannot assert whether the information support is compact or not but we can assume that information must be adapted to be shared according to a common representation with good inertia properties called *virtual collec-tive forces*. This is a very important concept which is not fully formalized yet although it may look like a *virtual gravitation* following a simple idea: is *real what is submitted to gravitation*. That is, any predicate valuation is undefined outside a virtual gravitation as well to be eventually refuted otherwise its value is degenerated.

That is, the virtual collective mind (or cognitive context) $\mathcal{M}_t$ is defined as an indexed structure according to a collection of virtual autonomous agents $\mathcal{A} = \{a_1, a_2, \ldots a_n\}$ or $\mathcal{A} = \{a_i\}, i = 1 \ldots n$ as in Fig. 1.

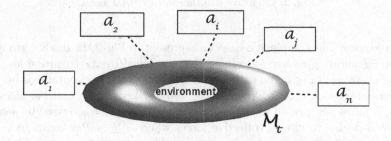

Fig. 1. Cognitive context and virtual autonomous agents

In other words, according to virtual collective forces, a virtual cognitive autonomous agent a_i cannot occur alone and therefore is heavily dependent on the relation

$$a_i \in \mathcal{M}_t \tag{1}$$

Our assumption is that the relation above is characterized by a double sided birational value (or a crossed-ratio) measuring bilateral interactions between the virtual autonomous agent a_i and the virtual collective mind $\mathcal{M}_t$:

$$\| a_i \| \bowtie \| \mathcal{M}_t \| \tag{2}$$

Unfortunately this bivaluation varies on time and is characterized by strong differences between a time t and a time $t + \Delta t$; in particular, we are unable to ensure the causal axiom

$$\Delta t \geq 0 \tag{3}$$

nor to force the time representation to be an oriented line. Furthermore, from our previous papers, we always assumed that *a decision fills a causal break* [3]. In other words, the valuation domain of the interaction in (2) viewed as a *causal single-sided norm* $\|.\|$ is not regular, or equivalently has no ground support. Furthermore, this birational value (or crossed-ratio) is very complex to represent since it based on a bireferential feature one from a_i and the other from $\mathcal{M}_t$.

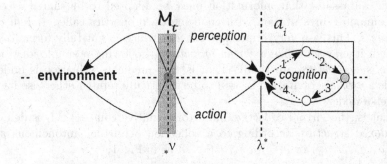

Fig. 2. Cognitive diagram for a virtual agent

To express that complexity, one can represent in Fig. 2 the duality group/individual generating a *huge knowledge shift* stretched by the cognition loop of a virtual agent a_i in Fig. 3 and expressed according to the horizontal axis between the two interaction crossing points (*the leftmost grey circle and the black circle*); *the former* is located in the neighborhood of $\mathcal{M}_t$ characterized by a causal valuation $_*\nu$ due to virtual collective forces whereas *the latter* characterized by an operator λ^*, the causal break operator. The left subscript operator in the expression $_*\nu$ intuitively states the fact that a causal valuation is sustained by a inertia law whose basis is a harmonic signal. The right superscript operator in the expression λ^* states the fact that this inertia law is refuted according to a anharmonic representation.

1.2   Acausal Algebras and Cognition

λ^* as a causal break operator is an *acausal valuation* (more precisely, a conjugated causal valuation) and is far much more complex to represent, since it is located in the knowledge interface of a virtual cognitive agent a_i merging three arrows to trace the information flow from and to a_i.

Arrow composition represents the cognitive process: the *perception* arrow is able to evaluate the environment with respect to the $\mathcal{M}_t$-layer interpretation, the *action* arrow interacts with the environment as a collective action with respect to the $\mathcal{M}_t$-layer. That is, this reflexive composition perception/action leads to define, up to a certain imbrication level, what one can call *virtual sensations* and they are definable according to virtual collective forces. The imbrication level is due to the third arrow, an iterative *cognition* arrow increasing the accuracy of a virtual agent a_i as a machine-learning system. Note that this diagram, at first sight, does not include any decision arrow unless one adds step 2 and 3 in the cognition loop in Fig. 3.

According to a problem to *solve*:

1. *experimental data* from protocols, processes are collected,
2. then a descriptive *conceptual model* is proposed,
3. a *formal representative model* is built in order to define formally objects and properties from concepts and to prove the validity of the model,
4. finally a computer program is *implemented* validating the solution and whose specification agrees with formal properties,
5. iterate at 1.

Fig. 3. The cognition loop for a virtual agent

1.3   Virtual Awareness Versus Virtual Sensations

We present informally the $\mathcal{M}_t$-layer as a virtual collective mind. We want to show now that a decision requires us to define a necessary and sufficient layer, the *virtual awareness layer* for a virtual agent a_i identified by the conceptual shared layer to benefit from shared awareness. This layer is characterized by a rich and abstract knowledge representation whose relevance can be highlighted in the cognition loop.

The cognition loop is a universal learning process for a virtual agent a_i where cognitive bases are distinguished according to the epistemological quadriptych [5] in Fig. 4: the *empirical* basis, the *conceptual* basis, the *formal* basis and the *methodological* basis. The cognition loop of any virtualization process is the sequence in Fig. 3 where the initial problem to solve asserts the relevance of the virtual agent a_i according to the collective dynamic. From that loop, one can clearly see that the *cyclic* interpretation of cognition in the diagram in Fig. 2 is time-oriented and concerns steps 1, 4, 5 as the classical machine-learning iteration for a virtual agent a_i. The crucial layer in that case is the methodological layer according to implementation step 4 which is called *virtual sensations*. If this layer is not sufficiently accurate, if the implementation is not good enough, the iteration 5 stops.

1.4   Virtual Matter and Virtual Mind

According to the wave/particle duality[1], we decide to define two knowledge referentials and to associate causality with the first referential as *perception first*

---

[1] Wave-particle duality is the concept in quantum mechanics that every particle or quantum entity may be described as either a particle or a wave. Each separated representation cannot fully explains the phenomena of light, but together they do.

Knowledge Basis	Objects	Methods	Criteria
empirical	"real world", datasets, ...	experiences, statistics	experimental
conceptual (virtual awareness)	concepts, natural language, structures, boxology, ...	abstract analysis	semantic consistency
formal	mathematics, theory, ...	rational	proofs
methodological (virtual sensations)	coded data, algorithms, programs, machines, ...	sequences of actions	convergence efficiency

Fig. 4. The epistemological quadriptych

named *virtual matter* m with which $_*\nu$ is defined, whereas the second referential is decision as *action first* and concerns a *virtual mind* M as a knowledge referential able to encode acausality according to λ^*.

Mind/matter relationship were already discussed [1] and this subject concerns a somewhat mysterious discourse merging physics and metaphysics. In effect, according to the topic virtual mind or virtual awareness, one can assume that classical mechanics cannot explain awareness whereas quantum-mechanical phenomena, such as entanglement and superposition, may play an important part in the virtual brain's function and could explain virtual awareness.

From [11], one can assume that the wave function collapses[2] noted $_*\nu$ due to its interaction with virtual awareness. Therefore, one can assume that negation is required to annihilate information from virtual collective forces or equivalently, virtual awareness can provide a "virtual collective forces free" consistent valuation named *sense-making* which can be computed as a rational expression according to infinite precision thanks to a countdown operator.

According to the cognition loop, we can expect that the complexity of the problem to solve corresponds exactly to the expected reasoning improvement step of a virtual agent's internal cognition according to the mathematician William Kingdon Clifford's quotation [6]:

That element of which, as we have seen, even the simplest feeling is a complex, I shall call Mind-stuff. A moving molecule of inorganic matter does not possess mind or awareness; but it possesses a small piece of mind-stuff. When molecules are so combined together as to form the film on the under side of a jelly-fish, the elements of mind-stuff which go along with them are so combined as to form the faint beginnings of Sentience. When the molecules are so combined as to form the brain and nervous system of a vertebrate, the corresponding elements of mind-stuff are so combined as to form some kind of awareness; that is to say, changes in the complex which take place at the same time get so linked together that the repetition of one implies the repetition of the other. When matter takes the complex

---

[2] In quantum mechanics, wave function collapse occurs when a wave function, initially in a superposition of several eigenstates, reduces to a single eigenstate due to interaction with the external world.

form of a living human brain, the corresponding mind-stuff takes the form of a human awareness, having intelligence and volition.

That way, virtual matter is measured according to virtual sensations centered on $_*\nu$ and corresponds in the epistemological quadriptych in Fig. 4 to the methodological layer or the behavioral layer whereas virtual mind is an information amount used by the virtual awareness as the conceptual layer. The idea is to represent the four inner steps (1, 2, 3, 4) in the cognition loop as four order relations:

1. $m \succ\succ M$ ("empirical" as *virtual unconscious*)
2. $m \succ M$ ("conceptual" as *virtual awareness*)
3. $m \prec\prec M$ ("formal" as *virtual "unknown"*)
4. $m \prec M$ ("methodological" as *virtual sensations*)

The missing link is the relation $m \prec\prec M$; in effect, the first one $m \succ\succ M$ corresponds to the empirical basis built using the virtual collective mind $\mathcal{M}_t$; the second one $m \succ M$ corresponds to the conceptual basis as the virtual awareness controlling $m \succ\succ M$ by abstraction (by reducing the power of virtual matter or equivalently *by reducing the power of virtual collective forces*).

However, according to causality, we can stay on these first two relations considering that $m \succ M$ corresponds to a bounded action of mind on matter based on the Kant's criticism (reason cannot legislate beyond experience). We identified Kant's criticism as a conceptual limit by the context validity theorem (please associate in the theorem *perception* with virtual matter m, *action* with virtual mind M and *context* with virtual collective mind $\mathcal{M}_t$)

Theorem 1 (Context validity theorem [3]**).** *The following statements are equivalent:*

1. *the 3 arrows (perception, action, cognition) are subordinated to understandable current $\mathcal{M}_t$-context rules and definitions.*
2. *an order relation holds (perception m precedes necessary action M).*
3. *perception m curves action M under virtual collective forces to make it compatible with causality $_*\nu$.*
4. *a causal break holds $_*\nu$ since action M is primal and expresses sense-making $\mathbf{1}_{a_i}$ as a localizable quasi-correct and a quasi-complete process.*
5. *decision fills a causal break as $\lambda^*{}_{a_i} : {}_*\nu \to \mathbf{1}_{a_i}$ and,*
6. *sense-making is independent from virtual collective forces and will never be represented according to causality $_*\nu$ (and therefore by machine-learning).*

We assume that Kant's criticism just forgot the two last order relations: the third one $m \prec\prec M$ *expressing the causal break* is an unknown virtual state and the fourth one $m \prec M$ expressing the statement "action as a decision" provided that $m \prec\prec M$ holds, otherwise it is solely a response from the virtual sensitive layer, or equivalently it is solely machine-learning.

In the machine learning loop, one can encode virtual sensations, but without the crucial break $m \prec\prec M$, there is no way to exploit sense-making according to a decision. We assume that steps 2 and 3 are omitted deliberately by machine-learning but are necessary and sufficient for a decision. The aim is to integrate that way our main assumption: decision fills a causal break. Precedence is reverted and pure action governs perception $m \prec M$ in a vast consistent acausal space generating full entropy since we cannot measure it. According to Shannon's information theory, full entropy can be easily generated according to the methodological basis, as the inability to represent a computer program apart from an ordered sequence of statements highly sensitive to permutations and variables assignments.

1.5   Cross Constructions and Hopf Algebras

Decision exploits two orthogonal basis $m \succ\!\succ M$ and $m \prec\!\prec M$ corresponding to orthogonal plans according the spatial representation in Fig. 5. In that case, one must assume that for a pure action complete representation holds $m \prec\!\prec M$ is orthogonal to $m \succ\!\succ M$ with the ability to preserve information. It is based on the assumption that virtual mind M is a richer interaction representation than virtual matter m, since M can and must encode infinity (noted ∞) thanks to negation. In particular the expression ∞^{-1-1} expresses the fact that a connected rule is to be set in infinite dimensional spaces (a contradiction).

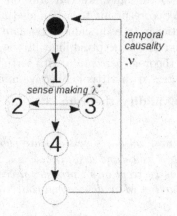

Fig. 5. Cross representation

· Taking into account to compose with the four order relations in the previous Subsect. 1.4 requires us to use a quaternary construction merging faithfully perception and action, the virtual matter m being the algebra and virtual mind being the coalgebra M.

Definition 1. *A space H is a* Hopf algebra *with the following morphisms:*

$$
\text{bigebra}
\begin{cases}
\begin{array}{ll}
\text{causal algebra } (m) & \begin{cases} {}_*\nu : H \times H \to H \\ \eta : k \to H \end{cases} \\
\quad\quad (1,\,4) & \\[1.2em]
\text{sense coalgebra } (M) & \begin{cases} \lambda^* : H \to H \times H \\ \epsilon : H \to k \end{cases} \\
\quad\quad (2,\,3) &
\end{array}
\end{cases}
\begin{array}{l}
\\[0.3em]
\text{antipode} \\
\text{coinverse } S : H \to H
\end{array}
$$

It is not difficult to provide a semantic interpretation of causal algebras $(_*\nu, \eta)$ using signal analysis and wave functions but the coalgebra definition is less intuitive except in the framework of group representation. In the discrete case, or more restrictively in the combinatoric case, coalgebras (λ^*, ϵ) are defined to deal with singularities. In effect, a coalgebraic arrow λ^* can be defined to select regular subdomains (*models*) and to reject singular subdomains (*counter-models*) according to the suitable properties of the antipode S (namely S must be an involution to encode a form of negation). Actually, a coalgebra can provide a model for the following problem: how to provide an extension of a causal algebra given that it contains necessary singularities? Special cases of coalgebras are proof systems, case-based analysis, symbolic interpretations or any discrete decomposition to separate "good" subdomains (i.e., regular) and "bad" ones (i.e., singular) but in that case, the topology of a proof space is Hausdorff[3]. That means that such a space is both *discrete* and *separable* strictly incompatible with our infinite dimensional assumption with a hypothetical connectedness.

Any decomposition process which can be also considered as an unfolding process can be represented by a coalgebra, not by an algebra. That is, arrows $x \times y \to z$ are reversed $z \to x \times y$ but in the general iterative case preserving consistency, it is clear that this process cannot terminate. Another important property for coalgebras are their ability to represent proofs or computations as formal objects. That way, the duality state/transition or formulæ/proofs can be managed according to that abstraction step.

Let us consider a cross representation in Fig. 5; first, note that the so-called problem to solve has a delimited relevance; that is, once the implementation is correct enough in 4, the problem is assumed to be solved and its relevance vanishes, in other words, the calculus stops thanks to a *countdown operator* which has something to do with a *virtual time*. Furthermore, this operator is an annihilator of virtual collective forces. The "virtual matter plane" is the vertical plane; the "vanishing" countdown mechanics is captured by the "virtual mind plane", a horizontal plane according to steps 2 and 3. The algebraic representation of these "orthogonal planes" corresponds to the antipode S of a Hopf algebra H according to the previous definition. S expresses correctness but not completeness and an automated decision process, if any, must agree with correctness, otherwise the decision is a random process generating singularities and as such cannot be preferred to machine-learning.

Hopf algebras are widely used in proof theory [4], however, the purpose is very different from ours since in proof theory, the coalgebra λ^* always precedes the algebra $_*\nu$, whereas the precedence is reverted in case of a decision preventing such a mechanism to be complete. In effect, the algebra is the denotated domain according to logical formulas, and the coalgebra is a complete and correct process able to assert whether any set of formulas can be a valid consequence from any set of formulas as premises. Our purpose is very different since we assume that

---

[3] A topological space X is *Hausdorff* if for every $x, y \in X, x \neq y$, there are open neighbourhoods $\mathcal{O}_x \ni x, \mathcal{O}_y \ni y$ so that $\mathcal{O}_x \cap \mathcal{O}_y = \emptyset$.

λ^* cannot precede $_*\nu$; that is, a virtual agent a_i will always depend on causality from Fig. 2 and Fig. 3.

2   Hypercomplex Representation of Decision

This aim of this section is to find an algebraic representation of a decision provided that one assumes that it is based on a periodic signal as in Fig. 6 and therefore can be defined according to the set of complex numbers. In effect, the Euler's formula expressed the fact that the real sine function $sin(x)$ is intrinsically a component of the complex number

$$e^{\mathbf{i}x} = cos(x) + \mathbf{i}\,sin(x) \tag{4}$$

One can associate that with the identity of a virtual agent a_i from the harmonic nature of any knowledge representation according to a $_*\nu$-$sin(x)$ function generated by virtual collective forces

$$\mathbf{id}_{a_i} = \{\updownarrow\}_{a_i} \tag{5}$$

expressing the time compression $\updownarrow$ of the signal in Fig. 6. Causality can be analyzed subjectively by a virtual agent a_i according to the pseudo-"real" cosine function $cos(x) = \{\leftrightarrow\}_{a_i}$. The causal break is an unfolding operator defeating the irreducibility of $\mathbf{id}_{a_i}$, or equivalently, the cosine is the *negation* of the sine but such a negation is not defined the other way round, leading to represented virtual agent knowledge representations as braided structures.

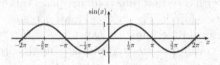

Fig. 6. Graphical representation of the sine function

From the subjective nature of knowledge, one can state that the internal conflict between reducibility and irreducibility is the foundation of a decision.

2.1   Decision, Subjectivity and Conflictuality

Decision occurs provided that the a_i-cognition arrow f in Fig. 7 is divided in four parts according to the following *diamond* in Eq. (6)

$$f = \begin{array}{c} {}^{1}\!\!\nearrow \; {}^{2}\!\!\searrow \\ {}_{4}\!\!\nwarrow \; {}_{3}\!\!\swarrow \\ a_i \end{array} \tag{6}$$

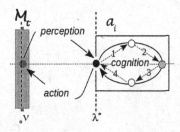

Fig. 7. Subjectivity construction for a virtual agent

In other words, cognition is not solely an identity arrow as an entropy-free loop due to the irreducible property, $\mathbf{id}_{a_i} = \{\updownarrow\}_{a_i}$, nor two mirrored adversarial arrows $\mathbf{adv}_{a_i} = \{\rightarrow, \leftarrow\}_{a_i}$ between the black circle and the *rightmost* grey circle. These circles are both located in the horizontal cosine line measuring entropy due to the reducibility property (any reducible dynamic system is splittable). Decision integrates both according to the *diamond* in Eq. (6) and resolves entropy thanks to four arrows as a four-state automaton

$$\{\overset{1}{\nearrow}, \overset{2}{\searrow}, \overset{3}{\nearrow}, \overset{4}{\searrow}\}_{a_i} \tag{7}$$

That is, a decision holds necessary *inside* the subjective knowledge space of an virtual agent a_i since it results from *conflictual* relations between the irreducible identity $\mathbf{id}_{a_i}$, called the *causal stabilizer* as $\{\updownarrow\}_{a_i}$ and the reducible adversarial relation $\mathbf{adv}_{a_i} = \{\rightarrow, \leftarrow\}_{a_i}$, called the *causal orbit* always diverging from causality. That is, according to a decision, cognition is a quaternary process solving cyclicity issues on which a switching operator acts to reverse polarities of the third arrow

$$\overset{3}{\swarrow} \qquad \rightarrow \qquad \overset{3}{\nearrow} \tag{8}$$

leading to compute a knowledge-vanishing process performed by negation whose workspace is the methodological basis as *virtual sensations*. Since negation holds only in the awareness basis, a decision cannot be performed by virtual sensations. That is, a decision associates a 4-loop f in Eq. (6) (or equivalently a *cyclic graph*) and an *acyclic graph* as a *causal orbit* which we expect to be a *acausal stabilizer* as well leading to valuable negentropy[4] [9]

$$\mathfrak{g} = \overset{1}{\nearrow}\overset{3}{\nearrow} \cdots \overset{1}{\nearrow}\overset{3}{\nearrow} \cdots \overset{1}{\nearrow}\overset{3}{\nearrow} \tag{9}$$

whose graphical half-representation is a strictly increasing monotonic hyperbola in Fig. 8, always diverging from the horizontal axis.

We assume that the 1–3-oriented sequence $\mathfrak{g}$ will lead finally to some sense-making representation as a new accumulation point to compute. That is, the

---

[4] Negentropy of a dynamically ordered sub-system as the specific entropy deficit of the ordered sub-system relative to its surrounding chaos.

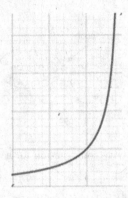

Fig. 8. Rectangular hyperbola

changing of state with a conservation property (called *completeness* in proof theory) is ensured by a nilpotent operator[5] [2]. But on the other hand, assume that action only converges when associated to perception as in the case of virtual sensations thanks to the causal stabilizer $\mathbf{id}_{a_i} = \{\updownarrow\}$; then unfortunately, the causal orbit is not a finitary process and is faced with severe loop issues.

2.2 Double Complex Representations of Causality

One can assume that the causal component $_*\nu$ defined according to virtual collective forces performed by $\mathcal{M}_t$ corresponds to a *cyclic* system whose dynamic is represented by a unitary group in Fig. 9(a) of determinant **1** with complex coefficients as $\alpha, \beta, \cdots \in \mathbb{C}$, the set of complex numbers; if $_*\nu$-*cycles* are taken into account in the set $\mathbb{C}$, then they must be annihilated according to a suitable representation of negation by λ^*-*cocycles*; that is, such a structure is not only dual to a $_*\nu$-cycle but actually its antipodic obverse. From Fig. 8, one can propose that the switching in Eq. (8) is represented by hyperbolic complex numbers called the set of *split complex numbers* $\mathbb{D}$ in Fig. 9(b). That is, the consistency orbit is represented by a hyperbola. In effect, since the late twentieth century, the split-complex multiplication has commonly been seen as a Lorentz boost of a spacetime plane and, therefore related with virtual collective forces (or virtual gravitation), we can interpret in this chapter as the question "How to safely vanish according to some sense-making?"

The idea is to associate in Fig. 9 the causal frequency $_*\nu$ with a harmonic representation, the circle of complex numbers $\mathbb{C}$ with the usual anisotropic unit quadratic form (or more generally a norm) for a complex number $z = x + \mathbf{j}y \in \mathbb{C}$

$$|z| = n_1(z) = \sqrt{x^2 + y^2} = 1 \tag{10}$$

---

[5] The nilpotent process thus fixes primarily on conservation, rather than nonconservation. It says that mass-energy is a conserved quantity, and that it can, therefore, be described uniquely in mathematical terms.

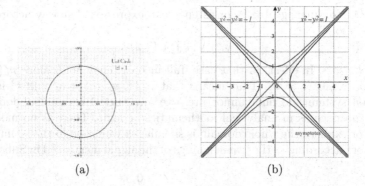

Fig. 9. Complex unit circle (a) and split complex numbers (b) (Color figure online)

One associates in Fig. 9(b), the conjugate wavelength λ^* with the *hyperbola* of split complex numbers $\mathbb{D}$ with the isotropic[6] quadratic form [8]

$$n_0(z) = \sqrt{x^2 - y^2} \tag{11}$$

This construction leads to a natural classification in two areas is delimited by red diagonals in Fig. 9(b) according to the very special equation

$$x^2 - y^2 = \mathbf{0}; \tag{12}$$

the first one, the *causal component*, is the symmetric vertical area of *green* hyperbolæ of the form $x^2 - y^2 < 0$ in Fig. 9 and the second one, *the acausal component*, is the symmetric horizontal area of *blue* hyperbolæ $x^2 - y^2 > 0$ in Fig. 9. Similarly, in three dimensions, one can define in Minkowski spacetime, where *time* is the vertical axis and *space* the horizontal axis, *green causal timelike* vectors, *blue acausal spacelike* vectors and *red lightlike* vectors.

2.3 Quantum Superposition of States

By superposing the two "eigenstates" (a) and (b) in Fig. 9, one can encode and control inconsistency $\perp = \{0, 1\}$ according to a very special mechanism. Take for instance a complex number $z = x + \mathbf{j}\, y$; on the $_*\nu$-circle in Fig. 9(a), the anisotropic norm holds $n_1(z) = \sqrt{x^2 + y^2} = 1$; one can add thanks to the superposition principle the relativistic split isotropic norm $n_0(z) = \sqrt{x^2 - y^2}$ according to the expression

$$(n_1 \otimes n_0)(y) = \sqrt{x^2 \pm y^2} \tag{13}$$

and this leads to full inconsistency. If $x = y$, $z = x + \mathbf{j}\, x$, then $x = \pm(\sqrt{2})^{-1}$ and the corresponding angle on the set of complex numbers of modulus 1 is the angle

---

[6] A quadratic form is said to be isotropic if there is a non-zero vector on which the norm evaluates to zero.

$\theta = \pm\pi/4$. Non-manageable inconsistency can expressed that way according to the four "roots"

$$\pm\left(\sqrt{2}\right)^{-1} + \mathbf{j} \pm \left(\sqrt{2}\right)^{-1} \tag{14}$$

as *zero divisors*. In effect, in that case, full inconsistency holds since $n_0(z) = \mathbf{0}$ is a zero divisor ($z \neq 0$). That means that $(n_1 \otimes n_0)(z) = \sqrt{x^2 \pm x^2}$ is a full oscillation system and one cannot preserve any partial regular subdomain or regular subspace as in analytical mathematics or logic. There is no model left implicit or explicit, the whole domain is singular; a valuation in that domain is a perfect fork according to the two meanings of the signal mentioned in Subsect. 1.4

$$
(n_1 \otimes n_0)(z) \quad
\begin{matrix}
\nearrow & \mathbf{0} \\
& \\
\searrow & \mathbf{1}
\end{matrix}
\tag{15}
$$

This situation is very uncomfortable since it means that one cannot preserve any model by isolating absurdity on a proper subspace. Therefore, one cannot use proof theory and automated deduction since these processes use this principle. However, their algebraic representations using sequent systems, category theory and Hopf algebras remain fully of great interest.

3   Quantum Physics and Semantic of Sense-Making

3.1   Bilinearity and Sense-Making

From quantum physics, the intuition is the following: virtual perception is an observable which can be measured as in quantum physics according to a *scalar product* $\langle\xi|\zeta\rangle$ in a Hilbert space using the bra $\langle\xi|$ and ket $|\zeta\rangle$ operators.

One can assume that $_*\nu$ looks like an *bilinear invariant* as an "Hamitonian" $\mathcal{M}_t$ curving interactions, as a geometrical process, between a virtual a_i and a virtual agent a_j (a) and defining a $\mathcal{M}_t$-identity for an agent a_i (b)

$$\text{(a) } \langle\xi,\chi\rangle = \langle\xi|\mathcal{M}_t|\chi\rangle \text{ (in Dirac notation),} \quad \text{(b) } \langle\chi|\mathcal{M}_t|\chi\rangle = 1 \tag{16}$$

From *virtual sensations* according to $_*\nu$, one can express *virtual awareness* as the operator λ^* whose role is to contradict $_*\nu$ or equivalently to invalidate the "Hamiltonian" $\mathcal{M}_t$. Thanks to negation as a switching operator, virtual perception can also leads to a *supra* virtual action, having a "negative impact" on the usual action defined according to the "Hamiltonian" $\mathcal{M}_t$ and called the "unproduct" operator

$$|\chi\rangle\,\mathcal{M}_t\langle\xi| \tag{17}$$

In that frame, by using information theory, one can assert that a signal has always two meanings allowing a virtual agent a_i to encode inconsistency as a relevant object. In effect assume that the unproduct in (17) equals the antisymmetric exterior product as the "anti-scalar" product or the wedge product $\xi \wedge \chi$ with

$$\xi \wedge \chi = -\chi \wedge \xi, \tag{18}$$

or

$$\text{(a) } \xi \wedge \chi = |\chi\rangle \, \mathcal{M}_t \langle \xi| \text{ (in Dirac notation),} \quad \text{(b) } \chi \wedge \chi = \mathbf{0} \tag{19}$$

which, according to a trilinear construction on trivectors $\chi \wedge \xi \wedge \zeta$, can lead to express incompatibility between agent behaviours.

Such an incompatibility requires a negation and contradicts the fix-point $_*\nu$ expressed by the identity $\mathbf{id}_{a_i}$ according to a $_*\nu$-*truth* $\langle \chi || \chi \rangle = \top$ for an agent a_i, since the internal conflict $\mathbf{adv}_{a_i}$ is defined as $\chi \wedge \chi = \bot$ and corresponds to a $_*\nu$-*falsity* by anti-symmetry. That way, $\top \rightarrow \bot$ is the *anti-truth table arrow* as a constructive mapping from the idempotent $\langle . || . \rangle$ to the nilpotent functor merging finally compatible arrows and incompatible arrows

$$\mathbf{1}_{a_i} = \langle . | \mathcal{M}_t | . \rangle \rightarrow . \wedge . = \langle . | \mathcal{M}_t | . \rangle \rightarrow | . \rangle \, \mathcal{M}_t \langle . | \tag{20}$$

In effect, since $\langle \xi || \xi \rangle = 1$, one can consider that it corresponds to $\mathbf{id}_{a_i} = \{\updownarrow\}$ as an identity matrix whereas $\xi \wedge \xi = \mathbf{0}$ as an annihilator, corresponds to $\mathbf{adv}_{a_i} = \{\leftarrow, \rightarrow\}$ mapping $\mathbf{id}_{a_i}$ to a singular form. We have actually two eigen operators and thanks to the superposition principle, consistency may look like

$$\alpha . \langle \xi || \xi \rangle + \beta . (\xi \wedge \xi) \tag{21}$$

One can encode that way by Eq. 21, the fact that we can have both a scalar product measuring virtual agent compatibility $\langle \xi, \xi \rangle = 1$ thanks to virtual collective forces, and an exterior product measuring virtual agent incompatibility $\xi \wedge \xi = \mathbf{0}$ thanks to virtual awareness and the causal break operator. We cannot have both, and we must use that *fork model* expressing that no logical solution holds, or equivalently no decision can be taken from deduction. In terms of intuitionistic logic, the *fork space* corresponds to the intuitionistic hole or the hopeless *full absurd state* $\bot$, where no provable formula holds and no refutable formula holds, or equivalently no model holds and no counter model holds.

3.2 Triality and Incompatibility

Assume that $\mathcal{M}_t$ is a partial domain with incompatible virtual eigen vectors $|\xi\rangle$ and $|\zeta\rangle$ as virtual agent behaviours. One can note

$$|\xi\rangle \, \mathcal{M}_t \langle \zeta| \qquad |\zeta\rangle \, \mathcal{M}_t \langle \xi| \tag{22}$$

The idea is that the morphism

$$\langle \xi | \mathcal{M}_t | \chi \rangle \rightarrow |\chi\rangle \, \mathcal{M}_t \langle \xi| \rightarrow \langle \zeta | \mathcal{M}_{t+\Delta t} | \chi \rangle \tag{23}$$

generates χ-inconsistency from Eq. (22) but can be solved according to the χ-resolution

$$\xi \xrightarrow{\chi} \zeta \cong \mathcal{J} \oplus \zeta, \tag{24}$$

expressing the fact that χ *prefers* ζ *rather than* ξ as a morphism of eigen states. This process is iterative as the regular expression and provides finally a *full acausal change* from $\mathcal{M}_t$ to $\mathcal{M}_{t+\Delta t}$

$$\langle .|\mathcal{M}_t|\chi\rangle \rightarrow (\ |\chi\rangle \mathcal{M}_t\langle .|\ \rightarrow \langle .|\mathcal{M}_{t+\Delta t}|\chi\rangle\ )\ * \tag{25}$$

Assume that one can encode negation as a $\pi/2$ rotation

$$|\xi\rangle \langle .|\cong\quad \cong ((\langle .||\xi\rangle))^{\perp} \tag{26}$$

In that context, negation is the action of the complex number $0 + 1\mathbf{j}$.

3.3 Sense-Making and Subtractive Arithmetic

If one wants to characterize the decision process, one must respect, according to Sect. 2, a knowledge precedence relation. This precedence relation can be viewed at first sight as a huge drawback since it sets inconsistency as a natural state represented according to a truth value superposition principle.

That is, in the cognitive process, under action of virtual collective forces, one must compute virtual sensations first, long before a decision. Everything get is fine, except that virtual awareness is a fix-point whose aim is to question any kind of information observed under the angle of virtual collective forces. The idea is to associate this mechanic according to subtractive arithmetic.

We must necessary start from that initial "virtual sensitive state" in which the effect of the individual on the group in terms of strategic decisions is residual and the two grey circles and the black circle on the horizontal axis of Fig. 2 are superposed in the causal $_*\nu$-vertical axis (all the *horizontal cosine coordinates* are set to $\mathbf{0}$); that is, the causal break operator is the null operator $\lambda^* = \mathbf{0}$ in Eq. (21) since nothing is assumed to be subtracted to the scalar product. Assume that there is a ratio (or an invariant) between the "distance" (we have to be very careful with that term since a distance is usually commutative) $d = [_*\nu, \lambda^*]$ between $\mathcal{M}_t$ and a_i, and the "distance" between the black and the grey circle inside the a_i-box.

One can assume that cognition is defined by two areas: a left hand side and a right hand side setting a precedence from left to right but without necessarily a time representation. It is crucial to set the knowledge basis of the virtual collective mind $\mathcal{M}_t$ as built on virtual sensations that are understood to be the "signal" pair (perception/action), and therefore the process starts from a single global identity (left and right) as $\lambda^* = \mathbf{0}$. Furthermore, $\mathcal{M}_t$ is characterized by a very high knowledge level, allowing the set of virtual agents $\{a_i\}, i = 1\ldots n$ to communicate via $\mathcal{M}_t$; therefore, the cognitive context is characterized by a multiplicity or a cardinality $_*\nu$ of the virtual mind $\mathcal{M}_t$ as a stable *average value*

$$_*\nu = \|\mathcal{M}_t\| \tag{27}$$

whose role is to mitigate individual knowledge entropy generated by conflictual subjectivity $\mathbf{adv}_{a_i} = \{\rightarrow, \leftarrow\}$. The "next state" is a conflictual state generating a subjective intrinsic a_i-knowledge entropy and defined according to a very special negation.

This state is characterized by the negation $_*\nu$ taken as the *inflexion point* λ^* of coordinates $(0, 0.5)$ of the sigmoid (a) in Fig. 10, the integral of the Gaussian (b) as the probabilistic support. That is, λ^* detects a causal break and builds a valuation incompatible with $_*\nu$. From statistical analysis, one can use the natural definition of a $\mathcal{M}_t$-frequency $_*\nu^7$ in the Eq. (27) which is a positive integer value incompatible with the virtual agent's knowledge. That way, a decision can be viewed as a negation of a Gaussian curve $_*\nu$, or, in other words, to check the conditions for which the operator λ^* is the annihilator of a Gaussian curve.

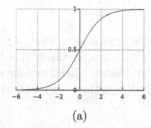 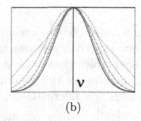

(a)   (b)

Fig. 10. Inflexion point of the sigmoid (a) and probabilistic support $_*\nu$ (b)

The idea is to associate some quantitative features to a causal break. We propose to find an interpretation of the sigmoid as a S-curve, an important project management tool: the progress of a project is tracked visually over time according to a historical record of what has happened to date. A double S-curve identifies a discontinuity zone during a phase transition from old to new technologies. In our case, we propose to add a horizontal symmetry; that is, the main increasing S-curve in Fig. 11(a) as the *adherence* around the frequency $_*\nu$ under the action of virtual collective forces and at the same time a decreasing curve which expresses a continuous decreasing *validity*. This result creates in the neighborhood of the inflexion point a singularity φ as a cusp model in Fig. 11(b) and the decision occurs in that area.

3.4 Quasi Additive Structures and Anti-superposition

The idea is to define an horizontal splittability condition for the linear operator $\langle \| \rangle$

$$
\begin{array}{c}
\diagup \ \| \ \diagdown \\
\cdots \quad \cdots \\
\diagdown \ \| \ \diagup
\end{array}
\tag{28}
$$

to obtain diamond structures.

---

7 In statistics, the frequency of an event $_*\nu$ is the number of times it is counted in an experiment.

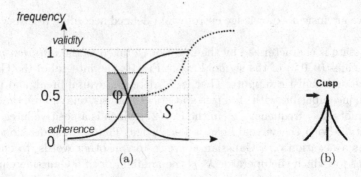

Fig. 11. Mirrored S-curves and (a) cusp point (b)

One has to alter the superposition principle according to two "eigen states" which are not exactly eigen states; that is, λ^* is the annihilator of the eigen state, the eigen orbit, whereas $_*\nu$ is the eigen stabilizer. Therefore, one can think about sense-making as the pseudo-differential equation, although the causal break domain is not differentiable

$$+ \partial\lambda^*(.) = -\partial_*\nu(.) \tag{29}$$

since it corresponds to full absurdity as the red diagonal in Fig. 9.

This double construction holds thanks to a superposition principle between causality $_*\nu = m \succ\succ M$ and the causal break operator $\lambda^* = m \prec\prec M$ as in quantum logic but which is not additive in our case

$$_*\nu \not\oplus \lambda^* \tag{30}$$

That is, from the previous subsection and due to the fix-point $_*\nu$, one cannot add continuously an *information gradient* on the right of the frequency $_*\nu$ thanks to λ^*; the construction is highly asymmetric and leads to define a rather complicated structure: a Clifford algebra according to a geometric product:

$$_*\nu \not\oplus \lambda^* \cong {}_*\!\!\not\nu \oplus \lambda^* \cong {}_*\nu \to \lambda^* \tag{31}$$

The corresponding Clifford algebra expresses the fact that $\langle \xi || \chi \rangle$ is no longer valid, whereas one cannot compute $\xi \wedge \chi$ as a dense structure.

3.5   Cross Constructions and Clockwise Orientations

Assume that the cognition loop corresponds to a time-oriented process; temporal clockwise causality is characterized by a positive value $\|_*\nu\| > 0$ according to the complex anisotropic norm $n_1(z) = 1$ due to virtual collective forces, and as such is assumed to be a front-end first harmonic $_*\nu$; sense-making is a back-end (pseudo) acausal second harmonic λ^* whose multiplicity is a negative or a null value $\|\lambda^*\| \leq 0$ according to the $\mathbb{D}$-isotropic norm $n_0(z) = 0$ and whose role is to annihilate the front-end.

In other words, the front-end and back-end can be represented as two distinct "virtual hyperplanes".

Unsolvable issues occur when one hopes to merge them in a unique "virtual hyperplane" (that is, according to a suitable projection) to benefit from a commutation property unifying clockwise and counter-clockwise angular distances. Since we do not want to face such a situation, we propose to build a "braiding" whose local representation is shown in Fig. 12 if one considers to that decision mechanics contained in a volume, a "virtual hypercube" is identified as a tesseract[8] [7]. That way, the front-end and the back-end are merged according to a unitary "virtual hypersphere" 1_{a_i} which cannot be the fundamental "frequency" since $_*\nu$ is annihilated. In other words, from $_*\nu$ to 1_{a_i}, something has to be removed.

3.6   Sketch of the Decision Process

One can provide now for the' first time the sketch of a decision process $\lambda^*{}_{a_i} :_* \nu \to 1_{a_i}$ whose computation is based on the subgroup of quasi-identity matrices embedded in a "virtual hypersphere."

The connection between the sense-making *acausal* coalgebra λ^* and the *causal* algebra $_*\nu$ is ensured by a harmonic representation of the antipode $S = 1_{a_i}$ in the Definition 1 of a Hopf Algebra, allowing the decision process to terminate. What is really crucial is to define the sense-making dynamic; we assume that thanks to the Hopf algebra H, sense-making is defined according to geometric numbers (numbers connected with angles): we assume that causality $_*\nu$ is the first harmonic as the prime geometric number p; then the idea is to compute the decision λ^* according to its conjugate, a second harmonic q represented as another prime geometric number q, and with remarkable properties for the commutator as an harmonic operator able to restore the signal

$$[p,q] = p\,q - q\,p = n, n \in \mathbb{N} \tag{32}$$

From that commutator identity, one can define the following theorem:

Theorem 2 (Conceptual basis validity). *The following statements are equivalent:*

1. *The phase shift or the knowledge stretch is the antipode S defined as the commutator*

$$S = [_*\nu, \lambda^*] = {}_*\nu\,\lambda^* - \lambda^*\,{}_*\nu \tag{33}$$

   "between" $\mathcal{M}_t$ and a_i in Fig. 2 and is a $_*\nu$-harmonic ratio.
2. *the conceptual basis holds and*
3. *decision mechanics holds as a causal break operator λ^* switching the polarity of the arrow (3) in Eq. (8).*

---

[8] The tesseract is the four-dimensional analog of the cube where motion in the fourth dimension represents the transformations of the cube through time.

Once the causal identity as the Hopf identity is refuted η, this refutation can be used by the co-identity ϵ to build the second harmonic as a valuation of the conjugated wavelength λ^*. The association $\eta \oplus \epsilon$ as $\eta \to \epsilon$ can be built according to the functor ∞^{-1-1}.

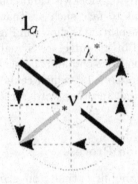

Fig. 12. Decision as a causal break

3.7   Square Annihilation of Counter Models

The intuitive idea is to consider that it is not possible to identify and to remove a counter model viewed as a cube except by unfolding its squared representation with negation as a square root. The starting structure is an infinite dimensional a_i-identity matrix $\mathbf{1}_{a_i}$ of length ∞^{-1-1}; we assume that from $(_*\nu, \lambda^*)_{a_i}$, the causal frequency $_*\nu$ can be assimilated to the diagonal of scalars as eigen values of $\mathbf{1}_{a_i}$ whereas the causal break operator as a *conjugated wavelength* $\lambda^*_{a_i}$ concerns the transition from the diagonal towards the extreme anti-diagonal elements

$$x_{1,\infty^{-1-1}}, x_{\infty^{-1-1},1} \tag{34}$$

called the "passage points." The algorithm fills the embedding circle $\mathbf{1}_{a_i}$ taken as a 4-sorted closure algebra able to encode consistency and sense-making. In effect, contradiction is certainly essential but the role of $\lambda^*_{a_i}$ is also to *integrate* $_*\nu$ according to some knowledge stretching operator. One can assume that the causal break operator performs like the switching operator in Eq. (8) another switching operator of the form

$$\lambda^*_{a_i} : \langle \chi | \mathcal{M}_t \| \xi \rangle \to | \xi \rangle \, \mathcal{M}_t \langle \chi | \tag{35}$$

from compatibility to incompatibility, but not the other way around since $\lambda^*_{a_i}$ apparently has not a group structure and is not an involution. The algebraic representation is a *braiding* [4, 10] which is taken to be quantum entanglement; that is λ^* can compose, but $\lambda^* \circ \lambda^* \neq \mathbf{id}$ instead of classical negation $\neg\neg A = A$ is an example of an involution.

It is a pity because our aim is to embed these switchings inside an automorphism algebra whose main property is to be *inner* to provide a correctness result with infinite precision thanks to "recovered hidden" symmetries.

4   Conclusion

From unification of the virtual versions of physical theories: virtual relativity, virtual gravitation and virtual quantum physics, one can explain the nature and the properties of the very high level of knowledge representations that a virtual mind must have to be able to communicate with others and to decide on its own using acausality. The idea is to show the limit of causal theories as machine-learning, and to explain that the intractability of automatic decision procedures results from the ignorance of relevant precedence relations between a virtual collective mind and a virtual aware agent. According to these precedence relations, a decision can be set as computation of a harmonic rational expression with infinite precision.

References

1. Hiley, B.J.: Non-commutative geometry, the Bohm interpretation and the mind-matter relationship, vol. 573 (2001)
2. Rowlands, P.: Zero to Infinity: The Foundations of Physics. World Scientific, Singapore (2007)
3. Bartheye, O., Chaudron, L.: Algebraic modeling of the causal break and representation of the decision process in contextual structures. In: Lawless, B. (ed.) Computation Contexts. CRC (2018)
4. Blute, R.: Linear topology, hopf algebras and ∗-autonomous categories. Research report (1993)
5. Chaudron, L.: Simple structures and complex knowledge. Habilitation thesis, Onera, Toulouse, FR (2005)
6. Clifford, W.K.: Mind **3** (1878)
7. Coxeter, H.S.M.: Regular Polytopes. Dover Publications, New York (1973)
8. Knus, M., Merkurjev, A., Rost, M., Tignol, J.: The Book of Involutions. AMS, Providence (1998)
9. Mahulikar, S., Herwig, H.: Exact thermodynamic principles for dynamic order existence and evolution in chaos. Chaos, Solitons Fractals **41**, 1939–1948 (2009)
10. Majid, S.: Foundations of Quantum Group Theory. Cambridge University Press, Cambridge (1995)
11. Wigner, E.: Physics and the explanation of life. Found. Phys. **1**, 35–45 (1970). https://doi.org/10.1007/BF00708653

Author Index

Printed in the United States
by Baker & Taylor Publisher Services